GENESIS,
the Book of Beginnings

GENESIS,

the Book of Beginnings

Dr. Danny K. Hill

XULON PRESS

Xulon Press
2301 Lucien Way #415
Maitland, FL 32751
407.339.4217
www.xulonpress.com

Unless otherwise indicated, Scripture quotations taken from the King James Version (KJV)–*public domain*.

Printed in the United States of America.

Paperback ISBN-13: 978-1-6628-1012-1
Hard Cover ISBN-13: 978-1-6628-1220-0
Ebook ISBN-13: 978-1-6628-1013-8

Acknowledgments

Thanks to all my friends in the many churches which have inspired me along the way. There is one which needs mentioning who has been a tremendous help to me and that is Mrs. Janice Spivey. She spent hours editing this book.

Dedication

I want to dedicate this to my wonderful wife, Brenda, of 52 years, for inspiring me to write this book. Had it not been for her encouraging me along the way, I am sure it would not be completed. She has been a true helpmeet for me over the years. I also want to thank many of our preacher acquaintances for pushing me to what they thought was the right thing in writing this book. Special thanks to my lifelong friend and confidant, Rev. Robert Vannoy. Then to my current pastor and friend, Rev. Bill Bradley for his help and encouragement to help me see this through. How could any of this been possible without the Lord? I thank Him for all He has done.

Table of Contents

Chapter 1

One must understand **Genesis Chapter One** because it is the Foundation chapter for the entire Bible. If you do not understand this chapter, you will never understand what the Bible is about, who it is about and why written. If this chapter is not real, then none of the Bible can be trusted.

But, Thank God, it is true! **Chapter One** gives us the Biblical account of creation and how it all began. Who started things in motion? What happened to the creation itself? For that matter, it gives us the historical account of creation. How that God Almighty made what we see around us.

Therefore, there is not one shred of scientific evidence that the theory of Evolution can be correct. Even theistic Evolution has no scientific basis.

When you read chapters like **Psalm 8** and many more, we note very quickly why the heavens exist. In the first six verses, we will see God's crowning work accomplished in man's creation. The heavens were made first, according to the direct Creation of God himself.

The first verse says, "In the beginning, God." Since Jesus himself is the Jehovah God of the Old Testament, we will see Him as the Creator. The Apostle John wrote and said, "All things were made by him, and without him was not anything made that was made," **John 1:3**.

We also find another statement by Paul in **Col. 1:16, 17**, "all things were created by him, and for him; and he is before all things and by him, all things consist."

In other words, if God is not holding everything together, everyone and everything would fall apart. You have to ask the question of who God is, is He just a Creator. Why would God do those things? Our text says He is, before all things, with no beginning and no end. The Creator is the cause of all things, and He is the explanation of all things. Therefore He is the destiny of all things. It is not enough to regard Jehovah as a God or as one among many. Neither should He be considered as just the God of Israel. He is Jehovah, the one true God, for there is no other God greater than He.

There is no question; He is the Creator of Heaven and earth. He is not just superior to the gods of the surrounding nations; he alone is God.

Years ago, some people confused God and His Creation. He is the God of Creation, not just God in Creation. He is more than that; He is my God alone. "In the beginning, God created."

That beginning was when God created time. Time began with creation.

Before creation, there was only eternity. It has been correctly said, "God was and is and ever will be." God always was. He exists outside of time. In eternity past, there were no stars, no sun, no moon nor earth. Nothingness existed itself, the night of oblivion. It is nothingness far worse than just emptiness. For how long this nothingness lasted, humanity will never know. Why there was nothing is something we must never try to comprehend for God is infinite, and we are finite.

The Bible describes Heaven and earth as yet unmade; we can say there was only empty blackness and void and darkness upon the deep. God lived in total bliss and majesty when time was previously unknown.

Then He called light out of the darkness, and He called order out of chaos, yet the question remains where God exists and where is His home?

The answer to that question is He came from nowhere. That is theologically correct and biblically sound for we read in **Hab. 3:3** "God came from Teman. And the Holy One from Mount Paran." In its secondary meaning, Teman means nothing or nowhere. God came from nowhere because there was nowhere for God to come from and to come from nowhere, He stood on nothing.

The reason he stood on nothing was there was no place to stand.

Standing on nothing, He reached out his hand where there was nowhere to reach and caught something when there was nothing to find, hung something on nothing, and said, "Stay there."

Our finite minds can never comprehend the greatness of God. God is so real we find Genesis does not attempt to explain God but tells us what He did.

Re-wind for a moment. In the very first words of Genesis, you hear these words, "in the beginning." This first verse assumes the being of God. It implies His eternity, His omnipotence, His absolute freedom and sovereignty, His essential goodness, and His infinite wisdom. "God" of **Gen. 1:1** is "Elohim," a Uni-plural noun.

"Created" is a singular verb and requires a unique subject. Overwhelmingly, the Bible asserts one God. It is hard to be more straightforward or clear. There is a genuine and powerful God!

Genesis 1: 2 says, "And the earth was without form, and void; and darkness was upon the face of the deep. And the Spirit of God moved upon the face of the waters."

There can be "no form and void" with or without darkness. Here is a tremendous revelation of truth. This revelation may come down to be accurate, referring to matter. The matter is not God, but without God, it is meaningless, dark, and useless. This meaningless may also be true of intelligence if there is no God. Too many people worship the intellect. This meaningless may also be said of the soul. Here is a tremendous opportunity for change, but it has to be under the Holy Spirit's brooding power. Matter can be changed.

The transformation of the mind is possible. The brain may know and yet be in utter chaos. "If our Gospel be hidden, it is hidden unto them that are lost." "We have the mind of Christ." God made the soul like the earth, without form, without light, without life, but not without God.

From the description in **verses 2, 3**, we begin to learn what God created. It says then He called light out of the darkness, and He called order out of chaos. This verse describes the fundamental aspect of the earth which God created. Many interpreters say that the Hebrew word translated was in the phrase "the earth was without form" should have been translated "became."

Became is a secondary meaning of this Hebrew word, and this translation is only contextually possible if it warrants it. The original text refers to its state of being. The earth was without form and void. In its original state of the planet, this means that the surface was not yet perfect since God had not completed his creative acts.

The first thing God created was the matter. From Matter, He could and did systematically make all things. When God told Moses to write the words "without form," it means formlessness, confusion, and emptiness.

Here is what God did with the earth. It was like a potter who takes a lump of clay and as he lays it on the potter's wheel and then begins to mold and make it into what he wants. He took his best and began to shape and transforms it. The words "without form and void" do not mean or refer to one great catastrophe. God did not make a mess the first time and then had to remake anything.

Our text says, "The Spirit of God." Where ever He is, He removes the darkness and imparts beauty, giving life. The word "moved" means flutter, move, shake, hover over, and brood over. The image the writer is using is that of a mother bird hovering above her nest. There is one more r place we find this word used in this way, in **Deut. 32:11**, where God is described "like an eagle stirreth up her nest, fluttereth over her young, spreadeth abroad her wings, taketh them, beareth them on her wings." So the image of the Holy Spirit is very much maternal. We see God the Holy Spirit, like a mother bird, tending and nurturing what He has already created, bringing it, or just saying it.

Some men never understand the power of God and what He wants to do in their lives. Most of their lives become marked with a lack of purpose. Nothing has changed. Man is still the same. God expects us to have changed lives after we put our trust in Him.

Think of some of the people mentioned in the Word of God. Lot wanted a pasture more than the things of God. Gehazi wanted the seeming security of material things and the prestige of this world. Ananias and

Sapphira wanted position and notoriety in the early church, but they tried to deceive by performing a wicked act against the Holy Ghost. Ammon, a man who hungered for the wrong things of life, sat at the king's table and starved his soul. But there are men whose hearts cannot be bound by this material world. They hunger for the things of God. They seek a Holy God. The Holy Spirit of the eagle stirs within them. It keeps them restless and wanting something more from God. Sometimes it can be a lonely road. I have found that it is in the hours of loneliness that God does some of his greatest works. "It was in the lonely grief of Elijah that he heard God's voice. In the lonely path of faith, God came again to Abraham, telling him to leave his homeland and seek a new country. It was in the lonely hours following Peter's disgrace he found God.

Think back, and you will find it was in the lonely midnight hours that Jacob wrestled with God. It was in the loneliness on Mount Sinai Moses would get God's Law. In the loneliness of her barrenness, we note Hannah saw God fulfill her prayer. It was in the loneliness of her weight on her shoulders that forced Esther to approach Ahasuerus. It was in the loneliness of that dark dungeon that Daniel received his great vision from God. It was in the loneliness of the prison pit that Jeremiah found a renewed burden for the people. It was in the loneliness of the prison that Joseph felt the presence of God. It was in the loneliness of the prayer in Gethsemane that the Lord labored, doing work for His Father. He was only just a stone's cast away from the disciples, but it may have been a million miles that separated them. It was loneliness in Bethlehem's stable where Mary cared for the baby Jesus. It was loneliness as she stood at Golgotha, watching her son. "God uses the schoolhouses of loneliness to teach his servants.

Philippians 3:13-14 says, "brethren, I count not myself to have apprehended: but this one thing I do, forgetting those things which are behind, and reaching forth unto those things which are before, I press toward the mark for the prize of the high calling of God in Christ Jesus."

One of the world's most recognized poets, John Milton, had to sell his copyright of "a paradise lost" for $72.00. Robert Louis Stevenson would battle with tuberculosis but would write some of the greatest classics of literature. On his way to being acknowledged as the greatest dramatist of all ages, William Shakespeare held horses at the London theatre door for sixpence a day. Homer struggled with blindness writing "the Odyssey" before almost reaching immortality among the philosophers and literary giants.

John Bunyan cheered himself in a prison cell by making a flute out of his prison stool while writing "Pilgrims Progress" and "the Holy war." Helen Keller struggled with her obstacles of being deaf and blind and turned adverse circumstances into positive assets.

We know Mr. George Frederic Handel had paralysis on his right side.

His money was gone, his creditors were going to imprison him, but he rebounded and composed the greatest of his inspirations, "Messiah."

One renowned sculptor had to work in an orphanage, modeling a lion in soft butter before his chisel ever tasted the marble. Hallelujah choruses are not born in a vacation condominium but a jail cell-like Paul in *Acts 16*. It's all a matter of perception. Stand up to the harsh old world.

Stand, as the anvil when the stroke of courageous men falls fierce and fast. Storms but more deeply root the oak whose brawny arms embrace the winds. Stand, like the anvil, noise and heat are born of earth and die with time: the soul, like God, its source and seat, is solemn, still, serene, sublime! Paul said in *2 Timothy 4:7, 8* "I have fought a good fight; I have finished my course, I have kept the faith: henceforth there is laid up for me a crown of righteousness, which the Lord, the righteous judge, shall give me at that day: and not to me only, but unto all them also that love His appearing."

The eagle who longs to sore for the heights will not be content to stay on this earth. I'm going through! I will soar above the storm. I will hope for the greatest. I will do the will of God. I will defeat the enemy. I will proclaim the Gospel as long as there is breath in me. I will. It is what God Holy Spirit can do for you, instilling within us the desire to go on for God.

In the Holy Spirit, we can see His person and power. He moved. He hovered, He quivered over, and He brooded over, put energy in, and moved over!! Our salvation by the Holy Ghost is that moving over us. What a beautiful thought!!

I believe that the Trinity was involved with creation as well as in our salvation. It is all done by God the Father, God the Son, and God Holy Ghost. The job of the Holy Ghost or his task is to look after and protect us from the world's things and the flesh and the devil surrounding us. Yet, often we think He is unreachable, too hard to find, and hard to understand. We think of the Holy Spirit as the third person, and thus, we expect little. No wonder we do not see God the Holy Spirit doing very much!

If we could only understand that God is not "way out there." He is right here, right now. Do you know why we don't see God doing things in our lives? Cause we can't see. The ole sin nature has blinded us. The devil is doing the best he can to keep us from seeing God for who He is.

When we think of the Trinity of God, we find many having a hard time understanding this concept.

The simplest explanation of the Trinity is simplest explained by me saying this: I'm a father, I'm a son, I'm a preacher, I'm a brother, I'm a husband, I'm a son-in-law. These are all that I am just as when we say God the Father, God the Son, and God Holy Ghost. They are all God, and respectfully who they just tell us something different about Himself. If I don't have any problem being each one of those characteristics about myself, then do you think God would have a problem being, Father, Son, or Holy Ghost? Did you know that all three of the Godhead had something to do with your salvation?

We can say God planned our salvation. God, the Father, has selected me. God, the Son, has purchased and saved me. The Holy Ghost performed it and has sealed me. I have heard it said, "God thought it, the Son bought it, and the Holy Ghost wrought it, the preacher preached it, the devil fought it, but thank God I got it." We serve a real God, a powerful God, and a living God.

As we have said, Genesis is the book of beginnings. When we say beginnings, we are not speaking of God himself but of what He did as far as humanity is concerned. We find out what God did. Everything made was made by Him. We call them the creative acts of God. He created the heavens, the earth, and all that is in them. In them, we see the beginning of the material universe, the sphere of the divine revelation of grace. We understand the start of the human race, the subject of the divine revelation of grace. We see the beginning of sin, the cause of the divine revelation of grace. We understand the origin of divine redemption, the character of the divine revelation of grace. We see the beginning of the nations, the scope of the divine revelation of grace. We see the birth of the Hebrew nation, the channel of the divine revelation of grace.

We see the beginning of the life of faith, the outcome of the divine revelation of grace. This book is all that is needed to understand the rest of the Bible and to understand God.

This book is the beginning of sin and its effect on humanity. This book is the beginning of time, and in this time that God has given man the innate ability to know what He desires.

And we will learn from this desire what can be the ultimate end of the man himself if he will but trust this God for all of his beings.

From the New Testament, we find that Moses is the human penman of Genesis. "And beginning at Moses and all the prophets, he expounded unto them in all the scriptures the things concerning him." See *Luke 24:27*. We also find these words written by Luke, "And He said unto them, these are the words which I spake unto you, while I was yet with you, that all things must be fulfilled, which were written in the law of Moses, and in the prophets, and the Psalms, concerning me." See *Luke 24: 44*.

As soon as you begin to read and study Genesis, you can see God's purpose for us. It is that we might know the real history of God's Creation and who He is so we might learn from Him.

It is not hard to notice this world in which we live. Man is trying to destroy everything right and good.

The world is turning so anti-God all you have to do is show people the Bible and they either run or hate you. They have tried many times to destroy it but to no success. "And they are written for our admonition, upon whom the ends of the world have come." See *1 Cor. 10:6, 11*.

Not only to know that God is the Creator of all things, but Genesis gives us the necessary information to provide mortal man the ability, the intelligence, and the Spirit essential for fellowship with Him.

In its pre-inception, we find that when Heaven and earth were yet unmade, when there was only empty blackness and void, and there was darkness upon the deep, and when the time was unknown, God lived in total bliss and majesty alone, as we have said before.

"And God said, let there be light: and there was light." See *Genesis 1:3*. Light is the most basic form of energy. Energy is related to matter and proven by Einstein's equation e=Mc2. The velocity of light is in this equation. The written word may speak of this when it says the Spirit moved in the darkness over the formless earth. From here, we know God divided the light from the darkness. We do not know the nature of this light, nor do we know the source.

Many today believe the Gap Theory is correct. I would beg to differ with them, and I think I can show you where they are wrong. First, it is a severe mistake to ignore the tremendous implications and influence of the Theory of Evolution. The fundamental principle of Evolution; their concept of development with its increasingly complex organization contradicts the impregnable established laws of Thermodynamics. What is this, you say?

Of course, there are two of these.

The Law of Energy Conservation is the same as the first law of Thermodynamics. This law states that energy can be changed into a different form, and it does not appear to be either created or destroyed. We know that matter and all physical phenomena are various forms of energy.

There is tells us no creating is going on today.

The second law of Thermodynamics states and I will not try and use a technical form that says that all physical systems, if left to them, tend to wear down and become disordered.

In other words, machines wear out, processes run down, and organisms die. These two laws have been scientifically verified thousands of times through experiments from the nuclear level to the astronomical level and with no known exceptions. They indicate that what we know as original creation is running down.

This second law states that the universe must have had a beginning and eventually run down, and the first law, on the other hand, says that the universe could not have created itself.

Some adequate cause must have created it; we know it is the God of Heaven!!

The so-called Gap Theory is incorrect by being both unwarranted biblically and impossible scientifically to prove as some would suggest a gap being in-between *Gen. 1:1 and Gen. 1:2.*

Exodus 20:11 states that in 6 days, the Lord made the Heaven and the earth, the sea, and all in them is. Thus nothing in the world or sea could have been made before the six days of creation. The Gap theory is supposed by it advocates providing time for the geological cycles, which are then terminated by a great cataclysm leaving the earth without form and void.

However, the geological age, based on the principle of uniformities, denies a worldwide cataclysm. *Gen. 1: 2* does not describe the earth after a long time and catastrophe but rather from the beginning of history.

Initially, the earth matter was without form, referring to the fact that the waters covered it and possibly contained most of the substances necessary in completing creation. Isaiah said God had not created the earth in vain to be forever empty but rather formed to be inhabited. See *Isa. 45:18*. It is essential to recognize that *verses 2-31* do little more than expand upon *verse 1*.

They do not fully explain creation. These verses do not prove the Gap or Evolution theory. The stated Biblical facts at hand must be accepted by faith.

As you begin to read, you will find a pattern to these six days of creation. We can say formlessness changed to form, and emptiness changed to habitation.

Look at the days as God made them. In *verses 3-5*, we have Day 1, where God made the light.

In *verses 14-19*, which is Day 4, we have God making the luminaries. You know what they are, the sun, moon, stars. In *verses 6-8*, we find Day 2; we see God creating the air. We call it the upper expanse. In *verses 20-23*, you have God as the catalyst for making the water or the lower expanse. On Day 5, God created the fish, birds. In *verses 9-13,* Day 3, we see God created dry land and plants. In *verses 24-31*, which is Day 6, God created the animals and finally, man. We see in this way; the first three days remedy the situation of formlessness. See *Genesis 1:2*. The 4 through 6 Days deal with the state of 'void' or 'emptiness' of *verse 2*. Notice the relationship between Days 1 and 4, 2 and 5, 3, and 6. For example, it takes air and water to support the life of the fish and birds.

We must consider at least two more thoughts in this text. First, there is an order of six days.

In its context, we see, "this account is arranged systemically, with each day building upon the creative acts of previous days." Secondly, there is a method involved in the creation, a process involving the change from chaos to cosmos, and disorder to order. While God could have spontaneously created the earth as it is, He did not choose to do so. The text's clear impression is that this process took six literal 24 hour days, not long ages.

Instantaneously is the keyword of today. We know this as the world we live in. However, it should be very evident God is not on our timetable. Man is the crown of God's Creation. First, man is the last of God's Creation. The entire account of creation builds to the making of man.

We understand God made man in His image, yet we acknowledge

God made man in His image, but he reflects the truth that man rules over God's creation.

Do you not know, God is the Sovereign Ruler of the Universe? Man, by extension, is the Ruler of the earth. By His mercy and grace, God has delegated a small portion of authority to man for ruling His Creation. In this sense, too, man mirrors God. God shows us man's worth, which is directly related to his origin. No wonder we hear such frightening ethical and moral positions proposed today, which are prevalent before our very eyes. In his sins, man has come to the place where he has no morals, no guilt, and no shame for what he is doing in God's very eyes.

It has been corrected stated that "Any view of man's origin, which does not view man as the product of divine design and purpose, cannot credit to man the worthiness God has given him."

It has been said," our evaluation of man is directly proportionate to our estimation of God."

Note how clear and simple our text is. It is the language of regular human speech taken at face value. The first and literal meaning of the Hebrew word "Yom" means a natural 24 hour day. Unless the context forces us to assume another meaning, we must accept that first meaning. When the O. T. associates "Yom" with a correct numeral, it refers to a solar day of 24 hours. See *Gen. 7:11; 8:14; 17:12*; etc. One of the keys to our understanding is that Moses specifically speaks of evening and mornings as a Jewish day. From this text, we see in the days of creation the great interchange of light and darkness. They must be regarded not as a time of duration of years, but merely 24 hour earth days. Contextually, this is the best explanation. See *Exodus 20:9-11*.

We find that God created the heavens and the earth in six days and then rested on the 7th day. The word "rested" in the Hebrew is the word "Shabbat," defined as, to cease, cut off, and put to an end. Therefore there has been no other creation by God since the 6th day. So then the view of the long periods would do violence to the law of nature.

Remember, on this third day, we know God created the plants, trees, and grass of every kind, and yet there was no sun. For these plants to live for such a long time, it is contrary to nature's laws, if we accept the third say to be a long time. Even if we were to change these days into long periods of "time," they still could not answer the question as to "how" it all began. Emphatically God pronounced all of His work to be very good.

This goodness certainly does not refer to millions and billions of years of struggle, death and disease, pain, and suffering as some claim the fossils give the record before this "2nd creation" of God.

In *Genesis 5:5*, we have the account of the good ole age of Adam. He lived to be 930 years *old*. If each day were to represent a long time, then if Adam's life began on the 6th day, he too would have to be millions of years old, and the Scriptures would be a lie.

For me to believe this Gap theory that we have looked at, at least three things would have to happen: They would have to produce a specimen of something created out of nothing. They would have to provide a specimen of Evolution from non-living matter and make it a living thing. Then they would have to produce structural development from animal to man, including man's spiritual being. So, it is very obvious to each of us from God's program that the earth has received particular attention, for it is on the planet that God will eventually establish His coming kingdom.

We should ask ourselves another question, and that is why did He take six days to perform the acts of Creation when He could have just spoken it into existence instantaneously? See *Exo. 31:12-17* for an explanation to this question. The seven day week has no basis outside of the Scriptures.

Comparing Scripture with Scripture, we understand God's command to work six days and rest one day of the week. That is why He deliberately took as long as six days to create everything.

He set the example for man. Our week today is patterned after this principle. If He created everything in six thousand million years, we would have an irritating long work week. Much of the creation account does not give us much detail into those events. But given the information we have, we know in six days God finished His Creation. God saw everything was in harmony and right at the end of the six days of creation. So then each of God's creatures was placed in an environment ideally suited for them. How can we determine that God made the earth with age? *Genesis 2:11, 12* give us the answer. Notice the mention of the gold, bdellium, and onyx. This passage proves these things did not take billions of years but were literal 24 hour periods. Everything God made He completed in six days.

The earth and everything on the planet were made full, mature, and perfect.

With the appearance of age, this creation proves that God brought forth a man and a woman who were mature adults from the first instance of their existence. The result also included a balance of all chemical elements so that the earth could support life. It is only reasonable and consistent with His character and His revelation of Himself in this creative process that God would create the entire universe a complete, operational, and functioning mechanism. See *Rom. 11:33-36* and *Heb. 11:3*.

As we have seen, some people believe there was a very long time interval between *verses one* and *two*, which would account for a long time for it to take place in their geological cycle. What happens then is we must accept the possibility of two creations. They say the first creation was in *verse one*, and the second creation in *verse 2*. The void, the chaotic state, would indicate the destruction of the first world. And then there are four more chapters to give us the fall of another creation. There seem to be two primary reasons for inserting the "time."

One is to cover the time of the creating of the angels and the fall. The second is to build a bridge between the biblical account of the creation of 6 days and the evolutionistic geology theories, which would require a long, long time according to their thinking. Knowing would help explain the time necessary for the formation of rocks, minerals, and salt accumulation in seas.

The most common explanation of the period between *verse one* and *verse 2* is when Lucifer fell, and in rebellion, the first earth destroyed. See *Jer. 4:23-28; Isa. 14; Ezek. 28*. These are the verses associated with this teaching to back up this thought. What is the answer? Between *v. one* and *verse 2*, we have the word, "and." The term "And" is a conjunction. It connects *verse 1* with *verse 2*. Therefore, *verse two* cannot set forth God's re-creative act, which would have been necessary if there had been great destruction.

In the language itself, there is nothing to suggest such an interpretation. It is logical because of this to put *verse one* and *verse two* together without a break. When you read the context of chapter one, it makes it easier to see that this is the correct interpretation. Why?

If we take the two creation theories, we must consider that Moses devoted one single sentence to the account to create the first world and then added another part to the verse to describe its destruction. He then continues with an entire chapter to describe the creation of the second world and, as we have said, devoted four Chapters to account for the destruction of the second creation by way of the flood. Most Christians do not realize that this theory is a product of evolutionary thinking and not practical science.

Evolutionists look at the geological structure and see years and ages, while the creationists look at the same geological formation and see God's mighty hand. The difference is where their faith is. To explain this further, if we place ages between *verse one* and *verse two* is to imply that the evolutionary processes were in operation during that time. So the correct view is to accept the six days as being literal days.

I believe the real clincher is that it would require a pre-Adamic race and explain the presence of fossils of people who were supposed to have lived before Adam, and then they died. Yet they would have been killed by not committing sin but allowing Satan to destroy what God had made.

The Bible makes it very understandable that sin is the reason for man's death, not Satan.

Admittedly if we accept the one creation account, which brings about several questions, we should ask. Like when we're angels created? When did the rebellion of the angels take place?

The only reasonable answer to these and many other questions is that God just did not see fit to give us all of the solutions that may arise, and there are some things that God never intended us to see. Therefore we call it a veil placed over our eyes. We must, at some point, accept what God had done just by faith in Him.

In many respects, then we see Genesis as virtually the leading book in the Bible. The purpose of the Book of Genesis is to make it possible to understand the rest of the Bible. Everything happens and hinges in Genesis.

From the second day onward, we have observed a systematic upward unfolding of God's creation plan. It is to bring order and beauty out of chaos and forming matter into wonders.

All of this is seen in ***Gen. 1:6-8***. The second step of creation was dividing primordial chaos into an upper and lower sphere by creating the first Heaven. The Hebrew word firmament is "Rakia," which means a spreading out like a tent or a canopy. By creating a layer of gases, we find God surrounded our planet with what we know as the atmosphere, which to the human eye appears like a majestic blue canopy in the sky above us. This sphere is approximately 60-100 miles thick, consisting chiefly of two gases; 78% nitrogen & 20% oxygen.

This sphere forms the air we breathe, making life as we know it possible on this planet.

So far, as has been scientifically determined, no planet has the type of atmosphere that is breathable except earth.

The canopy over and around the earth, called the firmament, must have been made of invisible water vapor, extending fart into space. They provided a marvelous canopy for the earth, shielding it from deadly radiation coming from outer space. This canopy produced what is known as the greenhouse effect. The waters under the Heaven still refer to the ocean and waters.

Designed by God, we note the canopy's purpose was to create a climate that was ideally suited for the first humans.

Webster's dictionary defines weather as "the state of air or atmosphere concerning heat and cold, wetness and dryness, calm and storm, clearness and cloudiness, or any other meteorological phenomenon."

One definition of climate is the average weather of a place or region over an extended time frame. One characteristic of the weather is that it does not remain the same for very long.

There were three basic things which took place on this the third day. First, you have the separation of the liquid from the solid matter in primordial chaos. The second was the creation of the seas and the formation of the continents in one mass. Then third was the covering of the dry land with green vegetation. Then He took all this and formed what we know as the earth and hung it in space without beams or cables and set it in a rotating motion.

This rotation's speed has never changed, but as we will see a little later, planet earth's tilt has moved from its original setting.

What a sight this must have been. The angels were witnessing the birth of the first planet in the universe. Think, how they must have shouted for joy when they beheld all of the cosmic forces released when God said, and "let the waters under the heavens be gathered together unto one place, and let the dry land appear."

Let us consider these events when this incomprehensible force started in motion. Think of it, here is a mass of primordial chaos, formed into a planet, and when its liquid contents changed into solids, it reminds us of when we squeeze the water out of a sponge. It is like a giant ball releasing its contents in a bucket or just as a baker might form a lump of dough into a loaf of bread.

Imagine what an awe-inspiring sight must have been when the continents and islands rose from the deep with the mighty splash as if monstrous whales were coming to the surface. We see matter becoming rock and atoms moving to form the minerals of the earth. Here we see gold became gold, silver became silver, and all the metals and minerals became what they are, and each is given its specific place in the mass of matter whereby a planet was in the process of being formed. What must tremors have vibrated when all the waters under the heavens were set in motion to gather into one place, rising with a tremendous roar?

All of this happened because God spoke it! In **verses 9, 10**, we have implied that a great geological process was taking place. Great upheavals produced all this through pressures and volcanic activity. Here brought about a significant distortion of the earth's crust. It once was all flat, now rugged, but directly it caused the land to appear. No plants could grow without this taking place. In the present economy, it must have soil, water, light, and chemical nutrients.

God did this by making everything full-grown, explicitly in the creation of man. All of this happened because God spoke it!!!

After the land and sea were separated, God formed the dry land into a suitable habitation for man and all other living creatures by providing it with an atmosphere and water without which life would be impossible. God, when creating vegetation, created it with varying sizes, colors, and shapes. He places rivers, lakes, and seas, oceans with mountains and valleys and flatlands.

He filled the interior of the earth with an abundance of a population of animals and bio-chemicals of countless varieties for practical use and man's enjoyment. He then covered the sterile surface with a layer of fertile soil to make life and growth possible.

Finally, when all of this took place, God wrapped the new, infant planet unfinished, born into infinite space, a beautiful area of vegetation, different colors, smells, and unique designs full of fragrance and beauty. Here is our earth, the planet on which we live, which God set in motion on the third day. The world went into ecstasy in science's achievements in creating a space capsule for space travel.

More than that, a man was able to travel into space and come back. Yet, most people today completely ignore the Creator's infinitely greater works and refuse to honor and glorify Him, who made everything. With man's inability to see God for who He is, what is revealed to us is the very nature of man himself. Can't you see the creation account describes the character and attributes of God?

There are many misconceptions concerning God in our world today, and reading through Genesis corrects this thought. You cannot read Genesis without seeing the character and attributes of God. We know God is a sovereign and all-powerful God. This is the key to understanding how different He is from all the rest of this world's gods.

As you study Genesis, you will find no creation struggles. Nor does God overcome opposing forces to create the earth and man. Instead, God creates with a mere command, "let there be."

These are order and progress.

In reading, you will find that God does not experiment but skillfully fashions the creation of his omniscient design into being and, as we will see, man, is His ultimate achievement. We can describe God as no mere force but a person. God is no distant cosmic force, but an ever-present personal God. The fact man is created in His image is repeated often in the Word of God. See **Gen. 1:26-28**.

As we have said, Man is a reflection of God. Who we are is a reflection of the very being of God.

In **Chapter Two**, we will find God provided Adam with an opportunity to work alongside a helpmeet daily in the Garden. See **Gen. 3:8**. We know God is eternal.

Interestingly, you will find other religions do not proclaim their gods' origin, but Genesis declares from the beginning God is.

In this discloser of God, we find He immediately is active in the creation account. We also know God is good. We know creation did not take place in a moral vacuum. Morality is a very fabric woven into a design.

Note in our text that the expression "it was good" is used many times.

The word "good" implies not only a moral value placed on a man but the fact he is complete and useful to God. Therefore, those who hold to atheistic views of the origin of the earth see no value system but are accepted by most people.

At the time when God decided to create that from the beginning, which was nothingness, it was excellent. He just wanted to create.

Through His Creation, we see God's attribute of graciousness and goodness evident; **Matt 5:45**.

On the one hand, man is so God-like in his creative genius that he can imitate the Creator.

Then, at the same time, he can be so utterly blind and perverse and so dazed by his conceit and pride that he cannot see the truth about himself. The man should have humbled himself and acknowledged his finite capabilities and accepted who God was as the Creator of the universe's origin. But he would not and in his hatred for the things of God would rather believe in the perverted imagination he had made of himself and the things around him.

What sinfulness is man? Then we turn around and give this absurd theory and superstition a national blessing. We have the U.S. Supreme Court ruling in its wisdom that every child ought not to be taught the origin of Creation by God had instead taught an unproven theory is disturbing to me. An Omnipotent Creator of Heaven and earth to whom all men are responsible is an unconventional thought. They only have one option today, and so they try and get rid of Him by reasoning Him out of this universe from the beginning. See *1 Timothy 1:21-24*.

If we accept by faith the creation story as the simple, literal truth, then we immediately have a way of understanding all of the facts of geology in its proper perspective. Although the evolutionist has no final answer to which came first, the chicken or the egg, *verse 11*, answers this question. It is undeniable that the chicken came first.

Notice, God did not command the seed to bring forth; he commanded the earth to bring forth vegetation. The vegetation itself was to produce seed that would germinate more vegetation.

The parent always existed before the offspring, minus the belly button! God does not say it is going to be good; He said it is good. He put the lights in the firmament of Heaven on the 4th day, *verses 14-19*. Remember that this is not the beginning of light. We saw that in *Genesis 1:3*.

So what is the purpose of the two greater lights? It is merely to divide the day from the night, *verse 14*. That question should lead us into asking ourselves the question as to when did God create the sun, moon, and stars.

Do you know when??? Again the answer is in *verse 1* of *Chapter one*.

Even though God created them on the first day, their usage came to bear on the fourth day, setting them apart to give light on the earth. See *verse 15*. The phrase, "let there be lights" is literally, "Let there be light-bearers, places where the light is. The subject is light-bearers, or light-holders, not the light itself. These lights provide a beautiful parallel to the believers being the light of the world. See *Matt. 5:14-16*.

A Christian is supposed to be the light of the world. Here in the same sense that the sun and the moon are the light-bearers. For Christians, we have Jesus living in us. Nothing should prevent that light from shining to others and pointing them to Jesus. God's purpose in centering the light in the sun, moon, and stars is obvious. See *verses 14, 15*. It was to provide day from night.

It is to be for signs and seasons, days, and years. See *verse 14*. It is to give light to the earth.

There were days and nights before the 4th day, insomuch as God divided the light from the darkness on the 1st day. On the 4th day, God assigned the sun, moon, and the stars to regulate light upon the earth.

Notice now, some of the stars were small, some were large, some were off to themselves, some were in clusters, some were dim, and some were bright. All of these heavenly bodies were set in perpetual motion, each moving in its orbit. Each of these maintains the constant distance from each other and travels through space faster than a speeding bullet. All have continued in their respective orbits without interruption or collision, each maintaining its timetable with absolute mathematical accuracy.

That is why David, as a lad, could sit on the hillside around Bethlehem and reach his harp and sing. See *Psalm 19:1-6*. These signs were to declare the glory of the Lord. See *Psalm 8:1-4*. More so, these signs were given to man to establish how to find his way from one place to another. Another reason was they were used to predict future events and to provide divine judgment. See *Lk. 21:25-27* and *Joel 2:30, 31*.

Not only will these light-bearers be for signs but seasons. The early Babylonians seemed to have been the 1st to develop the study of the stars. They mapped out the heavens and located many great stars and constellations. They established the calendar year of 365 1\2 days. They predicted the eclipse of the sun and the moon. We are confident the wise men who came from the East to Jerusalem, seeking the newborn king of the Jews, were undoubtedly Babylonian astronomers.

The movements of these heavenly bodies fix days and years. The earth's rotation around the sun determines a one day cycle. This set in motion the signs, seasons, days, and for years.

Man needed navigational aids to direct and guide him. Therefore we have these heavenly bodies. Through these Heavenly bodies, God created what we know as a gravitational pull to divide the climate into seasons.

Duly noted, we have the four seasons of spring, summer, fall, and winter.

So they were not just for astrology and the signs of the zodiac or fortune-telling. Animals, plant life, and all humanity needed light and heat upon the earth. Light and heat upon this earth is the main reason for these heavenly bodies. Life can't survive without the existence of the sun and moon and the stars.

Man measures the time it takes for light to reach the earth from the planetary bodies in terms of light-years. The question comes to mind how that if stars are so many light-years away from the earth and the distance light can travel in a year's is determined in this way, how can we see the light of these stars if they are so far away??

The answer to this question is that God, when He placed the heavenly bodies in space, brought the light from the earth to the stars or made them like He did planet earth, with age built-in. The light of these stars fixed on the 4th day of creation would give age. In *verses 20-25*, we have the creation of living things: the 5th and 6th days. Up until the 5th day, God had to prepare the earth for living things and man.

On this the 5th day, he begins the creation of living things. We see God created fish, fowls, and whales. We could say all ocean life. Each life created was to bring forth after its kind, *verse 21*.

While there are variations within each species or kind, there is no evolution here. The thought is of mutation versus Evolution. One kind does not produce another type.

The third day was the beginning of life on the earth with the creation of plant life. Life, in and of itself, is incomprehensible, even in plant life. Even more mysterious is the creation of conscious life. Plant life is a living thing, but it is not a conscious living thing. Plant life is not aware of its environment, nor does plant life has sense organs. It does not feel. It does not choose where it will live. It does not recognize its offspring. Now we do not have time here, but sometimes you need to take a very close look at an egg's contents. We do not have the time to tell you of the numerous things that must occur before an egg can hatch. How could all of this happen?

How could these little creatures, not endowed with human intelligence or creative imagination, do all of the things necessary to hatch an egg? Who taught them the birds, to build a nest, find the right kind of food to eat? Who regulated the timetable for the hatching period? How did the mother bird know that her brood had taken the place of the eggs? Now they required food for them to survive? Who told the mother bird that those little birds came from those eggs?

If they had evolved, how did they survive before these changes took place if it took millions of years to come about? How did they learn the skills necessary which are essential for them to survive, or before the foods they needed to eat came into existence? How can the different species confine themselves to a specific kind of food, and only found in a particular place?

Why do they continue to stay within those boundaries and limitations if they evolve?

Some birds feed on fish, others on rodents, and others snakes, some just worms, and some are only strict vegetarians, not to mention that they sometimes had to travel great distances to get their food. How did they acquire the knowledge of where to find these foods and then to have the skills necessary to get it?

Since some say they evolved, which came first, the shape of their bills or their food habitat came to mind. You could write a book just on the questions you should ask. Who taught the birds to sing, and where did they learn the songs they sing, or why are their different songs to sing? Why doesn't the crow have a voice like a canary? Another interesting thing concerning fish and birds is their ability to migrate. Interestingly both fish and birds migrate.

Some fish species and birds leave their natural habitats locally for some unexplained reason, only to return to the same place they had gone before, years apart. Who told them when to leave and when to come back? How can they find their way through uncharted routes, lousy weather, and even night's darkness? On the other hand, animals are conscious of their existence, whereas plants are not conscious of their presence. One thing unique about animals is they understand and sense their environments. They have sense organs. Animals are aware of feeling in that they can see, they can hear. They are mindful of heat and cold. Animals can feel hunger and thirst. They can select their food. All animals can recognize their offspring, and they have child-like attitudes and mentalities. Who told them all of these things? The answer is God did.

The last animals to be created on the 6th day were mammals. With the creation of mammals, animal life reached its highest form. The word "mammal" comes from a Latin word," the mother's breast." Mammals are creatures whose young get nourishment with the milk of their mothers. There are several distinguishing characteristics that separate mammals from all other animals God made. Mammals give birth to their young.

Another unique attribute of mammals is they have highly developed brains and nervous systems. Also, mammals breathe utilizing lungs. Mammals have their bodies covered with hair, some more, some less. Mammals have four limbs. In studying them, mammals have vital organs very similar to men. Mammals have always lived within the realm of humanity. Mammals, some of them, are very faithful and unselfish servants to man.

Mammals begin their lives at the moment of conception. Conception means that a living female cell, called an ovum, has been fertilized or penetrated by a male cell. These two cells collide and become one fertilized living cell. This one cell is the beginning of a new life, which contains all the distinguishing characteristics of the adult in that species. The mother nourishes this new life until it can take care of itself.

We know that man is the crown of God's Creation. He is the reason God created, and ***Gen. 1:26-31*** records this event for us. God created man to be the Ruler of all that He made. The man was to have complete dominion over everything created on the earth. Two chapters deal with the account of the creation of man, both in *Gen. 1* and *Gen. 2*. In *Gen. 1:26*, we have revealed to us the purpose of the creation of man. In *Gen. 1:27*, we have shown for us the pronouncement of what God did. In *Gen. 2:7*, we have revealed to us the procedure of how God did what he did.

In Gen. 1, God emphasizes man's relationship to the material universe. Man is God's crowning work.

In Gen. 2, man is presented as having a spiritual capacity that no other creation made.

As we have stated before, man is made in the image of God. No other created begin was made this way. Man's creation was distinct from that of other creatures in that God breathed into his nostrils the breath of life. In giving him life, God permitted man by a simple command to do certain things. Yet these bounds were made not to allow the man to disobey what God told him to do. His liberty consists of loyalty in keeping the Word of God.

Only he was conscious of there being a Creator.

Man can commune with God. Because of this ability, we say the man is the crown of God's Creation, for no other creature has that ability. In *Genesis chapter 1:24*, we find something very unique about the man.

Man consists of body, soul, and Spirit. That part of man we see, the material part, will one day be changed into immortality. Therefore a man will always exist somewhere. This body will be resurrected at a later time. The believer will receive a glorified body. Man has a soul which no other creature has.

In man's soul is where is the seat of his emotions, desires, affections, etc. are *Psalm 42:1-6*.

In the scriptures, the "heart" is synonymous with the soul.

If the man only had a body, he would be like a tree. Yet, man has a soul which gives him self-consciousness, like the animals. Man has an intellect that is a mind, and he has sensibility, that is, emotions, and has a will, which is the power of choice.

However, the most crucial part of man is his Spirit. The Bible sometimes calls it the "inner man."

It is that part of us that is God-conscious. We cannot see it or feel it, but it is part of every human being, even if they declare themselves an atheist. See **Prov. 20:27**.

Man has a kinship to God that is higher than that of God has made, **Acts 17:28**. The likeness is a resemblance or similarity. Man resembles God in that he has personality. Also, we know man is in the likeness of God in that he has purity. However, man can choose, and he may decide to go in the wrong direction from God. Man resembles God in that he has power. His creative acts demonstrate God's strength. Even in a fallen state, a man shows a shadow of that power through self-government, language, thought, originality, and organizational ability.

The purpose of the Spirit of man is to give him the ability to communicate with God. The inner beings of man, call it consciousness or Spirit, controls man and are far more important than his appearance. What a man possesses is not nearly as important as whom he is. Man, made in the image of God corresponds to the words, "after his kind," **verse 25**.

As God's representatives, man is to have dominion over all God created. We see this in **verse 26**.

We have the emphatic proclamation of man's divine origin. In Creation, God intended man to walk in fellowship with Him, but he rebelled against that directive. But now, through God's son and His love, we have that same opportunity to have fellowship with Him. See **verse 27**.

We can see three distinct steps in man's creation. First, the man was formed from the dust of the ground, then God's breath in his nostrils, giving him the breath of life. Their man became a living soul. So we see that man came from the earth. Scientists tell us that, indeed, men came from the elements of the planet.

There are some puzzling things concerning the similarities between a man and some animals. However, they are best explained by each having one designer and Creator, rather than using the theory of Evolution to explain it. One thing to note is the fact we share the same environment. See *I Cor. 15:39-41*. Though sin has marred man's image, it can be restored through our being born again today. The resurrection described for us in *I Cor. 15:42-49* that restoration will be complete one day.

In *Gen. 1:26*, we have these words, "let us" the plurality indicated here is in keeping with the Hebrew word "Elohim," used as God's name throughout the creation account. As revealed earlier in the scriptures, God is a trinity, which means there are three persons in the one Godhead.

There is no plurality of God's; instead, the man was created in God's image, after His likeness, emphasizing the similarity between man and God.

Note that this is not necessarily a physical likeness because God is a spirit and has no physical form. Some verses are hard to understand, but we have other verses that help us understand God's mind more. *Eph. 4:24* tells us a little about what God meant when He said He made us in His image. The new man spoken of is created in God, or after God, righteousness & holiness. Neither of these attributes is visible at any time.

But that is part of the image of God. This new man is regenerated as distinguished from the sinful man. The regenerated man is the one who has become a partaker of the divine life and nature of God. God proclaimed no other creature would be like him. The man was God's final creation.

The new man results from a person receiving Christ as his Saviour and becoming a new creature.

We see this profoundly taught in *1 Cor. 5:17*. The whole purpose of the believer is that which Christ has formed in him. Look at *Gal. 2:20* and *Col. 3:10*.

In *Genesis One*, God creates everything and calls it good. Creations' purpose was to glorify God, yet humanity failed in his one duty. If we accept Christ's restoration, you can return to God's original objective and have the Creator's hope for eternity.

Chapter 2

Beginning in *Chapter 2*, we have man's creation, which was God's final creative act. The man was the final touch and crown of all His works. There have not been any more creative acts by God. What God does now is to sustain that which He has made. See *Heb. 1:3*. God, by His omnipotent power, holds all things together. He fixed immutable laws in all things ordered and by which all creation fulfills the objective for which intended. He holds the earth suspended in space. The earth travels around the sun at tremendous speeds rotating on its axis. Here is what regulates every clock made in the world. Day follows night, and season follows season. The sun continues to radiate light. The birds continue to feed and build their nests, and so all things continue as God has ordained them to be.

When God completed creation, we read, "It was very good," *verse 31*. God had created a perfect world, perfect in all of its detail. There were no thorns and thistles in that world, no disease, and no sin.

The earth brought forth abundantly of everything needful to provide for man's wants, comforts, and pleasures. In God's desire for the man in his existence, he would not need to struggle with survival. There would be no arctic cold. No disease. No disorders. No earthquakes. No aging process. No suffering. No death.

On the 7th day, God rested not from fatigue but in the joy of His creative works' achievement. He could enjoy His creation because there was no sin. The 7th day is a particular subject of divine favor, making it Holy and sanctified. See *Genesis 2:3*.

This seventh day was set apart for a Holy purpose. God's Sabbath was not merely inactivity. It was a cessation of the work of the six creative days.

Blessed in our text means God gave the creative acts his Holy approval and rested from creating.

Sanctified in the text means God set that day apart from the days of work to rest. God rested from his labors not on man's 7th day but man's first day on the earth. The command for man to rest came 2500 years later and was given to Israel by Moses. See *Neh. 9:13, 14; Ex. 20:8-10; John 1:7*. This rest of God is symbolic to the rest of the believer in Christ, note *Heb. 4:9-11*.

The believer's Sabbath rest is not limited to a specific day or year. We enter it when, as believers, we cease to struggle in the flesh and live the Christian life by God's power and might. In *Ephesians*, we see Christ has already provided everything the believer needs to have rest in God. Indeed, God did not intend for man to be lazy after his creation.

The man had two responsibilities. That was to keep the Garden and stand the testing of the free will God was going to give him. *Gen. 2* provides the background to the events recorded in G*en. 3. Gen. 2:8-17* is dealing with the Garden. Eden was the name of a specific region, and the Garden was in the eastern part of that region. In *verse 10*, it tells us of a river in the Garden.

From this river ran four more rivers. The Tigris and the Euphrates are two of these rivers. No one knows what the other two were. Today the heads of the Tigris and the Euphrates are about 2000 miles apart. These are indications that there have been some significant changes since the days of Adam. See *verse 15*.

As we think about man's creation, we can't help from thinking about how some people have the idea that God did not create man, but by being evolved from an animal, you know this as the theory of Evolution. From our studies, we can conclude man and animals are in any way related. The animal kingdom cannot transmit knowledge from one generation to another. No animal has or can experience a real sense of guilt when it does wrong, nor develop consciousness of the judgment to come. No other animal has a desire to worship the one true God. Immortality is not something an animal understands. No animal has ever learned to read or write. No animal has ever learned to cook its food, make its clothes, or make work tools. No animal has ever honestly laughed at something humorous.

A man stands alone *physically*; he alone can walk upright. A man stands alone *mentally*; he solely can communicate in a sophisticated manner. A man stands apart from all other creatures.

Spiritually, he alone can know the mind and will of God.

God made man different from how He made any other being! Without being so repetitious, we adamantly say the man was made in the image of God. God is a trinity, so man is a trinity. Man has a body, and he has world consciousness. Then, man can understand death, hurt, and sorrow. Man has a soul, and He has self- consciousness. Man has a Spirit. Therefore he is God-conscious.

One of the exciting things about man, as we have said, is he is in God's image. One of the primary meanings of this is that man has free will. Freedom is an inherent part of human nature. See *Gen. 1:26*. We find the world's influences, the flesh, and the devil can make a man do things he would not normally do through our own experiences. Many scholars over the centuries have debated the subject of the free will of man. In my studies, I have concluded from the Scriptures that God does not predetermine our choices. It is especially true concerning God's will. See *Matt. 23:37*. We can choose between good and evil, for the choice is ours to make whether it is right or wrong in God's eyes. Study the following verses. *Deut. 24:16; Job 19:4; Jer. 31:30; Rom. 14:12; 2 Cor. 5:10; Rev. 22:12*.

This freedom gives humanity the power to be deliberate, determined, and creative in choosing plans, purposes, and life directions. Through this freedom, we find we can have a right relationship with God and others. There have been many times in making choices those powers from without having influenced us. See *Mark 7:23; Rom. 12:2*.

From the instant sin became a part of man's nature, we understand the principle of making unwise choices. *See Gen. 3:6*. More than that, we find the influence of sin upon our lives limits the very God-given freedoms. See ***John 8:34***. The Christian life can be a struggle until you understand the power of sin upon your life and seek God's power through the work of Jesus. See ***Rom. 7:19-24***.

In these following verses, we see through Jesus Christ and God's work in salvation, regeneration, and sanctification; we can be free to function as God created us. See ***John: 3: 2-36***.

This freedom of our ability to allow Christ through the Holy Spirit to guide us in making the right decisions is ours to make. See ***2 Cor. 3:17; Gal. 2:16-20***.

The most significant influence of our lives should be that Christ-like Spirit is demonstrating love to others. See ***2 Cor. 5:14***. He should allow us to make the right kind of decisions for the glory of God. We can say that frequently we have allowed our freedoms to influence us in selfish ways. See ***1 Pet. 2:15-16***.

Freedom of our will is to choose to obey and serve Christ, bringing glory to Him. We should use this to cause us to want to follow Christ in all things and serve His purposes on earth and glorify Him. See ***Rom. 6:17-23***.

The purpose of our free will is we are provided the opportunity to know Him and the power of his being. We see this in ***Matt. 12:50; John 7:17; Eph. 6:6; Jas. 4:15***.

As we all have failed God in the sense of sin, we are all born now with the sinful nature, and we need Christ and his salvation to help us make the right choices. See ***Rom. 10:12-13***.

Glorifying Him should be left to the individual's free choice to accept or reject salvation and accept our decisions' consequences.

Now, I have said all of that to bring you to a particular point. I want you to think with me what took place on that day, the day God made man. Having already made the earth, we find Him reaching down and taking some dirt and molding it until he has a man. There is not a doubt that all the creatures He has made are watching intently. The difference between these one and all others is that he will have the power of choice. The choice either to choose right or wrong is God-given. That will be called free will. Within the power of choice, we see man will have the ability to love, hate, know good and evil, and what responsibility there is in this decision making.

Over the centuries, man has made some awful choices, and as time has gone by, man has forgotten his maker many times. But God has a plan, knowing what man would do. He made that first man, someday allowing His only Son to come to this earth and doing something created man could not do. That was paying for the sins he would commit against a Holy God.

There would be a time when He would come in the flesh and be rejected by humanity and be hung on a tree because they would not listen to Him and accept him. But, that was the plan for God knows all things, even the rejection of man. He loved us so much He was willing to let His Son do a work we could not do. Enough to create us, die in our stead for the sins we would commit against Him. Oh, how much He cares!!

He was making man that day; I am sure He must have felt the pain that created man would bring Him throughout time. Why didn't He make the man obey Him instead? The answer is because if you remove choice, you remove love. What pain there must have been in the heart of God as He made man.

But what joy of knowing that man would be able to commune with Him now and for eternity.

Now was the time for the breath of man to be placed in man. You could see his chest rise.

Suddenly we see the man moving and breathing, but God could see the Spirit of the man stirring more than that. Unequivocally the seen and unseen creatures of God were amazed at what was taking place. Man is made so different from all the rest of God's creation. Man, given a choice, what a thought!

Now, it is our choice!! Remember, God made you. Are you going to love Him back in return?

In understand **Chapter 2**, it must be studied in the light of **Chapters 3, 4.**

Chapter 2 aims not to give another account of creation in general, but to supplement *Chapter 1* and describe in greater detail the nature of man.

Chapter 2 begins with a brief review of the creation events and then continues with a more detailed account of Adam and Eve's creation. It gives us a description of the Garden of Eden, the place where God first placed man. It continues with establishing marriage as an institution of God, and the program that God gave made and man's responsibilities placed upon him. As God's image, we understand that throughout the rest of the Bible it deals with man's relationship to God.

Chapter 2 bridges the gap between *Chapters 1* and *3*. *Chapter 1* speaks of creating a perfect world that had received the pronouncement of being "very good" in God's eyes. As a result of the fall, God's masterpiece world now has a curse upon it, which we will see in *Chapter 3*.

Chapter 2 is necessary because it supplies the essential background for all of this. So then *Chapter 1* shows how this world came into being. *Chapter 2* is an account of the events that followed creation and what man did in the Garden and God's given responsibilities.

Here in *Chapter 2*, we have two trees. One is for life. One is for testing.

Man needed to exercise choice according to God's will or face the consequences of a stubborn attitude toward Him. It was there at the tree of knowledge of good and evil that God provided the focal point for the man to decide for God or himself. Adam could know good and evil because God created him in His image. The exercise of man's will demonstrates that he has dominion over the other creatures of this earth. But for a man to use his freedom of choice concerning good and evil, he needed to face decisions that would involve him in learning to say no to temptation.

There were and are moral issues man has to learn to face. This issue was not whether he would know good from evil, but whether he would continue sound reasoning in following God's known plan. Because man failed in this test, he now had an experimental knowledge of the difference between good and evil.

We know the tree of knowledge could not impart in itself the truth of good and evil. It was not the fruit that was the problem. It was man's disobedience that brought spiritual ruin to man.

We should remember that God had given man all he needed without deciding whether to obey or to disobey God.

The command of God forbids a man from partaking of the tree of good and evil knowledge.

God kept this one tree as a test for man. The test boiled down whether he would choose fellowship with God or go on his own against God's Word and take the forbidden fruit.

It is doubtful whether the tree of knowledge of good and evil had any more attractive fruit on it than the other trees in the Garden. The future of the whole human race hinged on what Adam and Eve would do with that tree.

It wasn't a hard thing that God asked because He had given man everything he needed. Just one thing not to do and that did not eat of the fruit of that tree. God even warned the man that he would die both physically and spiritually if he ate that tree's fruit.

The phrase, "thou shalt surely die" is fundamental, *Genesis 2:17*. The biblical meaning of death is separation, either physically or spiritually. We know the man was created primarily as a spiritual being and the body secondary. It was not the body that God wanted fellowship. It was the spiritual essence of man.

In the very moment man disobeyed God, he died spiritually. Therefore, separation came from God. See *verses 16, 17*. The man did not die physically on the day he disobeyed God.

However, the seeds of death had been sown; decay set in, and eventually, men did die physically.

Because Adam partook of the fruit, we acquired our sinful nature. Following death for all who follow Adam in life will see all have sinned and come short of God's Glory. See *Rom. 5:12; Heb. 9:27; 1 Cor. 15:25, 26*.

From these verses, we must conclude a person born into this world is already spiritually dead. See **Eph. 2:12**. Man does not have to sin to acquire the sin nature, nor does he have to sin first.

He is born with that nature. Our sinful nature puts each person in a state of condemnation when he enters the world, according to **John 3:18**.

When Adam and Eve sinned in the Garden, we admitted it was not the devil that made them do it.

Adam chose to sin against God. He knew he was disobeying the Word of God but freely wanted to do so.

While **Genesis 1** describes an order from chaos to cosmos, or disorder to order, **Chapter 2** follows a different pattern. God knew from the beginning man would need help. Man lacks in many things, but God provided what we need, as shown in the following verses. In **verses 6-17**, we see no shrub, no plant, no rain, and no man. These are satisfied by the mist and the rivers, the man, and the Garden, as we see in **verses 6-14**.

The lack we see in **verses 18-25** is, simply stated, "No helpmeet for Adam." This helper is provided divinely in the last part of **Chapter 2**, as we will see.

Let me emphasize that Moses does not intend to give us a chronological order of events but a logical one. He intended to describe the creation of man, his wife, and their setting.

These become critical factors in the fall, which occurs in **Chapter 3**.

In **verse 6**, we first mention how water is supplied on the earth by the word "mist."

This word means "spring." Spring gives us the idea of a river with running water, making it possible for all life, including the vegetation, to be watered. In part, this could explain some of the work Adam performed in keeping the Garden. It should be easy to follow God creating the Garden, and in that Garden was a water supply for man to drink. How else would that which God had made survive? See **verse 9**.

There are two trees mentioned here. You have the tree of good and evil knowledge, and the other is the tree of life. See **verses 16-17**. Interestingly, we can only hypothesize how Adam conveyed this command of God to his helpmeet. I wonder if she got the message.

No matter what took place, I am sure that she understood what God meant as told by Adam.

The man was in this paradise. It was for him to enjoy this wonderland surely, but he also cultivated it according to *verse 5*.

Now Adam's creation is described more fully in *Genesis 2:7* than the verses in *Chapter 1*.

Realizing later, he, as not created like other creatures must have been a humbling fact for Adam. Another difference in Adam's creation stems from the fact that his life-breath is God's inspiration, as seen in *verse 7*.

There was no mythical Garden God created. Every part of this paradise description leads us to understand that it was a real garden in a precise geographical location. There are specific points of reference given to help us identify the location of the Garden. There are four rivers named, but only two of them exist today. That should not surprise us knowing the cataclysmic flood which took place. Therefore, for us today, it would be impossible to locate this Garden.

The Garden of Eden was a place different from what we think of today. First of all, from the Scriptures, we see it was a place of work. Most men today dream of paradise as a place where they could lay back and never work again; some would say Adam experienced Heaven on earth.

However, there were restrictions in the Garden. Many people today mention Heaven as a place where they could do anything they want to do.

Knowing how beautiful the Garden of Eden must have been, a state of beauty and bliss, it cannot be thought of as a place of unlimited pleasure for later; we will find Adam had many jobs. While Adam was able to do most anything he wanted, there was still God's command, which forbids him from eating that tree's fruit.

Heaven is not what many think of today. It is not a place of just experiencing every desire one could think of, but Heaven is a place of knowing and understanding fellowship with God.

Here is how we become being a servant. As you can see, servanthood is not a new concept discovered in the New Testament.

God was showing Adam meaningful service adds purpose in life. Later you can see God described Israel as a cultivated garden, a vineyard in *Isaiah 5:1-2*. Then, in the New Testament, you will find Jesus spoke of himself as the vine and we as the branches.

We see this illustrating again how much the father loves and cares about us. See *John 15:1*.

Paul described the ministry of a servant as the work of a farmer, for the Christian. *See 2 Timothy 2:6*.

In the Scriptures, we often find the church described as a flock, indicating we do have a job. After salvation, you will find out there is still plenty to do for the Lord.

As Christians, we should see the work of the Lord as a blessing and joy instead of duty or drudgery.

In *Genesis 2:18-25*, we have described for us man's helpmeet. One requirement is left to do.

God has made the earth, all the things, and creatures therein. It was God, who placed man in the Garden to cultivate and keep it, yet, there is one thing lacking. All the animals made by God have a companion but not Adam. Note *verses 18-25* and see God meet the need.

Adam's mate was an extraordinary creation, a 'helper, suitable for him", reading *verse 18*.

God wanted to create a helper, not just a slave, and this helpmeet would not be inferior to him.

To better understand what God wanted, look at the Hebrew word "*Ezer*." It was a word that Moses liked. See *Exodus 18:4*. In context, you will find it refers to God as man's helper.

See *Deuteronomy 33:7, 26, 29; Psalms 20:2; 33:20; 70:5; 89:19; 115:9; 121:1, 2; 124:8; 146:5*.

The Hebrew word implies a helpmeet. There is in no way implied inferiority or such. In a way, this is consistent with its usage; God is helping men by the women. What a beautiful thought.

How far above some designs this is. Then, Eve is a helper who works with and answers Adam, for he is the headship's human race.

Today men have the impression that a wife or woman needs to be just like the man. Have you ever noticed when you have the right partner in a relationship, how, just looking from the outside, it would appear they were incompatible?

It is by divine design God made us this way. Therefore we understand incompatibility is one of the purposes of marriages! God has appointed conflict and burdens to teach us how to grow spiritually in the home to become one flesh. These are to be secondary to the high and holy purposes of God.

God made Eve so she could correspond to Adam physically; there is no question. She also honored him socially, intellectually, spiritually, and emotionally.

When I counsel those who plan to marry, I do not necessarily seek to discover the many similarities. When talking with a man and a woman, especially in marriage counseling, they need to know each other better. Many times I have explained it will take years to now another person in marriage. God made us all different by design, and this is what will bring about a healthy marriage.

Before creating this counterpart, God first whets Adam's appetite. God uses the creatures He has made to help Adam in what was to come. The animal's march by Adam, and names them recognize they are coming in pairs, a male and female. There is no doubt he is thinking of this, but more than that, this naming the creatures shows the rest of creation that Adam has the headship over them. See **Genesis 1:28**.

How carefully Adam must have noted the unique characteristics of each creature brought before him. How long it took, we do not know. As Adam watched these creatures paraded by, he realized there was a void in his life. There is no doubt he must have talked with God about this. It was in these conversations he understood the void was he had no mate.

Perhaps it was at this point of his need; God put Adam in a deep sleep and from his rib, He fashioned a woman. Then He presented the woman to Adam. Stop and think of how he must have felt when he saw her for the first time? See *Genesis 1:23*.

The name of Adam's mate is "woman." The English translation accurately picks up the play on the two words. In Hebrew, man would be pronounced 'ish; the woman would be 'ishshah".

While the sounds are comparable, the roots of the two words are different. Properly 'ish may come from a parallel Arabic root, carrying the idea of 'exercising power,' while the term 'ishshah" may be acquired from an Arabic parallel, meaning 'to be soft. See *Genesis 2:24*.

From this account, we understand the process God has established.

What is a man to do but leave his father and mother, and in the KJV, we find the word "cleave" to his wife? See *Genesis 2:24*.

It means to hold on to, to have only one, or the only one.

There is an interesting word here in our text. In *verse 24*, we have the word "therefore."

Why is it there? Men were to leave his parents to take a wife.

Without preaching a message here, we see the implication of not forsaking the responsibility for taking care of his parents in their later life but in the sense of being dependent on them.

Look at these New Testament references; *Mark 7:10-13; Ephesians 6:2, 3*.

From these verses, it is apparent man is to cease living under their headship and control, and he is to function as the head of a new home.

What is interesting in this is that the woman only transfers headship. She was once subject to her father and mother, and now, after marriage, she is to be subject to her husband.

To put it in today's vernacular, marriage is much more than just a social event. God considers it a sacred institution in its original intent. As we have said, we understand Adam preceding his wife in the creation, and we know this is why the husband is to exercise headship in marriage. See *I Corinthians 11:8-9; 1 Timothy 2:13*.

That brings us to the role of the woman in the church. Here this was not just Paul writing his idea, nor to the culture of his time. Here was a revelation from God. See *1 Corinthians 14: 34*.

No passage in the entire Bible so concisely defines the things which count in life.

The woman may have it difficult, but think of what the man must now do. Before marriage, the man was to be submissive to his father and mother.

Now, in marriage, he becomes the head of the home. As has been noted, the husband-wife relationship is permanent, while the parent-child bond is temporary. Even if the parents are unwilling to end the dependent relationship with his parents, it is still a son's responsibility to do so.

It has been said, "To fail to do so is to refuse the kind of bond necessary with his wife."

In this relationship, you can see the husband and wife are to be co-equal and co-reigning together.

That can only happen if both are willing to leave their parents and make a bond together.

They become one flesh. As years have gone by in our marriage, we find each other answering each other without asking questions. When young and lacking experience, couples begin as individuals wondering how they will become one. But as you strive to follow the command and will of God, you begin to see what He intended for them. We should ask, what is the reason for its mention here in Genesis? First of all, there were no parents to whom Adam or Eve was born. We know from the account in our text Eve's inception was directly from the rib of her mate, Adam.

The original union involved no parents, for the wife was a part of her husband's flesh. This last verse is not accidental. It describes for us a great deal that we need to know in *Genesis 2:25*.

For example, sex did not begin with or because of the fall. We know that procreation and physical intimacy were God's intentions from Adam and Eve's time. See *Genesis 1:28*. Today the world yearns to assume that they have invented sex and that God only seeks to prevent it.

Apart from God, there cannot be the sex God desired for man. We have turned God's will in sex upside down. Call it ignorance or even bliss, but it is not the way God meant. With our calm, collected, and sophisticated thinking, we know all there is to know about sex in our generation.

"How naive are those who have never had sex before marriage," we believe. Yet many times we have said that in life, it is better not to know some things. Many times we have heard it say, it was just sex being innocent. There is no such thing as sweet innocence. See *Matthew 19:4-6*.

Then there is one last thought that needs mentioning before we close this chapter.

Life's meaning can only be understood through men being created in God's image and likeness.

What we see today is not what made us in the image. Sin has taken away what God instilled within us, and only through the finished work of Christ can that image be restored. See *Ephesians 4:23, 24; Colossians 3:10*.

So many times, we have it all wrong. We think work is a curse, but that is not true. Work gives the purpose of blessings and a fulfilling of what God desires from us. Note *Genesis 3:17-19; Colossians 3:22-24*.

Do you understand the institution of marriage as God intended? Think about it as we marry and get to know each other. That is only a reflection of a deeper and richer fellowship that God wants us to have with him daily.

Chapter 3

A s we have said, Genesis is the "book of beginnings." Nearly everything that we know about humankind began in the book of Genesis. There is the beginning of man, the beginning of time, the beginning of organic growth. In *Genesis 2*, we saw the beginning of the woman. *Genesis 4*, we will find the origin of worship and death.

Through this chapter, we see nations, governments, and kingdoms established. We will soon see another new beginning after the flood. This book will find the origin of slavery, jealousy, and idol worship, but five significant things are happening in *Genesis 3*.

Indeed, this is one of the fascinating chapters of the entire Bible. Here is the foundation for humanity and his living today. It is not only our living for today but how to make preparation for eternity and how to get there.

In this chapter, we see the injection of sin into humanity. I would ask myself this question, "did God know that man would sin?" He did know so that the answer would be yes. See *Rev. 13:8; Acts 15:18*. Then you have those who would say that if God knew what man would do, why would He create them? The reason is simple. He knows the beginning and the end. God already had a plan. He had a plan in eternity past. So, in reality, God knew before He ever made anything that would happen to His Creation? God also knew the beautiful results of salvation and how redeemed people would give eternal glory to Him.

In our text, we see the question of sin and what is wrong with today's world, plus Satan's introduction. From the beginning, the devil is the evil one. We will learn much about him here in this chapter. The history of man brings us to an immediate question. In the original state of man existence, was he primitive? Did he go through the Stone Age and Bronze Age and whatever? What does the Bible say?

To answer that question, God, in creation, made man in a state of maturity and perfection.

In other words, he was made fully mature with age and did not have to grow up. God created man with the capacity and facility of mind to reason, think, and do things.

I can say he lacked nothing when he was in the Garden of Eden.

God made man perfectly. This perfection was in his body, mind, and soul. Apart from Scripture, we can see the evidence of history is on the side of Scripture. The Egyptians got their civilization from the East, Greece from Phoenicia, etc. Historically, there is no indication of a nation of savages ever rising from a state of barbarianism to being in a civilized country.

The oldest records and writings prove that the standards of a civilization long ago were exceeding high. The entire human race had its origin from a common center, and that center is the seat of all civilization founded in the Middle East.

So the theories that man passed through the different ages have no scientific proof. We must believe the authority of the Bible. It states that man had perfect knowledge.

In this chapter, we have Satan's devices, and it shows us how powerless man is to do right.

When it comes down to depending upon our abilities to defeat the devil, there is no power of our own whereby we overcome.

This chapter also records the spiritual effects of sin. From the time of the first sin to the present man, all man wants to do is flee from God's presence and all that God is.

Another question we should ask is, what is a man to do? It is not a simple answer to the question, but the Bible does have the answer. It has been said, "it is one thing that a creature should be treated according to his character and quite another to account for his having that character."

To begin with, the Bible reveals to us the principle of representation. This principle is the ground on which the penalty of Adam's sin has come upon us. But on the positive side, we have Jesus Christ, who is our representative and substitute for our sin by going to the Cross in our place. Here is one who bore my sin in my place and took the penalty of my sin upon himself to have eternal life. This eternal life is with and through the God of Heaven, and there is no other way to attain this but by Him alone.

There is nothing I could do to gain or attain Heaven. On the one hand, we receive the penalty for sinfulness. On the other hand, we have the reward of subjecting ourselves by Faith in Christ Jesus.

Yet another question we should ask ourselves is, would Adam have died, had he not sinned?

Was his body made in an immoral state, had he not sinned? From the Scriptures, it is understandable that if Adam had not eaten the fruit, he would have never died. The second point is less clear, but the Apostle Paul states that we have been born in the earthy image.

That means that our present bodies are like the body of Adam as created.

Then his body no less than ours requires to be changed, according to **Rom. 2:7**.

This chapter also reveals God's attitude toward the sinner. Although man seeks to cover up his sins by his own devices, God has graciously provided a covering suitable by meeting His standards.

This chapter reveals to us the beginning of the prophecies of Jesus Christ. In this chapter, we see how man became sin and cannot approach a Holy God except through a mediator. This chapter reveals to us the destiny of Satan, our greatest enemy. This chapter explains to us how evil came to be in our hearts. This chapter shows how God is not the author of sin but that man, by his own free will and choice, brought his state of purity to an end.

An important thing to remember about man is that God could have created him differently, but chose to make him in His image.

First, I want us to look at Satan. We see the temptation of Adam and Eve. See *verses 1-5*. In reading the text, we would think, "ask ourselves, how did Satan approach Eve? Look at *verse 1* then *2 Cor. 11:13-15*. To be sure, Satan is no fool. He has much wisdom. Satan has great understanding, and he knows how to use that wisdom against man to defeat man. Note *Ezek. 28:17*.

Notice how subtle he is in *verse 1*. He does not reveal who he was and that he was God's enemy. Interestingly Satan used the highest form of animal life to deceive Eve. He did not come to her and tell her how much he hated God. I also find it very interesting that in the beginning, God told Adam to keep the Garden.

"Keep" carries with it the thought of guarding and protecting. That would include "keeping" his help-meet. See *Genesis 2:15*. With the unrest and local outbreaks and all the race implications of today, I could see the Civil Liberties Union or some such organization having the audacity to come before God, filing a lawsuit against God in defense of a minority her being a woman.

Since they were placed outside of the Garden and now could not have access to what was once their home, many would today say it was an illegal eviction. Besides, we know God based this eviction on a sinful act committed by both Eve and her husband in the privacy of their own home between two consenting adults. And, they would say, the punishment was far too excessive for the crime committed. All they did was eat some fruit. Surely that could not be a crime in this world? Then to say this small thing they did would affect the whole human race.

To be sure not. Some do not take the Bible seriously or literally have little difficulty here.

His, in our understanding, would be against a Holy God.

Yet many today see the narrative in *Genesis 3* as being a myth or just a symbolic story. I encountered a nearby college professor who did not believe the message of **Genesis 3** was real. Indeed, he was a Bible professor in college and did not accept the details of the fall.

Have you ever wondered why Eve is the only one in the narrative speaking here? Why was their punishment so great while committing only one sin? Why did God think this was such an evil sin, and why did God punish them so? Explanations will be coming forthwith.

The answer reveals itself because we would not know what God meant about sin if we did not have the first three chapters of Genesis.

We understand what God made, he made perfect, and all you have to do is leave it to man to mess it up. We have seen all of creation had God's stamp of approval on it. All you have to do is read the *first two chapters* to know God loved what He had done. It is because of that one sin in the Garden that introduced sin to the rest of humanity. Because of the sinful nature, it did not take very long to see evil in the entire human race.

Our text does not take long to find the hideous crimes committed by a man in his heart's imagination. Why **Genesis 3** is so essential is revealed to us in the text.

Knowing how the devil is and how a man reacts is why the world is the way it is today and has been for over 6,000 years. More than just the sins of the heart's imaginations, we have before us how that Satan will tempt man and the strategies he will use against us. **Chapter 3** helps us to understand why women have such a hard time following the commands of God. And there are thousands of questions to be asked here.

I am sure you can think of a few to ask yourself. There is one thing for sure here: I have no regrets in studying this great foundational chapter for doctrinal purposes. It is very descriptive in God's dealings with the entrance of sin into the human race and the consequences of man's disobedience to God's will. More than that, we will find a beautiful narrative in studying this chapter that reveals the Grace of God. He goes and seeks out the sinner and provides the necessary coverage for the sins man committed. Involved with this revelation, God promises a Saviour for all humans if they accept his free pardon for sin.

Now the serpent suddenly appears in ***verse one*** rudely and without introduction.

Adam and Eve were in the Garden, probably doing what God had told them. We should expect to find them there. They were not looking for the serpent to appear on the scene. As we would say today, he came out of nowhere. What a surprise. I know this serpent is one of God's creations.

Not knowing if it was an actual snake, what matters is that this creature was being used by Satan, described as a dragon and serpent. See the following verses; ***2 Corinthians 11:3 and Revelation 12:9; 20:2***.

As impressive as some are, there will be many unanswered questions about the origin of evil in our text. They are simply not provided to us. We must trust God by Faith.

Moses intends to bring to our attention the fact of sin and how man came to understand sin.

One of the most intriguing things here is how Satan comes before Adam and Eve. His approach was subtle. Notice, at first, he does not challenge Eve's Faith in God. Satan may manifest himself as a Madelyn Murray O'Hare, but he is often an "angel of light." Paul talks about this, for ***2 Cor. 11:13-15*** says, "For such are false apostles, deceitful workers, transforming themselves into the apostles of Christ. And no marvel; for Satan himself is transformed into an angel of light. Therefore it is no great thing if his ministers also are transformed as the ministers of righteousness; whose end shall be according to their works."

Today, in our pulpits, we have preachers who call themselves men of God who may be holding a Bible in one hand and preaching an unholy alliance out of their mouths.

Satan knew what would cause Eve to doubt the words of God.

He said it is significant, but just like today, it is not just what they say, but what they don't say is just as important. The words, 'Yea hath God said," in ***verse 1*** is dripping with innuendos.

What did Satan mean? Rebellion reeks here from Satan. No, that is not what God said, did He?

Moses used the word," the Lord God." In the Chaldean, this means Yahweh, the Elohim. Satan, on the other hand, just said, God.

From this it indicates his hatred toward God. Can't you see what the devil is doing here? He is the deceiver, the one who all he has to do is create doubt in a person's mind, and he knows this will lead to disobedience toward God. He was only inquiring about the fruit and what God had said about it. He twisted what God said and what Eve thought to cause doubt to enter in.

Don't you see with him talking with her and mind doing the talking in actuality, Eve and Adam switched roles. Could God make a mistake, Eve?

Satan had succeeded in doing what he set out to do. It was not just to get her to eat of the forbidden fruit. Sin always goes much deeper than this. They were not following the plan of God. Remember, therefore, Adam was the head of authority in the household. By them switching roles, the chain of command changed. The man took the submissive wife's position, and Eve took the part of the headship of authority, the decision-maker. It is man's responsibility to lead the wife and not the other way around.

Satan initiated the conversation, and if he challenged the rule of God or even the Faith of Eve toward him, that conversation would have ended right then. Instead, he stated he just wanted her to make things clear for him. We all are so full of pride, assuming we know best, it does not take long to see the error performed here.

In all of this conversation recorded for us, it is of great interest; Satan does not mention either the tree of life or the tree of knowledge of good and evil. He only talked about the fruit itself.

In turn, Satan took her mind off the abundant provision of God. In so doing, all she could then think about was the restrictions God had placed on them. If only Adam had mentioned the Grace of God to Eve at this moment.

Here, you see a total misrepresentation of what God said and his severity of the punishment if they did not follow God's will. She did not understand eating the fruit would bring physical and spiritual death. Satan was sharp in questioning God's Word. Since we have the Word of God in our hands today, we should know anything that causes you to doubt the Word of God should make a red flag go up in front of you. How did Eve respond to the words of Satan? We see this in the next couple of verses, as seen in *verses 2-3.*

She started right. She testified of God's blessing, *verse 2.* But then she spoke of the restriction God had placed on them. We see this in *verse 3.* You can see her mind and heart working here.

Doubt is entering in, and covering herself, she adds to God's word. See *verse 3* and *Prov. 30:6.*

Adding to the Word of God is always a dangerous thing to do.

Many are doing this today, with versions and perversions of the Word of God. Satan renews his attack on Eve. Listen to his words in *verses 4-5,* "And the serpent said unto the woman, thou shall not surely die: for God doth know that in the day ye eat thereof, then your eyes shall be opened, and ye shall be as Gods, knowing good and evil." Satan was subtle in his first attack, but here he is, replaces deception and doubts with a denial of God's Word. What is he saying? He denies God's Word and the fact that God does not and cannot lie. See *verse 4.* Satan works in the religious realm. He substitutes his word; see again *verse 4.* Can you see him questioning God's motive, *verse 5*?

We all know Satan can make some very enticing promises that he had no intention of keeping, and they are always better than what God is offering. God's warnings were not understood as the promise of certain punishment but as the mere self-centered deity threats. We may wonder at the presumption of Satan's denial, but it is my opinion that this is the direct cause of what weakened Eve's opposition. How could anyone be wrong, which was so specific?

Many today are convinced more of a teacher's dogmatic tone than their teaching's doctrinal truthfulness. Arrogance is no assurance of doctrinal accuracy.

The record of the fatal blow of Satan is in ***Genesis 3:5***. Many have tried to determine the precise method Satan is using. His words are to remind us, in his opinion, we lack something.

God has held back on us, keeping the very best for himself, but He would not allow it. All Satan wanted from Eve was to eat the fruit, and then she would be like God.

In our text, we acknowledge Eve did not know what evil was.

But, she did not need to experience sin to know what it is. I find an illustration of this play upon human curiosity in the book of ***Proverbs***: ***Prov. 9:13-17*** "a foolish woman is clamorous: she is simple and knoweth nothing. For she sitteth at the door of her house, on a seat in the high places of the city, to call passengers who go right on their ways: whoso is simple, let him turn in hither: and as for him that wanteth understanding, she saith to him, stolen waters are sweet, and bread eaten in secret is pleasant."

This thinking of what God had done is the key to Satan's offer. The destructive process has begun. The seeds of doubt are there. In her dialogue with Satan, we see she was already entertaining evil thoughts about God's character and care for her.

The process of her falling into sin had begun. In contemplating her actions, we will now follow her desires in partaking of the fruit against God's will.

James 1:13-15 says, "let no man say when he is tempted; he is tempted of God: for God cannot be tempted with evil, neither tempteth He any man: but every man is tempted when he is drawn away of his lust and enticed. Then when lust hath conceived, it bringeth forth sin: and sin, when it is finished, bringeth forth death."

This thing called sin is the very nature of all of humankind. No one is exempt. No one has escaped sin except the Son of God.

For now, I want you to realize what happened here. Here, as we have said, is the first mention of sin in the Bible. As we study, we will sin in all of its characters. Sin is attractive and pleasurable. But in the end, sin destroys. Sin is like cancer that spreads through the body.

You can find no cure but one. *James 1:15* says, "Then when lust hath conceived, it bringeth forth sin: and sin when it is finished, bringeth forth death."

Can I say to you today that if you are involved in the practice of sin, are you on the road to death and Hell? Notice what happened when Cain fell into sin.

Gen .4:5 says, "But unto Cain and to his offering, he [God] had not to respect. And Cain was very wroth, and his countenance fell."

Then in *Gen. 4:8*, we find these words, "it came to pass, when they were in the field, that Cain rose against Abel his brother, and slew him." Imagine the regret, the heartbreak, and the sorrow that Adam and Eve were going through as they buried Abel. I am sure that you will find sin always brings much pain, heartbreak, and regret. One man's sin brought this result about.

When you think of those who have fallen under the pressure of Satan's devices just like Adam, imagine how heavy the guilt of his sin must have been every time he tilled the very ground he was walking. Every time Adam passed by the grave of Abel, it reminded him of his sin. You will understand before this chapter ends that sin is an offense to Him in God's eyes.

We find in the New Testament these words, *Matt. 18:7* "Woe unto the world because of offenses! It must need be that offenses come, but Woe to that man by whom the offense cometh!"

Offense" means a trap-stick (bent sapling), i.e., Snare (fig. cause of displeasure or sin): an occasion to fall (of stumbling), offense, and a thing that offends is a stumbling-block.

I know in jungle warfare, soldiers would take a tall young sapling, and then bend it over with a rope loop tied to the top of the tree, and when the enemy would come by and trigger that trap, it would throw them high in the air, leaving them hanging to the mercy of the enemy.

Many have said, including Satan, that the best defense is a good offense. As we continue our study, we see the fall and the immediate results of that sin. See *verses 6-7*.

First, we see the disobedience of Eve, ***verse 6***. See also ***1 John 2:15-17***.

She listened; this is the test. She looked; this is the temptation. She lusted; this is the trouble with all of humanity, and then she lost by her willingness not to resist by partaking of the fruit.

That has been the tragedy for all of humanity since that day.

One of the intriguing things here is Eve is where God told her not to be. Where was she at, and why? She was beside the tree where God had he told them not to partake. Why stand there allowing the devil to tempt if God said to not eat of it? Had she not been there, there is the possibility she would not have sinned at that time. Notice that the tree of life does not come into the conversation. Eve's inward struggle was not the two trees but the fruit on one of them.

Through the leading of Satan implanting thoughts in her head, she thought there must be some unique quality in that fruit. She had to find out the truth.

It did not matter Satan had not told her the consequences of eating this fruit. His deception was great, so much so she could not resist his power and influence. She only saw the forbidden fruit. Undoubtedly, having studied that tree for some time, she finally determined that the benefits were too great not to partake of the forbidden fruit.

Adam must have known the promise of punishment and the consequences, not a word from him. Was he afraid to say something to her? What is wrong with Adam? Even more was the fact that Adam was with her when she reached out, touched the fruit, and then brought it to her mouth, taking a bite.

God help us all at this point.

Moses describes the deception and disobedience of Eve in six verses, but only a part of one sentence to record Adam's fall. Why? There are two words Moses gives to us in this narrative that answers our question. They are, "with her," in ***Genesis 3:6*** see also ***1 Tim. 2:14***.

I have contended for many years in this whole text, Eve was never alone with Satan and that Adam was always by her side. Yet in all of this, there is never a word from the man.

In this account, if Adam was present, and I believe it to be a real possibility, we can see why it was easy for him to partake of the fruit without a word. If Adam were not present throughout the dialogue between the serpent and his wife, one could still understand what happened.

Eve could have gone and found him and told him she had eaten of the forbidden fruit.

Adam could consider what they did. It was asking her questions would help him understand what would happen if he ate the fruit.

Did eating of the fruit help her to understand things better? Did she feel any immediate effects from eating the fruit? Was she feeling sick or anything? Through the text, I convinced Adam knew after Eve partook of the fruit what the outcome would be. He took the fruit, and I believe understanding God's Mercy would soon follow, even though he had broken God's commandment.

He must know how much God loved them. Oh, but what a tragedy. Man is so weak. In retrospect, Satan has many weapons he can use against us. He has had six thousand years of training, and he is very good at what he does. In our text, He has already cast the seeds of doubt in Eve's heart. In her mind and heart, she says, "And when the woman saw that the tree was good for food," You say what is wrong with this? She should not even have been looking at the tree. Sure it was good to look at, and it had fruit on it. She looked, and this triggered the lust of the flesh. See *Gal. 5:16-21.*

Continuing then in *verse 6* we see it was, "And that it was pleasant to the eyes," She looked, which is the eye's lust. How many sins begin with a look? Do you understand how subtle and smart the devil is?

Then we see these words, "and a tree to be desired to make one wise." Here is the sin of the pride of life. What danger is she facing now? Sin has now entered into her heart. Once that takes place, there is action to the born. So we see the result of her sin in *verses 6-8.*

The next words in the Scriptures are terrifying to me. ***Verse 6*** says, "She took of the fruit thereof, and did eat, and also gave unto her husband with her, and he did eat." She ate and then gave it to her husband.

Sin is not just one sin for sin always leads to another, and the direct result is that one who sins frequently leads others to sin. Sin spreads. He ate of the fruit also. See ***I Timothy 2:14***.

Gen. 3:7 says, "And the eyes of them both were opened, and they knew that they were naked, and they sewed fig leaves together and made themselves aprons." It is stated correctly, "Sin has its consequences as well as its punishment."

Satan does lie and deceive, and he will never tell you the whole story and what will happen in the end. How often have you done something, knowing it was wrong but did not understand your actions' consequences?

They immediately saw their nakedness, knowing their sin had brought God's separation and shame to their hearts. A new experience was beginning called guilt and remorse. The glory they once had, and the innocence of not knowing sin was now gone. Even as they shared this, I would think there is no consolation here. I do not believe they understood what fully had happened. That sweet fellowship with God was now gone. There will be separation from Him because of their disobedience. Accordingly, that one they had loved to fellowship with, they began to fear. They could not bring themselves to face Him, so they hid.

They were alone. What could they do? Instantaneously, they died spiritually. Also, physical death had begun. Note what we find in the Word of God in ***2 Thessalonians 1:9***, which says, "who shall be punished with everlasting destruction from the presence of the Lord, and the glory of His power."

The sad fact is God did not do this. It was accomplished by the hand of man, specifically Adam. Then the sinful nature entered their souls. There is separation and now alienation from God. Man chose sin rather than fellowship with God for eternity in innocence. Hell is God giving men both what they want and what they deserve. See ***Revelation 16:5-6***.

They knew they were naked. What does this mean? They lost the righteousness of God about them. In innocence, they were not aware of their nakedness. Now that the veil of purity has been lifted and taken away, they saw themselves as they were. They were without God.

Therefore their eyes, because of sin, were opened.

Man would have never needed clothes if he had not sinned. Here is why men and women need to dress modestly today. In the text, we ask what they would do now. They did the same thing that everyone who comes face to face with sin does today. They tried to cover it up. But to no avail.

Nothing can compete with the righteousness of God. The man now is no longer holy and righteous and innocent. Now he is a sinful man who has to face a thrice Holy God. No matter what man tries to do, it will never reach the mark of God's holiness. The reason is that it is the nature of man to want to produce his remedy and covering for sin. See the following verses, *Job 14:4; Psa. 49:7; Isa. 64:6; Rom. 3:10-12*.

Oh, we have tried many times to hide from God, but you can't. See *verse 8*.

In context, we see God's love from *Genesis 3:5* by Him, providing a way to bridge the gap from man to Him. God has always sought after man. He is the one who has done the seeking.

It was God coming to the Garden seeking Adam and Eve. His impressive design began questioning Adam and Eve while they hid, or so they thought, from Him.

Satan's questions were to cause Eve to fall. God's questions were designed to bring the restoration and reconciliation of man eventually. One intriguing aspect of these sequences of events is the order of the pronunciation of the consequences of the curse.

God pronounced first on the serpent, then Eve, and finally Adam. In seeking God's direction, we see in God's initial dealings with man. Man is the first in our context, then the woman and then Satan.

Note this is God's chain of command. They each destroyed this order. Notice Adam is the first questioned by God. *Verse 9* says, "And the Lord God called unto Adam, and said unto him, where art thou? *Verse 10* starts, "and he said, I heard thy voice in the Garden, and I was afraid." See what coward's sin makes us. How did Adam answer God when confronted?

The very thought of Adam and Eve seeing God must have brought fear in their hearts. He said, "Because I was naked, and I hid." *Verse 11* says, "And He said, who told thee that thou was naked? Hast thou eaten of the tree, whereof I commanded thee, that thou shouldest not eat?"

God knew Adam was naked and that he had eaten of the forbidden fruit.

But God wanted Adam to confess it with his mouth. He wanted him to tell the truth. God knows all things before we ask for them, for He is an all-knowing God, yet many times He wants us to ask for necessities for our knowing our needs.

Therefore, we may know He is a gracious and loving God willing to forgive us. It is to bring glory to his name. We read in our text *verse 12*, "and the man said, the woman which thou gavest to be with me, she gave me of the tree, and I did eat."

Now we see the true nature of man! The pride of Adam comes to the surface! In arrogance, there is no acknowledgment of any sin. He answers in absolute disrespect towards God, enmity against his wife, and resourcefulness regarding him. Here, he quietly reflects upon God and says to Him," and the man said, the woman which thou gavest to be with me."

It was like him saying to God, if you had not given me that woman, I would not have eaten the forbidden fruit. However, as you recall, he was with her the whole time and did not question or take charge of the conversation when he had the opportunity.

Here is the core of his sin. He allowed her to take his role as a leader, and he took her place as the help-meet. He gave up his rightful place, and we see the results of all of this. Sin entered in.

Blame her all he wants, but in the end, God gave just punishment to Adam, for he is the head and not her. He did listen to her, and he also listened to Satan and chose not to do anything when he had the opportunity. Can I say as we live in a world today of blame-shifting and saying it is not my fault, I would tell you that God knows the truth and, therefore, will punish accordingly. He punished Adam. Do you think He will do less with you?

You listen to your corrupt heart and see what happens.

The reason is before us. God compels no man to sin. We bear that and the consequences of sin alone unless we are willing to admit and confess that sin before a thrice Holy God.

Without a doubt, our text reveals a clear example of free will found in the Bible. Adam had a choice. Eve had a decision to make. That decision was to do evil in the sight of God. They chose to do evil in the sight of God. They thought they could lay the blame on someone else. Satan did not make them sin. He showed them a lie, and they believed it. They both consented in their hearts to sin against God. They placed their will in the place of the will of God. Given their conversation with God, we can see the lie, the contempt, and the disrespect.

It goes deeper than this: we see enmity against God by the woman and man. Man is always trying to figure out how he can get out of things, especially in sin. How many times have we heard those caught in sin act like it was someone else's fault? Evil can only separate from fellowship, from the heart outward. Continuously we meet those who are so proud that they are unwilling to confess their sins before a thrice-holy God. Why is it so difficult to bow before Him? Adam was no different from us. He said, "The woman whom thou gavest to be with me, she gave me of the tree, and I did eat." See *Genesis 3:12*. Here are fifteen words that will be immortalized forever.

Then you find these simple words, "and I did eat." It was if he had something caught in his throat. He could not get the words out. At this time, he was not ready to face the shame of what he did. He had to think about it. He had to consider what he had done and what God was saying to him. What we see is pride. Only until pride brakes can we have a clean heart before God.

The only thing God will accept is humbleness for sinning against God; repenting of those sins.

It is easier just to blame others, but this will not grant us access to God. Remember the words of David after he had sinned against God. ***Psalm 51:4*** says, "Against thee, and thee only, have I sinned, that thou mightest be justified in thy sayings, and clear when thou judgest."

Here is the language of none but those who, like David, are willing to confess their faults and are genuinely sorry for their sins against God Almighty.

Is this what Adam did? I think not. Instead, we see no brokenness, no desire to get right with God. All we see is his blaming others for what he had done. Notice ***verse 13***, "and the Lord God said unto the woman, what is this that thou hast done?" She had disobeyed God, obeyed the devil, and ruined her husband. You will note this is quite a contrast from the way God had made her. Remember she was to be a help-meet! God says, "What is this that thou hast done?"

What is God's purpose here? She needed to be shocked and made aware of her sin and the dangerous consequences of her crime.

To hear God speak must have been like thunder in the ears of the woman and the man.

In the eyes of God, the Law must be preached to self-righteous sinners of which they were.

Without a change of heart and a real confession of sin, there can be no peace. Like the people at the base of Mount Sinai, when they saw and heard the thunderings and lightings, we must come before Mount Sinai and come face to face with our sin, not another's, but ours, fearing Almighty God unless we repent and turn to Him for forgiveness.

Only then can our hearts be glad, and our burdens lifted. That ole saying is true, "you have to get them lost before they can get saved. You cannot get a person saved until they first realize they are lost and on the way to a devil's Hell.

It is not necessarily the thunderings and the winds that cause people to understand.

Sometimes it is the small still voice of God speaking to their hearts through the Holy Spirit's work in one's life.

There are other times when we must face our sins and bring us to the place of repentance.

Notice God's approach to Eve. "And the Lord God said unto the woman, what is this that thou hast done?" "And the woman said, he serpent beguiled me, and I did eat." See *verse 13*.

Notice she did not say I sinned in taking of the fruit. We still see the unbroken heart. The pride of her heart is still there. God here indicts her with sinning against Him. How could she deny the fact?

What happens next is what we call blame-shifting. Eve takes her blame and lays it on the serpent for she said, "the serpent beguiled me, and I did eat." See *verse 13*.

She should have said that she was blamed for talking with the serpent instead of talking it over with her husband. Who was the problem here?

She should have said it was her fault and not the failure of her husband.

That would have been a confession of guilt and blame, and it would be a genuinely repentant heart. That is not the case here. Both are full of pride and arrogance, hard-hearted, refusing to listen to the words of God their Father. Instead, she said in *verse 13*, "the serpent beguiled me, and I did eat.

Remember what Adam said in *verse 12*, "The woman which thou gavest to be with me, she gave me of the tree, and I did eat." Nothing they could do would correct the sin. I am so thankful for this particular text that shows us the great Grace of God, which teaches us that salvation comes only from the Lord.

In their state, wouldn't you think they would be crying out to the Lord for forgiveness?

Here they were, spiritually and soon physically dead, and as the Bible describes them, children of wrath and without God, destined to a place called Hell. Now they stand before God, condemned but not willing to confess their sin. They should have said what they had done and fell on their faces pleading for God's Mercy. Could God forgive them with the attitude of their hearts? They had each eaten of the forbidden fruit. They both had acted on disobedience.

They both knew the will of God and forsaken it. We see no remorse for turning their backs on the Grace of God. They had broken the heart of God, and it was if they did not care, nor were they concerned about the consequences of their sins.

If God did not do something, how could he be just in His dealings with man? The paradox is before God. If He does let them go without being punished, what would they do and more, and what would Satan do? Wisdom designs a plan of how God may be just and yet merciful; be faithful to His Law, punish the offense, and at the same time, spare the offender.

What we see here is a fantastic scene of divine love. This plan had been in the heart of God through all eternity. It is hidden to the eyes of creation itself and the man himself! But still, there is no repentance from man.

However, God had known what man would do. He going was not caught off guard, and He was not surprised by the outcome. Punishment is forthwith coming and not withheld, but there would also be grace and mercy extended to the man and woman. This Mercy and Grace would come in the form of a Saviour. However, there was no reprieve for the serpent and Satan.

Note the wisdom of God in **verses 14, 15** which says, "And the Lord God said unto the serpent, Because thou hast done this, thou art accursed above all cattle, and above every beast of the field; upon thy belly shalt thou go, and dust shalt thou eat all the days of thy life. And I will put enmity between thee and the woman, and between thy seed and her seed: it shall bruise thy head, and thou shalt bruise his heel."

With joy in our hearts, this text gives us the first mention of the Savior. We will see God's plan placed into motion. This plan has always been Jesus Christ, for **Eph. 1:4** says, "according as he hath chosen us in him before the foundation of the world, that we should be holy and without blame before him in love."

The plan of God was not a mere afterthought. There has never been any other plan like the plan of God.

I have preached many times that nothing ever happened to God that surprised Him? His plan is not a plan of desperation. We may think God is not in control of the universe or humankind's destiny, but that is not true. We can say with confidence; God has never been nervous or upset about anything. God's plan of the Redemption of humanity has always been the same from eternity past. He always has had a Savior for man. In the mind of God, before sin entered in, there was a coming Saviour. Before God created man, before man sinned, His plan was in operation. The goal was for Christ to come and die on the Cross and rise again. Through prophecy and the fulfillment of prophecy, we saw God proclaiming there would always be a sacrificial Lamb of God to remove the world's sins. As I said, this plan of Redemption began in the very heart of God in eternity past. Before creation, God has set the wheels in motion.

The man was given free will, the right to make a choice, and chose his life direction.

God, knowing man would make wrong choices had a plan. Listen to **Rom. 8:32** "He that spared not his own Son, but delivered Him up for us all, how shall he not with him also freely give us all things?" Please read **1 Cor. 15:1-4**.

As God pronounced judgment upon the serpent, all Adam and Eve could do, was seen in horror and listen to God's words. By now, they realized that pain and suffering were coming, not only to them but also to humankind. What disgrace was before them?

Their status had changed because of the fall. Adam could not stand as our representative.

Instead of our representative, he stood just only as a sinner man before a Holy God. Their only recourse was to plead the innocent lamb's blood whose blood was shed for them and cry out for God's mercy. Adam and Eve were now prisoners of the sin nature, without the strength to resist the powers involved because of their sin. The truth is if we will see our sin, confess our sin, and repent of our sin, we can have eternal life found in Jesus Christ.

Jesus Christ is the second Adam. In the first Adam, we have death, and in the second, we have Life everlasting. The only correct course for humanity to take should be to come to God, imploring him to give them mercy and faith, whereby they shall lay hold on Christ's righteousness. It is this faith that God will accept. Our hope in Christ's work on the tree at Calvary, out of love and gratitude for our Redeemer in saving our souls from Hell, is necessary.

This atonement for sins would bring about the fulfillment of God's promise whereby He would bruise the serpents' head and destroy his power and dominion over them.

How much did Adam and Eve understand? They knew and appreciated much more than we give them credit because we will see sacrifices instituted at the end of this chapter.

Where should those skins come from, but from animals, specifically a lamb, slain for sacrifice, of which God originally made them coats?

In the next chapter, we will find Abel and Cain offered sacrifices unto the Lord. In the New Testament, we will find the Apostle tells us that Abel did it by faith, knowing God's promise to his mom and dad. Eve said when Cain was born, "I have gotten a man from the Lord," or, as has been noted by others, "I have gotten a man, the Lord, the promised Messiah." See *Genesis 4:1*.

She understood what was to come! The whole purpose of Redemption is in the person of the Lord Jesus Christ. We see Satan bruising his heel when he tempted Him for forty days together in the wilderness. We see Satan bruising his heel when He was born, and intense persecution started against him during his public ministry. We see Satan bruised his heel, when our Lord complained, that His soul was exceeding sorrowful, even unto death, and He sweats great drops of blood falling upon the ground, in the Garden. We see Satan bruising his heel when he put it into Judas's heart to betray God's Son.

As Christ walked through the Garden that last time, Judas comes with his band to take him and have him nailed to that accursed tree. He would cry out, "my God, my God, why hast thou forsaken me?" Yet, in all this, the blessed Saviour, the seed of the woman, bruised Satan's accursed head, for, in that he was tempted, He was able to rescue sinner man. The Bible says, "By His stripes, we are healed. The chastisement of our peace was upon Him." See *Isaiah 53:5*.

By dying on that cruel tree, He destroyed him that had the power of death, that is, the devil.

As a result of this, God triumphed over them, spooling principalities and powers and since has made a public show of them. God has fulfilled this promise. There will be an eternal enmity put between the woman's seed and the serpent's seed forever.

All are sinners. Therefore, by designing the sinful nature, the flesh will persecute those born after the Spirit.

Who should this surprise? It is the devil and his co-Horts desire, for they hate God. It did not take long for this hatred to show itself. We know Cain rose against Abel and slew him.

Persecution had continued through all ages before Christ came in the flesh, as the Bible's history, and especially *Hebrews 11*, plainly shows. It raged exceedingly after our Lord's ascension, Witnessed by many as we note in Acts' book. It is now screaming and will continue to rage and show itself, to the end of time, to a higher and higher degree in these last days. But let not this disappoint us; for in all this, the woman's seed is more than a conqueror, and bruises the serpent's head.

You see this illustrated in the Israelites, the more they were oppressed, the more they increased.

The battle was also real of the Apostles; the more they were persecuted, the more the Gospel spread. So that Tertullian compared the Church in his time to a mowed field, the more frequently it was cut, the more it grew. Mark it down my friend, the blood of the martyrs will run freely in these last days of the Church.

Beginning in the book of Acts and through the ages, we wonder and stand with admiration of God's plans. We see how Satan has been relentless in his attacks against those who have tried to further the Gospel. Though the devil has tried to stop God's plan, and try he will, he will not succeed in his efforts. In the battle down through the ages, he has been defeated time and again. The Word of God has and will prevail over the power of the devil. ***Genesis 3:15*** says, "I will put enmity between thy seed and her seed; it shall bruise thy head, and thou shalt bruise his heel."

This battle still rages today and, at times, more intense than at other times. We know that there are two seeds; it is called the seed of the woman and the serpent's seed. Scriptures call it the flesh lusting against the Spirit and the Spirit warring against the flesh. Knowing our two natures, the one in the flesh and the other is the Spirit; we see the constant war going on within us. Another way to put it is to say there are two natures, one of the flesh and the other of the Spirit. In the end, grace shall prevail over the sinful nature, and the woman's seed shall bruise the serpent's head.

The text's promise ensures believers' blessed victory over sin, Satan, death, and Hell itself.

Many people just do not understand that after salvation, the ole sin nature remains with us and is as corrupt as ever, and as I would say, "Vexing our souls."

We may often lose the fight with the devil and his cohorts, but the victory in battle belongs to God, for we know what Christ did in that place called Calvary. However, I have read the last book of the Bible and found the answer that in the last days, the Lord Jesus will present His Church, without spot or wrinkle, to His Father. As Satan rejoiced that day when Adam and Eve fell, we can celebrate today that through the finished work of our Saviour, Jesus Christ, there is coming a day when all of Heaven will shout for joy in knowing our Saviour reigns. "Then shall the righteous shine in the kingdom of their Father, and sit with Christ with Him on high." See ***Matthew 13:43***. "And let us not be weary in well doing: for in due season we shall reap, if we faint not." See ***Galatians 6:9***.

Heaven is looking mighty good, right now.

Just in the conclusion of this section, we have found that ***verse 9*** gives us the first question of the Old Testament, "Where are thou?" Interestingly the first question of the New Testament is," where is he?" Know this, that sin is the transgression of God's will. We see this plainly illustrated in words, "What is this thou hast done?" See ***verse 13***.

Here is the total result of all of man's sin. God said, "Bruise thy head." See **Genesis 3:15**. Here the meaning is God would send a redeemer to repurchase us at Calvary in God's plan for the Redemption of man for his sins. When Jesus hung upon the Cross, the devil was defeated forever. He lost his battle against God and man at the Cross.

He is a defeated foe, forever destined to be in a place called Hell. Yes, the devil looked like he had won when he "bruised the heel" of God, but it was short-lived for on the third day, the victor arose from the grave and defeated death, Hell, and the grave forever.

I feel it is essential to take the time to discuss Adam's sin, and that this sin nature was imputed to us. We find the word "impute" is used 11 times in Scripture. See **Rom. 4:22-24; Rom. 5:12-14; Rom. 4:5-8**. Mark this as one of the essential doctrines in the Bible. This word imputed means to put on one's account or the giving or reckoning or to account that something to a person.

There are three stages in which Scripture deals with and uses this doctrine of imputing.

Adam's sin, since he is the legal and federal head of the human race. Again look at **Rom. 5:12-21**. Just as we receive Adam's sinful nature, so is it that we can have God's righteousness through Christ imputing our sin on His own body on the Cross? See **2 Cor. 5:21**.

Through Christ, by faith, we receive his righteousness, being credited to those that believe. See **Phil. 3:9**. It is not our righteousness which we are saved by but only His. These all relate to one another, as we will see.

When we read, our sins were imputed to Christ, or that He bore our sins, it means he did not sin. All that is means is that He assumed or took our place for deserving justice for our sin in a place called Calvary. Note **1 Pet. 2:24; 2 Cor. 5:21**.

He knew the Law's just demands and took our place on Calvary to answer those just demands. As to the righteousness of Christ imputed to us, we had nothing to do with it.

You see, at death, Christ becomes our representative, just as Adam was our representative in the beginning, and in Christ, we can all be made alive, just as in Adam all die. God, when one accepts Christ as their Saviour, gives us the gift of His eternal righteousness. He puts His righteousness on our account, taking away our sin, the penalty of sin, and then the guilt of sin.

When God states that we are righteous in His eyes, which means our account had been settled with Him and the Law.

The debt we owed and needed to pay, and could not, Christ bore in our stead.

The Law's just demands were death, and Christ took the Law's requirements, placed them upon Himself everything that I owed, became our substitute on the Cross, and met those demands. Now when God sees us, He sees a sinner saved by His Grace.

When we say that Adam's sin is imputed to us, which does not mean we committed that sin, but by our union with him, if we had been there, we would have done the same thing he did.

That is, we would have partaken of the fruit too. The sin nature he passed to us ensures we would have done the same but becomes the very ground of condemnation because we are born with sinful nature.

In our language of today, justification means, just as if I had not sinned. That is to be declared righteous before a Holy God. So then the Scriptural doctrine is this: God placed Adam as the federal head or representative over the whole human race, recognizing him as it were on probation in the Garden not only for himself but for all of humanity. Had Adam not sinned, he and all of us would have remained in a state of holiness forever. As he fell, we fell so that the penalty of that sin came upon us as it did on him.

There is a reason, and this is what we need to explain next. It is our union with Christ. Think about this: everything that was said to Adam, God spoke to him in his representative capacity. The promise of life was for him and his seed forever. Adam's dominion over the earth belongs to all of us today. All of the laws and commands against him in the case of sin are upon us.

The parallel drawn between Adam and Christ by the Apostle Paul directs us to this. Adam fulfills many types, especially Christ. The consequences of this are to be the same in both Adam and Christ.

What probably would help is to prove to you that this is not just an isolated fact. Note the following examples. We see this illustrated in the curse pronounced on Canaan, which later fell upon his ancestors. See *Ex. 34:6, 7*. We see this represented in Esau's selling of his birthright, which shut out his descendants from the promise. We see this in the children of Moab and Ammon. They were excluded from the congregation of the Lord forever because his ancestors opposed the Israelites when they came up out of the land of Egypt. You can see this when God said to Eli that his house's iniquity would cause no more sacrifice to be given in his home forever. Remember, God told David that the sword should never depart from his house.

In the New Testament times, when Jesus walked the earth, and the Jews cried, "His blood be on us."

Today that sin still weighs down the Jew scattered to the four corners of the earth. This principle runs right throughout the Word of God. As we have stated, the whole plan of Redemption relies upon this same principle. Christ is the representative of His people, and He imputed His righteousness on our accounts. We are set free from sin. See *Rom. 5:12-14*.

We now, though still, a sinner have a new legal standing before Almighty God. See the following passages; *Rom. 1:17; Rom. 3:5; Rom. 3:22, 25, 31; Rom. 10:.3*.

No man who believes the Bible can shut his eyes to this fact. In the following verses, *verses 16-19*, we have the sevenfold curse God placed upon man and creation. He cursed the ground that man walks upon. He told the man that all the days of his life would be filled with sorrow.

He said that instead of there being no problem taking care of the Garden, thorns would grow up in the middle of it. Instead of enjoying the pleasure of looking after the Garden, man would have to work all of his life. Because of sin, man's end would be to return to the dust of the earth. He could live with God for all of eternity.

Because of sin and its consequences of sin, God, in His kindness, would keep man from the tree of life and not allow him to partake of it so that he would not live without God for all eternity.

What a gracious God He is.

However, sin separates man from God. No longer would man have fellowship with God.

In His abundant provision, God provided a way for man to have fellowship with Him once again through the blood of Jesus Christ. We ask the question of how Christ has met those needs in my life. See *Galatians 3:13*.

There should never be a doubt in our minds; Christ has met every requirement God demands. See *Rom. 3:19; 8:20-22*. Isaiah says He was stricken for me in *Isa. 53:8*.

In the New Testament and the Old Testament, we find He bore the pain of our sins.

Note the following verses. *John 19:1-3; Prov. 22:5; Isa. 5:6; Matt. 15:7*.

Let me tell you; He sweated on a place called Calvary so I would not have to.

Read the following verses: *Luke 22:44; Ecc. 1:3; Eph. 4:28; 2 Thess. 3:10*.

He took the dust of death so I would not have too. Read *Psalm 22:15; Job 1:21; Palms 104:29*.

From the Scriptures, we find He fulfilled the curse. Read *Zech. 13:7; John 19:34; John 14:6; Heb. 10:18-22*.

Jesus suffered separation from God, so I will not have to be. See *Matt. 28:46; Deut. 31:17, 18; Isa. 59:1*.

Separation from God was hard to endure. Maybe more than all of the physical suffering He had to go through. Now we have a more exalted place than Adam as the Sons of God, exalted to Heaven, joint-heirs with Christ. We have a decisive stand in his righteousness before God.

Christ gave us His righteousness for us to know the pardon of God. Now we have the opportunity to have a closer walk with God than Adam, for we are now members of the body of Christ.

As this chapter began and now comes to a close, with God having to put Adam and Eve from the Garden and protect its entrance to the tree of life, had He not clothed them in His righteousness, they would have been lost forever.

I want to begin this section with some lessons from the fall.

We will see this in *verses 20-24*. The first lesson we learn from the fall is the inherited necessity of the Gospel. We will see this in *Genesis 3:20*. The second lesson we learn from the fall is the saving substitution of the Gospel. We will see this in *Genesis 3:21*. The third lesson we learn from the fall is the present protection of the Gospel. We will see this in *Genesis 3:22-24*.

In our text, we must recognize at least two things. By Adam calling her the mother of all living, he understood God would use her to produce the seed of promise, as seen in *verse 15*. I am sure Adam did not know all there was to know, like when or how, but he knew it would be through her.

Then secondly, he understood the necessity of the promised seed because he understood the impact sin was to have on us all.

Eve means life, as at the beginning of life. At the beginning of life, Adam realized that their sin passed down to all their offspring. Giving her the name, Eve, showed her the mother of all humanity and all fallen humanity. As we have said and worth repeating, the Bible states, "that in Adam all have sinned."

From the moment we are born, we are sinners. We do not have to sin to become a sinner. The race of humanity was affected by the disease called sin from the first person born to the last. We've talked about that as the reason that Jesus had to be born of a virgin. If Christ had been born of an earthly father, He would contain tainted blood, thereby having the original sin nature.

But he didn't. Jesus not only lived a perfect life; He was born free from the sin nature, which we have all inherited from Adam. Eve then was the mother of all of fallen humanity. The good news of a Savior is what fallen humanity needed to hear.

Something else we can learn from the fall is the saving substitution of the Gospel, seen in *Genesis 3:21*. Adam and Eve had sinned. They had violated God's command. God had given Adam an A or B choice. It was either obey me and live or disobey me and die. He disobeyed.

So the only thing he could expect was death. God gave him a choice, and he willingly chose the option that brought death. From the very beginning, God designed it so that the wages of sin is death. God's justice would be served if He had immediately destroyed Adam and Eve and sentenced them to eternal Hell punishment. Think about what happened when Satan led the rebellion of angels. God immediately cast them out of Heaven and condemned them to eternal punishment. He made no provision for their Redemption. They were not allowed to repent.

Their sentence was instant, and it was irrevocable. That's what God's righteous justice demands, immediate and eternal damnation for sin. It would be death.

If God allowed sin to go unpunished and violated His death requirement, He would no longer be just. He would be unfair, and His righteousness is no longer pure. But God still loved Adam and Eve.

You say, how much did He love them? Enough to provide a way for their Redemption, so their sins must be covered without violating His justice and righteousness. He provided a way by providing a substitute. He shed the blood of an animal as an innocent substitution for their death.

But can you imagine how Adam felt when God had to kill one of the animals that Adam had named?

Remember that they had never seen death. God slaughtered an animal right in front of them.

He slaughtered the lamb and clothed them in its skin. Now, this wasn't like wearing a fur coat.

It was like clothing themselves in the one who had died as their substitute. God's demanded justice because an innocent victim died in their place, as their atoning substitute.

God's love gave as He provided a substitute for them so they might live.

He clothed Adam and Eve in the pure garment of the one who died for them.

Besides being clothed in an innocent animal's skin, we have the covering of Christ's righteousness. That animal skin temporarily covered Adam and Eve's sin. But it also pointed to the need for an eternal covering. It was an infinite atonement for sin, provided 4000 years later on the Cross at Calvary.

Except for this time, instead of God sacrificing an innocent animal, He sacrificed his son.

Jesus Christ, the eternal Son of God, willingly gave His life as a substitute for your sin, for my sin, and Adam and Eve's sin.

While that first incomplete sacrifice looked forward to Christ's perfect sacrifice, your salvation looks back. Look back and cling to the Cross in faith, believing that Jesus died as a covering for your sins. Because, just as the coats of skins served to cover Adam's sin and shame, Jesus' blood covers your sins and mine.

Finally, the third lesson is the present protection of the Gospel. See **Genesis 3:22-24.**

Notice the reference to the trinity in **verse 22.** "Man has become as one of us." Some people believe this was a sarcastic comment by God. I don't see that. I understand that when man's eyes were ripped open to sin's ugliness, he saw something he wished he had not seen.

It is evident; God never intended him to see violence and separation. Since God sees everything, He saw it. But He never intended for man to view it.

So, when he, man, ate of the fruit, his eyes were opened to a world that only the triune God intended to see, a world of not only the good that

God had shown him but a world of evil and sin and pain and suffering and rebellion.

Now, through his eyes, he saw all this horror. And even though God had provided atonement for their sin in covering animal skins, they were still under the curse.

They still had to deal with pain and toil and suffering, and sin. To put it in today's terms, they were saved but still living in a fallen world. But God's Grace shined through once again.

God saved them by providing an atoning sacrifice, but He also protected them from themselves.

He cast them out of the Garden. Was it punishment? Yes.

But even more than that, it was protection. The more significant part of it was for the protection of man.

God, the Father, Son, and Holy Spirit, cast Adam and Eve out of the Garden for their protection. If they had been able to stay, how long would it have taken before they had eaten of the tree of life had they stayed?

Note that the first mention of the tree of life is first here. Was it hidden before? Probably not. Did they know about it? Probably.

Remember, the command was to eat of any tree except for that one tree.

He just had to eat of it. Now, God specifically protects him from eating of the tree of life.

He protects him from living forever in sin.

Eating of that tree would be detrimental to the human race. Imagine living in a fallen, cursed world without the possibility of dying, living forever, and struggling with Satan's temptations forever.

Can't you see the mercy of God in all of this?

He is living, wrestling with his dying flesh's nature, and only accessing God through a mediator. He put them out of the Garden and separated them from it with an intangible barrier that they could not cross. That's how much He loved them. And that's how much He loves us. He loves us enough that He protects us. He provides us protection from ourselves in our daily lives. No matter how bad we've ever been, we never as bad as we could have been.

He provides us protection from Satan. He only allows Satan to tempt us up to what we can handle. Nothing comes to us from Satan that hasn't already passed through God's gracious and merciful hands.

Finally, He provides us protection from the curse. He numbers our days so we won't have to struggle with our flesh forever. He also promises a new heaven and new earth that are not marred by sin and the curse. And He promises we will walk with Him forever without separation or boundaries. God protects us just like He did with Adam and Eve for that's part of the Gospel. And God revealed it over 4000 years before the New Testament was ever written.

He showed us the inherited necessity of the Gospel. All have sinned and not just by our actions.

We have all sinned in Adam, and his sin passed down to us. God showed us the saving substitution of the Gospel. Nothing we can do is sufficient to cover our sins, and corruption results in death. Either our death or the death of a substitute must be first met. The blood that our Lord Jesus Christ shed on Calvary is the perfect substitute for our sins. It is the only thing that can cover them and wash them white as snow. God showed us the present protection of the Gospel. God had a plan to keep us from struggling with sin. It is all of faith in Him. He doesn't want us to fight through a fallen world eternally.

He protects us from how bad things can be in our daily lives. And He eventually protects us when He calls us home to be with Him.

The question is, will you be going home with Him? Have you recognized your inherited need for the Gospel? Have you accepted His saving substitution for your sins? He desires nothing more than to provide you permanent protection. All you have to do is ask.

So that brings us to the aftermath of the fall, as seen in **verses 20-24**. I want you to notice something here. I want you to witness Adam's Faith. God has just pronounced His curse upon creation because of sin. He has said that man will now experience death because of sin, but he also has said that the woman's seed will crush the serpent's head. Now, before Adam and Eve, God pronounces a sentence of death. But Adam believes by faith in the promise of the seed of the woman. This is the reason for the name change to Eve, which literally means "life." In other words, Adam understood what God said, and he responds in Faith, **verse 15**.

And then God covers them with the skins of animals. The animal skin is a picture of the atonement that is to come. The Bible says, "Without the shedding of blood, there is no remission of sins." We could say forgiveness of sins here. And so the blood of animals is shed, and Adam and Eve's nakedness is covered. But the sacrifice of animals can only cover in, but the sacrifice that is to come will obliterate sin and wash us whiter than snow. And lastly, God drives them from the Garden of Eden.

Sometimes, you'll hear people say things like, "God didn't want them to eat from the tree of life because He was afraid of them becoming too powerful." Their removal from the presence of the tree of life is an act of mercy.

Eternal condemnation would have been their state if they had eaten of the tree of life. Remember the words of the ordinance of communion? "Wherefore whosoever shall eat this bread, and drink this cup of the Lord, unworthily, shall be guilty of the body and blood of the Lord." Note *1 Corinthians 11:27*. See God's Grace in action.

So God drives them out of Eden. They have lost paradise. They've lost walking in the cool of the day with God. They lost their relationship with, and their fellowship with Him was destroyed.

They will suffer, and their work will be burdensome, and childbearing will be painful, and men will Lord over their wives, and there will be sadness, pain, and suffering.

Now we see the cherubim. They are guarding the entrance into the Garden of Eden. Adam and Eve can no longer physically enter the Garden. The cherubim always represent the divine presence and glory and Mercy of God, described by the fire and the sword. It was there between these cherubim God had made the Mercy seat. Now, the man, instead of having no way back to the Garden, found instead that God in His Grace had provided just what sinful man needed.

Remember that they could no longer come in the very presence of God. No longer would he be able to walk with God in the cool of the day. All of that was gone. Man's only hope was that God would provide a place set aside for man to come and worship, where God in His divine presence would be there on the Mercy seat between the two cherubim. The only way to approach God and that is through a blood sacrifice. God expected them to perform this to meet with Him.

God taught this to Adam and Eve after sinning by slaying a lamb in their stead and providing blood atonement through that substitute. All men would indeed be barred from entering the Garden and from partaking of the tree of life, but it is also equally valid that the Mercy seat's purpose was to keep open access to God! Notice what we read in *Rev. 2:7* "he that hath an ear let him hear what the Spirit saith unto the churches; to him that overcometh will I give to eat of the tree of life, which is in the midst of the paradise of God."

I see some things God gave to man after the fall. He gave him a promise of a Redeemer who would destroy the work of the devil. God gave them clothing symbolizing the righteousness of Christ. God put the Mercy seat up at the Garden's entrance, indicating all who would come and worship God; there would be salvation.

Let me tell you what has stopped. When you set in Church and listen to a preacher preaching, it does not matter what you do religiously. God is no so much concerned about outward appearances as He is with the heart. You can genuflect, shout, nod your head, sleep, anything, but unless your heart is stirred, what have you done? We have said and will continue to say there is only one way to God, and that is through Christ. We can do what we want, but that will not appease God.

It is only by acknowledging the blood sacrifice of His only begotten Son for the forgiveness of sins. Doing something on our part is not in God's plan. We come only by faith in Christ alone.

That is where the Christian life begins, and for that matter, it ends. The natural approach to God is cut off. What does he say? See *John 14:6*.

As a child of God, we have to realize what has taken place. The Apostle Paul says, "I am crucified with Christ: nevertheless I live; yet not I, but

Christ liveth in me: and the life which I now live in the flesh I live by the faith of the Son of God, who loved me, and gave himself for me, according to *Gal. 2:20*.

Until the curse of death is satisfied in God's eyes, no man can come to Him.

We know salvation, but until the body's resurrection occurs, we cannot be in His presence.

As Hebrews declares to us, the glorious truth of the matter is that the blood of Jesus Christ has opened a new and living way into the holy place.

There is coming a day when this will take place. See *Heb. 10:20*.

In these 1st three chapters, we learned about the world that God had made and the mess we made of it, but the rest of the Bible is about God's plan to clean up that mess for His glory and good.

People must reach the age of understanding before they can comprehend God's meaning by the punishment of death. God speaking to them opens their minds and hearts.

They become self-conscious of this fact. Further, we see how that individual is aware of the shame, guilt, and then fear of being separated from a Holy God.

Pride frequently enters in, and they want to blame others for their inherent sin, nature, and consequences. They come to see just what God meant when He told Adam he would surely die.

What can the sinner man do? Enslaved by sin, bound to die in those sins, spend eternity in a place called Hell. What can he do?

The next step is that of repentance. As we have studied, we see God's skilled hand, tenderly, graciously, leading the guilty couple down the path of sins awareness, showing them their wrong. Repentance consists of two things. First, there is an awareness of the direction of temptation. It comes from within. God helped Adam to see that. His sin was not that Satan made him do it. That sin arose from something within.

Second, they had to confess it was their sin and no blame-shifting. They had to come to the place where pride had to step aside and acknowledge their sin was they ate of that fruit.

It was not until they were willing to confess their sins before God could they be forgiven.

Only then can Satan be defeated, and his judgment pronounced.

Here, God opens man's eyes to the necessity of their clinging in dependence upon God, which is the only place of safety, security, and strength in life.

After this, we noted is an act of Faith on Adam's part. See *verse 20*.

We understand as soon as we see the link established in God's statement to the serpent about the woman where he said: "I will put enmity between you and the woman, and between your seed and her seed; he shall bruise your head, and you shall bruise his heel" which brings us right back to *verse 15*.

Then *verse 20* deals with the same thing. It is only till then we see the name change of the woman to Eve. The word Woman is the Chaldean word "Ishsha." The blessing was in response to God's promise of the coming seed. This word, "woman" means God called her "out of man."

Then, as Adam changes her name to "Chavah," the actual Chaldean word, she is now the mother of all living instead of being out of the man.

Therefore in *verse 20*, there is an indication of Adam's understanding that a race of men and women is to come from Eve; thus, she is to be the mother of all living.

God had just pronounced judgment upon man and said to Adam, "In the sweat of thy face shalt thou eat bread, till thou return unto the ground; for out of it wast thou taken: for dust thou art, and unto dust shalt thou return," and Adam understands, from that, that he is now to become the Father of a doomed race, that, because of his sin, that which he begets is doomed to die. See *Genesis 3:19*.

This truth is just as sure today as it was the day God spoke it to Adam.

We begin to die when we are born, and the process goes on until it results in the inevitable conclusion of the grave.

I am always faintly amused by the medical profession's optimistic reports about the immediate increase of lifespan, though I am sure this is progress and is somewhat right.

Now, as we have said, the battle rages.

Death is man's destiny. Though much knowledge is acquired in the medical field, there is certainty man will one day die? Adam realizes that this is true. Now, all who accept the finished work of Christ become part of the family of God. Interestingly, Eve understood this first. We see this in her name change.

Throughout the Bible, you can notice that Biblical characters have a name change many times, indicating a change in nature. The name changing is about faith and their belief in God.

Later in *Genesis*, we will learn that God changed Abram's name to Abraham, and Abram's wife, Sarai, to Sarah. These name changes are significant and have much spiritual meaning.

Jacob had a name change to Israel, which means a prince of God. However, his original name means supplanter, a liar. All through the Scriptures, you will find this to be so.

It is always God doing the changing.

Like the New Testament, you will find Simon's name changed to Peter the rock. Think of Saul of Tarsus to the title Paul. As Saul, he was a man of power and conceit. Like Paul, his name means little. That is what we are in the eyes of God, and this is how Paul saw himself.

All through the Scriptures, you have this significant change of name.

It always refers to something that has occurred within, which has changed the person's whole nature.

In the case of Eve, we find she was not only to become the mother of humanity, but she is also to be the mother of those who would find life through Jesus Christ.

The thrust of this whole chapter is before us. Either accept the way of God or take the devil.

What will you do?

Act on faith in God's Son or refuse and reject Him, as many millions have done.

If they chose not to repent, God would grant them their desire to go to a devil's Hell.

Will you trust in the grace of God for salvation? See *Ephesians 1:6*.

Again we are clothed with the righteousness of Christ. We are given his legal standing before the Father. This account beautifully pictures all this. But notice why God requires the clothing. We see a dress for God's benefit is not required. Before they sinned, Adam and Eve wore the righteousness of God. They lost that righteousness the moment they sinned. With His Holiness, they needed no clothing. To them, it did not matter.

In thinking of this, it is evident God did not require them to have clothing on as we know of it today. It did not, and would not have bothered them. Dress is for public or personal appearance's sake. God desired they understand that standards for them had changed.

Now it was acceptable for them to wear clothing. Clothing is adequate for us today, and we see several stories in the New Testament that relate to this.

Think of the Prodigal Son. The first thing the Father did for him was to clothe him. In Gadara's demoniac story, we can read where when the demons were cast out of him, he was dressed, sitting at the feet of Jesus and in his right mind. See *Mark 5:15* and *Luke 8:35*.

In our text here in *Genesis*, it is essential to understand God did all the work for them.

He killed the lamb, and He clothed them. They did not. They had to let God do it.

That is in keeping with the step of faith needed by them. They had to learn to trust the way of God. We must let God do this to us.

Many have indicated there seems to be some inconsistency in this last section. See **Gen. 3:22-24.**

How often had God prodded us to come to Him and retreat from all outside pressures and come humbly before Him? It is to take by quiet faith that He promised to supply, will you partake of his patience and power and meet the circumstances of sin. We can do this with a mind at ease, no longer fearing the penalty of sin, trusting in His finished work.

Do you understand what God was doing? Here lies God's function of the tree of life.

Last, again we have the Altar. An Altar is a place designed or separated for worship unto God, a fellowship place with God. It is a place where we give our praises and prayers unto God.

An Altar symbolizes holiness and represents God's presence, a higher place where untarnished (spotless, blameless) services are given to God. An altar is a refuge and comfort for God's child from the troubles of this world. An Altar should be a place where petitions happen for others' wellbeing inspired by the Holy Spirit. We know today the Church serves like an altar where Christians fellowship with God. In the Bible, God's men built Altars after He had filled His promises like Moses, Abraham, Isaac, Solomon, etc.

In this chapter's conclusion, I want to tell you of The Greatest Story, Redemption. Can you imagine now what is happening? They removed from the Garden, never to enter again. What once was their home now is a forbidden place. We will never understand Eden's loss to its fullest until we reach the other side in a place called Heaven.

As a famous radio broadcaster would say, " now the rest of the story." You remember Paul Harvey on the radio?

We should be thankful God would allow His only begotten Son to rise off the throne of Heaven and come to this wicked world, not giving up on humanity, but loving us so much He left the splendor of Heaven to die for me and you on a place called Calvary.

Adam and Eve did not know the full story of Redemption, but two thousand years after Christ came, we know how much He loved us. That is the story of Redemption. God was keeping Adam and Eve from making their way back into Eden. It must be His way or no other way to be redeemed. So much so, He was willing to join us outside of Eden.

Listen to **Heb. 2:14-15**, "Forasmuch then as the children are partakers of flesh and blood, he also himself likewise took part of the same; that through death he might destroy him that had the power of death, that is, the devil; and deliver them who through fear of death were all their lifetime subject to bondage."

Thank God He did come just like He promised. He did break the chains of sin hanging around our necks. He is our only hope of Redemption. Once again, we hear from God's Word in **Rom. 5:20** "Moreover, the Law entered, that the offense might abound. But where sin abounded, grace did much more abound."

I am so glad that whatever tragedy we face, whatever sin may raise its ugly head, can be pardoned by grace far more significant than our sin.

In God's eyes, it is not a stalemate with good and evil balancing each other out.

Understand God has a beautiful warehouse full of grace to give to every sinner.

I am sure man sought Eden for a long time, but one day our eyes were opened to the fact He gave us much more than Eden.

He gave us Christ, His only Son. That is the more excellent Redemption story.

Chapter 4

G en. *3* reveals the root of sin. *Gen. 4* exposes the fruit of sin. *Gen. 3* focused on individuals, specifically Adam and Eve. *Gen. 4* will focus on the family and society itself. *Gen. 4* tells what happened after Adam and Eve sinned. *Gen. 3* tells us the sin committed against God. *Gen. 4* tells us if we sin, it will be against God and man.

Because of Adam's sin, his descendants all receive the sin nature, and then the entire human race will find sin and misery.

We do not have indicated the amount of time elapsed between *Gen. 3* and *Gen. 4*. It is quite likely that many more children than Cain and Abel were born. It tells us that Adam was 130 years old when Seth was born, and yet Seth was only the third child referred to in Scripture.

From Scripture, there is no doubt that Adam and Eve had many more children.

Cain had a wife, as we know. How and who is the typical question. The answer is obvious. It had to be a sister of his. There was no law against marrying close relations back then because the human race had not yet deteriorated where the blood factors caused problems. We do not know how many people were living during this time, but it could have been thousands.

In our text, we come to Cain and Abel. Both were born after the fall after Adam and Eve were placed outside of the Garden. They were both sinners because they had inherited the fallen natures of their parents. Both required a spiritual rebirth. We believe both accepted the teaching and instruction of how they would now worship and fellowship with God. You could, in all practicality, call this chapter the results of the fall. When we think of God's judgment and punishment of sin, we reason ourselves just what we can get out of that sin before paying the consequences.

As an illustration, taken from "The Fruits of the Fall," I once heard was a story of a man and wife, who decided to go to a drive-in movie. When they arrived, they thought the price was too high and plotted to put one over on the theater's management. The husband climbed into the car's trunk when they were within a short distance of the drive-in.

They had made a plan that his wife would let him out once they were in the drive-in. They got in, but then the plans went southward. Hold on; there is a problem here. The wife got in the car and found out the husband had left his keys in his pocket. He was the trunk with no way to get out of the vehicle.

All in all, they had to call the rescue squad along with the police. He had to be cut out of the trunk of the car.

Such is the path of sin. The ride is often short, and the price is way too high.

At first glance, in **Chapter 3**, taking the forbidden fruit and eating seemed like a trivial matter, a mere misdemeanor. But **Genesis chapter 3** makes it clear that it was a matter of gravity.

The result was men have chosen to believe Satan rather than God.

In their opinion, Adam and Eve had concluded that God was tough and severe on them.

It was the idea of the serpent. The serpent had suggested Eve try the fruit. Indeed, Satan asserted that no harmful effects would occur if they partook of the fruit. He told them they would be as gods, knowing more.

But in this **Fourth Chapter of Genesis**, it does not take long to see that Satan's promises were nothing but out-right lies. It is now we see the real wages of sin begin to appear.

Next, we see the fruit of the fall in Cain's life seen in **Genesis 4:1-15**. Soon we will have Adam and Eve having their first child, a son named Cain. His name is probably a play on words.

It sounds similar to the Hebrew word, *Quanah*, which means 'to get' or 'to acquire.' In today's vernacular, his son might be called "Got."

The name's importance is that it reflects Eve's faith, for she said, "I have gotten (*Qaniti*, from *Quanah*) a man child with the help of the Lord." We may never know the precise meaning here, but we see the son was a gift from God. While he is a type of the flesh, the earthy, and the natural man as he was the firstborn. You must read further in *1 Cor. 15:46-49*.

Eve understood that one of her children would be the linage that would bring about redemption.

If this is what she thought, we know disappointment was at hand. Adam and Eve knew a redeemer was coming from God's promise, and who would not have thought that redemption was at hand?

That is what we believe today that Jesus could come at any moment. We live in a world today that mocks us concerning a similar promise of His second coming, knowing it has been two thousand years since He left earth the first time.

Abel's name meant 'vanity,' 'breath,' or 'vapor,'' which may speak of his life's brevity. *James 4:14* says, "Whereas ye know not what shall be on the morrow. For what is your life? It is even a vapour, that appeareth for a little time, and then vanisheth away." He is a type of spiritual or second-born man. He was a keeper of the sheep, as was the Second Adam. *John 10:14* "I am the good shepherd, and know my sheep, and am known of mine."

Perhaps Eve had learned the consequences of sin did not go away so quickly. Her life and those who would come after her would involve struggle, heartaches, and trials filled with much sorrow as they worked to repair the damage done by what they thought they could do.

In essence, Cain was the symbol of Eve's hope, Abel, of her despair.

Both were born by natural means. Both received the sinful nature from parents. Both were children of death and not life. *1 Cor. 15:22* says, "For as in Adam all die, even so in Christ shall all be made alive."

Often in life, we have said our children were like night and day. So were these two children for they had different occupations as they grew up, **verse 2**. However, they were both taught about the fall, judgment, and the remedy. Abel was a keeper of flocks in their occupations, while Cain was a tiller of the soil. Interestingly nowhere does Moses imply that one of these occupations is inferior to the other? We will see Cain's problem was not in his means of livelihood but the man himself. See **Gen. 4:3-5**.

Years later, the Israelites who first read these words of Moses would have little difficulty grasping Cain's sacrifice. They would know and understand that it was a matter of the heart. They would see that man could not approach God without the shedding of a lamb's sacrificial blood. Later, other offerings could be given but not to come to God.

Indeed all were made aware of the different sacrifices.

The very first thing we discover in our text is that Cain's offering fell short of God's requirements of the Law. Of course, Moses had not given the written Law at this time, but God had given commandment of what and how they were to come to Him.

Three things become instantaneously apparent about Cain and his offering to God.

He had the Wrong Offering. He had the Wrong Attitude. He had the Wrong Motive. We do not know what God shared with Adam or his sons, but we know that they understood what God wanted.

We see this from the words God spoke to Cain. See **Genesis 4:6, 7**.

God's question implies that Cain's anger was ill-founded. We will see that Cain's anger was not justified at all. Many times have we seen people get mad over nothing? There are some things they understood better than we, even Cain.

From our text, we can read between the lines and comprehend Cain had a problem. It was not understanding or lack of instruction. Already, God told him the "how" and the "why." That should have been enough for God to accept his idea.

A hamburger stand may let you do it 'your way' as the commercial says, but God will not.

From the Scriptures, we learn that Cain had a form of godliness but denied the power thereof.

As a friend of mine has said, 'You can go to heaven God's way, or you can go to hell any way you please.'

Cain had some religion; he did not have God. Yet, He believed in God, and he wanted God's approval. However, self is in control or at least, so Cain thought. It is our will against the will of God.

So we ask what you will do.

For most people, the way of God is not the terms they like. That is the reason Hell has religious people residing there. The problem is before us. We find Cain did not want to approach God through the shed blood of an innocent Lamb. He wanted to give God what he could do; we call this the fruit of his labors. Naturally looking at the situation, Cain had a green thumb, and he wanted nothing to do with bloodstained hands.

Men today are no different from that. We live with a world that wants to claim they believe in God, and many say they believe Jesus is the Son of God. But just like the demons, they want to approach Him without the Holiness of God. *James 2:19* says, "Thou Believest that there is one God; thou doest well: the devils also believe, and tremble."

At least the devils know who God is, and they have a right to tremble. Most men have no fear of God. They refuse to bow the heart; this is the same as the devils themselves, refusing to submit to the Lord. They refuse to accept the work on the Cross as payment for their sins. Are they good enough to be accepted by God?

The message of the Gospel is straightforward, as taught us from the Holy Writ. They can think as they please God but no matter because the truth will come out. Abel brought the first fruits of the flock, a type of Christ. See *verse 4*. He got a blood sacrifice and in *Heb. 9:22*, "And almost all things are by the law purged with blood, and without shedding of blood is no remission."

Abel followed the pattern of *Gen. 3:21*.

It was a faith offering. Listen to *Heb. 11:4* "By faith, Abel offered unto God a more excellent sacrifice than Cain, by which he obtained witness that he was righteous, God testifying of his gifts: and by it, he being dead yet speaketh." And *John 14:6* says, "Jesus saith unto him, I am the way, the truth, and the life: no man cometh unto the Father, but by me." Also, *Acts 4:12*, "Neither is there salvation in any other: for there is none other name under heaven given among men, whereby we must be saved."

1 Pet. 1:19 says, "But with the precious blood of Christ, as of a lamb without blemish and without spot:"

There are many more passages like; *Luke 22:20; Acts 20:28; Romans 3:25; 5:9; Ephesians 1:7.*

Man will never understand it was a gracious God who gently sought out Cain to confront him with his sinful anger.

Cain knew what God was doing to restore him by warning him of the impending danger he faced. He had time to repent, but he would not.

How stubborn can we be?

Interestingly, different from what man would do, we find God does not compare Cain's offering with Abel's.

The issue was not the difference between the two brothers. God told Cain again of His standard for worshipping Him. Yet, his attitude was that of rebellion and rejection of God's standard. All this had nothing to do with his brother. God could have scolded Cain or punished him as a parent would a child. God wanted Cain to accept His plan, His way of worship. All Cain had to do was submit his will to God's will, and everything would be fine.

However, Cain decided to eliminate his brother and his offering by murdering him. Remember, they both brought a sacrifice. Getting a sacrifice was not a problem. It was the "why" and the "how," which was the problem. Cain's sacrifice was only the symptom of the problem. The problem was Cain.

Verse 7 is pregnant with the implications of what has happened. Cain thought the way to get over his depression of being rejected by God was to kill his brother. He would feel better if he got rid of the competition. This lead to guilt, and that guilt turned to anger. No doubt, he was angry with himself, but he took it out on the wrong person, as we know.

We know his brother was innocent and only trying to help him.

He was wrong in his hatred toward his brother and his God. He was wrong in the murder he committed. Cain chose to ignore God's gentle prodding to get him to turn from the way of self and follow God's will, let him be fully aware of the dangers ahead.

Sin was at the door, just waiting to enter in. It was his master. However, sin has mastered us all, now Cain is faced with the decisions he had made and would be held accountable for his choice.

He needed not to have succumbed to sin, just as we should not, because God always gives sufficient grace to resist any temptation.

Reading *1 Cor. 10:13* says, "There hath no temptation taken you but such as is common to man: but God is faithful, who will not suffer you to be tempted above that ye are able; but will with the temptation also make a way to escape, that ye may be able to bear it."

Cain waited till they were alone in a field. There no one would see what he was going to do.

He killed his brother. See *Deut. 22:25-27.*

I want to stop here and park, so to speak about what has happened. There is a problem that is raging like a wildfire today, and I want to confront it. There is a choice in the making. Will it be salvation by the blood or the way of Cain? Note these following verses: *2 Cor. 11:14, 15; Jude 11; Rom. 10:3, 4; Jer. 23:6.*

I remind you, God has a right to demand righteousness. However, there is righteousness sought after by all of humanity. Every human being worldwide wants to be accepted by his holiness. It seems every man is watching and scrutinizing every other man today.

This country and that country are watching what we are doing on our side of the world.

They want to see if we are infringing on someone's rights.

It saddens my heart in knowing this demand for this kind of righteousness, which is just self-righteousness, has found its way into most pulpits worldwide. It has infiltrated not only the world but churches. No longer in pulpits do we hear the preaching against this doctrine of self-righteousness. No longer in pulpits do we hear of preaching on the fundamentals of the faith.

By that, I mean doing what God says the way God says it. Read some of the sermons by some of the old preachers of years gone by, and you will know what I mean. Today we have sermonettes or messages on moral issues such as; As a Christian you should be kind and helpful, and fulfill all the social needs of this world, Or you should love justice, that is of the kind that is of the world, Or you should show mercy and don't be so harsh and cruel to others.

Let every man do as he pleases, and nothing will happen, right? The phrase for today is for us to do good and be kind. If you think it is correct, it must be, right, right?

The final thought lying behind this kind of reasoning is that he who possesses such a character is going to heaven for what he has done. He can stand before judges with confidence and have no fear of punishment. The men of today are being taught he need not fear the Judge of all judges.

For when he stands before Him at the judgment seat, everything will be alright. Man thinks because indeed, if he is a righteous man here on earth, then God must accept that same righteousness in allowing him into a place called heaven.

Today in the land wherein we live, that is the teaching in nearly every pulpit. All of that sounds good and is very sweet to the ear. Do you see anything wrong with that teaching? No matter.

What is wrong is that it is just not the Bible!!!

Because this righteousness that is being taught, preached, and believed does not depend upon faith in Christ and His shed blood to get you or me into heaven. It is all of the works.

This righteousness with which we have been speaking about indeed gives a semblance of honor to His name repeatedly.

But the Christ it presents is not the Christ of the Cross. The Christ of Bethlehem is the baby in a manger, for he is not a threat to what they are doing. He is the Christ who walked this earth as a good man.

There are many descriptions of him. We all want to look upon the beauty of his life, and we each want to feel the tenderness of His words. We all can recognize the helpfulness of His deeds.

His titles are many. He is known as a great prophet. He is a great man, and He is the great physician. He is also a great expositor. Everything about Him is excellent. We are called upon to follow in the steps of this great man. He has done all manner of good.

He did learn to be unselfish, and to carry the burden of others is making the world a better place to live. But with elaborate talk about His life and character and all the appeals concerning His example, He never leaves Bethlehem's environment. He never reaches the Cross.

He is not a problem to be faced as long as he is allowed to be the manager's baby. However, if He does not reach the Cross, then humanity can never be saved. There would be no clear understanding of why He went to the Cross in the first place. When you begin to examine this righteousness preached, you will find that it denies the Cross and refuses to accept it as the grounds of approaching thrice Holy God. Nor do they believe He is the only source of true righteousness, which we need and is the only acceptable means of approaching this Holy God.

Today the death of Christ on the Cross is not considered necessary for the redemption of our soul. Many do not believe that the sacrifice of His life and blood that He shed on Calvary is the only hope of attaining the righteousness which a Holy God will accept. Many times out on the doors, we find people who believe Christ only provides an acceptable way before a Holy God.

Every time we confront these people with the question, "why did Christ die and God allow him to suffer the way that he did if you can do something within yourself to attain salvation and go to heaven?" They cannot answer this question.

It is evident as a man looks at his nature, culture, and development of our way of life; he thinks he is self-sufficient. Therefore, God must accept him for who he is and what he has done.

In short, Cain's offering is today's language around the globe.

You remember that offering don't you? There was an altar piled high with the vegetables and grains of the field. It probably was all covered with figs, grapes, oranges, all kinds of vegetables.

It must have been covered in flowers smelling sweet, all under a clear blue eastern sky.

No doubt, it must have been a breathtaking sight.

It must also have been very satisfying to Cain, witnessing the labor and toil and handiwork he had achieved.

But listen to what God said to him in ***Gen. 4:3-7***. His offering was an insult to God. Why did God refuse such a beautiful offering? There are several reasons to explore. One, because of Cain's sin nature, he was a sinner. God cannot; God will not allow sin in His presence. Next, it is because of his relation to God. At present, Cain had none. Next, because it is the revealed truth of God in that he would not listen.

His teaching from his parents was there was only one way to approach God.

That was only through a blood sacrifice. I am sure Adam told all of his children this.

Next, because of Cain's persistence in presenting this offering from the very ground, he walked on, which God had cursed, defying God Himself. Because of Cain's insistence in denying the truth known to him, which gives direct verification of what he was taught, he was in rebellion to God.

Next, because he deliberately turned his back on God's revealed will of how to worship.

Next, we see his self-righteousness in exalting the fallen nature through the offering he brought to God. Again, it is because he denied the way of the right sacrifice in not giving a blood offering to God. God had told him he had sinned and that there would be separation from a Holy God.

He thought he was better than God's sentence of death upon him.

Another reason is that Cain ignored God's demand for atonement for sin, performed in God's way. God demanded a substitute for his sins and not the fruit of the ground. Frankly, Cain could care less about what God wanted, for he wanted to do what he wanted to do. He insisted on approaching God on his terms. Next, because he treated God as if he were like himself, one who would accept whatever he desired to do as long as it was "good."

Nothing was wrong with the offering Cain brought, except it was not what God had told him to do.

If this were preparation for a meal at a table, that would have been great. However, it was not a meal. It was to be a sacrifice unto the Lord. Cain was now standing upon ground which God had judged and cursed. Like his father, he stood outside the gate of Eden, away from God's presence, placed under death's sentence, with no way to bridge that gap between himself and God.

However, God had made provision for this. From the fall, God had declared man and woman alike guilty and that no good was in them. Therefore, a man in his sin cannot stand before a Holy and Just God. Man is a sinner. God will not allow sin before him, nor will He allow sin into heaven. If he did, he would be less than holy. Therefore, because of man's ungodliness, he must die according to *Rom. 6:23*. Fallen man is a reproach to God.

But if one has taken advantage of the liberty and freedom of which God had so graciously given him and is willing to give up his will for God, then that man can stand before a Holy God on the grounds of the blood atonement.

Man has abused that privilege and forever has marred his image and relationship with the God who loved him. There is nothing God could do except pronounce the sentence of death upon man for his sin. As indicated before, God provides salvation by the shed blood of an innocent lamb, slain on the altar of sacrifice. That altar for Adam and Eve and their children were at the East Gate of the Garden of Eden.

While Adam and Eve were in this state, God revealed Himself as a God full of grace. He slew an innocent animal as a witness to their sinning against Him. There was no approaching God with sin not covered until this sacrifice took place. He taught them they must apply the shed blood of that sacrifice for their sins by placing that slain, innocent lamb on that altar. We know that before a man can approach God, man must satisfy the demands of the Law of God. Adam and Eve saw the type of sacrifice God had made. After the lamb was slain, God took that skin from that innocent lamb and made it a covering for Adam and Eve to wear.

As by testimony of being forgiven, the sacrificial shedding of the innocent lamb's blood had to be slain and then placed on that altar. The covering was made of those sins so they could then approach a Holy God. Now they can stand accepted before an Almighty God who is Holy.

All of this was a shadow, a picture of the Cross of Christ. It was the prophecy that the death of Christ would become atonement for sin. It was this atonement that would satisfy the demands of God's righteousness against the sinner man. By his death, burial, and resurrection Christ would become the cloak of covering, the justice that God demanded.

We must realize it is death not of my own, but a substitutionary and voluntary death by someone else, giving me lifeblood that allows me to come before a Holy God. The atonement for sin will enable me to be accepted by Him as if I had not sinned. Now God agrees with the offering of Christ and His shed blood for me, in my stead, in my place, washing and taking away my sins.

What purpose would I have accomplished by shedding my blood? Coursed in my veins is nothing but the sin nature having what the Word says is filthiness and vileness. How could I stand before Him in this state? Thank God, it is His blood, which has made me whole again.

God does a beautiful thing in our life when we accept the sacrifice of Christ in our stead for the remission of sins.

God imputes Christ's righteousness to our account. That sets me free from the penalty of sin and curse of my ole sin nature. Now it is not my righteousness, with what I have done, that God looks down and sees in me. The righteousness of God himself wrought and has given to those who believe, through the finished work of Christ on Calvary's Cross that covering we need.

How do I know that Christ has done what he said he would do? The proof of the pudding is in the fact of the literal, bodily, physical resurrection of Christ from the grave and His ascension on high.

That indeed proves for us that His righteousness was indeed sufficient and that He is indeed my righteousness. Christ came, spotless, pure, perfect, as the second man, Adam, the new head of the human race to be the giver of spiritual life, indeed the righteousness of God himself.

Approaching God based on the sacrificial death of Christ, the believer can find himself acceptable before God. Here he stands in the beauty of His Holiness, having eternal life, given to us by His only son. Jesus willingly gave his life that I might live forever in a place called heaven.

So then, the teaching of Adam and Eve was that the only way to approach God after they had sinned was it must be through a blood sacrifice.

God had shown them what they needed to do if they desired to come to God and have fellowship with Him.

Cain knew this. His parents had taught him the Gospel of the blood. Yet, despite all this, Cain decided to bring an un-bloody offering to God. Again this was an insult to God.

You may still want more proof of this. It was an insult because Cain ignored the fact that now there is a gulf between man and God because of man's sin. He missed the truth of the pronouncement of the sentence of death upon himself as a sinner man. He ignored what God had already done in bridging the gap between man and God through the blood sacrifices.

He ignored what God had said and brought an offering of the ground cursed by God.

He refused to view himself as a sinner, one who needs a Saviour and the only one who can satisfy God's demands. In doing these, he was exalting himself as knowing more than God himself.

Cain is now a natural man. He is of the flesh and not of the in Spirit. His offering of the ground made with the hands of man is that of a self-righteous man. Him being self-righteous enough to believe that his righteousness was good enough that God should accept it.

Man sees himself like this today. Sure he will admit for the most part that he may have sinned a little here and there, but nothing so severe as to keep him from the presence of God, and nothing to make him be cursed with the curse of death and sent to a devil's Hell. Many tell us today say they believe in God.

Believing in God, this is the main thing, they say. Yet, nowhere do we read Cain did not believe in God. Indeed the opposite is exact since he made an altar of an offering made with his own hands to that God.

Today such things as Hell, punishment, judgment, indeed they are not relevant for us. The world of today refuses to accept the Word of God. To believe so means you are very narrow-minded, cruel, haters of everyone else. To think that you must be very narrow-minded. To live not harming anyone, or committing any of these great sins, doing the best I can, that is the key, or is it? So our conclusion is this: Self-righteousness is unacceptable before a thrice Holy God. Cut and dried.

So let us dig just a little deeper. This offering by Cain exemplifies such an attitude as we have been describing. It does set aside God's estimate of the man and replace it with man's assessment of himself. However, the truth the Bible so clearly teaches, which so many in the world reject today, is not a question of what your opinion may be or what you think about yourself.

It is wholly a question of what God thinks of you as a natural man, as a sinner man, as a man of this world. You may or may not have a reasonable opinion about yourself. Morally speaking, you think yourself just, fair, and right by those around you, justifying yourself. You may even have a clean enough life, and your fellow man may not hold anything against you. No matter.

Your estimate of yourself nor those around you will not count for you as you get ready to stand before a Holy God.

Incidentally, God has in His Holy Word, given his estimate of man, to know what He thinks. Listen to these words in the following verses. ***Rom. 3:10-12; Rom. 3:23; Rom. 5:12; Gal. 2:16; Gal. 3:20.***

Whatever has been the reasoning of God that leads him to this conclusion, that is, in His estimate of man after the fall, seeing that it is His nature to do right and to make a sound judgment and because He is a Holy and Just God then we must agree with Him of His view of man.

He cannot lie. Therefore He cannot ignore or look over or condone any sin, no matter how small it may be in our eyes. We are all guilty. We are all sinners. We all have the sin nature.

When a man thinks he has found another way, self- righteous man tramples underfoot the assessment of God of man found in His Word.

That is an insult to God. This offering of Cain and others like him put away the fact that God sent his only son to die on the Cross for them to fulfill the climax of all sacrifices.

All must believe to be saved. If they refuse to believe Christ and His work alone can bring salvation, they will spend eternity in a devil's Hell. See the following verses. ***Heb. 9:27; Heb. 7:25-27; Heb. 9:11, 12; Heb. 10:4.***

Self-righteousness proclaims that a clean thing can come out of an unclean thing. It denied Christ's statement when He said that which is born of the Spirit is Spirit, and that which is born of the flesh is flesh. Self-righteousness hates the thought that the flesh will only produce flesh.

Under no circumstances can it produce anything but flesh. Self-righteousness refuses to see neither that between the flesh and the Spirit, there is a great gulf fixed which even God, speaking with all reverence, cannot bridge, nor a man in his efforts.

Noted earlier, Jesus Christ is the only way. It would be correct to say self-righteousness declares *John 3:1-18* to be false. Self-righteousness is willing to stand before a Holy God and offer him something that He already has rejected. Self-righteousness sets aside God's Word and exalts man's works, proclaiming man's righteousness on an equal level with a thrice Holy God.

There is a narrow way; the Bible says to receive righteousness, which is by the blood.

In our text, we see that God does not allow us to wait very long before knowing what He thinks about Cain's offering.

He rejects Cain's and accepts Abel's. Now let us turn our attention to Abel. Abel represents the second born, the second birth, the spiritual life. He brings before God an offering, an offering that is not very pleasant to the eyes. Here is something that causes the mind to turn away from and our stomachs to roll. In fact, to the human eye, it is repulsive to see. Why? Before Abel, there lay a lamb, spotless, pure, and perfect. This animal's life ended with a sudden quick stroke of the sharp knife he has in his hand, cutting its throat, letting it bleed to death, giving all of its life-giving blood. Every natural thing in man's senses would cause him to look with horror at what had just happened. Between the offering of Cain and the offering of Abel, there is no possible comparison.

Everything in the offering of Cain appeals to man. It is lovely, beautiful, in all of its ways.

On the other hand, Abel's offering had nothing, looking at it to cause others to accept it.

It was disgusting to see.

We can only imagine the look with sorrow and horror of what has just taken place. Our sympathies go out to Cain to consciously or unconsciously admire him in what he has done.

Why would Abel be so cruel, so heartless to slay an innocent little lamb?

But the offering of Abel was justified in the sight of God. In that hour, Abel takes God's side against himself. He believes what God has said about himself. It is true. In effect, he says: O God thy Word is right; I am a sinner in all that I am. Because of that fact, I have the sentence of death upon my soul. I am the one who should die. But I surrender my judgment of myself to thy understanding of me. But, O Lord, if I take thee at thy Word concerning your judgment of me, I will also take thee at thy Word concerning your grace.

Abel knew the promise God had made at the gate of the Garden of Eden. God himself provides in the form of a sacrifice of that little innocent lamb on that altar. There He shed that innocent blood for another, as it were, taking my place, bearing my sin and shame, becoming my substitute. He provided an alternative substitute for Adam and Eve covering them in the coat of skins. He took from the lamb giving unto Adam and Eve spiritual life.

Do you say if I come bringing a suitable substitute sacrifice of another, you would accept that for my sins? God says profoundly, yes!!! As long as that sacrifice is His Son! Abel's offering was full of judgment, condemnation, sin, sorrow, death. But it honored God in taking Him at His Word, and God met that act of faith with that promise of His Word. God accepted Abel's offering. God rejected Cain's.

Let us remember that acceptance and rejection had nothing to do with the individuals themselves. Abel was accepted because his offering pleased God. We must also remind ourselves that Cain had the same opportunity to be recognized, as did Abel. Remember, God asked Cain why his countenance was fallen? If Cain had only gone and gotten a lamb and shed its blood, he too would have been accepted by God.

Yet, he would not. It wasn't that he could not. He just would not. He stood by that beautiful offering even though it was an insult to God. Since that time, anyone who brings an offering before God from the labors of his own hands or anything has to do with his efforts will be rejected by God. That kind of offering is the way of Cain. It is the way of the flesh and not of the Spirit. It is the way of self-will and self-righteousness and not the righteousness of God.

Again what was wrong with the offering of Cain? The way of Cain is the devil's substitute. The instrumental thing today is if I think it is alright, then it must be okay. That is what the Bible calls self- righteousness. It is none other than the way of Cain. Look anywhere, and that is what you see. The philosophy is the same worldwide. It is in the sounds we hear in music. It is in the papers we read. It is on the internet to see. What man thinks is that he has found a better and easier way to go to heaven. It openly denies the blood of Jesus and the need for blood atonement. See *2 Cor. 11:14, 15*.

It makes them think that God is so good that there must not be a Hell. Some don't even believe that the devil is real. They think he is just a force or something in comparing the work of the Holy Spirit. There is nothing real about him. Do you not see what all of this will lead too?

If you deny who Jesus is. If you deny who the devil is. If you refuse, you need the blood atonement for the remission of sins. If you reject that, you must accept Jesus was born of a virgin.

If you deny, then you need a Saviour. Destroy the biblical teachings of Jesus, Satan, and sin and the need for redemption and see what happens. Even those whom accept Satan's presence but deny he has any power and limits his operations.

Can I say that these people have never made a more significant mistake in life? Satan transforms into an angel of Light. Then he can seek to do his most subtle work. We take away the repulsive image that so many of us have heard about him, and then he becomes the angel of Light. He uses what he knows will work against us. He has no fear of God. He already knows what the end times will bring. But He uses beautiful things. He uses exciting things. He uses pleasant things.

He uses pretty things. He makes everything seem reasonable. The only thing is he is not willing to tell you is the truth. He is not willing to tell you the result of following him.

He is not going to show you the awful reality of the consequences of your sins.

Interestingly, his ministers are not hideous monsters and creatures that come out after dark and from the earth's bottom. Here is not something out of a horror film. They show themselves as righteous, and we suck it up hook line and sinker. But it is not the righteousness by way of the Cross of Calvary. Think of the attitude of the devil toward the Cross of Calvary.

There had been one continual effort to keep Christ from offering himself there on that old rugged Cross and shedding His blood for my sins throughout history.

Since man's fall in the Garden, that has been the strategic plan of Satan. He knows nothing else, and the sad thing about it is it works very well. He has had 6000 years of experience of how to turn you to his way.

During the personal ministry of Christ on earth, Satan tried many times to kill Jesus before He got to the Cross. On the Mount of Transfiguration, he attempted to lead Christ into committing suicide by throwing himself down from the temple's roof. Later he incited a crowd at Nazareth to throw Christ over a cliff and kill him. After this, he put many conspirators into their minds to proclaim him as their king and declare open rebellion against Caesar's rule. Satan had hoped that Christ would die for treason.

It was in the Garden Satan desired to drive the blood out of Christ's veins, killing him before reaching the Cross. Even on the Cross, he tempted Christ with his greatest temptation.

Satan moved the crowd to cry out and say to Christ that if he were the Son of God, there would be nothing stopping Him to prove who He was, and then everyone would believe him and follow him.

That was all a lie for Satan is the father of lies.

Jesus knew that thousands of angels would follow him if he desired them.

The power at his hands was such all he needed to do was give them one glance, and they would have come. Had He bid them come, there would be no Redeemer of humankind. Not long after Christ said, "it is finished," the Bible says he dismissed his own Spirit to God.

That is a statement worth mentioning. It was Christ's willingness to give up his life for men did not kill him. Those wicked men around the Cross did not kill him. How could anyone kill God? Again he willingly, with joy in His heart, gave up His Spirit. No man killed him. No wound caused his death.

He was our sacrifice on that Cross for my sins and not for mine only but yours as well.

In all of this, Satan's attitude is he will do all he can to bring failure to all of humanity, and despite his shortcomings, he still hates the blood and the Cross of Christ. So this righteousness which his ministers preach is not the righteousness of the Bible. They are preaching righteousness without the blood and, therefore, no atonement. Anyone who does not preach righteousness through the Cross's blood is preaching righteousness, which Satan is sending his ministers to preach. If he can succeed, those who will listen to him will go to a devil's Hell and miss that place called heaven. Indeed if he could get men to be good, kind, and righteous without faith in the crucified Christ, he has won a great victory for himself.

We see this happening today. Every year, we see a loosing of moral standards and true Christians moving more and more to the left, away from God, willing to compromise some of the great promises in the Bible. That willingness of today's churches is creating a reaction to the Cross and the blood of Christ. Why?

If men believe and think that they can have truth and righteousness apart from the Cross, then the devil has won, making the Cross of no effect.

We accept God's Word on the facts of Hell, sin, punishment, and judgment.

As I have said earlier, if there is no hell, no sin, no punishment, and no judgment to be met, in the eyes of men, it will be alright to be good, kind, love one another, and do your own thing. God will have to take you to heaven if this preaching is right. What pleases Satan to no end is many more will be in his home called Hell. Satan desires to confuse minds about God's true doctrines, enabling him to substitute a false gospel, condemning many to Hell.

From the day he turned from God and lost fellowship with God, he has known his time was limited in his dealings with humanity.

As his days grow shorter, he works harder and wiser to see his deeds accomplished.

He is like a leper. No matter what he touches, he corrupts it. Men's minds and men's hearts are closed to the things of God. They cannot see it. Most men believe anything, except in the power of the shed blood of Christ. They say anything but the blood.

This ministry without the shedding of blood is a mouthpiece of Satan. Therefore when you hear a man talking about righteousness, test it, and see whether it has the bloodshed on the Cross of Calvary as its centerpiece or, in the end, something man can do. When you hear preachers testifying that all men are the sons of God by nature, no matter how true or sincere or enthusiastic they are, I can tell you they are the ministers of Satan. It is preaching righteousness without the blood that is the self-righteousness that will send you to Hell. This ministry of bloodless justice is a sign of the last days.

The signs are indicating the end is near. Now, most of the preaching from pulpits is nothing but lies with no truth in them. It is a time when this world will see its ruin through vain deceit. We see it as a time when a man would rather listen to the devil and his workers' lie than listen to God's Word.

It is a sign of the times in which our Lord spoke. It will be a time when false preachers will come in his name and preach righteousness, not God's righteousness. The coming of the Lord draweth nigh. There is soon coming an hour when He will come and take us to a place called heaven.

Later he will come back and be revealed in unlimited judgment upon a world fooled by the devil's righteousness.

So I ask you, do you know where you stand? If you are building on your righteousness, if you are offering that to God and expecting to find security in it, then it is high time you awoke and understood this deception is not of the devil but your pride.

Read these verses, ***Rom.3:10; Rom. 3:23; Rom. 6:23***. All of your righteousness, the very best you can do, is no better than filthy rags in a Holy God's eyes.

It is time you awoke to the fact that the significant issue is the blood of Jesus Christ. That was the issue between Cain and Abel.

The blood is the only difference between Cain and Abel, in the end. That was the difference on that night in Egypt at midnight years later.

Wherever the death angel found the blood of a sacrificial lamb sprinkled upon the door of a house, he passed over it, recognizing that the blood was the blood of a substitute; an innocent lamb had died in the stead of the ones in the house. Whenever he found a home without the shedding of the blood upon it, no matter the character of the ones inside, no matter how good they were, no matter whom they were or how much prestige they had, the firstborn died.

The difference between the saved of Israel and the lost in Egypt was the blood of the lamb. And that is the difference now.

If you are saved for time and eternity, you have faith by taking shelter under the Lamb of God.

You have claimed Christ as your sacrifice and personal substitute.

Claiming Christ under the bloodshed on that cruel tree as your substitute is the only way to be saved. You must be honest about this. Otherwise, you are under the condemnation of a Holy God with only judgment for your future. Therefore, He cannot and will not excuse your sin.

Christ's blood gives you title deed to a place called heaven and to the throne of God. See ***Rev. 7:9-15***.

There is a great crowd of people standing before God's throne accepted of Him. How did they get there? The Apostle John asks one of the elders who they are.

He tells him certain things concerning them and says that they have garments washed in the lamb's blood.

Don't you see the lamb's blood, Christ's blood that gives them the title deed to the throne, and God's presence? It is the blood of the lamb. Never forget it.

Verses 15-17 gives us a two-fold purpose regarding Cain. Cain got assurance he would not die a violent death at a man's hand from these verses. Also, it is a clear warning to anyone who would desire to kill Cain. God spoke directly to Cain. Where is the secrecy in this? God Word did not say, "Whoever kills you," but "Whosoever slayeth Cain." Could there have been many people listening to this judgment?

Next, we see a partial genealogy of the line of Cain. We know Moses wrote this. It is to show evidence of the ungodliness of Cain. It is to leave no doubt in anyone's thoughts. It is also to serve as a contrast between the genealogies of Adam through Seth in *Chapter 5*.

These next verses ought to break one's heart. It tells us Cain departed from the presence of the Lord. As a sinner man, he had no relationship or fellowship with God. He had refused to confess his sin and repent. Because of this, God put him out of the presence of the Garden of Eden.

In these next few verses, we see a lot of events taking place. Cities will come into existence.

As we have said, there are probably thousands on the earth. In these next verses, we see the beginning of Polygamy. Farming with animals will begin here. Music, which can be useful, but is often evil, had its inception here. Metalwork began here.

One of the saddest things in these next verses is the fact that murder continued here. After Cain left his family, he had a child named Enoch and named a city after him. Note this would be in direct violation of God's will, for God had told him to be a nomadic, a wanderer.

Then we find in our text another man by the name of Lamech. He, too, went against the will of God by taking two wives, Adah and Zillah. It was through their descendant's much progress was made in culture and scientific achievements. We must pause here to say that even man is not without the ability to produce excellent and beneficial things to humanity at his worst.

Have you ever noticed how God-given talents often erred to man's imagination rather than blessing God through that talent? Man is no different today. All his skills and abilities are used as instruments of sin.

The skills of the metalworker produced implements of sin like the making of idols. See **Exodus 32:1**. To a natural man's eyes, the line of Cain had much to give to the world. Yet, it should sadden our hearts studying the actions of man during this time. Notice just in this chapter how many new sins that are revealed to us. What happened to repentance and faith in God?

In the text, there is so much sin. Murder by Cain of his brother and then, Lamech even bragged about killing a young boy to his wives. His murder was brutal, bold, and volatile. Worst of all, Lamech shows disdain and disregard for God's Word, according to **Genesis 4:24**.

God had spoken words to assure Cain that he would not die. In God's warning to Cain, He must have told him how serious this thing was called murder.

God values all human life. In studying, you will find Lamech twisted and distorted the will of God. He had no concern for life itself, nor did he care about the things of God's. But then appears a glimmer of hope. We see the Grace of God in **Genesis 4:25-26**.

In the New Testament book of **Romans Chapter 5**, Paul, the Apostle has much to say concerning man's fall. But he also gives these words of hope. **Rom 5:20** says, "Moreover the Law entered, that the offense might abound. But where sin abounded, grace did much more abound:" Sin indeed abounded in Cain's line, but the chapter will not end without a glimmer of the Grace of God.

Looking back, Eve hoped for a redeemer through her firstborn. He would not come through the linage of Cain.

Note, too; God would raise another son after Abel where the Christ child would come. We see this in **verse 25**. His name is Seth. Seth, too, had a son, Enoch.

Imagine how Adam and Eve must have felt in their losing hope of immediate retribution.

In those days, there was a remnant that did call upon the name of the Lord. See *verse 26*.

God will always provide hope in a despairing, wicked, and cruel world. Thank God, we have the New Testament today to tell us what to do and the principles and practices we should and should not follow.

This account is not merely an account of two men, brothers, or of their ancestors, but a record of two ways, the way of Abel and Cain's way. See *Jude 1:1-11*.

Just for a minute, let's look at these verses in the book of Jude. He warns his readers of those who are spiritual counterfeits in *verse 4*. You know as well as I do that there are those in this world who are not saved, but they will appear to be and act like believers to pervert the true faith and divert men from experiencing the Grace of God. If you look at these verses, many men are like Cain. The world is full of the religious crowd, doing what they do in a self-righteous attitude and trying to name themselves.

Then, some genuinely saved are those who, like Abel, approach God as a sinner.

They understand and accept the shed blood of a perfect lamb, Jesus Christ, to remission sins. They know they cannot gain access to the throne of God any other way.

The 'way of Cain' is an ever-increasing proclamation today. Corruption comes by sin.

We can say it is God's abandonment for the will of man. Listen again to *1 John 3:11, 12* "for this is the message that ye heard from the beginning, that we should love one another. Not as Cain, who was of that wicked one, and slew his brother. And wherefore slew he him? Because his works were evil and his brother's righteous."

Today, we see the heart's outward revelation being magnified right before our eyes with men saying they love God but reject God's way. If Christ were living today, He would be put to death as he was two thousand years ago. *John 1:4, 5* says, "in him was life; and the life was the Light of men. And the light shineth in darkness; and the darkness comprehended it not."

A little later in this same chapter, we read *John 1:9-11*, "This was the true Light, which lighteth every man that cometh into the world. He was in the world, and he made the world, and the world knew him not. He came unto his own, and his own received him not."

There is little hope for those who walk in the way of Cain.

There may be the dishonest gains of culture or technology, but they must ultimately suffer Cain's fate. They will find only sorrow and regret one day when their life on this earth is over.

Thanks are to God, some have found a better way, the way of Abel, through the blood.

Luke 11:50, 51 says, "That the blood of all the prophets, which was shed from the foundation of the world, maybe required of this generation; From the blood of Abel unto the blood of Zacharias, which perished between the altar and the temple: verily I say unto you, It shall be required of this generation." Also, *Heb. 12:24* says, "and to Jesus the mediator of the new covenant, and to the blood of sprinkling, that speaketh better things than that of Abel."

The blood is our deliverance, and it is our cleansing agent whereby our sins are taken away.

We can rejoice in hope, knowing we will never be eternally separated from God.

Have you come to trust in the blood of Christ for your sin? Why not do so today. See *verse 17*.

God told Cain what not to do, and that is what he did.

God had told him to be nomadic, yet instead of being a traveler, he built a city. How could God bless something he had cursed?

Tubal-Cain was a descendent of Cain. He was into music, and we know, according to *Ezek. 28*, what Satan will do with music. Satan fell because one of the sins he committed was his music was corrupt.

In this chapter, we have a man pronouncing judgment on man. God is the Judge and not man.

There is a great debate over the sons of man and the sons of God. The emphasis is on the fact of the two lines, the natural line and the spiritual line. The context is not about angels taking over the world. In **Gen. 4:17-18**, we have the first mention of this man Enoch. For textual purposes, the Enoch found in **Gen. 5:21-24** is not the same man as in **Chapter 4**.

This man in **Chapter 4** was part of the wicked world. If you will notice, he was the great-grandfather of Lamech. **Chapter 5**, in the account of Enoch, as you will see, is a Godly man.

Then in the last verses of the chapter, we have another glimmer of hope, Seth's birth. God always has his man on stage.

There may only be a few, but believe God, He will make sure that the truth is heard and that man will have to answer it. As we have said, this is about the natural line and the spiritual line in the Bible. We will look in-depth at this in the next chapter.

Chapter 5

We begin a new chapter, and it is one of the saddest chapters in the entire Bible, for they all died. It is like walking through a cemetery. Notice you read that they were born, they lived, and now they are dead. Each person, each family, each generation all died.

As you read, God had told Adam that he would surely die in the day he ate of the tree's fruit. This chapter is the result of this. Amid this death, you have the incredible story of how God is preserving a line for Him to get glory and honor.

So let us consider this account. In ***Gen. 4:16-24***, we have the record of Cain's offspring.

We could say these Canaanites were progressive, or liberals using the vernacular of today.

Progressive in their way of thinking, progressive in their actions, they thought they had developed those gifts they were using.

They should have the ability to see their God-given talents, but they were blind to how they acquired them by being able to build cities and make all kinds of inventions.

In quite a contrast to them in ***Gen. 5:1-32***, we have the record of the offspring of Seth.

These offspring are the God-fearing line of the human race.

Interestingly, the Bible is quite when mentioning the great things said about them accomplishing earthly things. Perhaps as strangers and pilgrims, they were looking for something better.

I remember a story of an old Scots minister. I think he was in the book of Matthew's account of the genealogy. As you know, many of the names mentioned are hard to pronounce. He said, 'Abraham begat Isaac and Isaac beget Jacob, and Jacob begat Judah.' What followed made it funny.

He saw the list of names continuing and said they all kept begetting one another down this page and halfway into the next.'

If we are honest, most of the genealogies in the Bible, we skip them. In my studying through the Book of Genesis, I must admit I seriously considered doing the same thing, merely passing by **Genesis 5**. There is a verse of Scripture, though, which would not let me pass by this chapter. **2 Tim. 3:16** says, "All Scripture is given by inspiration of God, and is profitable for doctrine, for reproof, for correction, for instruction in righteousness:"

Nevertheless, we should read genealogies if we are going to learn from them.

In preaching the Bible, I have learned that the inadequacy is not in the text of Scripture we preach, but in the teacher or the preacher preaching from the text. That is kind of hitting the nail on the head. The fifth chapter of Genesis is one of many genealogies you will find in Scripture.

There are things we need to learn from this chapter, and it will encourage and instruct us if we are willing to take the time to go through it. The genealogies of **Genesis chapters 5** and **11** are not the only place you will find references to people in ancient times. The Egyptians had king listings of their lineages, and so did the Sumerians. The Hittites had royal contribution lists, the historical and chronological value of which is beyond doubt.

These ancient near eastern genealogies are instructive to determine the correct interpretation of some of the biblical records.

We learn from the genealogies God wanted to teach other lessons, not just for chronology.

In **Genesis 5**, at first glance, you would think that one only needs to add up the numbers contained here to establish the age of civilization upon the earth. For example, Ussher arrived at the date of 4004 B.C. for the events of *Genesis chapter 1* through genealogy listings.

However, individuals' naming did not necessarily imply that there was a continuous sequence following each name. Often names were omitted, and the genealogical lists were selective in the admission of families.

Let's take a closer look at Adam to Enoch found in *verses 1-20*. As we have said in previous chapters, we consider Adam to be the federal head of the human race. In looking at our text, this first verse has a remarkable statement. It says, "The book of the generations of Adam," *Genesis 5:1*.

This statement stands alone in the Bible, except found in *Matt. 1:1*. They are the only two statements made in the Bible like this.

What caught my attention is the contrast between the two. If you note, we find that Adam is the federal head of the human race. In contrast, we see Christ as the representative of those who has been born again. See *Matt. 1:1*.

Our text reveals the Scriptural introduction of why we read of the first Adam and the last Adam. We see the New Testament counterpart in *1 Cor. 15:45* "And so it is written, the first man Adam was made a living soul; the last Adam was made a quickening spirit."

Also, note in the *Genesis 5* text, we have the "likeness" of men compared.

God created man in His likeness, but there is more to this statement than that.

Note our text follows the wording from other chapters in Genesis.

We should ask the question, "Why do we read that Seth was begotten in the likeness of Adam, *verse 3*?"

The answer comes to mind Adam had taught his family about sin. I am sure he must have explained how sin entered into his heart, changing their lives forever. Corruption of the heart and mind is what we understand will happen in this changing world. To understand Moses and his writings about the meaning and application of the genealogy of *Genesis 5*, we have to take a closer look and compare and contrast the account in

Genesis 4. Usually, speaking *Chapter 4* gives us the genealogy of Cain, while in *Chapter 5*, Moses describes the Godly line of Seth.

In one sense, this is correct. It should be evident to the reader. *Chapter 4* depicts the ungodly descent of the human race, while *Chapter 5* records the history of the line through which the Savior should come. *Chapter 5* is not the account of Seth's lineage, but the family of Adam.

Look again at *Genesis 5:1-3*.

There is puzzlement in the first few verses. Moses has already told us some of this information. Why tell us again? Previously we saw the genealogy of Cain came to a dead end.

It began with ungodly Cain, ends with wicked Lamech, and is 'gone' by the time of the flood.

Moses begins *Genesis 5* with the terminology of *Chapters 1* and *2*, 'created,' 'in the likeness of God,' 'male and female,' 'blessed them,' to indicate to the reader that God's purposes and program for man did not stop.

What began in the first chapters was carried out through Adam's seed, but not through Cain's line but instead through Seth. The whole of *Genesis 5* is a description of the ever-narrowing line through which the Messiah will come.

There is a distinction between the two lines, and they are distinct. We can illustrate this by the two 'Lamech' of *chapters 4* and *5*. Lamech, the son of Methuselah, found in *Genesis 4:18* of Cain's lineage, was Polygamy's initiator, mentioned in *Genesis 4*. See again *Genesis 4:19*. As we have said, worse than this, he was a murderer who boasted of his crime, *Genesis 4:23* and made Light of God's words to Cain as we saw in *Genesis 4:24*.

The Lamech of *Genesis 5* is the son of Methuselah and Noah's father, who, as we know, was a Godly man. Need I have to say, he was not perfect, as we are not perfect, but he was a Godly man! He knew the fact of the fall of man and the curse God placed on the earth itself in the naming of his son. See below in *Genesis 5:29*.

Remember, the ungodly crowd did not care what God had said about the ground they walked on being cursed. But it does indicate his faith that God would deliver man from the curse through the seed of Eve. Already this had been instilled by the preaching of God through the family of Adam. Is it possible Lamech understood this deliverance would specifically come through the son God had given to him?

The Sethites were looking for the coming Redeemer, the woman's seed.

They knew their iniquity and their sin, and they were willing to admit that they were sinners. I believe you have to accept your lost condition before you can be born again.

I also believe they exercised their privilege of providing an altar of sacrifice at the designated place there by the Gate of Eden, where God had set a cherub and a flaming sword. Remember, the cherubim guarded the entrance to keep them from entering in their way.

They knew their condition and were willing to face themselves honestly, acknowledging their sinful nature, calling upon the name of the Lord. See **Rom. 10:9-13.**

We know a day of judgment is soon coming. No unbeliever will be able to stand under the judgment of God. God has left us here to be a witness to the world. We preach the judgment upon sin, and there should be a separation from this world of sin.

Unlike those who have rejected Christ, for the believer, we have this promise of eternal life.

In our text, Cain's descendants' account, we find no numbers were employed, while Seth's line has a definite numerical pattern.

Looking closely at each individual, you will find that individual's age at the son's birth. You will also find the years they lived after their son's birth and the man's age at his death.

One interesting fact to consider before we go on is that virtually the person's life falls into two parts, either B.C. or A.D. That is before the child and after the delivery of the child. This division is not without importance.

Another interesting fact is the length of the lives of the men in *Genesis 5* is remarkable.

In trying to figure out why they lived so long, man has used every imagination of his heart to do away with the length of their age. We know conditions were undoubtedly different before the flood. So, before the flood, there was a canopy of vapor water surrounding the earth.

This canopy kept the ultra-violet rays from entering the earth's atmosphere. Moses intended the length of the lives of these men to impress us.

I still want to address at least a thought here of why did they live so long?

We cannot know for a fact, but it would not be wrong to suggest possible reasons. It could have been because of the effect of eating the tree of life. See *Gen. 3:22*.

Also, the degeneration of genes would become deadly for hundreds of years. We also know atmospheric conditions were different before the flood. I also have determined the historical and spiritual significance is enormous. When you study, you will find that Adam lived during the first 56 years of Noah's father's life. In the text six times in these verses, it is said, "he died." "He died" is mentioned a total of 8 times in the whole chapter. Need I remind you that sin entered through Adam? We hear these words from the Apostle Paul in *Rom. 5:12* "Wherefore, as by one man sin entered into the world, and death by sin; and so death passed upon all men, for that all have sinned." Also, these words in *1 Cor. 15:22* "For as in Adam all die, even so in Christ shall all be made alive."

The great tragedy was not that the men of *Genesis 4* died, so did those of *Genesis 5*.

Their failure is the children of Cain were judged of God and did not survive, but that Noah, the seed of Seth, did survive. We know all men will die, but some will be raised to eternal misery while the people of faith will spend eternity in God's presence. See *John 5:28, 29*, and *Revelation 20*.

When you look at the world, we think that the children of this world 'have it made,' but the ultimate reality of their fate is they will die in their sins just like the ancient world did.

At judgment day, those rejecters will receive their reward from the Judge of all Judges.

Just as death came to Cain and his descendants, so did the end come to the Godly seed of Seth? In our thinking of the man Enoch, you find he is a type of all those who walk with God. In the judgment, death will not swallow them up. Thank God, they will be ushered into God's eternal presence, whose fellowship we will have for eternity.

As believers, we can look death squarely in the face without fear, for the sting of death was removed by Christ on the Cross, as was the 'seed of the woman,' promised in **Genesis 3:15**. What defined early men's destiny was whether or not his name was in the book of Cain or Seth's generations. And what narrowed the names of those listed in Genesis 5 were their sin and their faith in God. It was and is provided by the salvation He promised, and so it is today.

The final question is this, in whose lineage are you to be found? Are you still in Adam, or has your life changed, and now you are in Christ? See **Romans 5** for more information on salvation. Salvation is not complicated.

Otherwise, how could a child understand it? Admit you are a deserving sinner of God's eternal punishment. Understand you have to trust Christ.

He alone can take you to heaven. Not what you can do. If you do this, your name is in the Book of Life. If you have not done this, then you are in the first Adam.

While your works may have influenced men, they will not meet God's standard for eternal life.

Again, in which book is your name found? Secondly, in this chapter, I am reminded that the man's measure in God's eyes is evidenced in his children. How should this change our priorities and values when we look at it from this perspective? Cain built by his son, but Seth built into his son. Cain sacrificed his sons to succeed. Seth found success in his sons.

How often we need to hear of the words of the Psalmist in **Psalm 127**!

The psalmist reminds the workaholics striving for success; sacrifices usually come at a very high price. Most of the time, success comes at the hand of the family.

And he tells us that our children, which are God's great gift to men, are not given us in rising early and retiring late, but in resting in the faithfulness of God.

As you study, two things marked out the men of *Genesis 5*. First of all, they were those who were men of faith. We see two men who stand out here, Enoch, found in *Genesis 5:18, 21-24*, and Lamech, found in *Genesis 5:28-31*.

In the first section of verses, we will look at the man Enoch, whom the Bible says did not die.

We will also look at *Jude 14-16* and *Heb. 11:5* in conjunction with our thoughts here.

There is no doubt the kind of man Enoch was. When you look at a man like him, you begin to understand how God operates. Enoch lived in a time of great trouble and problems in his world. Yet, we find God raising a man who would preach the Word of God without fear.

Please note the verses in *Jude 14-16* which says" And Enoch also, the seventh from Adam, prophesied of these, saying, Behold, the Lord cometh with ten thousands of his saints, To execute judgment upon all, and to convince all that are ungodly among them of all their ungodly deeds which they have ungodly committed, and of all their hard speeches which ungodly sinners have spoken against him. These are murmurers, complainers, walking after their own lusts; and their mouth speaketh great swelling words, having men's persons in admiration because of advantage."

These verses tell us a lot about the man Enoch. Enoch's name means instructed, dedicated to the things of God. Enoch must have been taught early in his life about God and how to fellowship and worship Him. As time must have gone by, we find Enoch becoming more dedicated to the things of the Lord. Our text tells us Enoch was the seventh from Adam.

We know the number seven is the number of completeness, and for Enoch, he was complete in God.

Here is a man that loved God but not only God Himself but the things of God. He had what the world needs today, and that is, he walked with God. To walk with means to set in order, to always set Him before us. It means living a life obeying all of the things of God to our ability. He knew God's Word would be the rule for his life. We know, too, it should be the rule for our lives, no questions asked.

What it means is to have every intention of our hearts trying to please God in all things.

It is to seek His will and not my will in whatever things we do. He walked with the heart's attitude to make sure the grace he received from God was not in vain. Notice the indication is he not only walked after God as all good saints should, but he walked with God.

Did you catch it? There is a tremendous difference here.

He loved God and the things of God and was willing to set aside what he wanted to do for the things that God had told him He wanted him to do. See *Gal. 5:16-26*.

An interesting thing about his life is he did not start walking with God until he was 65 years old. Something must have happened at this time.

We know what this fact was. The birth of his child is what the influence was. That child's name was Methuselah. "Methuselah" means "it shall be sent," referring to the flood which came the same year Methuselah would die. After the child is born, we find he walked with God for 300 years. Maybe we should stop and ask ourselves what it means to "walk with God?"

I think we should list several things here. It should be a walk that requires agreement.

Here we are talking about an agreement with God, "for how shall two walk together except they are agreed?" *Amos 3:3*.

Regarding his walking with God, we can say there can only be one way: by faith in the Lord Jesus Christ's finished work for eternal life. Under the Old Testament economy, they knew nothing of Christ. I am satisfied that Enoch understood that a Redeemer would come to take away the world's sins one day. He knew this, and he believed with all of the heart, these things to be right.

I am also sure this is what he must have preached this to those around him. He understood he had to walk with honor and in love before a Holy God. He understood that we are to be consistent in all things in our lives, and he was willing to do just that. *Heb. 11:5*, six says, "By faith, Enoch was translated that he should not see death; and was not found, because God had translated him: for before his translation he had this testimony, that he pleased God. But without faith, it is impossible to please him: for he that cometh to God must believe that he is and that he is a rewarder of them that diligently seek him."

He was different from those around him.

Then Moses makes a strange statement here in the text. He says that Enoch was not.

That is, no one could find him, even his friends. He could not be found by his wife or the rest of his family. His enemies did not even find him, and I am sure he had some if he preached about God. He was not found among the living.

What happened to him would be a reasonable question to ask. "Who put him to death?" Do you believe the account recorded for us in the Word of God?

It merely says he was not. Many have speculated about this statement, and so have I in giving the analysis of what happened. We know he walked with God, and we have jokingly said that God said to him, "it is closer to my house, so why don't you come and stay with Enoch and he said, "I think I will, and he did."

No doubt, what God did was provide for him a home in a place called heaven. We know he did not see death. In the final examination of his life, we can confidently say that he was a preacher of his day who lived for God, so God took care of him. See *1 Sam. 2:30-35* and *Zech. 3:7*.

We understand that Enoch is a type of Christ who was translated bodily into heaven, a victor over death and the grave. He is also a type of the living saints that will experience the Rapture at the second coming. I can hardly wait!!

Sometimes in reading and studying God's Word, we don't stop thinking about the consequences of what is happening. Here is a man standing against the tide of the day and willing to put his very life on the line for the Redeemer's cause to come.

He knew judgment was coming and knew many would die and go to a devil's Hell if they did not accept his preaching. On the other hand, as God "took" him, this gives us an excellent insight into what will happen to those who believe.

Look closer now at the text. There are things previously mentioned worth repeating, but again I feel it is worth it. Elijah, taken by God, is, in itself, a critical and enlightening fact in history.

It has happened in no other case except Elijah, nor has any other living man been translated to heaven except the Lord Jesus. That fact was illuminating in a great many respects. And we accept it as fact to what took place with Enoch.

What does it show us? It showed that there is a future state in which humanity will live.

Man has a soul and spirit, and they are going to live eternally somewhere. See *I Thess. 4:17* and *1 Cor. 15:51, 52*.

In that future state, as the verses above show, the body will be changed too. The ascension of Enoch also brings us to the type of the risen Saviour. If Enoch could be taken up and was not, why could not the Lord Himself be taken up after that He died? If He died and rose again and was resurrected, why would we think it impossible for God's saint to be raptured? If we are taken up in the Rapture, that means we are to exist somewhere, right? For those who want to argue and say this is not true, I find great difficulty in their reasoning. Not only that, this means God does love us so much that He has made a place for us and that we will dwell with Him for all of eternity.

Who would deny this? Surely this would encourage the child of God to push forward, stand for the cause before them, being willing to endure for a short time the chastisement of this world for the Glory of God. Enoch and Lamech looked back and gasped at the fact that sin was the root of their troubles and travail. They looked forward to the coming Redemption God was to provide through their families seed.

That brings us to the second description of these men of *Genesis 5*; they produced a Godly seed through whom God's purposes and the program would continue. Throughout the history of humankind, God has always had His man on the scene. This time was no different.

He has His preachers of righteousness and to warn of the judgment to come.

Now we are not told that every person in the lineage of Seth were Godly people.

We can say they were all sinners in need of a Saviour. But we know that these were Godly men and that through them and their children, a line would continue through Noah right on down to the Lord Jesus Christ.

In the judgment, God brought the flood, destroying all humanity, but through Noah, He did preserve the coming seed, fulfilling *Genesis 3:15*. The hope of men has rested in the protection of a Godly seed.

What a lesson would this be to the Israelites of old to learn when you think about this protection of the coming seed? When the Israelites reached the land of Canaan, they would encounter people vastly different from the Egyptians. While the Egyptians despised the Israelites, they would not consider intermarriage.

On the other hand, the Canaanites would invite it, and indeed, they nearly destroyed Israel's nation because of their willingness to intermarry and show them other sins.

You will find this accurate by looking at *Genesis 46:34; Deuteronomy 7:1*, and *Numbers 25:1*, for example.

If they continued to intermarry with the Canaanites, that would be turning from God.

To marry with the Canaanites would mean to pollute the Godly line through which Messiah was to come. Can't you see the plan of Satan in all of this? He wanted to destroy what God was about to do.

A blessing would come to the people of Israel if they obeyed Him by faith and obedience. Don't you know He would look after them? They should have known, and more than that, they should have trusted the One True God. In the end, you know what happened.

Humankind was prospering, so they thought they did not need God.

Does that not sound familiar to us today?

I am sure that most of the world's nations had begun to put their trust, not in the living God, but the technology of the Canaanites and other countries around them.

They were improving the standard of life, but in the process, they left out God.

How was Israel to fight in a war without horses and chariots? They were forbidden to use the latest technological advances. The question is, "why?"

The reason is simple. Israel must trust in Him. Note the following verses. *Exodus 15:4; Deuteronomy 17:14; Joshua 11:6*. In years gone by, having alliances with pagan nations may have been the world's way, but it was never God's way, *2 Kings 18, 19*.

Chapter 6

I want to jump right in and discuss this "problem" that has bothered so many people.

I know the arguments for the first part of this chapter. Admittedly there is great difficultly here unless you are willing to be logical and contextual. Without either, several viewpoints are available for those seeking other references that give seemingly different views.

However, I have found that if you have to "stretch" to get your point of view, you are probably wrong.

We can let the Scriptures speak to us, and generally, you can understand what God is saying. There is no doubt we get things wrong, but I have noticed that when I try and fit what I think of in the place of what God is saying in a text, the answer lies in finding the problem is with the teacher and not with the word. Interpretation can be demanding and challenging, but we must at least try.

If we consider the context to be the first five chapters of Genesis and, more recently, *Chapters 4* and *5*, we have been observing Seth and Cain's two lines based on their parents, Adam and Eve.

The tragedy of *Chapter 6* is that these two lines, instead of remaining separate, seem to join together. Of course, this did not happen overnight. It was a gradual thing. It is so easy to relax your guard in the church, and what happens next? The world, as we know it, comes rushing inside the church. Before long, it is hard to recognize the difference between the world and the church.

As we have found, living for God is an everyday thing. To do this is what we call a separated life unto God. Today not many preachers are willing to do this, much less the rest of the congregation. See *2 Cor. 6:14-16*. Unless one is willing to dedicate himself or herself to the Lord, the results will be the same as found in *Genesis 6*.

When the co-mingling of the world with the Christian occurs, the final result will be wickedness developing. It is contamination from the world, the flesh, and the devil.

Then you have these words found in *verse one*, "And it came to pass when men began to multiply on the face of the earth, and daughters were born unto them." The importance of the expression, "daughters were born unto them," is not just that the female sex was increasing in number.

This phrase refers to a particular danger to all men, specifically those of Seth's Godly line.

Look at *verse 2*, "That the sons of God saw the daughters of men that they were fair; and they took them wives of all they chose."

In our text, I want to address first the fact they were sons. In Hebrew, it is evident these men were born into the family. There is also a suggestion that something was happening with them. When God moved Cain, it caused Cain and Seth to go in their separate directions.

But over time, we see something happening. We believe Cain and Seth. They began to meet again. Those that were born from Seth must have started to go down into the cities. Their sin had free reign. It was there they could do what they wanted in the flesh, and no one would stop them. By this time, the world was, as we have said, very corrupt.

More than that, we see the Cainites and the Sethites beginning to marry. Even though they must have known the consequences of their actions of listening to the heart instead of God, they would not stop.

Interestingly, the women in the text are the ones singled out. Usually, the men are the ones mentioned by their linage. The reason is evident that here they were particular targets and objects of temptation to man. Think about it, God made man, and then He created woman.

Adam knew the difference, and that difference is what attracted him to her. Nothing has changed in that regard. Man still has the same desires as when created by God. Man's natural attraction is to the opposite sex, the woman.

In trying to keep in context, the lineage of Seth concludes in **Chapter 5** with Noah and his three sons. We talk about Seth and his prodigy, but we must remember that all of humanity was wicked by this time. I believe that would include those, for the most part, born of Seth.

Of course, Noah was part of that family.

Throughout Scripture, we find it is not the majority that gets saved but a remnant. I believe that is the case here. Remember, there were no chapter breaks or divisions in the original language, which means that the narrative continued from **Chapter 5** to **Chapter 6** without interruption. That means **Chapter 6** follows what took place in **Chapter 5** with the line drawn between Cain and Seth.

I believe this interpretation is correct: the sons of God refer to the Sethites, whose lives were characterized by walking with God, plain and simple. We see it is in contrast to Cain's linage, whom was not walking with God, and therefore they were not the sons of God. From our text, the men of Seth's linage looked at the women of all races, not considering their marriage beliefs. It became apparent this choosing was without being concerned about their moral character or whether they had a desire to please God or not. Those initially seeking purity in their relationship to those around them had broken the promise of God. Now men didn't care who they married.

We know that by this time, the men of the world had become evil, powerful, and corrupt in all they were doing for the Bible says they were and are desperately wicked. In this instance, it seems the wickedness in the world had free reign. In regards to the sons of God, it is evident there is a great difficulty here. But I would say to you to look at **Genesis 4:25, 26** "And Adam knew his wife again; she bare a son, and called his name Seth: For God, said she, hath appointed me another seed instead of Abel, whom Cain slew. And to Seth, to him also there was born a son; and he called his name Enos: then began men to call upon the name of the LORD".

Notice what Eve said about Seth. She considered him another seed. I believe this is about the coming seed of Jesus Christ. We see this in *verse 25*.

In the next verse, notice that the men mentioned are Seth's children, and many of them began to trust in the Lord's name. The word Lord is all capital letters. Our text is explicitly speaking of Jehovah Himself. And I would say it was not the whole of the Seth family as already mentioned.

In essence, Eve was telling Seth and his family that she considered him the sons of God.

Then those of Cain would be the opposite of the sons of God. Instead, they would be the sons of men. There would be the inclination to say these were sons who were born of their parents.

On the other hand, Angels were never "born."

To address the thought on angels, we will say it is true that good angels are often called the sons of God, but this is about their natural relationship to God and not an official title, which they may have. If angels were God's sons, it is evident they would not have committed such a sin, as mentioned in our text. For those angels who did sin, speaking about Jude, the Scriptures seem to indicate their apostasy was against God in heaven, and He cast them out and overthrew them because of their wickedness. Just because Jude's next verse is about Sodom and Gomorrah, many have assumed Jude was talking about the angels mentioned in *Genesis 6*.

Back in our text, we know some commentators have introduced fallen angels as those being God's sons.

However, rather than mythicizing a verse, just interpret it simply and practically; it is better to stick with the obvious interpretation. There is no doubt some of this thinking has come from the mythology tales of gods who married beautiful women and made super races. Somehow this has penetrated the thoughts of interpretation of the Word of God. The union of the families and that of the Sethites is the most logical explanation from the context here.

As we see, those in disagreement with me can quote many verses to support their view; I know there are as many verses to support my opinion.

What I see happening is that the men of that day turned to the lust of the flesh to satisfy their physical needs rather than being patient and waiting on God to show them the woman they were to take to wife.

Spiritual character is not taken into consideration here. The emphasis of *Genesis 6:2* shows the sons of God were looking at and were choosing wives because they were beautiful. They should have been concerned with the heart, but all that mattered was outside appearances.

The phrase "sons of God" is often used in Scripture to speak of men on the earth. Just for reference sake, compare *Psalm 73:15; Deut. 32:5; Hosea 1:10* and *Deut. 14:1*.

In all of these verses, you have the same Hebrew root word, which refers to men and not angels. What makes it confusing and gives some justification for thinking that these are fallen angels is that the phrase "sons of God" can refer to angels. See *Job 1:6* and *Job 2:1*.

In these verses, they refer to good angels. Fallen angels, most of the time, are not called the sons of God. The sin referred to in *Genesis 6* is not fornication or adultery or adulterous lifestyles but that of mixed marriages of believers and non-believers. Another evident factor is that these sins' judgment only fell on humankind, for the Lord said His Spirit would not always strive with man, *verses 3, 6,* and *7*.

Consider this factor for thought. In *Genesis 1*, we see that what God created was to reproduce after his kind. Many verses in *Genesis 1* refer to this. In 5 verses it emphasized ten times that God's creatures would reproduce after their kind. See *Heb. 2:7-16*.

Another factor is that the angels are of a higher order than man, even though fallen angels can possess a man.

Back to the text, we see that the sins of *verse 2* have their result in *verse 3*. As we have said, God said His Spirit would not always strive with man. We know, though, God is a longsuffering God. God was willing to give those 120 years to repent, but they refused. See *verse 3*.

Every stroke of Noah's hammer and his sons was a stroke of God's judgment against all humanity. Humanity did not just become sinful. He had been since the fall. Now he is sold out to sin.

The critical factor involved here is to determine whether **verse 4** is a result of **verse 2**.

The giants of the earth did not appear only due to God's sons' union with men's daughters. **Verse 4** makes a general statement there were giants on the earth.

It does not say there arose as if these giants were a result only of the mixed marriages of **verse 2**. **Verse 4** is merely speaking of another class of ungodly people on the earth at that time. The word giant does not necessarily mean one of a tall stature. The Hebrew word is Nephilim. It comes from the root word Naphal. It means to fall in a general term.

Here it means to fall upon or to overthrow, to attack. See **Num. 13:32, 33**, for example.

Again, it does say that these men were of great stature. In **Numbers**, there is a distinction between the men of great size and those of giants. See **verses 32, 33**.

The Naphal were men of great violence. The sons of Anak were among the Naphal and often called giants. See **Deut. 2:10, 11**.

In the context of **Genesis 6**, these giants were men without conscious, without morals, without a care for human life itself. Whatever their greed and hardness of heart would let them, they did it. They were those who would try and see the best in people, and those men took great advantage of them.

They became an unsuspecting prey. Do you know how these wicked people worked? The same way these men operate today. It is always against the weak and the old and the unsuspecting.

In following the context's flow, it makes sense to say that because of this union with the ungodly in marriage, they had the reputation of being very violent, immoral, and having no God-consciousness. I think it is regrettable that the word giants have misled many into believing these were angels in the form of physical giants instead of great moral wickedness giants. See *verses 5-7.*

The sad fact is that as a result of these people's wickedness, God then pronounces judgment. "And GOD saw that the wickedness of man was great in the earth and that every imagination of the thoughts of his heart was only evil continually."

What a profound statement this is, "God saw." You understand that there is nothing God does not see. Try to hide and get the same result as when Adam and Eve tried to hide in the Garden. God knew then, and He knows now. The wickedness that is going on today will one day be brought before the Judge of all judges. Judgment is coming. It was coming then and will come one day for us.

But in Noah's day, by God's mercy and grace, He gave them 120 years. I can say many like me are amazed at God's graciousness of God today in allowing sin to run its course, allowing humanity the time to repent.

Next are some powerful words for us today. And they would not!!! Just as today, He saw the evil of men's hearts and declared it would get no better. *Eph. 4:19* says, "Who being past feeling have given themselves over unto lasciviousness, to work all uncleanness with greediness."

We know the Word of God is powerful. Can you imagine what they preached in their day?

Please read the following words very carefully found in *Luke 17:26, 27.* Then you must read the words of *2 Pet. 3:3-7* to understand God does not play around with sin. Judgment is coming.

We know God is not slack concerning His promises. He says He will do it. Mark it down.

As I have said, "God saw," *verse 5.*

Then we read *verse 6*, and it says, "And it repented the LORD that he had made man on the earth, and it grieved him at his heart." I am sure most of us know what a broken heart is.

Imagine how broken-hearted God was at humanity. Everything man needed to glorify Him and to have fellowship with him had been given him.

They had grown so hardhearted and calloused along the way of life they refused what they could have had.

It saddens our heart to see the world the way it is today.

We see those words of **Romans 1** reveal the truth right before our very eyes. No wonder God's heart grieves. There is much reasoning for Him to be angry with humanity.

Indeed His patience is about to run out just as in the days of Noah. Remember what the Psalmist said in **Psalm 7:11**," God judgeth the righteous, and God is angry with the wicked every day."

What a powerful statement, and it should break your heart.

Now we come to the story of Noah and the Ark. We come to the point of perhaps one of the oldest and most well-known stories in the world. From our studies, many people and cultures have an account similar to the flood found in the Bible. Therefore, we understand it covered the earth. Growing up often, we heard stories that could not be verified. We called stories like this "whoppers."

Honestly, this is an astonishing and unbelievable story. In our day and time, we tend to focus on the sweet, furry animals coming two-by-two onto Noah's Ark. We like to talk about animals and the rainbow. But we forget that every living human being, except for eight souls, died due to the flood.

When I say God saw, He did not see it as an unconcerned spectator, but as one injured and insulted. Like a loving father, one would look at a disobedient child, one not listening. My response to my children has been to punish them. Still, some will not listen. I have heard others say they wished their child had never been born. That is extreme, but it helps to understand how must feel at times. The Lord repented he had made a creature that was supposed to love Him and fellowship with Him. The Lord's heart broke because He had put a man on earth. Here he had given him everything, made him a comfortable place to live, and furnished him a beautiful home. No wonder His heart grieved. Grieved Him that man had turned against Him and forsaken Him. Forsaking Him, to the point, they did not want anything to do with Him.

And you wonder at the expression it "repented" the Lord? Can you blame Him?

Here was a world that hated Him after He made them and gave them a place to enjoy. Yet man rebelled against God, and no wonder it grieved Him.

Yet we understand He is not as we are as humans. Emotions or passions do not move him.

However, there is nothing that can cause God to be "disturbed," so to speak. He is the eternal, immutable God, and He hath no pleasure in the wickedness of man. The reasons are before us as we look. He is a just and Holy God and cannot and will not look upon sin. And being a just God demands that which is wicked and sinful be judged by Him. However, God knew what man would do when He created them. He knew what would take place.

Instilled in man's heart is the opportunity to fellowship and love a Holy God and he would not. We do not see God changing His mind, for He is immutable; therefore, He has one mind.

The Bible says there is no variableness.

On the other hand, what we see expressed is the change of His way of dealing with a man. Throughout the Scriptures, we see the hand of God used in many different ways.

Yes, God was pleased with what He had completed, but now man has turned his back on the God who created him, and God could not allow it to continue the way it was going.

Just as it is today, it is man's heart that has changed, not God. God repented that he had made man. But we never find God regretting that he redeemed man, though that was a work of much more significant expense because something extraordinary had to happen to bring that about.

It was the price of His Son, His only begotten Son, dying in my place to bring about that redemption. As a man, we let Him down, but His Son would not, even in death, **Rom. 11:29**.

Gen. 6:7 tells us when God repented that he had made man, he resolved to destroy man.

Did not men have the opportunity to repent of their sins?

It is one thing to say we are sorry for our sins, and that it grieves us to the heart, but what good is it if we continue in that sin to do it?

We do nothing but mock a Holy God. We have watched people pretend to change their minds, but there was no evidence a change had taken place. Neither did they change their minds. So He resolves to destroy man.

Listen to these words of old and understand God just will not put up with sin. Please read these words found in **2 Kings 21:13** and **Isaiah 27: 11**. God said, "Enough is enough."

They will not listen nor repent. **Genesis 6:7** tells us, "He was grieved in His heart."

God looked down upon the earth, and He saw the wickedness of man, the evil, the sin, whatever word you want to call it, and it broke His heart. It broke His heart because He is Holy, and He is pure.

To best understand what it means there in **Genesis 6:6**, when it says that God was "grieved in His heart," you need to look further, and you will find the same word used in Hebrew.

The story in **2 Samuel**, referring to King David's Son, Absalom, led a revolt against his father, David. Absalom succeeded in taking over the kingship, but in **2 Samuel 18**, Absalom died in the battle. There is a heart-breaking scene at the end of the chapter when King David learns of his Son's death. **2 Sam. 18:33** tells us, "And the king was much moved, and went up to the chamber over the gate, and wept: and as he went, thus he said, 0 my son Absalom, my Son, my Son Absalom! Would God I had died for thee, 0 Absalom, my Son, my Son!"

Not only was David moved to grief, but so were the people of Israel. See **2 Sam. 19:2**.

The Hebrew word translated "grieved" in **2 Samuel 19:2** is the same Hebrew word used in **Genesis 6:6** to describe the anguish of God's heart at the wickedness of Noah's day.

The same Hebrew word for "grieved" in **Genesis 6:6** describe how King David felt when he heard his Son, Absalom, was killed in his war revolting against David.

The Hebrew word for "grieved" in **Genesis 6: 6** describe how a loving father feels when Son dies before they have a chance to reconcile.

One of the truths that God tried to teach humanity in the Bible is that He is Holy.

Through the Old Testament, you can see how many people responded when they came face to face with a Holy God.

Do you remember when Moses ascended Mount Sinai to receive the law from God?

Do you remember what the Bible had to say about Moses' appearance when he came down after receiving the Commandments? The Bible said that his face shone. Scriptures tell us his face glowed and seemed on fire. That is what happens when you come in the presence of a Holy, Righteous God. Later, Job came face to face with that same Holy God. At one point in Job's life, after experiencing all the suffering and injustice in his life, he lost his family, his children, his wealth, his health Job was sitting there with boils on his body looking up to heaven. At that point, Job's friends were counseling him to curse God and die, but Job continued to ask, "Why, why, why, why?"

Finally, the Holy God of heaven came to answer Job's questions. See **Job 40**. Do you know what Job had to say when God showed up in **Chapter 40?** Note what he said in **Job 40:4**, "Behold, I am vile; what shall I answer thee? I will lay mine hand upon my mouth." Then in **Job 42:5-6**, "we have these words by Job, "I have heard of thee by the hearing of the ear: but now mine eye seeth thee. Wherefore I abhor myself, and repent in dust and ashes".

That was Job's response when confronted with the holiness of God.

Isaiah was another person from the Old Testament who saw God. In *Isaiah 6:5*, the prophet Isaiah witnessed God sitting on His throne high and lifted up. Isaiah heard the heavenly beings' chants saying, "Holy, holy, holy is the Lord of Hosts."

Do you recall Isaiah's response when he saw God? Make time to read the first verses of *Isaiah 6* to understand the reaction of Isaiah as he sees the throne of God. We should be awed in the same way he was. Otherwise, we are out of the will of God.

There is the only possible response when a person comes face to face with the Holy God.

One day soon, many of us will walk through a portal from this world into the next.

There is soon coming a day when we will walk into the light of God's holy day.

What a day that will be, when we hear the angels singing, "Holy, holy, holy is the Lord of Hosts." See *Isaiah 6:3*.

When that day comes, the brightness of the reality of God's holiness will shine, blinding us.

When that day comes, the Bible says that every knee shall bow, and every tongue shall confess.

Do you know why? We know because God is more holy than we can stand. You see, the question is not: "How could a loving God destroy the world?" The question is not: "How could a loving God send a person to Hell?" Those are the wrong questions.

The right question is: "How can a Holy God forgive us?" The right question is: "How can a Holy, Perfect, Pure God stand us in His heaven?" Those are some of the questions we should be asking because on the day we meet God face to face, God's holiness will demand nothing but justice.

But aren't you glad that as we read God's Word, it does not stop there? In all of God's grieving and repenting, we find God has a plan. My, what a God! Somewhere along the way, God had instilled in man that thing called faith. There was a man whom God had been dealing with in that wicked world. His name was Noah. We find the words, "Noah found grace in the eyes of the Lord," in *Genesis 6:8*. We see something unusual beginning to happen behind the scene in the world. Noah was doing what God told him.

As children of His, we are to live by faith. He had faith in the unseen God. Where did he get his faith? *Romans 12: 3* tells us, "For I say, through the grace given unto me, to every man that is among you, not to think of himself more highly than he ought to think; but to think soberly, according as God hath dealt every man the measure of faith."

You understand this is God-given.

We cannot believe unless God is willing to give us the faith to believe. If you do not believe God is so holy, pure, and perfect, knowing your sin breaks His heart, your sins will find you out. If your God is not that holy, then your God does not have enough love to send His Son to die.

Do you hear what I am saying? A paternalistic, condescending view of God's holiness cheapens His grace and the sacrifice of His Son. But oh, how we love to worry. We worry about the African tribesman who never hears the story of Jesus. We worry about the South American Indians living along the Amazon River, who the missionaries never reach. We worry about the Asian and the millions in the heart of China. Are they going to Hell?

I can only answer that question honestly. I do not know.

Do you know what will determine this? It is the knowledge they have in God. You say I have read the entire Bible, but I cannot find Africa. There is no mention of South America.

China is not in there. But the Bible tells about a God who is so holy that He hurts and grieves in His heart. And the Bible speaks about a God who so loves that He would rather kill a part of Himself than send any one of us to Hell. Now, I believe in a God like that.

And because I believe in a God like that, I think that God will do what is right with the African and the South American and the Asian. We are not from any of these places, including Africa, and that is the whole matter. We do not live in South America. Will we never go to China? We do not have any excuses. We know the truth. We have heard the story. And we choose. Our faith determines the outcome. In *John 3:17-18*, these verses teach us that Jesus did not come to judge the first time. That is not why He came. He did not come to judge us.

Instead, when God's holiness demands judgment, and when God's love delivers undeserving grace, your faith determines the outcome. What determination have you made?

Do you know what you believe concerning the God of Noah and the Ark?

Have you ever placed your faith in Jesus Christ to save you from judgment?

Your faith will determine the outcome. Noah saw the un-seeable. That is, he saw things not yet seen. He believed in God, but he also understood the Word of God. He knew God would hold man accountable for his sins, but he also understood that God was a merciful God.

That is how he came to believe. See *1 Cor. 15:1-4*.

We understand that real faith does not have to see to believe. Remember that is what Jesus told Mary at the tomb of Lazarus in *John 11:40* "Jesus saith unto her, Said I not unto thee, that, if thou wouldest believe, thou shouldest see the glory of God?"

Noah believed in "things not yet seen" for 120 years before the flood came. The flood came, and God fulfilled prophecy. From this, we can say Noah did not look at obvious things, but by faith, he looked invisible because they are eternal. There is only one way to come through the flood's judgment, and by faith, Noah and his family went through the flood's judgment and saw glory.

Note this is our definition of being moved with Godly fear. *Hebrews 12:28* says, "Wherefore we receiving a kingdom which cannot be moved, let us have grace, whereby we may serve God acceptably with reverence and godly fear." Noah's faith caused him to act with godly fear, leading him to repentance, thereby resulting in salvation through God's grace.

We see as important here that he believed God's promise of grace, but he also believed in God's promise of judgment. Noah, like all lost sinners today, has a choice; he could accept God's gift of eternal life or decide to live in his sin and, in the end, allow God to collect the wages of eternal separation from God's mercy. See **Romans 6:23**.

Noah's faith moved him in holy fear, making him obey God by building the Ark. Noah believed that God would judge man, as He promised, saying, "1 will destroy man which I have created from the face of the earth," **Gen. 6:7**.

How do we know Noah believed God? The proof is that he "prepared an ark. "Wouldn't you have said what others in Noah's day said he was a fool for building that thing out of gopher wood? It is no wonder what he must have had to put endure. Noah's work of faith was the principle, the driving force that led him to build the Ark.

We have the experience in our own life that a Faith that does not motivate works is dead and of no use, **James 2:17**. So Noah had been working for 120 years building the Ark.

However, we know that he did much more than that. The Bible, as we have shown, says Noah was a preacher. He preached on God's righteousness and what man should do, but he preached on God's coming judgment.

As in our time today, I believe the judgment of God is imminent. I also think Noah preached the same message we should be preaching today.

In Noah's day, he preached judgment was imminent, and we should be preaching that Christ is coming back, and that will usher in God's judgment on this world again. Of course, we know judgment was in the form of the flood. Today we can see, as I said, Christ, coming in power and glory.

Turning to the events and thoughts on the flood, we can say the world back then knew very little about God and what Noah was doing, but today that is a different story. Have you met someone who did not know about a flood of some type? You have seen jokes about it, pictures of it, movies about the search for the Ark, and even ceramic representations.

The flood is almost universally known, not including the Biblical account in the book of Genesis. This familiarity sometimes makes a significant obstacle to our benefit from a study of the flood. Most of us have the attitude there is nothing new, so what could they learn in doing a detailed analysis of the flood?

There is nothing here that would change a person's thinking or especially his behavior, right?

Some today will tell you they believe God sent a flood, but that is about as far as they are willing to take it.

Would that same God judge us today? Judgment is unquestionably a topic in this event, but thank God; there is a much higher point: God's saving grace. While we dare not ignore this text's lessons, let us not lose sight of its support.

There have been many books on the sin and destruction of the flood. There have been others who have focused their attention on the mechanics of the deluge. Then some try and seek its meaning.

These next few chapters describe God's destroying of the earth through a worldwide flood.

No doubt, the world is filled with those who doubt the fact of a universal flood. Some of these heretics just plain write the Bible's account of the flood off as a myth or make it a colorful story with some morals and life lessons to teach us. Others say there is some truth to the Bible's account, but the flood was only a local and not a worldwide event. Then there's a whole group of unbelievers; those who are actively striving to destroy the faith of those who believe the Bible's account of the flood.

Some come up with all kinds of "scientific reasoning" to prove the biblical account as untrue.

When it comes to God destroying the world through a worldwide flood, a good question is this: Do we have enough evidence to prove what the Bible says? The overwhelming answer is YES!

I want us to look at some of the geological features involved in a flood worldwide. Scientists and geologists have proven evidence of a worldwide flood. They have searched from the mountaintops to the depths of the oceans.

Traveling throughout the world, you can see the earth's terrain affected by a catastrophic event in our past. For example, you can see coal beds, various canyons, ocean trenches, salt domes, oil deposits, etc.

We ask the question, what is sedimentary rock? As its name implies, water is intimately involved in the formation of sedimentary rock. We know the earth's crust consists of approximately 75% of sedimentary rock. You can find this kind of rock and the many millions of marine fossils embedded in them worldwide. These fossils show a rapid and violent burial, for you will find fossilized jellyfish buried before they could decay.

From many different species, hundreds of animals have been found jumbled together in many different positions. Some of these fossils have other fish hanging out of their mouths.

In other words, this was an instantaneous act, for they were eating them. Some of the creatures were standing, some lying down on the rocks.

So what does this mean you would say?

The indication from all sources is there was a rapid death both to animal and plant life. Just like what would happen in a worldwide flood! Think of the Grand Canyon and many other canyons around the world. Just about every canyon has a river flowing through them, cutting deep into the ground. The only plausible explanation for these things is not by a little river flowing through them, but by some catastrophic water erosion.

Also, we should never rule out over 230 flood stories, gathered from all over the world.

We agree, they are not identical to the biblical account, but we cannot rule out what they say.

Of these accounts from around the world, you will find that they all agree on four major points. A great flood covered the entire earth. All people except a remnant died. Everything else disappeared from the face of the planet. God helped Noah to build a ship that was able to carry some people and animals to safety. This craft landed on a mountain.

For 230 different cultures to be all are talking about and remembering the same event, that should be enough reason to accept a worldwide flood that destroyed the world. We could spend a lot of time dealing with questions regarding the flood that are not addressed in the Bible's account, but maybe later.

First, I think we should talk about Noah's godly character; according to *verse 9*, he was a man who walked with God. Noah is set forth as a prime example of a holy man. Our text tells us that he was a man who walked with God; this illustrates that he was a righteous and blameless man. Outside of Christ, there has never been a man who did not struggle with sin. Neither was Noah perfect. Yet, Noah stood as an outstanding example of the manner of person we should be.

In our text, much is said about Noah and his righteousness. In God's eyes, he was a man righteous, blameless, and walked with God. What a description of a person's character!

It indicates that their heart is right and that their actions are right before the Lord. It suggests a relationship with God and peace with Him. It also implies an active seeking of God and a desire to be close to Him because they love Him.

Sometimes you will hear the question: how is your walk with God? What are they asking?

For one, it's a question that requires examination and reflection, are you walking with Him or not?

We would ask this: are you staying faithful to Him, are you obeying Him in all things, are you pursuing your relationship with Him? The joy of your salvation, are you experiencing it?

Those would be excellent questions to ask ourselves.

I want you to think about the obedience of Noah to the commands of God. You can see those in the following *verses, 6:22; 7:5, 9, 16*, found in Genesis.

If a person is going to be known for something, then known as one who obeyed the Lord has to rank real high with God. Noah is not known for paying "lip service" to God; they know him as a doer of God's will, obedient to God.

God's instruction to Noah was to build the Ark. Nowhere do we find him questioning God and His ways. He is willing and obedient to all that the Lord told him to do. Noah is so highly spoken of in our text because he is called righteous and blameless.

In the N.T. Jesus says, "Why do you call me Lord, Lord, and not do as I say?" Admittedly, this is an excellent question.

Noah was no hypocrite, his talk and his walk matched up. He claimed a relationship with God, and he showed it with his behavior with God. See *1 John 2:3* and *I John 5:3*.

When we think of ourselves, it's not too often that we honestly do not know the right thing to do.

The problem is that we just want to do what we want to do. But we need to be doers of God's word. God's commands are not burdensome. Evidence of our being the children of God is that we have hearts that say, "Yes Lord, I will do your will, because I love you, appreciate your love, and want to please you."

In this, we see the blessings that come when we do the will of God. It did for Noah and can will for us. See *Genesis 6:8*.

Genesis 6:9 details what God did for Noah: a man who found favor with Him? Just think about this for a moment. God makes Noah privy to his plans to destroy the earth. What that means is that Noah had a personal encounter with God.

God, in turn, conscripts Noah. He gets to have the privilege of building the vehicle of their physical salvation, which is typological of the coming of Christ and his making for spiritual salvation.

Not only did God save Noah, but he kept safe his whole family. The Bible never speaks of his family being followers of God, only Noah, yet they get blessed because of Noah. The same principle works today. Other people around us get run off the benefits of God blessing us.

His blessings affect our culture and society, our communities, our families.

That we would say is a real blessing, not just some material thing that excites us for a few minutes.

As God continued to work in the life of Noah, He makes a covenant with him. It is through this covenant we are blessed today, for we are Noah's descendants. The principle is before us.

Simply if we will honor Him, He will grant us favor and blessing. Therefore if we do, He will bless and reward each of us accordingly. In blessing Noah and his family in the same context, we see that the flood, which is a judgment of the world, comes just like what people think Hell is today.

It is incredible the detail God allows Moses to use here to describe the events preceding the flood and the events to follow. It is hard to make this into a fairy tale. You have specific details regarding the Ark's dimensions and how it's construction. You have details regarding the number of animals to take. You have details such as Noah's age when the flood came.

Then you have details such as seven days from now I will send rain on the earth for 40 days and 40 nights God says. You have details regarding the time they were to spend in the Ark.

Again you have specific details regarding what happened in the flood.

From reading and studying the description of the details here is can only be said that that was an actual worldwide event.

Many folks try to write off the flood as some sort of mythical event, but the details are given punch a hole in any "mythological story" theory. And when you begin to study, many of the scientific questions which would arise have been answered. Of course, there are many questions that we could stop and answer here.

As we have said, God said they were all to be fruitful and multiply at the beginning of creation. What happened and very interesting. Instead of being fruitful and multiplying, Noah's day's people were destroying the world themselves, so what does God say He will do? He would only do what humanity was doing themselves, destroy the world, except He would do it by a Flood.

The reason here is plain to see. It was because of humanity's wickedness. Instead of becoming Godly, the people in the world became more ungodly. Sin and rebellion is not something that God overlooks. God does not destroy and judge people for no reason. God destroys and judges those who deserve it. The flood is all about justice.

People are not good; we are all sinners, evil to our hearts' core standing before a Holy God. Because of people's evil, judgment, and death comes.

It's because of our sin that we need a Savior; that Savior is Jesus Christ.

The worldwide flood of **Genesis 6-8** points to the coming and final day of destruction, and so too does the destruction of Sodom and Gomorrah.

You will see certain distinctive parallels between Noah and Lot and the destruction that ensued with the flood if you study. One thing the Bible is evident is that a day of judgment is coming. There is coming a day when God will again destroy this world and sinful humanity. See **II Peter 3**.

Many scoffers exist, scoffers who deliberately ignore the evidence of the world's destruction by the flood. Those in the Ark were physically saved, covered, and protected from God's judgment, so are those in Christ. They are spiritually saved and protected from the coming judgment day of God.

I'm sure you'll find this interesting regarding an ark: In the Bible, there is another person whose life was saved by riding in an ark. His name was Moses. See **Exodus 2:3, 5**.

The same word for ark is the same word to signify the basket of bulrushes in which baby Moses rode the Nile River.

Before destroying the world by the Flood, God delivered Noah. Before the destruction of Jericho, God had Rahab delivered. Before destroying Sodom and Gomorrah, God delivered Lot. Before God destroys the earth on judgment day, God will take us who are his saint's home to himself. The wrath of God and judgment day is not something we as Christians need fear. Instead, think about Peter's words, which you must read in **I Peter 3:20-21**.

I would like to mention a message I once preached on the man Noah.

I took my text from *Genesis 6:7, 8*, and in *Hebrews 11:7*. The book of Genesis, especially in these verses, we have a bleak picture of a man. You would think men would learn, but after 6000 years of training, we see that man has failed God miserably, as we saw in *Genesis 6: 7*.

When men fail, he will either turn to God or turn entirely from Him. For the whole of humanity, God also chose to act in mercy, but judgment.

God chose in His Grace to gather a remnant, and that is what we find in *Genesis 6:8*.

In *Genesis 6:13*, we find God said He was going to destroy all living things. Here is the Divine Verdict of God on humankind. The interesting thing here, God explicitly mentions the "flesh." We all should know in the flesh; we cannot please God. See *Romans 8:8* with *John 3:18*. But in His Divine Verdict against humanity, we find that God also has a Divine Plan, *Genesis 6:17*.

In the many years of our preaching, not many will listen to the calling of God. You can see it is not a matter of whether it is service or salvation. Take a look at *1 Cor. 2:10, 11*.

The Divine Plan of God is pure. God will not tolerate sin, and He has made provision for those who will not accept His gift of grace. That is a place called Hell for those that are deniers of God. Then there is the Divine Warning of God. Notice *Gen. 6: 17*. There is no place to hide from God. But in the process of His warning to humanity, we find God giving men a Divine Invitation. See *Genesis 7:1* and *Matt. 22:1-14*.

In the thought here, we see God providing Divine Security. See the following verses, *Genesis 7:16, John 10:9*, and *1 Pet. 1:5*.

God was divinely careful in all that He did. Note that He remembered Noah and His family.

We can say the same for today if we believe by faith, then God will be careful in taking care of us for all of eternity. Course we know by now it was faith that led Noah to the Ark.

It is faith that will lead us to Christ.

In the trials of his life, God told Noah of the immediate consequences of sin.

These were words spoken by God to him. Don't you see he believes every word that God said to him? Never once do we read that Noah doubted God. His faith was just like ours. It is based on things not yet seen. The skies were clear. The heavens were silent. It had never rained. See **Genesis 2:6**.

The Bible makes it very clear he moved by his godly fear. The one in charge of our faith brings with that faith a deep conviction. Convictions that will make him do something.

So he built the Ark. How many laughed at him, we do not know. But it did not matter. He proved his faith by actually making the Ark. Moving faith is the only kind of faith in God He commends. That kind of faith will force you to do something.

In the process of doing something for God, we see it condemns the world. God told him to come into the Ark. He could have refused to enter in, but he believed God. When he went in we find God shut the door. After God shut the door, the rains came but not until they were all safe in the Ark.

Through his believing God, he became the heir of righteousness for all people. Faith brought his family into the Ark, and this is what brought their salvation. So it was after the Flood God gave Noah a divine commission. He told him to get out of the Ark so that he could live for Him. We have to be taken out of the world to return into the world as His servants.

Before we go on, I would like to present some parallels Between Noah's Day and the Second Coming of Christ's Day. To see this, you must read what Jesus said in **Matthew 24:37-39**. He is speaking of Noah in this passage and the way things were in his day. If you remember in our Genesis text, we saw the way they lived. What that means is they were in wicked and would not believe. Noah preached, and that same truth will be taught in the last days, but their unbelief will cause them to "know not."

Many today scream peace at the top of their lungs, but you can rest assured that judgment is coming and that Jesus is soon coming. We note the conditions of the world compared to the conditions of our time.

Then the earth was "corrupt" and filled with "violence." That sounds like today's headlines.

Whenever God's judgment comes, I have seen that God always has his man on the scene to ensure that those condemned do not have an excuse.

Interestingly the flood was intended to destroy humanity; yet, God designed the Ark to save. Remember **Genesis 3:15**? It says, "And I will put enmity between thee and the woman, and between thy seed and her seed; it shall bruise thy head, and thou shalt bruise his heel." Remember that?

The key to recognizing the flood event is to grasp the contrast between Noah and his generation. Noah was a just man; he was perfect in his time. That is, he was with God. See **Genesis 6:9**. What an epitaph!

Moses summed up the righteousness of Noah by writing, "Noah walked with God."

What does this mean? Here is highlighted the fellowship between Noah and God, the intimacy of their union. Here also is exhibited the unity of this relationship. It was an everyday walk; it was a reliable one, in the sense God could count on him. This relationship between Noah and God was based on God's information about the creation of man and his fall.

There is no doubt that all of his forefathers had taught him these things. Also, this would include the promise of redemption. Remember the verse we quoted just above?

As you know, many times, God just simply does not tell us everything that happened. Then there are some things we will never understand. This righteousness Noah had come from him believing God; we call that faith. Listen again to **Hebrews 11:7**, which says, "By faith Noah, being warned of God of things not seen as yet, moved with fear, prepared an ark to the saving of his house; by the which he condemned the world, and became heir of the righteousness which is by faith."

It was not the work of Noah, which preserved him from judgment, but God's grace.

Again listen to **Genesis 6:8**, which says, "But Noah found grace in the eyes of the LORD."

Salvation has always been by grace, through faith, not of works, but unto good works.

Isn't that what Paul said in **Eph. 2:8-10** "For by grace are ye saved through faith; and that not of yourselves: it is the gift of God: Not of works, lest any man should boast. For we are his workmanship, created in Christ Jesus unto good works, which God hath before ordained that we should walk in them."

In contrast to Noah's righteousness, you can see man's rottenness. Listen to these words in our text, **Genesis 6:11, 12** "The earth also was corrupt before God, and the earth was filled with violence. And God looked upon the earth, and, behold, it was corrupt; for all flesh had corrupted his way upon the earth."

We may have to walk in the world, but we can do this without walking with the world.

We have said many times as Christians; we may be in it, but not of it. Note that we may be in the world, and yet we are to walk with God. For you see, walking with God reveals something. It indicates there is a holy companionship going on. There is a common purpose fulfilled here. We can see God let Noah into the innermost secrets of His plan. I know you have noticed that God will reveal many things to us through His Word. When we are listening, that is when God reveals His will to us. Think about **Revelation 1:1-3**.

Noah was a man who wrought God's works, as seen in **verse 14** of **Genesis 6**.

God, in His grace, has chosen redeemed men to work for Him, and with Him.

Also, this is possible when we become willing to forsake our own will for following His will.

What happened to Noah? We can see the far-reaching effect of Noah's ministry. His family got saved. Through him, God was able to preserve the human race.

As I preached this message, I remembered the Ark and its significance, as seen in our text.

We have an authentic record of how God protected and preserved the human race. There are many traditions and stories of an Ark and the flood in the world. The Ark is a historical fact, but this also shows how history distorts when not grounded in God's Word.

Only those in the Ark would survive. That is why we preach that the Ark typifies Christ.

As they were safe in the Ark, so are we safe in Christ. Once they were in the Ark, true salvation was they could not get out until God let them out, and for those in Christ, they will never get out. That is why we say the Ark typifies security. When Noah entered, God shut the door, and no one could leave or enter.

Just as a thought, think with me that the light that Noah had come from above. The light we get today, the pure light comes from above. When we need light, we look to Christ. Think of this as well; *verse 14* tells us the Ark was pitched within and without. Pitch is a form of oil.

Oil is a type of the Holy Spirit. The pitch sealed the Ark. The Holy Spirit seals the believer until the day of redemption. See *Eph. 6:30*. "Pitch" also is in Hebrew, the word for atonement. Christ is our atonement for salvation. He is the only way to that atonement.

When you think about it, there was only one door to the Ark.

That door was typical of Christ, who is the door, the way to God. See *John 10:9* and *John 14:7*. Have you thought about what you were like before you accepted Christ?

Each person's background is different. Most of the time, you were more interested in self, not even realizing they were displeasing to the Lord. The sin nature responds in this fashion. The one thing we cannot change from the day we were born is we all have the sin nature. See *Romans 3:23*.

It is this seed, the sinful nature which stands between God and us. How good can you be?

Not good enough in God's eyes, for no matter what we do, say or think, our fundamental need is Christ and His work on Calvary.

Before the so-called age of accountability, when we learn of sin and understand its ramifications, we know what it means to be covered by God's grace.

After that, when we are aware of our sinful nature, we must get right with God through accepting the salvation of Jesus Christ.

God just will not allow sin to go unchecked. It does not matter who it is that is sinning. Most sins are like habits involving things we cherish and love, just as if they were our child. Not many are willing to give them up, not ready to change. Instead, we would rather explore more of some of our sins instead of turning from them. Satan wants this also.

Left unchecked, this is what happens: For example, one lie leads to another, maybe a bigger one, one reckless night on the town leads to another. Sometimes one errant relationship can lead to another. Just one time of breaking a traffic law may lead to the disregard of others.

Sometimes all it takes is for you to swear one time, take the Lord's name in vain, or allow something to go wrong, and before you know it, you do not even think about what you are doing.

The power of sin brings us to realize that just one bit of greed or lust leads to graver sins.

As soon as pride or jealousy enters our hearts, we instantly become haters of God and try to be like Him.

It then grows to active dislike or hatred. Relationships break down; friends pass away, and so it goes. Every sin tends to grow and become more prominent. We understand sin, left unchecked, will consume everything around it. Our sinful desires are never satisfied; they always want more sin.

Remember, not all sin may bring pleasure, but different sins may bring happiness to other people. We can say if sin weren't fun, there is a real possibility we could be living in a holy world today. If it weren't fun, to begin with, we would have stopped sinning a long time ago. See **Hebrews 11:25.**

Have you noticed we sometimes fall into sin for a season? Something happens, and our sin comes to light, but we don't care what others think until that happens. Evil can continue our entire lives; even life shortens because of some of our sins' consequences.

Many times the consequences of what we have done are far worse than others finding out our sins.

Although a graphic example, remember the pleasures of smoking when you were in your teens and pulling one over your parents? Looking cool with your friends will be nothing compared to the pain you will have later in life if you continue smoking. You will find it difficult to walk upstairs or down a driveway.

Did you know God has promised every man one opportunity to hear the salvation message?

As a sinner, you will be judged according to your knowledge of right and wrong. If you have heard the Gospel of Christ's shed blood on the Cross as the only sacrifice acceptable to God for sin, which was your opportunity. If you deny and refuse to accept Christ, you will die an eternal death rather than have eternal life with God.

You will need to act on the words and make a decision to follow Christ.

It was like God looking at the world in Noah's time; you look into your own heart, acknowledging your heart's wickedness is consuming you.

God doesn't check to see what percent sin you are at and then say, "we're having a special today," anyone with less than 30% on the sin meter gets in free. Sin is sin, pure and simple.

God will deal with sin. Following our initial conversion, you must come to repentance.

Thankfully, the sin inheritance from Adam is taken care of by Christ's sacrifice.

Simply stated, as we accept Christ's sacrifice for the remission of our sins, God has promised to remember them no more.

Know this; Satan will do all he can to keep our interest in sinful habits affecting us.

However, the more we listen to and follow God's will, Satan will have less influence.

In our text, we found God said I would destroy everything that He had created evil because it repenteth Him He made them.

Nearly all references to repenting by God have to do with humankind in some way.

Many scholars disagree as to what God meant here.

Suffice it to say He was saying He would repent if they were willing to repent or if they did not, He was going to keep His Word.

The word "repentance" is used the same as the way we would. Once we repent of our sins, what do you do? Are they gone forever in your heart, or do you allow them to fester and rot, so they grow again? What happens if we leave them in the depths of our hearts?

How will you answer this question? The key to that answer is, are we willing to search for help and guidance. We should ask God to explore the dark corners of our hearts and see some sin. Whatever you are leaning on to keep that sin in your hearts must be eliminated. See ***Romans 6:6*** and ***Ephesians 4:22***.

There were only seven clean and one pair of unclean animals with seven pairs of birds kept on the Ark if you remember. Along with the wicked people in the deluge, we find all animals and birds died. Seek God's face, and ask Him what things you should get rid of in your life.

There are sins laid out for us in the Bible we know are wrong, and then other things we may not understand and have to seek Him to know what He means. Note ***1 Corinthians 6:12***.

Some sins and habits are hard to give up and break in our lives, and God knows this, for He knows how weak the flesh is.

Having done His part, God now expects us to do our part. We must deal with the former life of sin. That is why God gave us the Holy Spirit to deal with our hearts in this matter.

He has given each of us certain character qualities and talents to help us in our daily living. We must be clean for Him to use our skills for His glory.

We could say God likes to clean up our lives, making us vessels for Him.

Somewhere deep down in our hearts, God had implanted a talent that can He can use.

Then there are talents and gifts He has bestowed on us that He cannot use and must be eradicated.

You will find this to be confirmed later on in **Genesis 8:20-22**.

Sacrifices unto God are a need if we want to be willing to be God's servant. That is why Noah is such a prime example. Noah understood this. I am sure this is why as soon as he left the Ark, the first thing he did was build an altar of sacrifice unto the Lord. His heart humbled; he wanted to start right before God. Sacrifices were to be used in coming before a holy God.

When God smelled those sacrifices, He made the promise not to curse the ground again.

God keeps the promises He makes.

For you and me, the only way to move God's heart is to be obedient to Him and love Him. Our purpose in creation is simple to talk with God and fellowship with Him. Oh, how we need to get back to that.

If you are like me, the salvation experience was as secure as when God shut the Ark's door. It started to rain, and after a short time, everything outside the Ark was dead. But, everything inside the Ark was kept safe. Think of the ease it would be if Satan, the world, and flesh disappeared when we got saved. There would be no giants to occupy our hearts and bother us day by day. Imagine, safe from them every day, serving God with no conflicts.

But alas, that is not the way God operates in our lives.

We have to fight the good fight, sometimes hand to hand with the devil and his cohorts.

As Paul wrote to Timothy in **First Timothy**, we have to fight against principalities and powers, things seen and things unseen. Faith believes this. Remember, however, we are not in this fight alone. We must lean on the power of God.

We are weak at best and no match against the devil. Try as we may, like the giants of old who lived during the flood, and they died, so we will if we are not willing to accept the requirements for the justification of our sins. We should understand by now we have an evil heart that needs fixing.

As the Scriptures tell us, we must seek out our salvation, watching and praying, persevering till Jesus comes to take us home. We must not allow the wiles of the devil to defeat us for the cause of Christ. At the end of things, we can say God was looking for a pure bloodline His Son could make his entrance.

Is there purity anywhere? How can we work for Him while in sin? Read **2 Timothy 2:22** and **Matthew 5:8**.

Chapter 7

As we come to *Chapter 7*, we see the Ark, and its supplies are finished and stored on the Ark, and now God calls for the living cargo to go into the Ark, see *verse 1*. The 120 years of God's grace has come to an end.

It was during those years that Noah preached the righteousness of God. There is no mention now of Methuselah, the oldest man who ever lived. When he was born, his name indicates judgment would come at his death for the earth. We know now is the time for Noah and his family to enter the Ark and the animals. It is so sad the rest of the world would not take advantage of entering into the Ark by faith. If only they had repented.

Given the opportunity, we wonder why people will not listen. We see the fulfillment of why people will not listen found in *Matt. 24:38, 39*. What right did Noah have over everyone else to enter into the Ark, we would ask?

Because it was by righteousness and his faith in God he could enter in. He was righteous not because of his works but by his faith. It was what he believed, not what he did, that determined his relationship with God. See *Hebrews 11: 7*, and these verses from *Romans 3:23-25* reveals that faith is the only way a person can become righteous.

One of the most potent verses for us is in *Hebrews 11:7*. Please study this carefully.

Then to understand what God says of sin in the New Testament, please study *Romans 3:23-25* in addition to our text.

When a person believes he will change. If there is no change in that person, this indicates this person did not accept by faith the work of God in Christ. Noah dared to believe God when no one would.

As we read in our text, **verse 4** tells us God gave Noah all the preparations to build and prepare the Ark. Think of this principle. It is pretty straightforward. If He gives you a task, then He will provide your necessities to do the Job if we let Him.

There is another principle at work here. God often hides His own before the storm comes; see examples like **Isaiah 26:20, 21, Revelation 7:4-8,** and **2 Thess. 2:6-9**.

When we read that Enoch was translated before God that he should not see death, does that mean God's child will not go through trials and problems in this life? We are sure we will face many difficulties in life before the end. Many have asked, "How did Noah get the animals in the ark?" See **Genesis 6:20-22** and **Genesis 7:23** for the answer. Simply put, God commanded them to come in.

Think of the Ark, just for a minute or two. Here is a vessel 450 feet in length and 75 feet wide, and 45 feet high. Noah's Ark had three stories, with a skylight on the opening that ran entirely around the Ark's top. That opening was 18" around the top. Therefore Noah could only look out and up while he was in the Ark. He could not look down and see the destruction at God's hand, which was going on. We know that the Ark had the capacity of 1.5 cubic feet of space, times 450. That is equivalent to 522 box cars. Suppose we could put 240 animals about the size of sheep in each boxcar, about 1,000,000 total animals on board the Ark. How then could Noah and his sons care for so many animals? The Bible gives us very little detail here, but we could offer a couple of suggestions.

One is that of Hibernation.

Hibernation is a specific physiological state in which normal functions are suspended or greatly retarded, enabling the animal to endure long inactivity periods.

So there is that possibility.

Then, of course, we could say that somehow God gave Noah and his sons the ability to take care of all the animals and have enough food. If not being in hibernation, we would speculate they were all young animals coming on board the Ark. *Verses 10, 11* give us the details of the source of the flood. That water had to come from somewhere? It says from the deep and the windows of heaven. What does that mean? God tore the doors of the earth open according to *Psalm 33:7*, which says, "He gathereth the waters of the sea together as an heap: he layeth up the depth in storehouses."

We also know, considering the fountains of the deep erupted dramatically. *Genesis 1:2* says, "And the earth was without form, and void; and darkness was upon the face of the deep. And the Spirit of God moved upon the face of the waters." *Genesis 1:6-8* says," And God said, let there be a firmament in the midst of the waters, and let it divide the waters from the waters. And God made the firmament, and divided the waters which were under the firmament from the waters which were above the firmament: and it was so. And God called the firmament heaven. And the evening and the morning were the second day."

So we can see from this that there was a vast body of water under the earth and a great expanse of water above the planet, an extended canopy circling the entire globe.

This canopy is what God used to create the flood.

Also, this is how God divided the waters of the earth. The windows of heaven describe for us the torrential rains that came from the sky. The violent rains descended from the canopy over the planet explain the abundance of water that flooded the earth. The seas raged over the earth's surface, rapidly rising to destroy and bury the old world and all that was in it.

Nevertheless, in the process, the water bore up the Ark's occupants, delivering them from the peril.

God was now taking care of Noah and his family. Noah entering the Ark is symbolic of salvation, which was because of his faith in God. We do not believe he would have entered the Ark if he had not considered trusting God. Once he entered, the first drops of rain began to fall. It was then that the people of the world understood the consequences of their sin.

If only they had been willing to repent of their sins. Before that day, they had refused to believe God. Now it was too late. Imagine the rage, the cries of those standing around the Ark as the rains came, and the flood began?

Now it was too late for the mercy of God. Judgment was at hand. Therefore they were destroyed off the face of the earth. They had had their warnings from God. ***Genesis 6:3*** says, "And the LORD said, my spirit shall not always strive with man, for that he also is flesh: yet his days shall be a hundred and twenty years."

God even told them how long He would wait before judgment came, and they still did not believe Him.

Then he had given them another sign. There was a preacher who preached the righteousness of a Holy God for 120 years. As much as that, he also preached the grace of God that they might repent, but men in the hardness of his heart would not repent and turned his back on the one that could save him, God.

No doubt, Noah grieved because of those who had refused to believe his preaching.

As preachers, we have often preached and seen people walk away, knowing they needed salvation and yet would not because of their hearts' hardness only to die in their sins.

Try as they might; no one could now enter into the Ark for God had shut the door. As we said earlier in ***Chapter 6***, the Ark was covered inside and out with pitch. Listen again to ***Genesis 6:14***, which says, "Make thee an ark of gopher wood; rooms shalt thou make in the ark, and shalt pitch it within and without pitch."

The Hebrew word means "to cover, to make atonement." As we have said, it is symbolic of the blood Jesus shed on the Cross. From Adam on down, they knew it was the blood that God would accept on God's altar. It is the blood that protects us from the condemnation of God. The conviction came upon Noah, but through his belief, God saved him. That is what He will do for us today. ***Romans 8:1 says***, "There is therefore now no condemnation to them which are in Christ Jesus, who walk not after the flesh, but after the Spirit."

Note that the Lord is our Ark today. You know the only way to be saved from the wrath to come is to believe as Noah believed in God. See ***Romans 8:31-39*** for more.

Just as Noah was declared righteous because of his faith, we can claim that promise through Jesus. ***John 5:24*** reports, "Verily, verily, I say unto you, He that heareth my word, and believeth on him that sent me, hath everlasting life, and shall not come into condemnation, but is passed from death unto life."

Noah had no reservations about trusting God before entering the Ark, and we believe he did not doubt God's word after entering the Ark.

Now, turn our thoughts to the arguments for the universal flood and fossils.

The Middle East, where the Ark rested, is a region that does not have an abundant rainfall.

If the flooding were local, such a vast ark probably never would have floated. If it had been a local flood and the Ark had floated, it would have ended up in the sea. It did not float downward but drifted upward away from the sea. The Ark landed on Mount Ararat, surrounded by deserts. The closest ocean is the Indian Ocean with the Arabian Sea as its nearest point. It was 1500 miles away from where the Ark finally rested.

In ***Genesis 6:9***, there are more than 30 indications that the flood was universal and not a local one. The flood's purpose was to destroy man and beast from the earth and the planet. In other words, the world changed along with men as they knew it.

What came out on the other side is different from the one they knew. Listen to what ***Genesis 6:13*** says, "And God said unto Noah, The end of all flesh comes before me; for the earth is filled with violence through them; and, behold, I will destroy them with the earth."

So, when we say it was a universal flood, which means the waters had to be high enough to cover all the world's mountains. Look again at *Genesis 7:19, 20*.

It says, "And the waters prevailed exceedingly upon the earth, and all the high hills that were under the whole heaven were covered. Fifteen cubits upward did the waters prevail, and the mountains were covered."

We take that to mean that the water was 23 feet above the tallest mountain at that time.

As we have studied, we saw a continuous downpour of rain caused the flood for 40 days and 40 nights. Almost instantaneously, there was an incredible upheaval within the earth as the waters from below broken up.

A local flood could not maintain its level of water for the time specified for over a year.

From the following verses of *Chapter 7*, we know that nothing survived the flood except those in the Ark. Both the Hebrew and the Greek languages reserve unique words for referring to the Flood of Noah. The Hebrew word is Mabbul. The Greek word is Kataklusmos.

There is a fascinating study available by many authors on this subject. We will forego it for the present time. The conditions which exist after the flood indicate a significant change took place at that time. Before the flood, there was a high canopy over the earth. Now it no longer exists. Before the flood, there were no seasons. Now there are.

Imagine the entire earth being approximately the same temperature? There was nothing about climate change back then. Now we have climate regions. Interestingly, we saw before the flood man was a vegetarian. After the flood, he could and did eat meat.

Think for a little while about the flood. As a result of the flood, there has been tremendous erosion from the rain, and great gullies came into existence. The Ocean basins enlarged themselves. There were great tectonic movements of the earth under the seas. On the lands were great Volcanic and seismic upheavals. With all the power water has, it is easy to say there was an unusual sedimentary activity. The sedimentary action caused the formation of many fossils.

Because of what was going on, Ocean canyons formed. Once the earth had been warm, a significant temperature change took place, which caused magnificent continental glaciers to form. Once there was the only body of land. Through the flood, the lands were divided and moved apart.

Then you have the emergence of lands, mountains, valleys on each continent. With the beginning of seasons, that means the rain, wind, radiation, and storms started. These great upheavals and pressures that came because of the waters caused the formation of coal beds.

From there, we can see that men would only live approximately 120 years and less where men once lived for hundreds of years.

Without getting so technically involved, we want to share some thoughts about the fossils.

Fossils are an area where many have done some research, but without getting as in-depth as some other writers, let us practically look at it.

Significant evidence in dealing with the sedimentary rocks concerning the flood is these deposits took place in only months, days, hours, or minutes. YeYears of study have proven the Evolutionary Theory to be wrong concerning coal forming in the swamps. More than likely, the massive amounts of coal found formed in the deep floodwaters. In many places, we can discover layers upon layers of tree bark embedded in the coal. These layers of bark eventually carbonized into coal deposits. With the heat and pressures involved, it did not take long for the coal to form.

It should be obvious then that dinosaurs and other fossils could not have formed the way evolutionary books suggest. Fossilization was quick because we see no signs of bacteria or erosion in them. Understand fossilization took place under unusual circumstances.

The presence of fossils in the different types of animals gives us a strong indication that something catastrophic occurred.

Using some catastrophic phenomenon is the only way to explain their existence for the fossilization we find today.

Enormous dinosaurs, large schools of fish, and many diverse animals have been discovered entombed by massive muddy sediments formed in the rocks. There are fossils found in the formations in what is known as sediments laden with water.

Logically, there is a question we must ask: What happened to those who would not get on the Ark?

Creationists have suggested there were millions of people who lived at that time. Where are their fossils? Why are they not in the sediments and rocks?

Why are there not thousands of fossils of humans in the rocks and sediment?

These are logical questions; we must find the answers. It seems reasonable, from studying the Scriptures, we should find human fossils in the floor strata, but there are none. With so much evidence and Scripture to prove the global flood, there must be an explanation for the lack of human fossils.

Interestingly, there are no undisputed human fossils found. We will try and answer the lack of human fossils as to our understanding. Perhaps the fossilized human skeletons closest to having been pre-Flood humans buried in Flood strata are those skeletons found at Moab, Utah (USA).

There is a story of two human skeletons found in this town. They were supposed to be 65 million years old. The time called the Cretaceous age, meaning sandstone. There is hardly a remote possibility of them being pre-flood human fossils, but we would think otherwise to listen to the news. There are no real confirmations to accept this claim, but it can be perplexing at best.

There is some evidence we can use to help us unravel this mystery. Think of the nature of the fossil records themselves. Most people do not realize that 95% of the fossil record consists of shallow marine organisms such as corals and shellfish in numbers of fossils.

We know there are trillions of tons of coal made up of algae and plant fossils.

That means only 5% of all fossils are something other than this algae or trees and plants.

Therefore the vertebrates (fish, amphibians, reptiles, birds, and mammals) make up very little of the fossil record -- 5% of 5%, which is a mere 0.25% of the entire fossil record.

So comparatively speaking, there are very few amphibians, reptiles, birds, or any type of warm-blooded mammals found, yet much has been said.

There are only about 2,000 skeletons worldwide in museums containing dinosaurs.

Many of these only have one bone to prove their existence.

Mathematically this means only about 0.25% of all fossils are vertebrate fossils.

Evolutionist goes so far as to say they have found one tooth of some kind of horse.

At best, this is shallow and has no scientific proof.

The smaller animals and organisms would be the first to die in flood as the deep breaks open, with the erosion runoff from the land due to the torrential rainfall concurrently burying them.

There would be no human fossils near the surface.

Most fossils of what evolutionists have said were pre-flood but are post- flood.

We can understand why, in this case, there are not many mammals fossils found in the so-called Mesozoic rocks.

What happened to the humans who went through the flood?

The analysis would be that so much debris destroyed them.

Perhaps also think of the power of the floodwaters and the turmoil involved in the waters' movement.

Therefore, they were not buried in the sediments and rocks but destroyed.

Think of powerful floodwaters coming from the sky and the earth beneath, seemingly boiling or turning over and over.

The result would be human bodies thrown about, and then there are large moving objects swirling round and round, crushing them. No wonder there was nothing left.

Have you ever experienced a flood locally?

From personal experience, it is a scary thing to be in a local flood.

Once the waters begin to move, there is no stopping it. When the flood started, it was over for the human race.

With the debris and other things floating violently, there is no way any flesh would survive.

We are sure the chemicals from volcanic like acid would react to destroy all flesh.

Then there are the upheavals in the earth, removing all traces of bodies floating around.

They would decay rapidly.

Then there is a significant temperature change with all the water pressure, and everything will be gone shortly. A change process called metamorphism would destroy whatever bones of shellfish, mammals, or anything else.

We have to consider the volcanic lava that would soon appear on the surface flowing, hot enough to melt even rocks with it being so intense.

We know all of these factors significantly lengthen the odds of finding a human fossil today.

Then, there is the thought that a drowned body would not sink but rise to the water's surface to be eaten by some animal.

There is a term for this, which is the differential suspension. That means any animal in the water would need some type of food to survive, and the animals would devour the corpses.

The bodies that were floating about would still have rapidly decomposed.

It is doubtful any bodies would have lasted very long at the rate the earth was changing.

They became sediment in the earth.

Mathematically it seems impossible for bodies to be preserved and remain on the surface of the waters. There would be nothing left for a scientist of today to discover, and finding a fossil of a human being would be minuscule.

In conclusion, there have not been any human fossils discovered. Perhaps more than this, we should understand the whole purpose of the flood. God said He would destroy man from off the face of the earth. We need to be convinced God intended to take every trace of humans off the earth and what he had done and destroyed it. Scriptures seem to verify this.

Some would agree with this statement where God said he would destroy the beasts of the fields and everything which had the breath of life.

Rightly, they point out there are records of animal fossils and not human fossils.

There seems to be a contradiction here. When God said, "every living creature," was that not so? Looking through the Bible, we can find that statement again when Israel's nation left the Promised Land's wilderness. The original inhabitants of the Promised Land were to be eradicated from the face of the earth. The will of God is precisely this.

God pronounced judgment on all of those nations because of their wickedness.

We understand that God's instrument of judgment was the nation of Israel.

They did not follow God's will, and as a result of their disobedience, they have had trouble with them since that time.

We also see that God issued the instruction to King Saul to destroy the Amalekites, judging their wickedness utterly. See *1 Samuel 15*.

Because King Saul was disobedient to God, it later resulted in his downfall.

It is not hard to figure out God meant what He said to destroy them utterly.

By now, you should understand God will not tolerate sin of any kind.

Sin carries its penalty, which is death, and we know every trace of sin removed in His eyes, which would necessitate destruction.

Knowing humanity, the way we are is not hard to determine if a fossil remain of some human existed were found, it would not be long before statues were erected and worshipped.

Do you not think God would allow fossils to remain to prove there was a flood in the first place?

They also serve as a witness against man and to the judgment of God by the flood.

The fossils which remain should serve as a reminder of how much God hates sin.

Before our eyes, we see the justice of God.

We have the results of that sin for the world to witness for the record.

Also, we have this record, thereby leaving us a testimony to Noah's Flood's reality and the trustworthiness of the Scriptural record. See *2 Peter 3*.

First, God destroyed the world by water; next, He will destroy it by fire.

This next judgment will be quick, swift, and in a moment.

Prepare now before it is too late.

The best determination of when the flood took place was around 3000 B.C.

The key verse to understanding the flood account is in *Genesis 7:17*.

It says, "And the flood was forty days upon the earth, and the waters increased, and bear up the ark, and it was lifted up above the earth."

We should give some thoughts and a timeline as to what happened here. From *Genesis 7: 17*, we find these words, 'The flood was 40 days upon the earth.' In Hebrew, the word for flood is Mabbul. Go to *Genesis 9:11*, and there is this word again. Here is a play on words. In English, the words "water" and "flood" many times have a similar meaning. However, in Greek, we will find the word to mean "cataclysm." This meaning is different from the waters. It would mean a sudden and violent movement of the waters. Since the word "flood" is not mentioned again until *Chapter 9*, we understand this indicates the flood is over. The continual rain, which was the most tangible expression of the Mabbul in *Genesis 7:4, 12*, had ceased.

In *Genesis 7:11-7:16*, the first day of the flood gives us the date.

Then, we have the statement that the flood began when the catastrophic events of the flood started. From *Genesis 7:17-7:23*, we see the cataclysm itself, introduced by the forward-looking statement that the turmoil would last forty days. Imagine it only took forty days for the deluge to cover the entire earth above the mountain tops. From *Genesis 7:24-8:4*, we see the statement, "the waters prevailed," indicates our comment above.

In other words, the rains had stopped, and the flood had reached its stopping point.

After the waters had covered the mountains, we see the timeline tells us it took ten months for the waters to recede enough to see the mountain tops.

Once that happened, it did not take long for Noah to send birds to see if they could find dry land. See *Genesis 8:5-12*.

In the next verse, *verse 13*, Moses sees land from the top of Mount Ararat.

In the following verses, *verses 14-19*, Moses tells us the date of the last day Noah and his family spent in the Ark.

The land was now dry enough to walk on. So we will try and put the events to help us understand the process. By this time, all life before the flood had been blotted out or destroyed. There would be very few fossils for man to find with the great upheavals and volcanic like flowing water.

In thinking of what had happened, the seas had erupted from the deep causing a great cataclysm.

Is it possible for the fountains of the deep to water the earth initially?

This breaking of the fountains lasted for forty days, and there was nothing but destruction.

There was nothing that was not touched by the flood. By contrast, the 330 days after the flood describe the beginnings of restoration, i.e., receding the new earth's waters.

We understand that the complete geophysical and ecological recovery may have taken much longer.

God told Noah to start loading the Ark 7 days before the 40-day flood began. We see this in *Genesis 7:4, 10*. This period started on the 17th of the second month, as we see from *Genesis 7:11*. In further reading, we find the word found at the end of *Genesis 8:24* means translation 'decreased' or 'abated.'

The Hebrew word is in other verses commonly rendered 'fail,' 'lack' or 'want.' Now *Genesis 7:6* states Noah was 600 years old during the flood duration, which excludes the flood from lasting longer than a year.

More importantly, the Hebrew words used for 'dried' and 'dry' found in *Genesis 8:13-14* carry meanings not apparent from most translations.

Just to give some background information, follow through these verses. In *Genesis 8:13*, there is the word, 'Dried' - Strong's 2717 - to 'parch' (through drought) by analogy to 'desolate' or 'destroy.'

In *Genesis 8:14*, we have the word 'dried' - Strong's 3001 - to 'be ashamed,' 'confused' or 'disappointed,' or water 'to dry up' and for herbage 'wither.'

What is important here is if the ground dried on 1/1/601, the flood had already ended! The Hebrew word for 'ashamed' in *verse 14* must be understood in the subject's relationship. Furthermore, the issue in this verse is not water, but rather the earth.

Any explanation of this verse has to explain why the earth had reason to be 'ashamed' on the quoted date 27/2/601. So the land was dry.

Before we close this section, let us try and answer five questions that need an answer to our way of thinking. A couple of them we have already touched on.

The first question I would like to answer is were there dinosaurs on the earth? There are dinosaur-like creatures mentioned in the Bible. The Bible uses ancient names like "tannin," meaning majestic, gigantic beasts. This term could include dragon-like animals such as whales or giant squid. It could have been reptiles like the plesiosaurs or other creatures.

For a better description, read *Job chapter 40*.

We think Moses can be talking about giant dinosaurs like the Diplodocus or the Apatosaurus.

These creatures were plant-eaters and were enormous with massive bones. The Diplodocus was large, and his legs so powerful he could carry a boxcar on his back. Another unique feature was that they were not afraid of anything. If we saw something as substantial as they were, who would not be frightened? Job says their tails were like cedars. The cedar was one of the most towering trees in ancient times.

Remember, the book of Genesis was written about 2,000 years before Jesus was born. It is interesting that after the dinosaurs died out, many people forgot about them. It was only till about 150 years ago scientists and geologists began to put some of their bones together for museums. There has been much consideration about what these dinosaurs were; we will leave that to the experts. There is one thing we know: God created them as huge as they were.

Scriptures are clear men and dinosaurs lived together, and they were the ones who ruled the earth at that time.

There was dominion given to man from the beginning over creation, and that would include the dinosaurs.

The next question I would ask is, was the land of the earth one single mass? In studies, we have noticed that man often changes his mind about things researched with knowledge.

We know that before the mid-nineteenth century, men did not recognize the continents were moving. Many in the scientific field would not accept what we know today as the continental drift.

They considered it fantasy until they discovered the tectonic plates were moving.

Long before this was proven, a creationist named Antonio Snider way back in 1859 discovered this, but most would not accept his theory until recently.

He understood Scripture saying at one time the seas were in one place, implying one landmass.

Then being one mass, the flood caused a separation of the mass into several continents.

Wherever we travel on the earth, there is a correlation of fossil types around the ocean shores.

Imagine a zebra and his stipes; then, we can understand the magnetic patterns affecting the water currents and the ocean floor's volcanic rock movement.

A theory is known as today "plate tectonics" describes this process.

Without being technical, we understand the movement of the tectonic plates in the earth.

If they move, an earthquake erupts. The same principle is true of the ocean floor moving.

There are three types of what is called deformation occurring on the ocean floor.

One is called extension, where the plates are moving apart.

The second one is called transformation, which is caused by what is known as horizontal slipping. That is when the plates move along a fault line.

The third is called compression or when one plate slides under another plate, for example, the San Andreas Fault in California. Do further study, and will find this to be interesting.

There is even a theory called seafloor spreading.

We know the earth's surface is not very deep before finding molten rock either in the water or just below the oceans' bed. We also know this molten rock rises to surface either in the water or on the earth's surface, creating a new crust. Sometimes it establishes islands in the oceans, and when a volcano erupts, we see the lava flow, which soon hardens and forms another layer on the surface. When this happens, if enough of these rock surfaces, it can change the earth's magnetic fields.

Interestingly we understand the poles of the earth have reversed or switched many times because of this. In closing our thoughts on this, we know the continents can move nearly six inches in one year.

So how does this fit into the Biblical account of the flood in Genesis?

From what is stated, the tectonic plates' rapid movement is possible, thereby fulfilling the flood requirements. Dr. John Baumgardner coined the phrase "catastrophic plate tectonic movement," describing the process.

That brings another question to mind, which teaches the theory of Evolution and fossils.

What about the simple beginning structures of complex organisms from the fossil era to what we have today? "Evolution demands transitional forms between species and paleontology does not provide them." In creating this theory of Evolution, Darwin was often embarrassed by the lack of evidence in the fossil records. There is no proof in many of his observations.

From the time God created the plants and animals, there have been no significant changes.

Many of the fossils verify creatures from the past as being identical to the ones of today.

There should be enough evidence in the fossils to prove the different transitional stages of Evolution from the amoeba to man.

From today, we find no supporting evidence found for the theory of Evolution.

There are various proofs today, which disprove the theory of Evolution. One such view is that of fast strata formation, which states the sedimentary rocks, instead of taking millions of years to form, took place in just a few short months or years.

Note, this would coincide with the flood account.

Think of the coal formations. We know the theory of coal forming in swamps is wrong.

The compression needed for the rapid formation of coal was generated by the abundant supply of water during the flood, causing a massive increase in coal deposits worldwide.

Fossilization requires extraordinary stipulations. Most Evolutionary books today cannot support the idea of how dinosaur and other fossils formed. Animals seldom fossilize unless buried instantly and deeply before scavengers, bacteria, and erosion reduce to dust.

Such conditions are scarce. Most of the fossils found to give the evidence they were formed by catastrophic conditions.

Without such conditions, there seems to be no credible way to explain their existence.

Enormous dinosaurs, large schools of fish, and many diverse animals are entombed by massive muddy sediments that hardened into rock. Almost all fossils located in ocean basins are found here. This is the wrong order for Evolution.

Nearly "up to 85% of earth's land surface does not have even three geologic periods appearing in 'correct' consecutive order" for Evolution.

Just in closing, we would mention that the Scriptures indicate and accept the flood as being a universal flood. For examples of this, see ***Psalm 104:6; 1 Pet. 3:20***; and ***Heb. 11:7***.

Also, Jesus made acclaim to the fact of the universal flood in ***Luke 17:26, 27***, and ***Matt. 24:37-39***. We that fossils produced by the conditions associated with the flood are found everywhere in the world.

Chapter 8

As we come to **Chapter 8**, we find that the work of judgment is now over. The horrific deed accomplished. Vengeance came because God is to be exalted and for those who will not listen, for those who will not accept Him, for those who will not; He will execute judgment on them.

We remember that God has no pleasure in the death of the wicked. That is what **Ezekiel 33: 11** says. Please study it.

Today's people are willingly ignorant of God's impending judgment, just as they were in Noah's days. I believe we live in the same atmosphere and conditions as in the days of Noah. People around us today defy the name of God. They mock His name. They curse His name. What is He to do? What can He do? I will tell you. If He did not spare that old world where Noah lived, what makes you think He will save this one?

From the Scriptures, we know God will execute judgment upon the ungodly.

Just read the book of Second Peter for clarification on that story, especially **Chapters 2** and **3**.

We can truly rejoice because God knows how to deliver the righteous and judge the self-righteous.

In our text, we see as a result of the flood; there has been a tremendous transformation taking place. The earth that Adam knew is not the way the surface is today. There have been many changes. When scientist tells us what they think, we can only reason from Scripture what was done at God's hand.

Let me give you a brief similarity as to what has happened. There has been tremendous erosion from the rain, and great gullies have formed. The ocean basins expanded. There have been great tectonic movements of the earth under the seas. There have been significant volcanic and seismic eruptions around the planet. Nothing has been unscathed by the flood.

For the first time on this earth, there has been tremendous and unprecedented sedimentary activity.

With all of the water's pressures instantly, they were the formation of the fossils and coals.

While this was taking place on the surface, much was taking place underneath the world's waters. Because of this, enormous geographical changes in temperature were causing magnanimous continental glaciers formed.

Climatically speaking, the South and North Poles are the coldest points in this earth's face with extreme cold at both ends. On the earth from pole to pole, we see the emergence of lands, mountains, valleys. As we have said previously, we see the beginning of rain, wind, radiation, and storms, never before seen on the earth. These all brought about the coming of the ice age.

One more factor to consider is the decrease in the age of those who now live.

For instance, you have the descendants of Noah. Just for the record Ham's descendants went south. Seth's descendants went north to Japeth. After the flood, Noah lived to be 950 years old. In the next generation, we have a man by the name of Eber. He only lived to be 464 years. Then, just a few generations after him, a man named Abraham only lived 175 years old. Just a few generations after him, a man named Moses only lived to be 120 years old. After him, the average age was 70.

In *verse 1*, it says God remembered Noah. God does not forget. Many Scripture verses tell us that God does not forget. Yes, you can see that the all-seeing eye of God is ever-present before us. In our text, we see God made the wind for a purpose. It was not just to dissipate the waters but for the same design as in **Exodus 14:21**, which says," And Moses stretched out his hand over the sea; and the LORD caused the sea to go back by a strong east wind all that night and made the dry sea land, and the waters were divided."

When God opened the Red Sea for Israel's children, He caused a strong east wind to blow all night. The purpose of that wind was to dry the earth, so the Israelites could cross over on the dry ground to continue their journey to the Promised Land.

This wind of **verse 2** of our text was for the same design. In effect, Noah was going to walk over into the promised new world God had made.

You tell me God does not take care of His little ones! See **Psalm 104:5-9**.

Many times we see a cause and effect happening around us just as we see here. God caused Heaven's windows and the deep to open fountains so that the earth flooded, but He also shut them up to stop raining. It took 221 days for the water to subside so that man could set foot on the earth once more. Haven't you noticed many times when God's wrath comes, then there comes a period of rest? Have you seen that as well?

We frequently say trouble comes in threes, but then there is calm, a rest that we can anticipate. If we have learned our lessons well for God is always trying to teach us something, there will be a rest period. Think about it. After the making of Creation, God rested from all His labors. After the flood, the earth rested, and in the process, God rested in the judgment given to wicked man. Today, we remember God's wrath fell on His only Son, and we can rest in Him. What does the text say about this rest? We are complete in Him. It was just like Noah was saved because he put his trust in God. There he found rest.

It is so exciting the typology and representations that are presented before us.

As you study the Scriptures, you can see several things I would like to mention.

For instance, the Ark rested on the 7th month on Mount Ararat. The number seven stands for completion and rest. Then you have the doves. They went out twice seven days apart. Had they stayed out, they would have died. The number 14 stands for death, for it was the Passover Lamb's day, slain after watched for four days. Comparing the Scriptures, you will find that our Lord and Saviour also were killed on the 14th day at the time of the Passover. The number 17 is also essential. It was the 7th month, but it explicitly stated it was the 17th day that the Ark rested on Mount Ararat. The number 17 often refers to the resurrection.

And so we see that Christ was resurrected on the third day, which would be the 17th of the month.

Our expectation and faith as a Christian is our belief in the resurrected Saviour of our souls.

After God's wrath was seen and experienced by Noah and the rest of the world, Noah had to trust Him in keeping him safe from God's wrath and believe that God would bring him through to the other side. Isn't that our desire?

There are many types here; it is almost impossible to mention in this space.

You have the doves, a type of the Holy Spirit, but you have the ravens who are a type of Satan, sin, and wickedness. Then you have the olive branch. We have read the olive branch is the universal symbol of peace. An interesting statement follows this, and that is, Noah looked.

What do you think he saw? He saw the evidence of God's judgment. That and of itself would be very discouraging.

Yet I am convinced he saw the possibilities before him. Was he ready to accept the challenge God had placed before him? How could he continue to stay in the Ark? He knew the land had dried. He knew that soon God would open the door to the Ark. What would he do when the door opened? Would he have the courage to step out on the land? He knew he was secure in the Ark, but he had to soon step out into a different world. He was going to have to be brave and courageous for a new life that would soon begin. See *John 15:1-16.*

Noah did step out into the new world.

The first thing God had told him to do was make a sacrifice unto the Lord. Not only was it for the Lord, but I'm sure Noah showed deep appreciation and gratitude for keeping him safe.

Noah's willingness to obey God's command prompted God to promise Noah He would be with him.

You can see this promise in **Chapter 9**. Here is what God purposed within Himself. Listen to these words here in our text. It says, "**Genesis 8:21-22** And the LORD smelled a sweet Savour; and the LORD said in his heart, I will not again curse the ground any more for man's sake; for the imagination of man's heart is evil from his youth; neither will I again smite any more everything living, as I have done. While the earth remaineth, seedtime and harvest, and cold and heat, and summer and winter, and day and night shall not cease."

What is God saying here? He promises never to curse the ground or destroy life as He had.

Herein we see the heart of God once again. He loved men more than anything, but sin requires judgment. Nevertheless, more importantly, we see this as only a temporary fix for sin.

He judged his creation, but the problem was that thing called sin, implanted in man's heart through sin is still there.

The remedy for this problem of sin is becoming a new man in Christ. You cannot wipe the slate clean and start over again without Him. See **2 Peter 3:13**. However, we know, though, in essence, this is what God will do with the physical earth, He will exterminate it with fire and make a new heaven and a new earth. See **Romans 8:20-21**.

The flood was only a temporary fix at best. Sin has to be dealt with permanently, which will be through the coming of the Messiah. It is then man can become a new creature, trusting the finished work of Christ. See **2 Corinthians 5:17**.

We don't need evil people destroyed, for we are all evil to the core. See **Jeremiah 17:9, 10**.

We can see God promising to bring about our final salvation to Noah when he made that first sacrifice.

God, as we have said, promised the earth would never be destroyed by a flood again.

Noah had faith based on this, and for that matter, so do we. Admittedly, there is much negativism involved in the flood. However, if you can see beyond the flood, you should see the matchless grace of God. Remember what *Genesis 6:8* said, "But Noah found grace in the eyes of the LORD."

When you think about it, yes, there was judgment, but I feel we can honestly say that all the earth's peoples experienced grace. For 120 years, they did not know they had it. The Ark would have kept them safe, if only they had listened. They had the opportunity to accept the truth Noah was telling them. The Gospel would be based on their faith.

He proclaimed there was only one difference between Noah and the rest of the world.

He accepted the grace of God, and they did not.

Not believing, not willing to humble themselves, they would not accept the Lord but chose to live and die in their sins. They did not believe God would judge them for their sins.

But Noah wanted a relationship with Almighty God.

He knew God meant business and did not lie; therefore, judgment was at hand.

In Noah's last years, he spent them walking with God, building the Ark, and proclaiming God's Word.

This promise evidences the grace of God. See *Genesis 8:22*. Here is the irony of our day.

In his sin, men have choices, either risk God's judgment by not doing anything or bow before a holy God and repent. Many today smirk and revel in their sins before a holy God and provoke Him to do something about sin. They do not believe His Word when He says; He will put things in order. Some believe God is dead or apathetic, unable to deal with their sin, showing nothing but hatred toward God. See **II Peter 3:8, 9**.

As believers, just like Noah, we believe God should have sovereign control over our lives. See **Colossians 1:16-17**. When you see the preservation of all things as they have been, day and night, summer and winter, springtime and harvest should prompt the Christian to bow the knee to God in praise and submission to His providential care.

However, the non-Christian has twisted this promise of God's providential care into an excuse for sin. Remember **II Peter 3:3-4**?

God will concede man to have time to repent, but just as in Noah's days, the day of grace will disappear and be lost forever. See **II Peter 3:10**.

The days preceding the flood would be like those heralding His final appearance to judge the earth. See **Matthew 24:37-39**. Look around you today and see sin is rampant, seemingly nothing to stop it. Men are going about business as usual, with no thought of a holy God, doing what they have always done. In the world's typical everyday life, there is nothing wrong with eating, drinking, marrying. Most would say today, what is wrong with doing things my way?

Why should there be a penalty for that? I think and, I work, I make my way, what is wrong with that?

Many know nothing about God's grace for they have shut Him out of their minds and hearts.

The work of the devil has deceived them.

We hear so many times that it has been 2,000 years, and nothing has happened toward Christ's second coming. They forget God is a long-suffering God and what He does; He does deliberately in His own time. God is gracious, but the wrath of God is guaranteed.

The people of Noah's day found this to be authentic.

Wrath and judgment are for those who are not under the blood. One glimmer of hope in this is while God's judgment is inevitable, that is not the delight of His heart.

We see this because there is not one instance of suffering mentioned in the flooding context.

Note this is another of the reasons why Noah could only look up inside of the Ark.

It was so he could not see the suffering and torment of those outsides of the Ark.

Noah built the Ark with no portholes and windows of any kind. Therefore he could not examine God's destruction. Only at the top was there an opening to allow the light to shine in.

From this, we should determine God does not delight in giving judgment. Nevertheless, don't forget, He will judge sin and those who resist Him. Don't be deceived by the work of the devil. When you are young, you have the idea you will live forever. That is realistic, but more than likely, not the way you thought. There comes a time when God says, "Enough is enough."

There is an illustration I would like to share. "A few years ago, I visited a woman who was dying from cancer. Because of her physical state, on my first visit, I could not speak with her. On my second trip, her husband came to the door and let me in. She had become sicker than the first visit. While I waited, her husband asked her if she wanted to see me, and she shook her head and said no. I never saw her alive after that.

For many years, preaching helps scrutinize how people think that they can wait until one foot is in the grave before deciding to accept Christ.

In all honesty, it seldom happens that way.

Why would you think you could live in sin and be rebellious against God all of your life and think before you take your last breath, expect God to accept you? It can happen, deathbed salvation, but very sporadically.

Many times we see God's judgment is often allowing things to take their course.

The flood account seems almost like creation reverted to the conditions of the second day of creation. See *Genesis 1:6-7*. In Colossians' book, we see our Lord Jesus Christ is the Creator and Sustainer of the universe. See **Colossians 1:16-17.**

From what we have already shared, it strikes us today men do not act like they believe God exists at all.

During the Tribulation Period, man will find out what it is to live without God. At that time, His restraining hand will be withdrawn, and anarchy will rule the day. More often than not, we see God judging by giving man precisely what he has been asking. Many will wish for the day they asked about God.

In the final consideration, let us look at the subject of the salvation of God. We will give you something to consider, which is relevant in the conversation. Some may not like it, but it is the truth. The salvation of Noah was restrictive in many ways. In his day, working on the Ark, he proclaimed only one message. That was repent and how to be saved. God has a way, a plan that all must follow for salvation. As the men of the day we're going about business as usual, they rejected what God was offering. Today, God is offering one way to salvation. See **John 14:6.**

God's plan for Noah and the people of his day was instructive. Plainly stated, those inside the Ark were safe. Those outside the Ark were lost and died a horrible death.

Yes, those in the Ark were sinners, deserving the same judgment as those outside the Ark.

The difference is they believed God. They all knew the difference according to the preaching of the Word. The thing is, many elected to ignore the facts of the wrath of God. It is so today.

The world is godless and wants nothing to do with this God. They say they will not accept His punishment of sin. However, the message is the same. The choice is still the same.

Only two choices are at our disposal. We must accept the fact of our rejection of Christ, or we are bound to accept His gift of salvation.

Imagine the suffering and pain Christ endured on the cross. It was because of my sin he hung their suffering the wrath of God. When we accept God's offer of eternal salvation, in that instant, it is as if we were there with Him. We see our sin nailing Him to the cross.

God gives free will to choose, and I accepted Christ. In the same regard, those who reject Christ by choosing to act against His love offer will suffer eternal damnation.

There is no difference just like those outsides of the Ark; they will suffer God's wrath.

Knowing about Christ today can no more save a man than knowing about the Ark saved men in Noah's day. Unquestionably, looking through glass, we can see the blood dripping off altars of sacrifice, and who desires to look there?

Seeing the replica of the Ark today, it was not appealing to the eye. Besides, who would want to live with wild animals and the smell associated with it. We can say the same about Jesus Christ. He came not from an affluent family. Before he was born, He was an enemy of the state. Even before He could walk, they were trying to kill him. The prophet Isaiah prophesied of Him 700 years before He walked the earth.

Isaiah 53:2 says, "For he shall grow up before him as a tender plant, and as a root out of a dry ground: he hath no form nor comeliness; and when we shall see him, there is no beauty that we should desire him."

There is the possibility of salvation was more appealing, more would accept it. That would not be a valid statement. The bigger problem is that we cannot embrace a Christian's road in real life until we have experienced it. It is not a lenient road to follow.

I have listened to today's preachers, and you would think life as a Christian life is a bed of roses with miracles along the way. Who wants suffering, pain, and heartaches? That does not sound very inviting to me.

Do you want to find real peace and real joy, and one day be delivered from this wicked world? There is only one way.

Peace and joy come from experiencing faith in the revealed Word of God.

Envisage Noah asking God what rain was and wondering what noise thunder would make.

Yet, Noah built an ark because he believed God and then acted on his faith.

There is a difference between academic and active faith. Both are on the principle of faith, intellectual faith is just head knowledge, but an active faith believes and will from the heart act on that faith. We know he understood, for he committed himself for 120 years building something he had never seen.

In our lives today, we, too, have to act on the faith God gives. As Noah was a preacher of righteousness, somehow I do not think he preached from a pulpit. Yet, every stroke of his hammer and every board he completed condemned the men of his day.

It was a warning to them that judgment was at hand. As Christian, do we not say the same thing with every step we take? Our lives should reflect this same message.

That is the message that Christ is coming back to judge this world of wickedness and unrighteousness. What will your neighbor say? I sure hope they know by your testimony.

Next, we come to the end of the chapter and find God making a promise to Noah.

Here I just want to lay the framework to talk about the covenant God made and what Noah did. We find Noah making a sacrifice proclaiming that he was a sinner saved by grace.

In typology again, we see that Noah's sacrifice pointed to the death of Christ.

He knew what it meant. One thing worth mentioning is that Noah's sacrifice was a sweet savor to God.

Listen to what *Heb. 13:15* says, "By him, therefore, let us offer the sacrifice of praise to God continually, that is, the fruit of our lips giving thanks to his name."

Is that not what we are to do today?

In these final verses, we have that promise of God. From then until now, the sun has risen on the just and the unjust. God has been working, calling out His people, establishing His Church, etc. God is waiting while the message of the cross is proclaimed to the world.

The seasons shall remain. This verse contradicts the old saying that you will not tell one season from another later on.

Next, we will discuss the altar, sacrifices, and covenant by Noah and God in *Chapter 9*.

Chapter 9

This chapter establishes a new beginning for the whole world. At this time, there is only Noah and his family. God had inaugurated a new way of doing things, and I want to cover it in this chapter. I am thankful that God remembers. Otherwise, He would not have acknowledged Noah. He could have just left him to take care of his own.

Graciously God has a plan and is willing to allow humanity to be a part of that plan.

It is all of grace. From the beginning of time, God gives grace to every man.

Now we see this evolving to light in full bloom.

You know God could have destroyed everyone, including Noah and his family, but He did not. We do not need to understand it, but God has always loved sinful man and made provisions for him that only God knows. What did He tell man now?

It was the same thing He told humankind in the beginning, to be fruitful and to multiply.

That is God's desire from the beginning and still is today.

By this time, we are beginning to understand some of the innovations that are going to occur.

In *Chapter 8*, we described for you the changes in the earth itself. Here in *Chapter 9*, we will see more great changes at God's hand and deal with humankind.

There was a time when humanity was able to co-exist with all animals with no fear.

After the flood, all of that changed. Now, man is to rule over all other life. All other creatures are to fear man. Just a thought here is this does not mean that the Beast would never rise against man. However, today, typically, animals instinctively fear man. In the process of the changes made, we find that God asserts man must understand he is to be Holy. God begins to lay the foundation of what the written law would disclose.

He instructs Noah in the way of life as it is now. He reemphasizes for Noah the sacredness of marriage, and it is a permanent institution that He has set up from the beginning. See the following verses; ***Gen. 2:22-24; I Cor. 7:39; Rom. 7:2.***

Not only does God speak of the sacredness of marriage, but God tells Noah that life in and of itself is sacred in His eyes, and for any many shedding the lifeblood of man, the punishment Cain received would not be the rule of the day. Man would now pay life for life. Today we call this capital punishment. See ***Prov. 28:17.***

How important is blood? Just take a look at the blood that Jesus shed on Calvary, and then you will know. Moses, in the law, incorporated all of this. Hence we would ask, why would God give Noah these restrictions? Solely to protect man from man and to point man to the Lamb of God's saving blood.

Later God would give Moses the Law. As we follow the hand of God moving, we see what God is doing and what man has done. Therefore God begins to work with man in a new way by making a covenant with man.

I feel it essential to take a closer look at what God is saying and, in return, look at how a man should react to this covenant. As we look about us today, we live in an age which desires no long-term commitments. I have, however, enjoyed the commitment made to my wife of 52 years. Many do not want a permanent marriage. The vows of today are not what they used to be. There are no permanent guarantees. They will stay with each other and see how it works out. If everything is like they want it, they will stay. Otherwise, they leave. Today, you had better read the fine print.

Today's contracts are complicated, with diverging meanings who know what the result is supposed to be. You would think this is just the way of the world. However, we see this same thing in Christian circles and even in churches.

When I was growing up, a man was as good as his Word. That should be our declaration today. God has written many contracts with men called covenants. He has dealt with man in this fashion.

Here in our text, we find the first instance of a covenant God made with man. The word 'covenant' appears in *Genesis 6:18*, referring to the Noahic Covenant of *Chapter 9*.

This Noahic Covenant is crucial to us for several reasons. As I write this, it is raining outside, and rather gloomily, too. Thankfully, God is in control, and many times before, we have said God can't lie, so the agreement He made with Noah is still in effect today. God used the Noahic Covenant as a pattern of what He would do later on. As I said, the Noahic Covenant is still in force today. Noah's covenant helps us understand the New Testament covenant instituted by the Lord Jesus Christ.

The covenant with Noah also lays the foundation for the existence of the human government.

Why there is much debate over capital punishment, today shows they don't understand this book we have been studying. Look once again at *Genesis 8:20-22*.

We are not quoting it here, but you must reread it to understand the implications.

In studies, we can say technically, *Genesis 8:20-22* is not a promise God gave to Noah.

Instead, it is a proposal confirmed in the heart of God. Reread *Genesis 8:21*.

We see the mind of God, telling us His purposes. Note these are not spoken directly to Noah.

That brings us to an age-old argument we see among theologians.

On the one hand, you have those who would be called covenant theologians.

From the other perspective, some are dispensational theologians.

The first group or spectrum uses these covenants for their purpose and interpretation.

They teach at the expense of the other covenants God made with man, including the Noahic Covenant.

For others of the second group will disparage the theological covenants and only stress the biblical covenants.

Surely there must be a balance one can attain. In *Genesis Chapters 8 and 9*, both of these elements God reveals to us. It is the eternal purpose of God for men to have the opportunity for salvation. He established this in eternity past. See *Ephesians 1:4; 3:11; II Timothy 1:9*, and *II Thessalonians 2:13*.

God gives Noah his purpose by making a recommitment to him. Have you gone before the Lord and asked Him to revive you again? To restore that inner joy and peace and zeal I once had. As the ole colored preached said, "sot me on fire, Lord."

Here is what we need for us today. Don't we need to recommit ourselves to God, even daily?

Philippians 3:8-16 tells us, and I wish you would look at it, how we can know Him, and the power of His resurrection. If we were that intimate with God, would there be a change in me, in the world as we know it? This covenant of God with Himself was remembered by God when Noah wanted to worship God by his offering up sacrifices to God.

Noah just did not know the sacrifices that were to come. But in the meantime, God resolves never to destroy the earth by a flood again. So we see in *verse 11* of our text in Genesis.

God knew what Noah would do, even as he stood before the altar and made sacrifices unto Him.

We know that righteous Noah, according to *Genesis 6:9*, will soon be found naked in a drunken stupor, as we will see later on in this chapter in *verse 21*.

Surely you can see the problem here. It is man's sinful nature, and no matter how many times God destroyed the earth, if one man were left, so would sin remain. He is born with this character trait. Here is the core reason of why his heart is evil. That is why we preach he must become a new man, a new creature in Christ. We see this purpose in *verses 21, 22*.

As we continue to look into this chapter, we notice as we have said a new beginning.

Now we have not only a new beginning but a new set of rules.

Here you must stop and compare Scripture with Scripture. It is evident by the similarity of these verses to *Genesis chapter 1*. Here in *Genesis 9:1* and there in *Genesis 1:28*, God blessed His creatures and told them to be fruitful and multiply. Here in *Genesis 9:3* and there in *Genesis 1:29-30*, God prescribed the food man could eat. However, some differences indicate that the new beginning is to be different from the old. God pronounced the original creation 'good' in *Genesis 1:21, 31*.

Initially, God told Adam to subdue the earth and rule over it. See *Genesis 1:28*.

After the flood, Noah received no such command. Instead of doing this, God placed in the hearts of animals to fear man. It is the mastery of man to subdue them and control them.

Fear is the reason dogs obey their masters. When he does, it is because he fears him.

We know Adam and his descendants were vegetarians from *Genesis 1:29-30, 9:3*, Noah and his descendants could eat flesh after the Flood from *Genesis 9:3-4*.

There was, however, one stipulation. They could not eat the animal's blood, for the animal's life was in its blood. God places a high value on life and wants man to understand this.

Note, this is why God told us to take an animal's life for survival and not ingest the animal's blood. Why would this be allowed after the flood?

There is a difference between a human and an animal, as we have elaborated on before.

Animals do not have a soul, and God intended to provide nourishment for man through them.

Because of the changing factors surrounding the flood, man needed more protein in his body to survive.

Another thing to consider about man is because of sin, he must learn; he can only live by the death of another; for God requires a substitute.

Consequently, we can understand how man must live by the death of animals.

How else can we learn to reverence life?

Before the fall were men of violence, as seen from **Genesis 6:11**, like Cain in **Genesis 4:8**, and Lamech in **Genesis 4:23-24**, who had no regard for human life. Read again what is said in **Genesis 9: 5, 6**. Man's life is precious and belongs to God. It is God's to give and His alone to take. Also, animals that shed man's blood must die. See **verse 5** and **Exodus 21:28, 29**. We have capital punishment to show others if one takes a life, there must be punishment fitting that crime. We see this in **verse 6** and **Numbers 35:33**.

In Numbers and Leviticus, there are many laws today you see. Suicide is mentioned in other passages like **Job 1:21**.

The bottom line is man is not to shed the blood of another. This statement is accurate; the blood is the life of man. We know this because it is verified here in **Genesis 9:4** and again in **Leviticus 17:11**. Besides many other considerations, must we not conclude that a fetus has blood at the beginning of life?

Must we acknowledge that to shed this blood destroys the fetus, is to violate God's command and be subject to the death penalty? Do we not believe God created man in His image, **Genesis 1:27**, and here in

Genesis **9:6**? Given this fact, murder is much more than an act of hostility against man. It is an insult to God.

Many times we take things personally when it comes to God, primarily if someone attacks us.

Murder is a sin against God and must be dealt with severely.

From **verse 6** of our text, we see another reason for capital punishment.

See how God affirms his reason for shedding the blood of the murderer.

Cain was left to the world after he killed his brother. Do you know why God did not kill him?

Maybe it is for us to see the consequences of allowing a murderer to go free. This world was and is filled with great violence both then and now.

Concerning capital punishment, we can say men act on God's behalf to fulfill God's will.

And the government acts on God's behalf in punishing the evildoer and rewarding those who do well. The evidence is in **Romans 13:1-4**.

Without capital punishment, it is easy to see permanent results. There are more crime and anarchy than ever before. Look at our streets today, and you will know the truth. See **John 19:10-11**. Man's sinful tendencies are also kept in check by his fear of the consequences of his actions. Without trying to make a statement, we can see that the society that loses reverence for life cannot survive for a very long time.

Thus, God instituted capital punishment as a gracious restraint upon man's sinful tendency toward violence. Hence, humanity can live in relative peace and security until God's Messiah has dealt a death blow to sin.

Thus, a new age has dawned; it is not an age of naive optimism, but one to follow God's commands. If we are willing to follow these commands, then there is hope for the future.

Now, this brings us to the point of looking into the covenant God made with Noah called the Noahic Covenant here in **Genesis 9:8-17**.

You might call this first covenant with God the foundation, for there are many characteristics in this one you will find in the others.

Our intention here is just to highlight some of the covenant's more apparent features.

First, we see the Noahic Covenant was initiated and dictated by God.

This covenant reveals the sovereignty of God.

Notice there is no obligation with this covenant. God made it for man to follow. See *Genesis 3:20-22*. There was no discussion with Noah. God's will must be fulfilled in this matter.

Once a friend of mine owned a car that was on its last leg. Finally, he decided to find another one, more dependable. He found a vehicle he liked but wanted to consider it more. However, when he got into his car, it would not start, leaving him unable to negotiate. He accepted their offer and paid the price.

Here is a good description of what Noah was to do. Besides, who would question God?

Secondly, we see the Noahic Covenant gives Noah and all successive generations this privilege. See *Genesis 9:12*.

As I have said, this covenant will be in force until God changes it, according to *2 Peter 3:10*.

This covenant with Noah is universal. It affects all men in these times. See *Genesis 9:9, 10*.

Next, the Noahic Covenant is unconditional. Interestingly, some covenants were contingent upon both parties carrying out specific stipulations.

For example, you have the Mosaic covenant. The nation of Israel had to keep this covenant if they wanted the blessing of God. If not, trouble lay ahead. Please read *Deuteronomy 28*.

There was nothing conditional about what God was doing for Noah. God simply made a promise to him. There would continue seasons, and the earth would not be destroyed again by a flood. While humanity received specific commands in **verses 1-7,** these are not part of the covenant. Technically, they are not part of the covenant.

Fifth, this covenant was God's promise never again to destroy the earth by a flood, **Genesis 9:15**. Later regarding the Scriptures in **2 Peter 3:10**, God said He would destroy the earth by fire.

Thankfully, the child of God is removed from the wrath to come. Noah is a type of this by being protected from the flood via the Ark.

Sixth the sign of the Noahic Covenant is the Rainbow, which God will put in the sky for man to see. Read **Genesis 9:13-15**. It is very precise in its description. Understand in every covenant; God gives a sign of His promise.

The Abrahamic Covenant is circumcision. See **Genesis 17:15-27**.

Then we understand the Mosaic Covenant is the observance of the law and the Sabbath day. See **Exodus 20:8-11** and **Exodus 31:12-17**.

The "sign" of the Rainbow is appropriate for Noah. The Rainbow frequently appears at the end of the rain, signifying the promises of God to Noah. More impressive is the Rainbow.

God designed it for His benefit. We know when God sees the Rainbow; He remembers his promise to Noah and his seed. It should bring great joy and comfort, knowing God's faithfulness, guaranteeing us eternal life.

When Isaiah wrote his book, there seemed little hope for the nation of Israel. There is always hope found in the Word of God. As they went through a dark period in their history, we understand why God showed them the coming Messiah. He wrote it to give them hope based upon their faithfulness. See **Isaiah 54:9, 10**.

The language of **Genesis 9** was employed by Hosea to assure God's people of their restoration. See what **Hosea 2: 18** says.

Jeremiah wrote of God's future blessings, reminding them of God's faithfulness in keeping Noah's covenant. It is worth the time to study **Jeremiah 31:30-37** and **Jeremiah 33:20-26**.

In doing so, compare those passages with ***Psalm 89:30-37*** for more information.

Those under the Old Testament economy looked forward to the coming of the Messiah.

In turn, we look back to what God accomplished on the cross through His Son, Jesus Christ.

Israel was laid aside in the matter of salvation, given Gentiles the same opportunity for redemption. Today, Jews await the completion of the Church age, and during the Millennium, they will see their Saviour, Jesus Christ. We know the Church age is soon coming to an end because God is faithful to His Word. There have been many things that come to pass in this generation.

Prophecy is being fulfilled right in front of us. God fulfilled the old covenant of Noah in the new covenant of Jesus Christ. I am sure the flood was dramatic and horrible, but think of the work of Christ on Calvary and what He endured to make way for our eternal salvation.

What can compare to that? Jesus instituted this covenant by His death on Calvary. As always, there is a sign. It is the institution of the Lord's Table. We call it communion. Many of the New Testament writers tell us this, and so does our Lord Jesus Christ. See ***Matthew 26:26-29***. Through Jesus Christ, we see the new covenant compared to the Mosaic covenant is superior to it.

Like the Noahic Covenant, God initiated the New Covenant, and he accomplished it.

Generally, all humanity will benefit from the grace of God. Only those saved can benefit from the blessing of the New Covenant. The New Covenant is by the blood of the Lamb of God to forgive sins and receive the gift of eternal life. See what our Lord said in ***John 6:53-55***.

The vitality of trusting in Christ alone is receiving Him for who He is and what He has done for salvation. The only condition for entering into the New Covenant's blessings is the expression of personal faith in Christ by receiving Him and His eternal life gift. See ***John 1:12*** and ***I John 5:11-12***.

Like the Noahic Covenant, those under the New Covenant do not need to fear the future outbreak of His divine wrath.

The Noahic covenant says God will not destroy the world again by a flood.

The new covenant of Jesus Christ says we are no longer under God's divine wrath if we put our sins in Christ. Again see *2 Peter 3:10* and also *Hebrews 12:24*.

What an extraordinary comfort in believing God's covenant can bring this to us.

As part of humanity, we have before us the truth, and we should continue precisely where we are to stand before a holy God.

Just as in the Noahic covenant, there is no negotiating with God.

God laid down the terms for eternal peace, and they are unambiguous.

Have you surrendered to Him? May God enable you to do so?

The end of our text deals with God's sign to Noah and his descendants, including us today.

Think of the blessing it is and a reminder day by day that God never fails to keep His promises.

We may fail Him, but that will never happen the other way round.

What is the significance of the Rainbow? As the Rainbow appears, it signifies that the storm is over. As believers experiencing the storms of life, we are waiting on the Rainbow; you know the one around the Throne of Glory. Listen to these words of *Revelation 4:3* "and he that sat was to look upon like a jasper and a sardine stone: and there was a rainbow round about the throne, in sight like unto an emerald."

The Rainbow is a type of the second coming of the Lord Jesus Christ, who will redeem those who have been saved by God's grace. I am not looking for the clouds to break or the rain to stop.

I am looking for the Son of God to break through the clouds and take me home.

While we are waiting on the storms of life to cease and the Rainbow to appear, we can still experience the peace of God.

There is nothing Satan can do if we trust in God to cause that peace to leave us.

Please read what Paul said to the Philippian people in **Philippians 4: 6, 7**. This peace comes when we take His hand, for He will never let it go.

I know you remember when Jesus told Peter to come into the water. Please follow this text in **Matt. 14:28-31**, which are the words of Jesus to Peter.

I am sure you recall what Job said to his friends in **Job 23:10**. He said, "but He knoweth the way that I take: when He hath tried me, I shall come forth as gold.

This peace comes when we walk in His will.

That is when He'll direct us. Listen to these words by the Psalmist in **Psalms 143:10**.

He said, "teach me to do thy will; for thou art my God: thy spirit is good; lead me into the land of uprightness."

Psalm 40:8 says, "I delight to do thy will, o my God: yea, thy law is within my heart."

Not only can we have God's peace, but we can also experience the Patience of God.

While David was waiting on God, God was working behind the scenes to bring about His will.

It would do you good to read, especially the first five verses in **Psalm 40**.

As you begin to read this Psalm, you will also notice that God is watching over every one of us personally.

That is just the kind of God he is. Did you know that we can experience the protection of God? For Noah and his family, the story was straightforward. All he and his family had to do was stay in the Ark where God placed them. They needed not to try and get out. We say the same thing today; don't get out of the ship! In the vessel with Christ, we have protection.

You remember the story of Paul and the time he was in a terrible storm. He had prayed, and God had told him to tell the crew to stay in the ship, and they would be safe. Read *Acts 27:21-25.*

What is an excellent story, for if we are outside of the ship with Christ, we are lost? In *verse 31* of this chapter in Acts, Paul continued, "Paul said to the Centurion and the soldiers, Except these abide in the ship, ye cannot be saved." But did you know we can experience the presence of God? There was a time when Jesus and his disciples were in a ship, and a storm came up with them. Here are some seasoned fishermen. They had been on the sea many times, yet at this time, they feared for their lives.

I think as you read this text, you will find that first of all, they had forgotten Jesus was on board the ship, and there was no way the boat was going to sink with Him on board. Somehow they missed that point. Follow the story by Jesus in *Mark 4: 35-41.*

One thing is sure, God is in our midst, no matter what we may go through

Look at the many lessons we can learn from this. Why should we fear what man would want to do to us? The worst thing physically is for them to kill us, but I would remind you to be absent from the body is to be present with the Lord, which is far better!

I remind you that 2000 years ago, the Lord Jesus Christ shed His precious, red, royal blood on Calvary to ensure me and you of an unsinkable Ark in which God has promised Heaven. That is enough to make anyone shout. Glory! As the hymn writers have written, the shore is still there.

God's promises are still trustworthy. I can even see the lights of home. How about you?

I would love to tell you a true story that happened many years ago. There have been times when theologians gathered from all over the world from different faiths and religions in London, England, to discuss religion. Perhaps one of the questions which need scrutiny is, "What separates Christianity from all other religions?"

That is a question we should know the answer. What makes it so different from all other faiths?

One time in a meeting for this sort, a man named C. S. Lewis was there. They proposed that question to him. His answer was straight but profound. He said as we should say, it's all of grace. The cross's message is that God's Son takes our punishment when God's holiness demands judgment. There is one verse that sums up that truth. We have heard this verse so many times, and many are afraid to use it. We see it everywhere. Even many people not saved can quote it. That is *John 3: 16.*

That verse is the absolute purest truth in the Bible. When God's holiness demands judgment, God's love delivers grace. When God's holiness requires judgment, and when God's love provides grace, what you believe about God determines the outcome.

We each decide who we will meet on judgment day.

We decide if we will meet the Holy God of judgment or the loving Father of grace.

When I was a teenager, someone gave me an answer to the question: "How could a loving God send a person to hell?" The solution they gave me was that God does not send anyone to hell. We each choose where we will spend eternity. Our faith determines the outcome.

If you do not believe in a holy, pure, and perfect God, know your sin breaks His heart; if your God is not that holy, then your God does not have to love you enough to send His Son to die for you.

I believe the bow was the very "Glory of God"! How close is God in those storms of life? Let me explain what I mean here. Let me give you something to ponder. I'm sure you are familiar with Shadrach, Meshach, and Abednego in *Daniel 3*.

Remember what God did for the three Hebrew boys? God looked after them in the fire. God's protection is assured for us as we trust Him.

Think with me of Isaiah in *Isaiah 6: 1-5*, and like Ezekiel, these two fellows saw the impending judgment upon Judah coming. Exciting things happen in a storm. In the storms of his life, Isaiah saw the Lord of hosts, high and lifted.

Another Bible character, David, in **Psalm 23**, like Ezekiel and Isaiah, David saw the Lord during the valley of the shadow of death.

I am also reminded of a man by the name of Stephen, in **Acts 7:54-60**. Stephen saw the Lord looking down from Heaven as he was about to die after they stoned him.

Paul was also stoned outside the gates of Lystra and left for dead, and during this time, God took him to the third Heaven, and he saw things no man can see.

We think of the man Elijah. Did you know the Lord appeared to him during his flight from Jezebel? Search the Scriptures.

For there, you will find a man by the name of Moses. Remember what happened? The story of the burning bush is not consumed. God appeared to him out of a burning bush. We would challenge you to do some studies on your own. These are just examples that come to mind.

We would pose the question to you, have you recognized in your life the presence of the Lord when you are going through a storm?

Let me remind you that we are not home yet, but soon there is coming a day.

We are just pilgrims passing through on a journey to a place prepared for all those who have accepted sin's free pardon. Think of a place where there will be no sorrow, no pain, and no tears.

No doubt, we will have a new song to sing, and it will be wonderful to have none of these things affecting us, but the most important thing is that we will see Jesus; He will be the theme of our song and nothing else.

I remember what Job said in **Job 23:10**, "but he knoweth the way that I take: when he hath tried me, I shall come forth as gold."

The rest of the chapter takes up with the new future. Don't forget that all that went into the Ark came out of it. The three sons of Noah are the inhabitants of the whole earth.

They were Shem, Ham, and Japheth. Now we find out Noah was not a perfect man, for we see he was a sinful man and his sons. Noah's sin was not planting a vineyard but in getting drunk from this vineyard.

Some may argue that Noah did not know about the reaction of nature after the flood.

But he did know about the sinful man. Even though there were a new beginning and a new world, there was still the same sinful nature.

Next, we have the sin of Ham and the curse of Canaan. You might ask, "Why does God record this incident?" The answer is because there was both blessing and cursing upon man.

You will find in the text that Canaan, the son of Ham, received the curse. Man would have tried to cover up this incident, but God let it be known.

Shem, another son of Noah, was to possess Canaan. Israel was a descendant of Shem.

The Canaanites were descendants of Ham through Canaan.

Japheth, another son of Noah, would enlarge. "Enlarge" is from the Hebrew word pathah and means to make room; extend. Japheth's descendants are all over the world, and many are in the most prosperous lands.

In ending this chapter, we find Noah and his sons lived long lives. For the most part, we know they honored those around them. That should be our goal today. We are to honor those around us the let the know God is still on the throne and doing well.

Chapter 10

In this 10th chapter, we find the origin of the nations and races in the world today.

Later, we will see that this scattering of all the people born was at Noah's hands and three sons.

We can say it is true that the only satisfactory explanation for all the races, nations, and languages found in *Genesis 9, 10, 11*.

The evolutionist has no possible answer as to where the races originated. Although the evolutionists deny the Genesis account, they often use the terms Semitic, Hamitic and Japhetic, to explain their views.

We can say that the nations, races, and locations of all the earth people come from these three men.

Generally speaking, we know that Japheth represents the European and Caucasian man.

They have grown exponentially in number and wealth, knowledge, etc. Their dwelling place today is Europe, Russia, Scandinavia, and America.

We also know the descendants of Japheth are called Gentiles. Later this will refer to all who were not Hebrews.

We know Ham's sin; men think that the race of people he founded was black because of the sin he committed. While the curse is on Canaan, it appears to fall on all the descendants of Ham. Perhaps the curse is primarily upon Canaan since this nation would be driven out of the Promised Land by Israel later.

Nothing can justify servitude and slavery by any means, but it does accurately predict it.

Therefore, we know most of the nations at Ham's hand reside in the world's southern parts. We also know their dwelling place today is Africa and the east, but many are scattered among other nations. If you were to read **Deuteronomy 7:1-4**, you will find that Israel was forbidden to intermarry with the Canaanites, a nation of Ham.

Then you have Shem. From him comes the Hebrew nation. Jesus was a Shemite. You will find that in **Luke 3**. One of the most exciting facts concerning Shem is that nearly all religions originated among the Shemite's. They started in the area East of Greece and the West of India.

Chapter 11

Not only were the people scattered, but here we find that instead of one language because of this scattering, we see the development of many languages. Today many advocate a one-world language, a one-world government, a one-world race, and a one-world religion, but they are wrong according to the Bible! What we can say is this. If it was wrong in Noah's day, then it is wrong for today. No matter how good it sounds or how great it could be, it is still wrong.

In Noah's day, their efforts to unify races and religions was in direct disobedience to God's Word. It is still true today. There is soon coming a day when one will stand and declare a one-world language, a one-world government, and a one-world religion. I tell you he will be wrong.

He will be the anti-Christ just as a man named Nimrod is a type of anti-Christ. He could not stand the fact of what God had said to him in that there were to disperse rather than stay in one place. He rebelled against God and His will and stopped in Shinar's land and built a city by Babel's name. Then other cities were built and later became known as Babylon.

Let me interject some thoughts on Babylon and this man Nimrod. Babylon means confusion.

The Capitol of Babylonia, located by the Euphrates River, is also called Shinar and Chaldea.

Nimrod first built Babylon after the great flood of Noah's day.

Listen again to these verses. *Genesis 10:10* "And the beginning of his kingdom was Babel, and Erech, and Accad, and Calneh, in the land of Shinar." *Genesis 11:2* "And it came to pass, as they journeyed from the east, that they found a plain in the land of Shinar; and they dwelt there." *Genesis 11:9* "Therefore is the name of it called Babel; because the LORD did there confound the language of all the earth: and from thence did the LORD scatter them abroad upon the face of all the earth."

The city of Babylon is always associated with evil and rebellion against God. Many conflicts have arisen by Babylon in history.

One of its most notable enemies overtime was the nation of Israel. And yet God used the nation of Babylon to judge Israel in the days of the kings. Nebuchadnezzar, king of Babylon, carried the Jews away captive and destroyed Jerusalem's walls and temple. You will find this right in the following Scriptures: *2 Kings 24-25; 2 Chronicles 36*, and *Jeremiah. 52*.

You can read *Jeremiah 52*, where you will find God destroyed Babylon after the seventy-year captivity of the Jews. Continue with these words of Isaiah in *Isaiah 13:17-22* for more information.

In the book of Revelation, God tells of the rise of another Babylon in the last days before Christ returns. These last days Babylon will be the embodiment of all the evil and rebellion of men throughout history.

We must learn from these verses. Listen to God's Word again, as seen in several passages I want to present to you. *Revelation 14:8* says, "And there followed another angel, saying, Babylon is fallen, is fallen, that great city because she made all nations drink of the wine of the wrath of her fornication." *Revelation 17:5* says, "And upon her forehead was a name written, Mystery, Babylon The Great, The Mother Of Harlots And Abominations Of The Earth." *Revelation 18:2* says, "And he cried mightily with a strong voice, saying, Babylon the great is fallen, is fallen, and is become the habitation of devils, and the hold of every foul spirit, and a cage of every unclean and hateful bird." *Revelation 18:10* says, "Standing afar off for fear of her torment, saying, Alas, alas that great city Babylon, that mighty city! for in one hour is thy judgment come." *Revelation 18:21* says, "and a mighty angel took up a stone like a great millstone, and cast it into the sea, saying, Thus with violence shall that great city Babylon be thrown down, and shall be found no more at all."

The Old Testament Babylon was both a historical city and kingdom and was also a prophetic symbol for future Babylon. Christ will destroy the final Babylon. The prophets repeatedly use Babylon in a symbolic sense. There are two Babylon's mentioned in the book of Revelation.

One is Ecclesiastical Babylon, which is apostate Christendom, supposedly headed by the Papacy.

The other Babylon is known as Political Babylon, or the seat of his power, the last dominion of the Gentile world before Christ comes to judge this earth. Ecclesiastical Babylon is "the great whore" as seen in *Revelation 17.* Political Babylon destroys those who oppose him that the Beast may alone be the object of worship. See *Revelation 17:15-18* and *2 Thess. 2:3, 4.*

As you can see, this is very descriptive of the anti-Christ. But remember that Nimrod was a type here, which gives us information on the character of the one called Nimrod.

There is one final verse I wish to share with you about the anti-Christ is *Revelation 13:15,* which says, "And he had power to give life unto the image of the beast, that the image of the beast should both speak, and cause that as many as would not worship the image of the beast should be killed."

You mark it down. If God could take care of a man by the name of Nimrod and his cohorts, don't you think that same God can handle the power of political Babylon and destroy by the return of the Lord in glory"?

So from these passages we have read, we can determine the type of person Nimrod was with looking at the future anti-Christ. We can know they both are lawless and rebellious.

Listen again to *Genesis 10:8, 9*, which says, "And Cush begat Nimrod: he began to be a mighty one in the earth. He was a mighty hunter before the LORD: wherefore it is said, Even as Nimrod the mighty hunter before the LORD." When you compare that with *2 Thessalonians 2:8*, which says, "And then shall that Wicked be revealed, whom the Lord shall consume with the spirit of his mouth, and shall destroy with the brightness of his coming:"

There is no doubt they are both rebellious against God. From the Scriptures, we learn they both are mighty and powerful. In *2 Thessalonians 2:9*, "Even him, whose coming is after the working of Satan with all power and signs and lying wonders." Again in *Psalm 5:6*, we hear these words, "Thou shalt destroy them that speak leasing: the LORD will abhor the bloody and deceitful man."

We find they both are kings. *Genesis 10:10* says," And the beginning of his kingdom was Babel, and Erech, and Accad, and Calneh, in the land of Shinar." They both will are associated with Babylon. They both filled with "pride."

"Let us make a name," Nimrod said in *Genesis 11:4* " And they said, Go to, let us build us a city and a tower, whose top may reach unto Heaven; and let us make us a name, lest we be scattered abroad upon the face of the whole earth."

Here is what the coming anti-Christ will do. *2 Thessalonians 2:4* says, "Who opposeth and exalteth himself above all that is called God, or that is worshipped; so that he as God sitteth in the temple of God, showing himself that he is God."

But through it all, we find God is still in control. He is still all-powerful. In the end, they both meet their doom at the hand of God. I love it when we can see the hand of God working before our very eyes. Let me give you their fate, as described by the Word of God. In *Genesis 11:9*, we find these words, "Therefore is the name of it called Babel; because the LORD did their confound the language of all the earth: and from thence did the LORD scatter them abroad upon the face of all the world.

Then we have two passages which tell us the end of the anti-Christ. They are *Revelation 18:2*, "And he cried mightily with a strong voice, saying, Babylon the great is fallen, is fallen, and is become the habitation of devils, and the hold of every foul spirit, and a cage of every unclean and hateful bird." These words in *Revelation 19:20* " And the Beast was taken, and with him, the false prophet that wrought miracles before him, with which he deceived them that had received the mark of the Beast, and them that worshipped his image. These both were cast alive into a lake of fire burning with brimstone."

So what can we say about Nimrod? He was a man who was full of pride. He wanted to make a name for himself. Look again at ***Genesis 11:4***, which says, "And they said, Go to, let us build us a city and a tower, whose top may reach unto heaven; and let us make us a name, lest we are scattered abroad upon the face of the whole earth." Who do you think was saying this?

They had a leader. Nimrod set himself up as the ruler of his world at that time. His name means to rebel. He was a rebel against God. Instead of expanding and covering the earth, he built a city and started a kingdom.

By this time, a nation formed against the will of God. They were one language and speech.

We can say that unity is exceptional if based on truth and not against God. We see this was not the will of God. It was a movement of self-will. Note "us" and "we', in these verses here in ***Chapter 11***. They left God entirely out of their plans. Their unity was against God and His Word.

Let me tell you what they wanted. They wanted a city, a new name, and wanted to stay together and reach Heaven their way.

False religion began at Babylon. Egotism, rebellion, and self-sufficiency seem to be the root of men's activities here.

While rebellion, arrogance, and unbelief are evident in the story, the underlying problem is fear. Following the flood events, once Babel became a city, man forgot God and began to see the work he could do with his hand with mortar and bricks.

Look around you. What would we do without transistors, integrated circuitry, all of the advanced technology? Men say they can put a man on the moon. Now nothing can keep them from doing what they desire. But let me remind you of something. God has an answer to their craving to have unification. God saw what they were doing. God knows what the results would be if man continued on the course he was on.

God had a plan, and He knows how to implement that plan for God knows all things.

We know the story of the Tower of Babel. We also know what God did in the process.

Because of what God did, see the results of His doing? Their language changed, their residence changed, and their plans changed.

Mark it down. God is the author of separation and segregation, whether we want to admit it or not. What caused this is sin. Otherwise, it would not have been necessary.

Can I interject a thought here that probably will not go well with some people?

Nothing in the Scriptures suggests that God wanted these families to mix and intermarry.

God separated the continents, which resulted in the oceans standing as barriers against man mixing races and religions. God set up the language barrier to separate and segregate still further. Nothing in the Scriptures even suggests that God divided their languages in such a way as to cause the descendants of Shem, Ham, and Japheth to mix.

Admittedly, it would have been so easy for God to have done so! I know that it is hard to follow the will of God. I also understand that the natural man desires company and unity.

But I would also hasten to say that unity is not the highest good, but purity and obedience to God's Word are critical.

Think of all the things happening in the world today. We see what is taking place in our world today in the name of religion. Ecumenism is the watchword of all religions today, but there is the cost of truth with religions' unity. Some religious leaders regard unity as a goal worthy of any sacrifice. I can tell you God does not. The reason is the Word of God is pure and holy.

Unity should not come at the price of that purity.

We have said many times God wants His people to be holy and righteous before Him.

We stand on Scriptural ground when we say this. Listen to these words in *Leviticus 11:44*. It says, "For I am the LORD your God: ye shall, therefore, sanctify yourselves, and ye shall be holy; for I am holy: neither shall ye defile yourselves with any manner of creeping thing that creepeth upon the earth."

I can just hear someone say; well, that is the Old Testament. Well then listen to what Peter said in *I Peter 1:16*. It says, "Because it is written, Be ye holy; for I am holy."

We live in a world today where that is not the norm but the exception of living. God help us return to when we honor God and strive to be Holy as He is Holy. For us today, the communication gap created in *Genesis 11* can only be bridged by Christ. The Old Testament prophets recognized the continuous effect of Babel and spoke of a day when it would be invalidated. See *Zephaniah 3:9-11*.

Today, we see too many superficial relationships and perform an artificial exercise, putting on a show that many will accept. These will be who will inevitably miss the meaning of life. Someone has said that the 'upper crust' is a few crumbs with a little dough to hold them together.

What disturbs me most is that the church has fallen into the same pitfall as the world.

I think today's people are obsessed with what we would call being busy when its purpose is to destroy spending time with God. These pursuits of engagement tend to give false security.

We have programmed ourselves right out of the will of God. We have made programs a substitute for living by faith instead of having devotions daily in God's Word and seeking His power for living.

God could have died 70 years ago in many churches, and they would not know it.

There is one thing worthy of our faith: God and the work we do by His might.

In Babel's days, men began to see their labors as the cure of living without God, rather than being a curse. They believed that their hands could assure them of some kind of immortality beyond the grave.

We do what we do today to set a memorial to man's achievements, never once thinking of the one who made them. Have you considered this is because man is so insecure of himself?

We cannot hide the fact that the root of man's sin is his absolute rebellion and having active aggression against God and His people.

When men rebel against God, I still believe the root cause is his insecurity. No matter what he may accomplish or achieve, it remains man lives this life with the uncertainty of what is to follow.

I am glad as a simple country boy; God showed me the way to eternal life. And that life is in His Son. Amid evil, God always has a remnant. In this case, Abram's father was Terah in *verse 24* of our present chapter.

When you count the ages of each of the generations mentioned in this chapter, you can see exciting things. For instance, we find that Shem did not die until Abraham was 150 years old.

So Shem and Noah were both living at the time of Babel. Interestingly the Bible is silent on what part they may have played in all of this. Soon we will begin our journey with this man Abram. Through the experiences of Abram, God allows us to learn four valuable lessons about His character.

Even though Abram failed these early obedience tests, God still makes it possible to learn from them and find encouragement in our own lives. God cannot compromise on His standards without violating His nature. Since He is holy, He must never do anything to compromise His holiness; since He alone is glorious, He will never compromise even in the Revelation of His glory.

The glory of the Lord appeared to Abram in Ur as His plan and promised revealed to Abraham.

Three points of the plan were revealed for Abram for him to follow. It is like it is when we allow God to talk with us. He told Abram simply to go forth from his country. First, to the land, He said He would show him. Again He said to go on and leave his relatives. Abram was to leave his father. Was that so hard to do?

God's power and glory were so persuasive that Abram, previously a worshipper of idols, willingly went forth as commanded, but only up to a point! Abram obeyed God only partially. Does this sound like many of us today? So what does Abram do? Abram only partially obeyed God. See what happened next. He took his father's household with him. He took his relatives with him. Specifically, it was his nephew Lot and family.

He went only as far as Haran and settled there, not going on into Canaan.

When he finally got to Canaan, he quickly abandoned the land and fled to Egypt to find relief from the famine.

Abram was limping along, getting into trouble as he went all because he did not follow the detailed instructions of the Lord. How could God compromise His standards and bring immediate blessings upon the one who would not obey Him?

Jesus addressed the same subject differently when He told His disciples in the parable of the talents that we are to be faithful in the little things if we ever want to know the joy of serving over many things. See *Matthew 25:21*.

It is so sad that Abram lost God's nearness with which God wanted to have with him. From the time of the appearance of the glory of God in Ur, we read that the Lord appeared to him again only after he had left Haran and finally come to the land of Canaan.

You understand that God can only fellowship with those of His who are in His will.

Abram could not fellowship because he had not done what God had asked him to do.

It was not until after Abram came to his senses that God revisited him. Listen to these words in *Genesis 12:7*. "And the LORD appeared unto

Abram, and said, Unto thy seed will I give this land: and there builded he an altar unto the LORD, who appeared unto him."

Although Lot was still with him, God honored his next step in the path of obedience by appearing once again, something He would not do again until after Abram got out of Egypt and finally separated from Lot.

We cannot partially obey the Lord, by getting what we want rather than what He has required of us, and then expect to abide in the presence of His glory. He will not compromise His standards or dilute the calling He has given for us to walk in His will!

Are you satisfied without God's nearness, without the fresh revelations of His glory in your life, without the unique assurance of His abiding presence?

We can learn from this that Abram's failures did not nullify God's faithfulness despite all of this. I am glad that God's faithfulness is not contingent upon our adherence, or should we say its lack. Paul wrote to Timothy, and in *2 Timothy 2:13* said, "If we believe not, yet he abideth faithful: he cannot deny himself."

God called Abram through no merit in this man and will not allow His faithfulness to be less than perfect in the face of our constant imperfection.

Once again, we discover further evidence that God's unconditional faithfulness is the basis for our relationship to Him, our confidence in His eternal promises, and our eternal security through His saving grace in Jesus Christ.

Solely from the world's perspective, Abram's delays in obeying the Lord, even his tendency to ignore the Lord's counsel before acting, proved to bring great abundance. The text tells us that by staying in Haran, he amassed great wealth, accumulated lots of possessions, and built quite an entourage during their delay. Listen to *Genesis 12:5*. It says, "And Abram took Sarai his wife, and Lot his brother's son, and all their substance that they had gathered, and the souls that they had gotten in Haran; and they went forth to go into the land of Canaan, and into the land of Canaan they came."

The same could be said of his stay in Egypt, brief and disastrous though it was. *Gen. 13:1-2* says, "And Abram went up out of Egypt, he, and his wife, and all that he had, and Lot with him, into the south. And Abram was very rich in cattle, in silver, and gold. But from God's perspective, what Abram had done was get more attached to the world and less devoted to what the Lord had in store for him."

It is just like the devil to step in and mess things up when you determine within yourself; you will obey God's voice.

I can tell you the truth. Just as you think you are on the right track, the world, the flesh, or the devil steps in and stops you right where you are. Most of us cannot handle demanding situations well, for we cannot trust God's hand.

Where does trouble exist? It has a way of finding us. Most of us have a magnetic on our backs when it comes to a crisis. Typically, danger comes from within. Here for Abram, it was his family.

We see conflict arose with Lot due to the competing wealth and the resulting strife among their workers. They were standing on the mountainside, and Lot knew that going into that mountain would have significant obstacles. Lot's desire was toward ease and the good life, which led him to choose life in Sodom and Gomorrah down in the plains. Later, we will see that while in Egypt, they picked up an Egyptian maid for Sarai named Hagar, who ended up being a significant contention source.

We honestly do not know what would have happened had Abram followed the Lord's will directly, but we are confident that the unlimited abundance of the Lord would have met every need he faced every day.

Would famine have been a problem had they gotten to Canaan in time to prepare for it?

Would he and Lot have been separated, and Lot's family destroyed had he left him behind?

Would his wealth have been proportioned to the Promised Land resources so that he would have provided more immediate leadership among the surrounding nations?

We need to ask ourselves some valid questions as we try to obey God's will in our lives.

Of course, the Word of God has the answer. Listen to *2 Corinthians 9:8* "And God can make all grace abound toward you; that ye, always having all sufficiency in all things, may abound to every good work:"

Abram did not give God a chance to prove His everlasting abundance's unlimited resources because he only obeyed God far enough to still be in somewhat control. When you think about it, we are doing the same thing. Think of what God could do with us if we would only listen and obey. *1 Corinthians 2:9* says, "But as it is written, Eye hath not seen, nor ear heard, neither have entered into the heart of man, the things which God hath prepared for them that love him."

Abram could not have known what God had known from all eternity: all that He had in store for Abraham and the blessings that the nations would enjoy. How could land be given to one from a foreign country, or could a childless man become a father to a great nation?

How could a relatively unknown individual from Ur have his name made great?

Ultimately, how a Savior would arise from his seed would bring forgiveness for all who would trust His name by faith. Abram could grasp none of these matters, and for that matter, even having a history to look upon and the Word of God to hold in our hands, we still have trouble believing God. *Jeremiah 29:11*, "For I know the thoughts that I think toward you, saith the LORD, thoughts of peace, and not of evil, to give you an expected end."

God in His Unsearchable wisdom knows why He does what He does, and He does all things for His pleasure and glory.

In the next few chapters, our prominent figures will be Abram and his nephew, Lot.

So we have come to the end of another chapter, and in the next few chapters, we will take a closer look at the man Abram and his nephew, Lot.

Chapter 12

Even the line of Shem had corrupted itself as we begin this chapter.

In His great Grace, God chose Abram to be the father of a new nation that would honor God and accomplish His will. See *Joshua 24:2, 3*.

But we know what man can and will do. He will either hesitate or rebel or do God's bidding when faced with the will of God. God had to call Abraham twice. The first time he only partially obeyed. If you go back to *Genesis 11*, you will find that Abram lived with his father in Terah in the land of Ur. When God spoke to Abram, he and his family traveled 600 miles to the land of Haran. As you read *Genesis 11*, you can determine through a quick study that Abram's parents hindered him from obeying God.

There is a saying which states that partial obedience is the half- brother to total disobedience.

When one gets out of God's will, you are no longer looking to God but will do what you think is right in your mind, and more than not, it is the wrong thing to do.

How many times have we thought we were doing the right thing and later found out we were not? How many times have we felt we were in God's will and later found out we were sinning against God?

In looking at Abram, we find he became self-willed in his decisions making. It seems to be such an easy trap to make one fall.

I look at my life, and over the years, I thought I was in God's direct will later only to find out I was not. Oh, so hard is to admit, but there is wisdom in saying so. Maybe it will help you not make the same mistake.

The question would come to mind why his parents were a hindrance to him obeying the will of God? Simply because they still worshipped other gods, and Terah did not know the God of Heaven. When you look at the Hebrew meaning of the Word Terah, you will find that it means delay. Abram delayed until his father dies. See **Genesis 11:32**.

As we begin **Chapter 12**, we have the second call of Abram. Those first few verses give us this description of God dealing with Abram.

Maybe we could ask the question, "Who is this man, and what makes him the exception to the day's rule?" When God came to Abram, did He find in him something that made him noteworthy, deserving of the privilege to be bestowed upon him? No, like us, he was granted the opportunity to receive God's calling by grace, not because of any unusual merit that commended him in God's eyes! To put it in today's vernacular, here was a middle-aged, 75 years old married man with an established family business and no children.

He had the advantage of living in an advanced civilization in Ur, probably the largest city in the Tigris-Euphrates area, with an advanced system of writing, educational facilities, math expertise, business, and religious records, great wealth, art, and impressive architecture, like the ziggurats with flowing gardens.

As far as his family history in the region, his was one dating back to Shem, one of three sons of Noah, and like the rest of the people of his area, were steeped in idol worship as the surrounding culture. Ur was down-river from Babel, along the Euphrates.

Looking at him, we can say nothing in particular stands out, which would set Abram apart as someone who deserved special consideration by God. He was one who would become the father of multitudes, the father of the faith, and most significantly, one who would come to be called "friend of God."

Instead, he and his family actually "served other gods," according to **Joshua 24:2**.

There is hope for all if God can find someone in such circumstances and bring blessing in and through them.

Looking ahead for a moment by the time Christ came, certain ones among the Jews thought that only by belonging to their version of Abraham's faith could one ever know God.

They believed that only by adhering to the law could one become a faithful follower of God, which they accepted.

They, like many in our day, could not accept the fact our relationship with God is based not upon our works, but that it is the gift of grace through His Son. See *Ephesians 2:8-9*.

Abram's righteous standing had with the Lord preceded the law by over four hundred years, for we can say his righteousness was by faith, not through the works of the law.

Abraham enjoyed the privilege of God's calling, as do all who come to know Him.

As you can see in *verse 1*, "The Lord had said," which is in the past tense, indicates that this refers to an earlier call. You can see this in *Genesis 11:31, 32*.

When God called him, it was a call to separation. Sometime you should do a study on what it means to be a separated people before the Lord. Only until the death of his father did he become free to do the will of God. Just of interest note, we are free when we receive the death of Christ as payment for our sins. God is still calling His people to separation. See *2 Cor. 6:17*.

Once he got back on track, we see his obedience was by faith.

Let's take a moment and look more closely at this promise of God. The call of God to Abram contained seven excellent provisions to those promises. God said, "I will make of thee a great nation, I will bless thee, I will make thy name great, thou shalt be a blessing, I will bless them that bless thee, I will curse him that curseth thee and in thee shall all families of the earth be blessed."

Let me make a note of these promises again. God said, "Now the LORD had said unto Abram, Get thee out of thy country, and from thy kindred, and the from thy father's house, unto a land that I will shew thee." *Genesis 12: 1*.

This promise came to Abram when he was still living among the cultured people of Ur's land in Mesopotamia, and the Lord did not explain to him, nor show him at that time where he was going to go.

Then God said to him in *Genesis 12: 2* "And I will make of thee a great nation, and I will bless thee, and make thy name great, and thou shalt be a blessing:"

For Abram, this promise must have been particularly intriguing since he and Sarai had been unsuccessful in having any children!

Yet, as we have seen from history, the Lord has kept this promise many times over.

He has demonstrated Israel and then with all who have been grafted into God by faith in His promises. Clearly, to Abram, this promise has been fulfilled, is being filled, and will be until Jesus Christ, the Messiah, comes back.

Then in *verse 2*, God said to Abram, "thou shalt be a blessing." Abram has a distinguished name from an unknown individual living in no meaningful manner in Ur to a more famous man than most who ever lived. Those who bless Abraham and those who curse him will experience the same results as they give to him. Those who dare to curse him will be condemned, and those who bless him will be blessed. See *Zechariah 2:8*.

Abraham received God's promise as a special blessing that would endure through the ages because God never reneges His Word.

But the most potent promise God gave Abram assured him that all the nations of the earth receive blessings in him. Through his seed, salvation would come to people from every tribe, tongue, and nation to know blessing in him. See *Galatians 3:16*.

When the Lord appeared to Abram while he was still in Ur, obviously that Revelation of the glory of God struck him so powerfully that he was willing to give up everything and do anything the Lord showed him to do. See *Acts 7:2.*

What led Abram to take such a radical course of departure from all that he had known for seventy-five years? Was it the conspicuous evidence that proved to him that God could be trusted? We can only speculate here other than what the Word says. There is no doubt it was the glory of the one who appeared before Him. Once he saw God's glory, every other question, every doubt, every point of concern and confusion, paled into insignificance by comparing the Lord God's incomparable greatness.

After this last meeting with the Lord, we find Abram set out by faith in Canaan land.

Our text says that he departed. Again it was by faith, but like many of us, it was a weak faith.

Everything Abram had, he took with him.

It never fails that if one steps out in faith, the devil is right to contest that step.

Note God speaks to Abram over and over again. Have you noticed that God will speak to your heart again when you walk with God, and the devil comes along? I have.

Because of God renewing His promise to Abram, Abram decides to build an altar.

Want to know how we can understand if he was in the will of God?

Think about this, while he was in Haran, God did not come to him, nor did Abram build an altar there. God has an order to follow, and it is this: obedience and then worship and communion.

If we could only learn this, then we would not be like King Saul was so many times!

Finally, he comes to near Bethel. Bethel means "the house of God" and Hai means "a heap of ruins."

Today we stand between the two, but to which are we closer? *I Tim. 3:15*, says, "But if I tarry long, that thou mayest know how thou oughtest to behave thyself in the house of God, which is the church of the living God, the pillar and ground of the truth."

Have you noticed in life that one can be in God's will one minute and out of God's will the next?

After building the altar to God, what does Abram do? He heads in the wrong direction. That is so much like us today. He headed toward Egypt the wrong way. Look at our text. Just let a little trouble come our way, and what do we want to do? Run. Oh, I wished I had been willing to fight more for the cause of Christ!!

Why did worship hold such a high place in Abram's values that he would devote much attention to it refusing to compromise his convictions to get along with his new neighbors, the Canaanites?

Whenever he came to worship, Abram remembered God's eternal promises given to him by the Lord Himself, not once but on several occasions throughout his life. Each time of worship was a time to remember and be renewed in his faith that every Word spoken by the Lord could never break. See *Luke 1:37*.

What He promises is as good as done, and worship serves as a reminder of His promises.

Abraham saw the Lord in His glory once before at Ur, and now again upon entering Canaan, Abram builds an altar as a reminder of God's glorious presence.

Memories of that glory can fade if we remove ourselves from places where it is most visible, so we need to come to worship to be reminded of our Lord God's beauty and presence. When we remember, note how other concerns become less significant in light of God's glorious presence! Far from backing down, from being ashamed that his God was different from everyone else's, Abram was bold about his worship.

He wanted to make it clear to all concerned that he served and worshipped the only true God, the everlasting God. Rather than trying to keep everyone from noticing that he believed differently, he seemed to call their attention to the Lord's unique nature!

I think we could learn from this as well. According to God's promises, Abram knew that he would be a blessing to the nations one day because God would bless them through him.

When we know that God is the Lord, that there is none other, and that He is as He has revealed Himself to be in His Word, what response can we give other than worship?

Abram learned to worship as he knew more of the Lord; worshiping is the only appropriate response before Him.

We say that Abram's family is God's example for all families. The family principles of righteousness, holiness, purity, morality, family values, and fundamental truth have not changed from Abram's day until today.

Why was Abraham was blessed so? It was because he maintained a personal relationship with God. That is the key to being in the will of God. See ***verses 1, 4, 7***. See also the following verses: ***Gen. 15:18; Gal. 3:19-29; Psalm 84:11***.

Walk right, and God will bless you. Abraham maintained a right relationship with God.

He was human and made mistakes, but he trusted God.

He built an altar wherever God led him. Look at his life. His first stop till his last, he was always worshipping God. Indeed, when he sinned by not obeying God, there were times when he went somewhere and did not build an altar. Those times he was out of the will of God, and it is very understandable. Famines should drive us to God. Famines should not force us to the world, which was, in this instance, the land of Egypt. You say, "Why do we have famines in our lives?" Mainly famines are used for discipline and testing. See the following verses for more information: ***Genesis 26:1; Genesis 42:5; Ruth 1:1; II Sam. 24:13***.

We can see what Abram was doing here. No doubt he was thinking the way most think today.

He heard that Egypt had resources for him to come and get, so he went to Egypt, where the supplies were of the world instead of trusting God's resources.

We know this is typical of much physical effort today in the churches.

Here he walked by sight rather than faith. When we turn to the world for help and fail to walk by faith, this will always lead to deeper sin. So what happens in Egypt shows us he was out of the will of God. Once in Egypt, you will do what the rest of the world will do.

Most do not know how to tell the truth. And in this instance, neither does Abram. Fearing lest, on account of his wife's beauty, the Egyptians should kill him, he asks her not to acknowledge that she is his wife, but only his sister. Note this is what is known as a half-truth. Course we know that a half-truth is a whole lie. Because of her beauty, Pharaoh, king of Egypt, took Sarai into his palace and then gave Abram very liberally to her account.

God afflicts Pharaoh and his household with grievous plagues on account of Sarai.

On finding that Sarai was Abram's wife, Pharaoh restores her honorably and dismisses the patriarch with his family and their property and, in effect, tells them they have to leave Egypt. Interesting, isn't it that God uses a heathen man to straighten out a "Christian" man.

Now Abram returns to a familiar place to him. That place is Bethel, which means the house of GOD.

Can we not parallel this with the church today? Of the truth, there has been a famine in the land. But no matter what our need, God can supply it, even during the time of famine.

Yet so many of us are like Abram at this point, not willing to trust God as we should. Elijah and the widow are an excellent illustration of what the church needs to see today.

Elijah had learned the lesson of trusting God, and when he found the widow, he is not going to say to her, we are just going to die together. No.

He told her God's will, and she was obedient to that will, and in return, God blessed bountifully.

The problem is the church has resorted to bringing in worldly things.

As a preacher, I have watched how the church's people have become less respectful of God's things. See how they have replaced reverence to God with an attitude of selfishness. God help the church.

Abraham had to return to the place where he left the will of God. He had to go back to Bethel. Here is the site we each need to find, the house of God. Only till we return can God bless. It is here that we can be in the center of God's will.

The devil is driving so many out of the churches today. He is keeping them out of the church.

Just look at the number of things he is using to do that. Used to Sundays was a day of family get together at the church. Now nobody has the time to go. Many people substitute television evangelist for going to the church. Many people will work, so the only time they have off during the week is Sundays, and they are going to do what they want.

I do not believe you can be in God's will as one of His children if you do not faithfully attend a sound, fundamental, conservative, God-fearing, Bible-believing church. What the church needs to do today is get back to sound doctrinal preaching. The doctrine that will tell you what is wrong.

Bible teaching is excellent, but there has to be a mixture of God-fearing preaching that He can use to stir the heart, revive the spirit within us, move us to the point we will do something. That has ceased in the churches of today. All preachers seem to know how to do is talk. Anyone can speak if you do not want to offend someone.

There is an offense to the preaching of the Word. So be it! That is how I got saved!!

Listen, I believe in the purity of the Word of God. I believe in the preservation of the Word of God. Notice preserved, not pickled. We accept the preservation of His Word. How could we trust God with our salvation for eternity? I believe it is in the blood for redemption. You can spill blood accidentally, but Jesus did it on purpose. I believe in living right. That is what can make you holy before a thrice Holy God. I believe in the bodily resurrection of Jesus.

When he got up from the grave, the Bible tells us that he took the napkin off his face and left it. That tells us He is coming back again. I believe in the Glory of God. Most Christians have their eyes on everything but the Glory of God.

The Bible tells us that Abraham looked for a city, no doubt where God's glory is.

I believe in the spiritual separation of the believer. When faced with separation from worldly things, it seems like most people will only separate when the preacher is around.

Maybe that is why pastors cannot go visiting like they used to. Men of old used to be willing to give their lives for what they believed. That will not fly today. There used to be what many of us would call "Spirit-filled worship."

Look around you today; Most people have lives full of hatred, strife, jealousy, envy, etc.

There is no wonder those on the outside looking in don't want to come in.

Where is the joy, where is the smile, where is God's peace, where is the love there used to be in churches? You can walk into most churches and feel all of these things that we don't need to have in our services. Where is the power of the Holy Ghost? We can't just blame it on the lay-people either. Most preachers don't weep anymore. Preachers indeed get hurt a lot when they give the congregation their heart and soul. They will undoubtedly do them wrong.

But it is also true that you still have to love them. Maybe if we loved these little children more, perhaps some of them would become preachers and missionaries!

God has not quit filling men with the Holy Ghost's power to expose sin in their preaching.

Now that I got that off my chest, maybe we should continue with our text!

While in Egypt, his nephew Lot was with him, and it was the world that would later influence Lot even though he knew what God was doing in Abram's life.

When you think about Bethel in the Bible, it was and still is today that place of surrender.

Bethel was and is that place of public testimony. What do we mean it was a place of testimony? For Abram, it was his testimony as to who God was to him. It was a testimony to the world as to who he was trusting.

From the experiences in life, we can say that anytime someone is willing to surrender to God's trust, He will begin to do something. He is going to test him to see if it is real or not. Naturally, God knows the answer, but He wants the person to know for sure.

Abram was no different. There came a famine in the land, so he did not stay and let God take care of him. Anytime you leave the place of blessing, there is only one way to go, and that is down. Notice Abram went down to Egypt. He should have stayed in Canaan. In leaving Bethel, he notices he turns from believing in God to trusting the world's ways. Notice what he did.

He got Sarah involved in his plans of lying, deceiving, and so on. Abram had to learn that any departure from God's leading will end up in failure. Yet we know he went with Abraham to Egypt.

He saw all that took place in Egypt, including all of the sins of Abram. Later it would influence him to sin against God.

Before closing this chapter, maybe someone would ask was, "why would even go to Egypt in the first place?" The reason he went to Egypt was that he knew those people. Not many people are willing to walk alone in this world. Remember, it is said, "The grass is greener on the other side of the fence."

The world always has something to offer to those who are looking. Nevertheless, a lie is a lie, as we saw happening with Abram. Interestingly we find believers rebuked by the people of the world. Abram had to learn that any departure from God will only bring failure.

Chapter 13

We come now to this chapter, which is divided into three sections. As we will see, the first section deals with Abram. The second section deals with Lot, and the last section deals with Abram.

In the last chapter, we talked about Abram's sins and backsliding and going down into Egypt's land, a world type.

As we have seen for the believer, the world only brings trouble. How often have we listened to those around us and our flesh, and all it got was sadness and sorrow?

As you know, it took a heathen to get Abram thinking right again, so now he heads back to where he walked away from God.

Many times a believer in sin needs to return to the place where his sin began to repent.

If you know where sin began, get rid of the problem before God. How true it is in that we see Abram now separating himself from the world, which is the land of Egypt.

I found that many times when I was out of God's will, he is still looking after us with the hope of returning. Such is the case with Abram.

Even though he was out of God's will, we find God using a heathen man to bless him. Separation from the world always brings blessings, but have you not noticed that the devil can use that blessing against you if you let him.

Sometimes we get overconfident, thinking that self was a part of the recovery. Not so, my friend. After his failures and foolish departures from God's course, Abram found that he accepted back to the Lord when he approached Him in contrite worship.

As we will see, Lot was with Abram, and somehow through Abram, he also acquired great wealth, and we will know that he had a different result with his blessing from God.

To Abram, it seems to have been a blessing, but not to Lot.

To lay a foundation for later thoughts, I believe it was at this time that they brought Hagar out of Egypt, which proved to be a curse. See **Genesis 16:1-3**.

Abram returns to Bethel. As we have said, Bethel means "The house of God." Here is the place for all sinners to get right with God. Think about this; separation is not only from something but to something. Abram returns to the altar and worship.

We have mentioned before, but it is worth repeating that when Abram is out of God's will, there is no altar or worship record. This time we do not see him making an altar or worshipping in Egypt.

Just as an interjectory thought, think about this: Hai means the house of ruin. The only thing between you and destruction is the house of God.

Throughout the accounts of his life, Abram calls upon the name of the Lord with his family.

I want to pause here and just mention some of those names of God for you. Adonai means Lord. Yahweh means LORD. When you see the word Lord in all caps, it means the Lord Jesus Christ the "I AM." Then you have the compound name El Elyon which means God of the Highest. Then you have another compound word El Shaddai which means God Almighty.

Another name we find in the life of Abram is El Roi. Here is the God who sees. Then you have El Olam. Here God is proclaimed to be the Everlasting God. And last we have the compound name Yahweh Jireh which means God who provides.

I mention them because we all ought to be overwhelmed at the abundant provision of our Great God as a child of God. Time after time, you will see Abram as he comes to the altar of worship, overwhelmed by God's provision.

Think about it; he returns from Egypt with greater riches than he had before he left Bethel.

When he returns to Bethel, we will find the Revelation of the promise God had made to him in learning about the Promised Land at the end of this chapter.

Later in **Chapter 15**, we will see the reassurance of the covenant promises God made with him. Later we will see God giving Abram a name change and the significance of it.

Considering all that God, by His mercy, has provided for you, do you not have reason to be overwhelmed and called to worship with a grateful heart?

But in the meantime, we have to talk about his nephew, Lot. In these next few verses, it is evident that Lot is also out of God's will. It is hard to understand how Abram could raise Lot, and Lot turn out the way he did.

Just the way David raised Absalom. Just the way I have raised my children, and they do some of the things they have done.

I remember what I did growing up, and this filtered into my present life with my children.

Note what these following verses say to us. *James 1:14, 15* "But every man is tempted, when he is drawn away of his own lust, and enticed. Then when lust hath conceived, it bringeth forth sin: and sin, when it is finished, bringeth forth death."

I believe the problem here was Lot had not forgotten Egypt and all those beautiful things.

Can you not see what was happening? Although Lot was out of Egypt, Egypt was not out of him.

When Lot turned from Abram, he turned from the way of faith. The strife he had was not between him and Abram. This strife was in him.

He sought the pleasure of his own and would not consider his uncle. Today we call it self- interest or self- righteousness.

He may have been a righteous man, but he was living by sight and senses.

Lot took the route of least resistance. He went to the plains instead of the mountains.

Lot chose the route of lustful reasoning. I say that because of what will happen later on in Sodom. He had his eyes on the grass instead of on God. We know from this that Lot chose the route of fewer restrictions. Look at the morals facing him. We must also address the fact of the consequences facing him. We can say this about Lot. He chose to leave the godly and go and live among the ungodly.

Our text tells us he pitched his tent. Would that be the opposite of following God? There is no reference in Scripture to him having an altar. That tells us he was walking by sight and not by faith; he was always looking at appearances. He looked for the best. He lifted his eyes.

He was leaning on his understanding and not trusting God. Because of this, Lot makes wrong choices.

So the Bible says that Lot pitched his tent toward Sodom. He did not move into Sodom at first, but later on, he did. We will see this when we get to ***Genesis 14:12***.

Many are making the same kind of mistake today. Let me give you an illustration of what Lot did. I would ask you the question, which way is north? Some would point straight up.

Others would look at a map and point to the top of the chart, no matter which way you are facing! How can you be sure? Unless you have a compass, you might find it difficult to answer those questions more than an approximate answer. But then, a compass alone will not give you true north, but only magnetic north where magnetic lines of force converge somewhere in the Arctic Circle, but not at the North Pole.

In the United States, if you stand at a precise longitude somewhere along a line between the Alabama gulf coast and Lake Superior, true north and magnetic north line up. But as you move east toward the Atlantic

Ocean or west toward the Pacific, you have to adjust the reading of the compass to take into account how far the needle has deviated away from true north toward magnetic north.

Since this is not a compass reading class, you will have to take my word for it.

If you were standing in the Grand Canyon and your compass showed north to be one way, you would start walking 15 degrees west of the compass reading for the north to make sure you were on course for true north. You have to make adjustments for compass declination or variation to ensure you are moving in the right direction to go due north.

In our context, we see that Abram and Lot had a family discussion. Others got involved, and I think that some of Lot's family's advice was not sound. They did not know the exact direction in which to go, and Lot listened to them anyway.

If we want to arrive at the destination we are pursuing, we have to make sure that we are working with sound and factual information about our direction. In the account of Lot and Abram, Abram asks Lot, "Is not the whole land before thee?" See *Genesis 13:9*. Lot had to make a choice, to go in one direction or the other.

As you can see in the rest of this chapter and if you read on into *Chapter nineteen*, he made a terrible choice, which resulted in horrible consequences. The Lord presents just such an option before each of us every day. "Is not the whole land before you? What will you decide about which way you will go? Today is the day to set the compass, to order the direction of your days.

There are necessarily three kinds of people in the world: Drifting wanderers lost with no bearings toward true north. They are rebellious run-a-ways who are defiant with no interest in the true north. Then, some prepared explorers are seekers with a clear focus on true north.

The first group needs to know that God is the way, and in Christ, we can find and know Him.

The second group probably knows that God is the way but have hardened them against Him and have rejected Jesus Christ because they refuse to find and know Him.

In either case, these folks are desperately searching and need direction in their lives.

We have a responsibility to show them the way and lovingly introduce them to the one who is the way.

The third group includes the church, the body of Christ, and we need to make sure that we are not losing our way.

There are at least four things in consideration here to make sure we are heading in the right direction. The first thing would be our destination. Notice, they were in Bethel. The mountains were on one side, and the plains were on the other side. The mountains would be hard to face. The plains and the cities would make like easier. Which would you take?

Listen to what *Colossians 3:1-2* says. "If ye then be risen with Christ, seek those things which are above, where Christ sitteth on the right hand of God. Set your affection on things above, not on things on the earth."

What Lot saw as not the promise of God but which way would be more comfortable.

We can say that living the Christian life is hard to do for us today, and the way of the world would be a more natural and more comfortable experience.

But I remind you that Jesus Christ is our true north, the place our hearts can rest and be at home, at peace in their right destination. The pure and most excellent end, the highest calling, the ultimate goal of every person is to live for God's glory!

Not only our destination but secondly look at the direction. Unfortunately, our focus can be confused when we follow false headings and allow ourselves to get lost by following courses that lead us away from our ultimate goal.

Magnetic north is like the best efforts of people to try to make their way to the Lord. ***Proverbs 14:12*** says, "There is a way which seemeth right unto a man, but the end thereof are the ways of death."

God has given wisdom to every possible advantage in the resources made available to us. He has placed the highly sophisticated compasses of life in our hands to help us reach our destination if appropriately used.

Biblical teaching and study opportunities, spiritually gifted people, financial resources, excellent facilities, and advantages we cannot fully appreciate.

But these can all become detrimental if they are not adequately used to find our way to the only destination that matters. There is nothing God would hold back from us, to put it in layman terms, which would keep us from heading in the direction God's will is for our lives.

Next, we see God has given us a description. Listen again to ***2 Timothy 3:16-17***. It says, "All scripture is given by inspiration of God, and is profitable for doctrine, for reproof, for correction, for instruction in righteousness: That the man of God may be perfect, thoroughly furnished unto all good works."

God has given us His Word to describe our path; to us, help us make the necessary adjustments to the compass readings to consider how far off we are from the convergence of true north and magnetic north.

If we allow Him to, He will keep us from deviating, from getting our direction confused, from losing sight of our destination; he will bring correction through His Word. Indeed, this describes who we are to be.

One seeking God's Word but more than that, we are to be like unto God's Word.

Finally, we see our determination. Listen to what ***Isaiah 30:21*** says, "And thine ears shall hear a word behind thee, saying, this is the way, walk ye in it, when ye turn to the right hand, and when ye turn to the left."

God has spoken to us with compassion to encourage us to stay the course, set the compass correctly, and turn neither to the right nor to the left as we seek Him. Just because we think we are heading in the right direction in the way, we seek the Lord does not mean we are. Few pioneers and explorers ever started their journeys intending to get lost; they just lost their bearings along the way.

We need to make sure that our destination is the Lord, not just the journey's adventure.

We need to be sure that the following direction will lead us to our destination and not deposit us at some wasteland far from where we want to go. We need to listen for the voice of the Lord for the description of how to make the adjustments we must make take place promptly so that we do not drift further away despite all of our efforts. We need to have the determination that nothing short of reaching the prize will do for us and make choices daily that will result in that glorious victory one day when we finally reach the destination.

Like Lot, the whole land is before you; your whole life is before you. We should ask you, "Which direction will you choose?"

As long as you will make the journey, why not head for true north, not the magnetic north's false heading? Why not aim for gaining all of Christ, not just moving generally in His direction? What could be more significant gain than reaching the destination, finding the glory of the Lord, and knowing Jesus Christ in all of his fullness?

Today there are subjects that are not mentioned from the pulpits.

That is the subject of backsliding. I would say that most preachers do not even understand the meaning or the process of how it happens.

As we have seen, Lot is a good illustration of not going about our business in life.

The pressing question is, "How did he get to this place of decision in the first place, and didn't he understand the consequences?"

We all make choices in our lives. Sometimes they are right, and sometimes they are wrong. Sometimes we make choices and think we are doing the right thing, and later we find out it was a bad mistake.

Later on, when we get there, you will determine the results and consequences of our choices. After that, we will see that he was involved in a war in kidnapping and oppression and torment by the citizens of Sodom due to Lot's choice. Later in his life, we will find out he lost his material wealth; he would lose his wife and commit incest with his daughters.

All these things happened even though Lot himself was a righteous person, according to Scripture.

The example of Lot should serve as a reminder of the importance of double-checking the decisions we make in our lives. There is no doubt some of the choices we make that significantly affect our lives. Take, for instance, the decision to follow Jesus!

It will determine your place in eternity.

Making this choice to accept Christ will bear on every other decision you make in life.

It will determine whether you follow God's plan or your will. The choices you make can have a lasting effect on your marriage, family, and service to God.

From a worldly viewpoint, your choices are important, for the job market can change drastically in an instant!

Also, think of the decision made when you chose your life long mate. Many times this will, to a great extent, determine your degree of happiness in this life. It also will have a permanent bearing on your children and their emotional well-being! Divorce today seems acceptable in our society,

We understand we all make wrong choices, even in our marriage partners. But understand this, once children come, there is no way to divorce and expect to change what you did.

You will always be the father or mother of the children you pro-created. You would think that choosing a place to live is not essential, but I would remind you it was here in this choice that Lot made his mistake.

We understand the nature of our "Sodom's" and "Gomorrah's"! I am sure you are thinking, how can I make the right choice? Well, it is not hard to do. Just ask God for wisdom. See *James 1:5-8*.

Maybe you would say, preacher, that is too late. Once we have made a wrong choice, what can we do? Do what Lot did. He recognized it, listened to the Angels, obeyed God's Word, and left Sodom and Gomorrah. Do what is right without reservation.

Peter repented after he denied the Lord. He made the right choice. Resolve to serve the Lord.

What did Paul do after persecuting the church? He accepted the forgiveness Jesus provides.

How can I say more than determining to love God? We are to love Him with all your heart and all your soul and with all your strength. Don't let pride keep you from following the will of God.

As we ponder on the example of Lot, it should serve to teach us that making the proper decision is very important. It should help to warn us not to make our choices lightly.

With many preachers in the past, "Remember Lot" the next time you have an important decision.

The final analysis belongs to you making the right choices.

In this final section of Chapter thirteen, there is more information on the man Abram.

After he went back to Bethel and separated from Egypt, he had the task of separating from Lot, his nephew.

I am sure this was a hard thing to do. Nevertheless, it was the right thing to do.

It was only after the separation of Lot did God once again spoke with Abram. Now God shows him what He would for Abram if he would follow Him.

In contrast between the two think about these things. Abram walked by faith, Lot by sight.

Abram was noble in spirit and generous; Lot grasping, greedy and worldly. Abram was a humble man, and we can say Lot was not. Abram looked for a city whose builder and maker was God. Lot looked for a city built by man to be destroyed by God.

Abram is the father of all believers; Lot, the typical backslider of the ages. Abram, is "heir of the world," while Lot lost all his possessions and died in a cave. In the end, we will see life's triumphs come after life's testing.

Chapter 14

As we begin this *fourteenth chapter*, there is a turn made in what is happening in Abram's day. Now we have millions of people and establishments, rulers and kings. The old sin nature is at work.

We see greed walking among men in such a way as never before as they want more and more.

Note, this is the first war recorded in sacred history. Its cause was the rebellion of Sodom, Gomorrah, Admah, Zeboim, and Bela, against their conqueror Chedorlaomer, a prince of Persia. He attacks them with his confederates, routs their forces, plunders their cities, and rests for whose sake this victory is recorded, carried away Lot among the captives.

Furthermore, now Lot began to see the folly in his choice and share in his bad fellow citizens' evil. The Canaanites had invaded the land. With the children of Shem, much was destroyed and taken off. Now they want it back.

For Elam, of which Chedorlaomer was king, descended from Shem, *Genesis 10:22*.

Amraphel king of Shinar, i.e., King of Babylon and some other kings, were together is commonly understood. Interestingly, the King of Babylon would need any associates in a war against such petty princes, as mentioned *in verse 2*. The king of Elam, whose quarrel this was, as appears from *verse 4*, could not fight with them.

The kings of Sodom and Gomorrah thought they could, with probably only a handful of people, in comparison to King Elam's army, rebelled against him after he had brought them under his subjection.

Therefore, we must either take Amraphel to have been some small prince in the Shinar country, i.e., Assyria; if he were king of Babylon, that monarchy was not very significant in the days of Abram.

Moreover, we must also look at the rest as names of some particular places, like Sodom and Gomorrah, over which Arioch and Chedorlaomer reigned. They were like the kings as those in Canaan when Joshua conquered it later.

From what I can gather, everyone was trying to get more and more. What they had was not enough. Greed and ambition were the root causes here.

From our text, we see they took Abram's brother's son, who dwelt in Sodom.

When you think of the choices, Lot made it is easy to see they were bad choices.

You would think one so near Abram's relation should have been a companion and disciple of Abram and wanted to be close to him, but he chooses to dwell in Sodom.

Therefore, he must realize that what happens in Sodom will happen to him.

We can know if we are under God's will, we are under His protection and care.

Stepping out of the will of God, we pull ourselves from under God's protection.

We cannot expect that the choices which are made by our lusts of the flesh should bring comfort without one day bringing some form of restitution.

Interestingly, there is a particular mention made of their taking Lot's goods, which must have motivated him with Abram's strife and his separation from him.

As the preacher spoke recently and said that much of the Old Testament is types and pictures of the Lord Jesus Christ, we can see some in this passage.

This war is a type of war to come, the great battle of the tribulation. So it is a picture of the end times. See *James 5:1-6; Matt. 13:22, 23; I Tim. 6:9*.

The evil ones of this earth will receive the just punishment when Christ comes to rescue His own at His coming.

For sure, we live in the age of wars. Out of the last three hundred years, there has been very little peace, and there will not until the Prince of peace comes! See *Matt. 24:6*.

Abram is here a type of Christ, our deliverer. He intercedes and helps us when we are taken captive by Satan. See *1 Cor. 10:13*. Near the end of this chapter, we see Abram doing precisely that, rescuing his nephew, Lot.

I have often wondered why Abram attempted to rescue Lot, especially since the problem they had. Thinking about this as Christians, we are to be an example to our wayward brethren and help them. I see Abram as a type of the Lord Jesus, who supports God's child when something happens in their lives.

No matter what they may have done in the past. As in the case with Lot, we find that we will be rescued one day from this world of sin as he was delivered. After reading the story of Abram's success in his rescue of Lot is just something to behold.

All he had taken with him in his attempt to rescue Lot was 318 men.

Now we come to the mention of Melchizedek, who is a type of Christ. Even more, we can say this was a theophany of Christ. Melchizedek is the king of Salem. It means the king of peace. Who else, but Christ is the king of peace?

Salem was the ancient name of Jerusalem. He brought forth bread and wine.

The tithe reminds us of the Lord's Supper. For in the Lord's Supper, we see Christ as the bread of life. Furthermore, we know Christ's priest-hood was after the order of Melchizedek. Read *Psalm 110:4*.

Before we go on, we see many typologies here. Speaking of Melchizedek, he has no human descent recorded. See **Hebrews 7:3**. We do not know anything about his death or his birth.

The Bible says he is like unto the Son of God. See **Heb. 7:3**.

Abram gave tithes to him, as we in **verse 20**, the first mention in **Genesis**. There is no indication that God told Abram to give a tithe to Melchizedek.

The Mosaic Law was still over 400 years away. Therefore Abram was not keeping any prescribed command or law of God.

Although Abram was Paul's chief example set down in the Bible for justification by faith, from reading **Hebrews 11**, Abraham may not have been the first. So it is with tithing.

As for Abram, we know that he was a pagan when God first introduced him to Abram.

Probably he may have known about but did not know anything of God personally. It appears that God used him to start all over again. That this why the New Testament writers make so much over him. Without reading between the lines, Abram's tithing to Melchisedec is apparent because he was giving gratefully, voluntarily, and systematically.

There should be no doubt as to Abram being very grateful to God for what He had done.

What a victory he had just won. There is not a possibility of success without God.

Not only had he been able to rescue Lot, which seems the only thing he had intended to do, but he conquered several kings and took spoil from them.

Maybe the thought came to him as to how he could show his thankfulness. There was no church close by, no temple, or anything like that. So an outlet did not present itself until Melchizedek brought forth the bread and wine.

It is here we once again find Abram worshipping the one true God.

We should ask ourselves, "What made Abram respond to Melchisedec in the way he did, and how did Abram know he could safely give tithes to someone he had just met?

One answer is that Melchisedec words were the first Abram had heard about God other than God himself, showing him who He is.

Abram knew something of the one true God. No accident was recorded here. No doubt, Melchizedek appeared at the right time and spoke, exalting God's name, and he felt that he was right in his heart. See **Heb. 6:13-7:4**.

As to what Melchizedek looked like, all we know is what the Hebrew writer states.

In reality, who was Abraham talking too? We do not know for sure. All we know is what Melchizedek said and did.

What did he do? He brought out bread and wine. We see this prefigured both the death and resurrection of Jesus and demonstrated a memorial would come after his death. Of this, we are sure.

What else did he do? He blessed Abram. When Melchizedek blessed him, he knew that there was a direct connection between victory he had just won and this man who had the bread and wine.

Melchizedek verbalized the blessings of Abram. Blessed be Abram. Melchizedek put into words what Abram knew and felt. Note to whom received the blessing and the credit. The victory and blessing went to God.

No doubt, Abram understood this. Here the God of Heaven is also the Creator of heaven and earth. From Abram's response, we know he believed that. How could he not, when he had just seen the person of this Almighty God?

Blessed be the God most high. God wants credit when it is due. He requires honor. God is saying he wanted Abram to respond to him, in the light of the victory he had just given him over his enemies.

Abram knew it was by the power of God that had won the day.

Not only was Abram willing to give gratefully, but he also did what he did voluntarily.

There was no Mosaic Law to be confirmed or conformed. Neither is there any indication that Melchisedec assessed Abram and told him to give a tenth. Melchizedek was not God's revenue commissioner. God puts all of us on our honor to provide voluntarily.

We are to give as unto the Lord. Note, too; we do not read of a promise of another or more blessings if we offer a gift unto the Lord. He gave because he was blessed. He had only one motive. He wanted to give in thankfulness to God.

Not only that, but we read in our text that he gave a tenth of all. That required some calculation on his part. There must have been a careful inventory taken of what he had just won. It was not an estimate; it was a tenth. It was not legalistic in any way because the law did not exist. If your employer pays you a salary or wage by estimating what he thought you should get paid, most would not be too happy. Abram was careful in what he gave.

That is our example. We follow Abram by faith so that we might be called the children of God. See, *Gal. 3:29*.

We follow Him in gratitude that we might be cheerful in our giving as he was. See *2 Cor. 9:7*.

Then we must ask the question as to whom did he pay his tithes too. The answer is Melchisedec. Who was he? He was Jesus Christ personified in the flesh. Christ is our most High Priest. Later, Moses will declare the priesthood to come from the tribe of Levi. We know Jesus came from the tribe of Judah. See *Heb. 7:14*.

When the Mosaic Law came into being, it made tithing legal and binding by the Levi. Read *Num. 18:21*. Thus Abram paid his tithe to Melchizedek. The tithe of Abram prefigures the giving to support the ministry of the Gospel. That is helping the local church today.

How did Abram know to give a tenth? I am sure we do not have all of the conversations between Melchizedek and Abram. Don't you know he must have told Abram what to do?

Chapter 15

W e are thinking of this *fifteenth chapter*, which reminds us that eternity belongs to God.

Time belongs to Man. When we read this, we see Abram needed something from God.

I think we are a lot like that. We need something from God.

Looking at the text, we understand why Abram says what he does. Kings are defeated, but that does not mean they will not come and attack him and try and get their belongings back.

So as he sits there and begins to reflect about his victory over the four kings and wondering what they would do, God says to Abram, "I am thy shield and thy exceeding great reward,"

in *verse 1*. As we think about this, we see that a shield is a defensive weapon.

God said to Abram that He would defend him if those kings came around to bother him.

Most of us have a problem.

We are looking at ourselves and realizing how insignificant we are. Abram, as with men, their memories are short at best. He had already forgotten how God had made some promises to him. We often forget what God has said He would do. Just shows us we have limited vision, or what we have said is tunnel vision. Of a truth, the flesh is weak at best.

Just as God was with Abram, so is He who has put our trust in Him for eternity's blessings.

We live in a day and age we see in much preaching; you can have riches untold and multiply your dollars to thousands and thousands.

God's word never tells us this will happen to every believer. It makes those who desire to follow the will of God angry that so many are misleading today. Very seldom do you see a "rich" child of God?

Jesus told us to lay up our treasure in heaven, not on this earth. Besides, we know that this world's things are only temporal, and we find no happiness in those material things that work iniquity.

I believe Abram understood the promise relating to that one, which was to come. And it would be from his family, in whom all the nations of the earth are should be blessed, but yet we see the doubt in his heart wondering how God would accomplish such a thing.

It is like preaching. Our job as a preacher is to preach the word. Then we know it is up to the Holy Spirit to use that word to move upon people's hearts.

Presently, Abram had no children.

We ask the question, how could God keep His promise to him? God once again promises him he would have a son. And, through his son, this heritage would be as the stars in number.

It is here we see the gap between Abram and the average child of God. As Abram believed by faith in what God said, it was counted unto him for righteousness. Read ***Romans 4:3*** and ***Galatians 3:6-9***.

When we get off track most of the time, we took our eyes off God. We quit trusting Him.

We are no longer dependent upon Him. Self-reliance always gets us into trouble.

So again, God tells Abram to look to Him. The Scriptures tell us there is nothing too hard for the Lord. Abram did understand that he had a new vision, a new commitment, new knowledge, and new promises. Then he once again saw the greatness of God.

Once he saw, he believed. We must be able to see as Abram did. We must consider what Abram did.

When this took place, our text says he went out and offered a new sacrifice to God.

When you believe there will be new commitments made. Be a friend of God by obeying Him, thereby showing we have God just as Abram did.

In the next few verses, we find in the covenant God is making with Abram a seven-fold prophecy. God said to Abram that his descendants would be strangers in a land that is not their own.

In this prophecy, he as told that in this strange land, they would have to serve. God goes so far as to tell Abram how long they would be in servitude there. It would be over four hundred years.

When you read Exodus's book, you will find Israel was in Egypt four hundred thirty years.

During this time, they would suffer.

In the end, God would judge the nation that they served. In the process of leaving, they would bring with them much substance. God spared Abram, and he would die in peace. It took four generations to return to Canaan. Note the following verses for background information: *Exodus 12:40; Psalm 105:37*.

You know we serve an Almighty God, all-knowing God. He is omniscient. There is nothing hid from Him. Therefore we cannot limit God.

Just a thought here in our text, we find Abram impatient with God wanting Him to accept his sacrifice in his time. So what does God do? He makes him wait until His appointed time. See *2 Peter 3:8* and *Psalm 90:4*.

We cannot; we must not try and limit God. He does not work on our schedule.

Remember the new vision based on the latest knowledge of Abram. Now there will be new promises added because of his faith. We need to look to God even after our schedule for something to happen is over, and we should wait. It does not mean God has quit working.

Do you get the idea here in this promise; in this covenant, God gives us a picture of His Son's work. This covenant surrounded the sacrifice of something Abram accomplished.

It will not be accepted until the time is right in the will of God.

So this covenant is based upon a sacrifice, as we see in typology, Christ's death.

If you remember, God made the promise to Abram in *Genesis 13: 15*. It says, "For all the land which thou seest, to thee will I give it, and to thy seed for ever."

Here in our present chapter, we see God keeping His promise to Abram. Look again at *verse 18*. It says, "In the same day the LORD made a covenant with Abram, saying, unto thy seed have I given this land, from the river of Egypt unto the great river, the river Euphrates." We cannot enter into the promised land and call it our home until we have accepted God's Son's sacrifice on a place called Calvary; the blood has to be shed in our stead before God can say, "have I given thee"!

Chapter 16

In *Chapter 16*, we see desperate people do desperate things to justify their lack of faith. Remember, when Abram and Sarai were in Egypt? They brought a handmaid by the name of Hagar with them.

In our previous chapter, we saw a man of great faith. In this chapter, we will see a man of great unbelief in those very promises God had just made to him.

I do not know about you, but it is hard dealing with impatience. I can only imagine what God must sometimes be thinking.

Is it hard to wait on God in your life? How often have we prayed and prayed about something and then finally gave up on God answering that prayer only to quit and almost in the next instance, see God's hand at work?

In our text, we see the unbelief of Abram is the cause of his impatience. As we said in the last chapter, we should, as Abram should have been willing to wait for God's perfect timing.

God had told him that he now had a son from his loins! I take that to mean him and Sarai.

God did not need man's help to do something.

In *Chapter 15*, Abram shows excellent faith. Here, he lacks the patience to wait on God and let God fulfill his promise to him. See *Heb. 6:12*.

You have heard it said patience and faith must go hand in hand. Sarah was saying God has failed me, and we have to do something. She should have said nature had failed me, but God is my resource. How different the outcome would have been.

Like King Saul, who, when he looked at David and then looked at the Philistine, said in *1 Sam. 17:33*, "And Saul said to David, Thou art not able to go against this Philistine to fight with him: for thou art but a youth, and he a man of war from his youth."

Yet the question in David's heart at the time was not whether He was able or not.

God was able, and he knew the answer to that question before he asked it. What do you do when you look for direction and conclude the answer is not there? How often have we said, Lord, what are you going to do? And before God does anything, we do something wrong!

We need to learn not to try and help God out. He does not need our help.

Have we gotten out of God's will by doing what we wanted rather than following God's will?

This sin of impatience can be a deadly sin. We must not try and fit God to our timetable or schedule but learn to wait in Him. Is it possible to attain this in our lives? I do not know if I will ever achieve this in my life. That is the greatest sin I face day by day. I know He simply wants us to walk obediently, following him. What can we do to help Him? How can the weakling help the Almighty? The flesh tells us we can.

Just like Abram and Sarah, we need to understand faith and patience go together. How often have we believed God and then became impatient for Him to do what He had promised and jumped in ourselves and tried to do it?

We wanted to do it, and when we tried to do it, we made a mess of things. The thing is it was not when God wanted us to do His will.

Not many years ago, a song came out, and the title of it was, "I did it my way," by Frank Sinatra. We are doing it our way instead of God's way. Why does God allow these quiet times in our lives, especially if we try to determine His direct will for our lives?

One reason must be that He is trying to prepare us for the answer He is about to give us.

Our little grandson at the time of this writing often says, "Papa, I want it right now"!

Sometimes it takes God time to prepare our hearts and minds and even others' hearts and minds. So He allows time to pass on. Sometimes it is to test our faith. Then sometimes, we can have absolute assurance that God is going to do something.

If He were to give us an immediate answer, our faith would not grow. So He allows time to slip by. All the time, we become more and more impatient, waiting for God to do something.

We just want God to get on with it. Remember, God will not ask us to do something He has already done. It is not our responsibility to figure out how, when, or where the answer will come. We should leave all of that in God's hands. That is God's business.

Surely they can be even to correct us if we let him. Since we know that God has promised, we should just trust Him to do what He says He will do.

Often I have found these waiting periods make us begin to allow our faith to waver, and we begin to wonder what God is doing.

The thing about God is that He knows how to get our attention. Sometimes like in the last chapter, He wants us to sacrifice unto Him. It is not that He has not promised He has.

Sometimes we need to have a new attitude. Occasionally there may be sin in our lives, and He wants us to get that right before moving on. We often come to these times of silence when He isn't saying or doing anything but waiting on Him. How many times has God been working behind the scenes to get things right, and we could not see it?

How often have we felt God's leadership, and then we just got into the middle of it and made a mess of things without waiting on him. Then God has to spend time straightening out the mess we just caused. If only we had waited for Him.

Think of the timeline here. We know Abram left Haran at the age of 75. He was 86 when his son Ishmael was born. See **Genesis 16:16**. He was 100 when Isaac was born. See **Genesis 21:5**.

Ten years have gone. Year after year waiting and still, there is no son, no descendant, and no heir. Time is running out for them physically. Like most of us, they begin to plan on what to do.

First, we will begin to see how Sarai starts to plan on helping God out.

Again, we see Eve's impersonation for Sarai, who is in the lead and taking the initiative.

We would probably respond in the same way. In Abram's day, for a Hebrew woman, not to bear children was a shame. It meant blame on the husband and especially the wife. She became, as it were, a rejected vessel of the community. Surely there delight is in having children, so it was very significant. Sarai owns a slave, a concubine named Hagar.

During that time, the custom in Egypt was that if the house's woman could not bear children, she could give her maid to her husband and be his wife.

Understand that while they were in Egypt, they were out of God's will at this time.

No doubt, Abram was satisfied with one wife, even though the day's custom was quite different.

The thought was that if the second wife could bear a child, that child became the possession of the first wife, therefore able to carry on the family name. What happened is this.

God will frequently make promises or give us indications or show us his will and then come a silent period in his reasoning.

We, in turn, respond in a hostile, fleshly way, trying to help God out while all the time, all we had to do was just waiting for God to move. So Abram listened to her.

Satan is subtle and very smart in that he uses the one we are closest to bring across and idea.

He knows we will listen to them.

We must be cautious in listening to the advice of those around us. No doubt, Sarai was as sincere as could be. Satan knew how to get them off track. He uses those close to us because they may see us suffer a little and don't like that. From Sarai's point of view, it was a very sacrificial thing to do. Inwardly it must have caused her much humiliation and rejection.

The advice we receive from others can be sacrificial and costly to them.

We should ask another question. The question is, "Is there advice consistent with what you know? Is it what God has shown you?"

If it is not consistent with God's promises and the principles, we must not obey, regardless of how wonderful it may seem.

How many times have you been in trouble because of this? Note this is where a lot of us get into trouble. The argument is; she is my wife, and they are just trying to look after our best interest. The issue is: is this the will of God? Sarai made a terrible mistake. It looked right, but it was not right.

So often we try to make a door or some way when there is not one. If only we would not force the issue and let God work it out. If you don't, you will be sorry for it and the results.

One of the primary reasons for our trying to help God out is thinking logically or reasonable or rational.

Our logic is to put God in our box. Do we think this works? Other women had done and were doing what she was thinking. That is the way the world is doing it. Not for one minute would God have you do what the world is doing. Instead, they are listening to the voice of the flesh or Satan. Never look around you for answers. Always take an upward step. We are to walk a different way from the world.

If God is silent, be still, and let a loving God give you the answer in His time. When Sarah convinced Abram to take Hagar as his wife, immediately, something happened. Here was a man, contented with his wife, now having two wives.

There was no doubt when Hagar became pregnant, that made things change. The blame solely rests on Sarai. Bitterness, hatred, resentment, hostility, division, anger, rejection all flooded into her soul.

Immediately she began to criticize her husband and Hagar. There became instant turmoil.

When we try and help God out often, the one we love most winds up getting hurt the most.

Abraham is now guilty of having sex with Hagar. Sari deals with Hagar by hard and harsh means.

Hagar leaves with Ishmael. Near a well, God promises to her that her son would be a father of many.

We know that the Arab nations come from Ishmael. We also know that God did not recognize the marriage between Abram and Hagar. We know that Ishmael was Abram's son but not the promised seed. See *1 Cor. 15:46*.

Let me conclude here by saying that Hagar and Ishmael represent law-works-salvation.

To be in the will of God, you cannot attempt to help God out.

There is no faith or grace involved. Ishmael is born after the flesh. Sarai and Isaac represent grace-salvation. We live by the matter of faith and trust in God, which leads to freedom and liberty in Christ. Isaac was born through this promise.

We see grace versus the law. It is evident, for it is the battle of the ages.

We find contrast in our text. Sarai, who is grace, had a handmaid by Hagar, who represents the law, being her servant. The purpose of the law is to be our schoolmaster bringing us to Christ.

Notice the results of their sins. There were thirteen years of barrenness for Abram. See *Genesis 16:16; 17:1*. Often there can be far-reaching results of sin. We see this in the Israel-Arab conflict down through the centuries till now. We discover the Muslim religion, and its founder Mohammed is the offspring of Hagar.

She is the wife of Abram. If only there had been no Ishmael, how the world would be different today.

Chapter 17

In this chapter, we explain the covenant God made with Abram in *Genesis 15*. At this time, he was ninety-nine, thirteen years after Ishmael's birth. I would think this was a long time for him not to talk with the Lord.

To begin this chapter, we find that God is called the Almighty God in *verse 1*. The significance is because the actual Hebrew here is "El Shaddai," which means I am God all-sufficient.

That is, He is willing to pour out a blessing to Abram. I am God who pours out blessings, which gives them richly, abundantly, continually.

Isn't it interesting that God does not outright condemn Abram for his sin but says to him, be thou perfect? An aged saint of God must expect to live more by faith and less by experiences as the years go. Sometimes, when we have cause to fear because of our sin, we should expect God's hand upon us.

Maybe this is the reason it had been such a long time since God had spoken with Abram.

Note the humble posture he appeared in before God. It is on his face. It is true, the closer our walk to God, the more shall we feel our sinfulness and vileness before him. The spots that were unnoticed in the twilight are apparent in the noon-day. God's desires from each of us are reverence and holy awe that should be upon our heart and countenance when we speak before God. It has been said, "When we go before God in worship, God will be found near us in blessing."

Here Abram once again faces God. Abram is weak and frail in all he is and has done.

In our human efforts, it does not take much to realize what kind of God he is.

Here God presents himself as the Almighty God.

It was Jesus who said in **Matt. 5:48**, "Ye shall be perfect, as your Father, who is in heaven is perfect." Nevertheless, what does this imply?

It means saved from all the power, the guilt, and the contamination of sin. Here is only the negative part of salvation, but it also has a decisive role. The ideal thought is we are to be perfect as our father, who is in heaven, who is complete. It is to be filled with God's fulness.

It is to have Christ continually dwelling in our hearts by faith. It is to be grounded and rooted in His love.

Remember how God created us? We are in His image and likeness, or at least before sin.

Before man broke the commands of God, this is his state. Furthermore, this is the state into which every human soul must attain who would dwell with God in glory.

Sin is gone, death is defeated, and Christ is reigning.

How would you like this to be part of your life? The privilege is yours for the asking.

You will then understand the omnipotent love, the infinite merit of the blood atonement.

Thank God, it does not stop there, for we have the all-powerful and purifying presence of the Holy Ghost in our lives.

In your state as a sinner, how could you possibly dispute God over being saved?

God makes it as plain as day to us that the blood of Christ cleanseth from all sin.

Interestingly, in our text, we have the number thirteen mentioned. That is an unusual number to be found throughout Scripture.

Here in our text, it represents thirteen years of unbelief, rebellion, and apostasy. See *Genesis 14:4*. The number thirteen in Scripture represents trouble for the child of God.

Records show Solomon took seven years to build the temple and thirteen years to make his house. See *I Kings 6:38* and *7:1*. There was the number thirteen connected with the sin of Haman in Esther's day. See *Esther 3:12, 13*. It was thirteen judges who ruled during the apostasy in the days of the book of Judges. In the Book of Revelation, is the word "Dragon" found 13 times? There were twenty-six unclean animals and birds in *Deut. 14*. Paul received 39 stripes.

Back in our text, we find Abram again is told he is to be the father of many nations.

When studying history, you will find the Israelites, Ishmaelite, Edomite's, and others who came from him. Later on, after that the Gentiles had been drafted in, we would become Abraham's spiritual seed.

Here is the reason for his name change in our text. Abram means "high father," but Abraham means "Father of many nations." The everlasting covenant was with Abraham and his offspring, which would include Canaan as an everlasting possession.

By God's order, Abram's name changed to Abraham, correspondent to the promise; I will make thee a father of many nations. A new name is a unique honor, but it is better still; it confirms his faith.

What God calls him; is what God wants him to be. Though the children are unborn, faith gives subsistence to the things we hope. We all realize we are descendants of Abraham, Isaac, Ishmael, and the sons of Keturah. But in a more elevated and extensive sense, he is the faithful father, his seed is yet more numberless, and everyone will become a son.

Next, in our text, we see circumcision, the sign of the covenant. You would probably ask, "Why, circumcision?" Why not some other way?

God used this part of the body, rather than in any other, to denote in particular, His covenant so that man would understand that it was and is to be a holy seed, consecrated to him from the beginning. It is a usual process for the pagans cutting and making marks on their bodies when they worshipped their gods. The purpose here was to show or designate that part of the male body to God's glory, which propagated humankind.

His was for the purpose or token of the Divine covenant made with Abraham and his posterity that God would multiply their seed and make them the stars of heaven. See *Genesis 15:5*.

Not only did Abraham get a name change, but so did Sarai. Her name would be Sarah.

Interestingly, the same letter is added to her name that was to Abraham's, and for the same reasons.

Sarai signifies my princess as if her honor were confined to one family only. Sarah represents a princess--namely, of multitudes, or meaning that from her he Messiah the Prince should come, even the Prince of the kings of the earth.

We could ask, "Shall a child be born to him that is a hundred years old?" See the faith once again of Abraham. *Romans 4:20* tells us that, "He staggered not at the promise."

Then we have Abraham's prayer for Ishmael: O that Ishmael might live before thee! See *Genesis 17:18*. If a man is a man of faith as Abraham was then, he would desire the best for his children. I believe this is the case with Ishmael. He prays that God would not forsake or abandon him.

Shouldn't our desire for our children be that they might live before and for Him?

Might they see God's grace, which we have seen and accepted and believe it and trust that grace for their salvation?

Just like God did for Abram, He will bless them and give them many blessings.

That is our desire. God answers his prayer, and it is an answer of peace. See *Genesis 17:20*.

Then God repeats his promise to Abraham and for his son to be born of Sarah.

God reminds Abraham that he will establish my covenant with him to be Sarah's birth through his son.

God promised a son but not of the bondwoman, but by Sarah. Sarah shall share with Abraham in the blessing; she shall be the kings and nations' mother.

This permanent sign will endure forever.

Today we use baptism instead of circumcision for the sign of God's covenant. Necessarily they mean the same. We now accept Christ and His gift of salvation by the work He accomplished, giving us a new life in Him. The rite of circumcision was bloody, painful, and humiliating. There is a clear picture and type which denotes repentance, self-denial, and a desire to follow Christ exemplified.

It is necessary as a sign to put away the filth of the flesh and become holy as He is holy.

Remember, Abraham did what God asked in circumcision, and so the example he was we see later his people would follow him in this rite.

He also says to sinners in general in **Isaiah 55:7**, "Let the wicked forsake his way, and the unrighteous man his thoughts; Repent, and believe the Gospel; and, except ye repent, ye shall perish."

God has also set forth the terms of the agreement by which he will supply blessing abounding.

Surely we all understand that we cannot have God's grace upon us without faith and obedience to His will.

However, we must also understand that just being in the will of the Lord does not guarantee to be exempt from suffering for Christ's cause.

Let me give you an illustration in paraphrase called "Pushing the Outhouse." As a young boy, I can relate to this story. The little boy, like me, lived in the country. When growing up, we did not have running water in the house. That meant there was no toilet in the house. There was a little building called an outhouse. Just about everybody hated to go out there, especially during the wintertime when it was so cold. As the story goes, the boy decided to push the outhouse into the water. Just saying, there could be a problem with doing this. Later, after the boy did his thing, his father came to him and told him they needed to make a trip to the woodshed.

Growing up, we all knew what it meant to go to the woodshed. Boy, would it hurt!

Well, like most kids being inquisitive, the young boy asked the dad why? The dad said because someone pushed the outhouse into the water, and he believed it was the boy.

Well, the boy told the truth and admitted it was him. Then he said something like what I would have said. He said, you remember when George Washington's father asked him if he cut down the cherry tree. He did not get into trouble. That is right, son, but he was not in the cherry tree either when he chopped it down.

Chapter 18

G od made promises made to Abraham and Sarah. The promise was a son would one day come and be the Messiah, the world's Saviour. Admittedly, most are impatient.

When it was made known to her, she would have a child; her response would be like today.

He had not yet been revealed, but God knew from what line he would come. Remember, this promise was foretold centuries ago. In God's process, promising them a son, we see that God often takes His time. By the time God revealed his plan and completed it, Sarah was past childbearing age. She laughed, but today we would say, "Are you kidding?"

Listen as God spoke these words to Abraham. *Genesis 18: 13-14*, "And the LORD said unto Abraham, Wherefore did Sarah laugh, saying, Shall I of a surety bear a child, which am old? Is anything too hard for the LORD? At the time appointed, I will return unto thee, according to the time of life, and Sarah shall have a son."

We are arriving near the end of Abrahams's life. Remember where he came from and the initial problems he had following the will of God.

In his leaps of faith, we can see grave doubts and flare-up along the way of his life, just like in the rest of us. As his experience grew in trusting God, we find that he had a firm belief in God's enabling power in the end. Like us, he often seemed to lack faith in God, but he was willing to try and succeed he did. He made his way to Canaan's land in obedience to the Revelation He received from God in *Genesis 12: 1-3*.

First, we find God once again visits Abraham in the form of three persons. We have a theophany of Jesus and two angels with him as they approach Abraham. Coming up to his home, Abraham sees three people, and when they arrive, he invites them in the custom of the day was to prepare a meal for the guests, and so he does.

As they talk, he finds that once again, God comes to speak with him and renews the promise of a son by his wife, Sarah. Sarah is in the back and overhears the prophecy and laughs because she is old and past childbearing age.

In the process, Sarah's reproved by God confirms the promise again. This time God rebukes her upon her denial.

Now the angels tell Abraham why they were there. They were going to destroy Sodom.

Abraham knows that his nephew Lot is there. Sodom and Gomorrah needed to be either restored or destroyed. According to the assessment of the Lord, and this was the only opinion that mattered.

The same is true for our nation today. Will we be a part of the restoration or participate only in its further destruction? Facing the inevitable catastrophe of God's judgment on Sodom, Abraham cries out for the Lord to withhold the severity of His condemnation.

He prayed that the Lord would bring forth 50, then 45, then 40, 30, 20, and finally ten righteous people giving sufficient grounds for calling a halt to His plan to destroy this wicked city.

Every time of restoration of a people begins with a persistent intercessory prayer by someone willing to take their case before the throne of grace.

With the corrupt nature of our land crying out against us, what shall we pray to see the restoration of the righteous reign of the Lord among us? It is challenging to break through to penetrate the defenses of people who have hardened their hearts to find safety within their chosen dark realm.

Abraham prayed, hoping that in Sodom, there were still some hearts reached, even some lives that were not so far gone that all flesh had turned to stone.

Today, as you pray, understand that we seldom can influence people toward the Lord and His righteousness. Usually, we have to learn to break up the fallow ground before we begin to see any progress for Christ.

I see something interesting in Abraham's prayer of intercession. God is a righteous, holy, and just judge, ruler of the earth. He wants all to know this. How much of our intercession arises from our concern for the name of the Lord to be protected?

Although Abraham may have been gripped by his concern for the people of Sodom, for his nephew Lot, his prayer reflected another fear that God's name not be called into question, that His ways do not give grounds for turning away from Him.

The ground for keeping our intercession persistent, never wavering, is the honor of the name of the Lord.

When the main reason for my praying is for God's name to be known as glorious and His reputation upheld with honor, I know that I agree with Him when I pray.

Throughout the Scriptures, we repeatedly read all that is done, do for His name's sake. See *Ezekiel 36:22-23* for an example.

As we see the needs of our church's culture and our own lives, as we pray for restoration and revival, we must do so by interceding for darkness to be pierced, for hard hearts softened, and for God's name to be protected and honored.

You understand that in a godless culture, they do not tend to spend much time thinking about the consequences of their actions. The passage in Luke, where Jesus speaks of Sodom, reminds us that most folks will simply ignore such thoughts and never attend to what matters the most. See *Luke 17:28*.

Observing today, no one seems overly concerned; no one seems to care about where the Lord fits into the scheme of things until it is either too late or until He breaks through, intervenes, and motivates people to turn from themselves and Him.

Restoration only comes when folks have their hearts turned back to the Lord, reminding us how essential a role prayer plays in all of this. When the Lord finally breaks through, we find three things motivating us to seek restoration, renewal, and revival.

Once we understand the actual, undiluted consequences of evil, no one needs to explain what fear is.

Abraham saw what was about to happen, and honestly, it scared him into his prayer for the protection of Sodom and his nephew Lot. His fear of the awful destruction of God's wrath poured out on Sodom prompted him to pray with boldness and persistence he had not demonstrated before.

People who have no fear of judgment, no fear of the Lord, no grasp of the pure offensiveness of sin, ramble along and forget that postponed is not the same as canceled when it comes to God's judgment.

Another motivation for seeking revival and restoration arises from compassion for those facing condemnation. What a powerful motivation if we take God's judgment against sin and evil because we realize how deadly divine justice will be upon all who have rejected God's pardon for condemnation.

From the way we function, one would have to conclude that either we are hard-hearted creatures who care nothing about our fellow human beings' souls or do not believe that condemnation will ever happen. Ultimately, not many fear judgment, and not many have compassion for the lost. How can there be restoration and revival with it?

Chapter 19

There is an illustration I would like to begin. Years ago, I heard a story about who was a better father. One boy said his dad could write something on a piece of paper called a poem, and he could get $100. The second boy told that his dad could write a few words on a piece of paper called a song, and he could get $1000. The third boy said that is nothing. His dad could write something called a sermon and that on Sunday's, it took four men to collect the money.

How many of you saw the commercials recently from a cable company where the son asks a question about the lack of cable channels and the father responds with the line, "we're settlers, we settle for things," implying that the users of other cable options were settling for less than the best?

Unfortunately, we have that same thing happening in the church world today. Many professing Christians are "settling" for less than God's best, and even worse, they are settling for what the world has to offer.

Lot is an example of just such an individual.

I want to start what I want to say in this chapter by taking you back to where the problem first began with Lot. We ask ourselves, "What was the appeal of Sodom?" You have to go way back to *Genesis 13:10*, which says, "And Lot lifted up his eyes, and beheld all the plain of Jordan, that it was well watered everywhere, before the LORD destroyed Sodom and Gomorrah, even as the garden of the LORD, like the land of Egypt, as thou comest unto Zoar."

You can understand in the flesh how Lot must have felt. All this time, he was with Abraham and had to do whatever he said. Being human means, you will and are going to make mistakes.

Now he had an opportunity to get out on his own and see if he could become wealthier, having a life of his own. Besides, he could live like he wanted to. But oh, the consequences of miscalculating the decisions he was making.

However, for the most part, we cannot comprehend the consequences of our actions and decisions.

Now the damage has been done. You would think he would live as he received teaching.

But not so.

One of the first things to go was his lifestyle. On his part, this was a crucial mistake.

For one thing, we know both Abraham and Lot were nomadic. They had no permanent dwelling place.

There was one objective Abraham had from God. He, in the book of Hebrews, is told he was looking for a city. God made it.

Lot didn't know about city life. He had never seen the bright lights of the city and all that goes on there. *Genesis 13:12* said that Lot "... and pitched his tent toward Sodom."

Originally, Lot must have pitched his tent in the plain of Jordon. However, it did not take him and his family long to move to the city. The way sin works are just going step by step in that direction, and you will find your goal. Before long, a radical change has taken place, and he does not realize it. We ask ourselves, "How did Lot become acclimated to Sodom?"

The word acclimated means to adjust to a change in environment or status. We see Lot got used to the dark! Remember that *Genesis 13:13* says the men of Sodom "were wicked sinners before the Lord exceedingly."

There is another story I would like to mention about Vance Havner. He went into a dimly lit restaurant and just ordered. He ate his meal by faith and not by sight. The dimly lit room and not being able to see fit our text. If you stay in the room long enough, you will eventually be able to see.

The illustration helps us see how Lot became acclimated to the darkness. He got used to the darkness. At first, he was uncomfortable. Gradually he became accustomed to the shades of sin and depravity he was experiencing. Listen to *2 Peter 2:7-8*, which say, "And delivered just Lot, vexed with the filthy conversation of the wicked: For that righteous man dwelling among them, in seeing and hearing, vexed his righteous soul from day to day with their unlawful deeds;"

The word "vexed" means sorely distressed or troubled.

With Sodom and Gomorrah having the problems of its lifestyles exposed, it is not hard to see the trouble Lot had.

What did Lot lose because he settled for something less than the will of God for his life?

We can start by saying that if you settle for Sodom, you will lose your values through a loss of moral direction. When he lived with his uncle Abraham, everything seemed so clear; right was right and wrong, but when it came time for him to make these decisions on his own, he did not see things as black and white but shades of gray. Notice again the context of *Genesis 13:8-13*.

Lot knew the reputation of the cities of the plain. What comes to mind when you think of Las Vegas, NV? Have you heard, "What happens in Vegas stays in Vegas, right?" Think of the city of New Orleans. What does that mean to you? "Laissez Les bons temps rouler!" We hear this Cajun expression, meaning, "Let the good times roll!"

There is a contemporary equivalent to Sodom in our culture, at least by reputation, if not, San Francisco, CA.

Lot knew what he was doing but chose to disregard the reputation of these cities. He lost his "moorings," his "anchor," his desire for material success overrode his inner compassion to do what was right. He lost his way, and the only thing that stood between him and destruction was our merciful God's intervention.

Have you noticed what happened with Lot? He lost his moral discernment. More times than not, this is what happens to us. There is a new and very telling statement from the Lord in **Hosea 7:8, 9**, which says, "Ephraim, he hath mixed himself among the people; Ephraim is a cake not turned. Strangers have devoured his strength, and he knoweth it not: yea, gray hairs are here and there upon him, yet he knoweth not."

How does your hair turn gray or loose, for that matter? The answer is obvious. Unless you are dealing with severe disease, it turns a hair or two at the time. My hair didn't turn gray overnight; it came over some time. The same thing happened in Lot's life. His ability to discern right from the wrong is impaired by his continued exposure to Sodom's corruption culture. As we see this downward spiral taking place in this digression, there was also a loss of moral discrimination.

Now we are back in **Genesis 19**. Lot had come to the point that he could not notice the subtle differences in his life. When you begin to compromise or cut corners morally, you also have difficulty with the details of moral and ethical living. Lot had his eyes closed to his surroundings and did not care what was happening, not even his family.

Can you imagine where Lot was moral if he is willing to offer his daughters to this mob?

Do you think the men of Sodom would listen to him now? It is true; if you settle for Sodom, you lose your voice to challenge those around you. See **Genesis 19:7, 9**.

When Lot stepped outside the door of his home, he could not challenge them, not even with his daughters' offer.

Have you said, "Don't judge me, or you have no right to judge me?" That is a famous slogan today. Lot's problem was a loss of influence. He had lived among these people until there was very little difference between the way he lived and the way they lived. In our text, we see that Lot could not change them. See **Gen. 19:14**.

The angels asked if Lot had any other family, and Lot went to them to warn them about what would happen.

Finally, we see the results of Lot's life on the margins of disobedience. He had spent these years in Sodom as a nominal believer without values and a voice for God when it mattered the most.

Next, we see that if you settle for Sodom, you will lose your values and your valuables.

The old saying is true, which says our lives may be the only Bible people read. There was no church in Sodom. Unfortunately, there was no witness there.

Israel's nation is in its infant stage in this chapter, but the one thing God required of them and us is that we be a witness for Him. We do not need to know much.

Just that there is one God, the Creator of all things, and He deserves to be honored and worshipped exclusively.

There is no doubt that Lot could have been a witness for God, but he failed miserably.

What happened to the godly character his uncle must have instilled in him.

Where were those qualities of a godly man and his conduct?

What did Lot lose? First and foremost, he lost his family. Would you accept that kind of lifestyle for your family? It says Lot "lingered" and had to be led out of Sodom by the angels. Look at *verse 16*. His sons-in-laws "laughed" in *verse 14*. According to *verse 26*, Lot's wife looked back toward Sodom. Do you say what is wrong with that? It showed she had a heart for that wickedness, and because of that, she became a pillar of salt. Someone said, "You got Lot's wife out of Sodom, but you couldn't get Sodom out of Lot's wife!"

Later in this chapter, we see his daughters "lay" with their father and were with their father's children, what a sad situation. See *verses 33-36*.

The real tragedy is that these young women had no Biblical convictions to stand as a "firewall" to prevent this behavior. They had no problem justifying their decisions and vividly demonstrated the rationalization that we see today.

Philosopher Herbert Spencer wrote, "Not education but the character is man's greatest need and man's greatest safeguard."

Chuck Swindoll wrote, "Character is the moral, ethical, and spiritual undergirding that rests on truth, that reinforces a life in stressful times, and resists all temptations to compromise."

Here is what God would do with us.

He wants to develop our character, refining it to honor Him. If we have the kind of character God desires, we can interpret His will for our lives.

We are living in a time that looks more and more like Sodom each day.

Let me tell you four things in the closing of this chapter that helps us see that are comparable to Sodom. First, there is a hatred of Scripture. In our culture, there is a hatred of the Bible and everything that it stands for. Look at the efforts to remove any mention of the Bible or the Ten Commandments from public life and thought. Christians have sat on the stool to do nothing and allowed this cultural cleansing to occur with all its implications.

No more is the Word of God mentioned in so-called seminaries and churches. There is a spiritual cleansing happening in our world today. And we just sit idly by as if nothing is going on.

God help America.

Second, there is a total loss of shame, morally and spiritually speaking. Listen to ***Jeremiah 8: 12*** "Were they ashamed when they had committed abomination? Nay, they were not at all ashamed, neither could they blush: therefore, shall they fall among them that fall: in the time of their visitation they shall be cast down, saith the LORD." Then there is ***Zephaniah 3:5***, which says, "The just LORD is in the midst thereof; he will not do iniquity: every morning doth he bring his judgment to light, he faileth not; but the unjust knoweth no shame."

Third, there is a direct lapse in society for anything right. There are no moral standards and no absolutes to govern behavior, and "every man does that which is right in his own eyes!"

The supreme judge of behavior is the man himself, for God is demoted from the churches, and man becomes more and more defiled.

There has been a total lack of separation from the world and the flesh in our homes and churches.

Lot's problem is our problem! Notice the churches around us today. There seems to be very little difference between the lifestyles of Christians and non-believers. Survey after survey reveals this disconnect between Christian creed and Christian conduct. Biblical separation has been marginalized and devalued to the degree that the church has very little influence on God's culture and good!

What does the Bible say? Please read *2 Corinthians 6:14-18*. Here is a commentary of us today. The question is, why? Sodom had no Bible, but Sodom did have Lot, and he had no influence for God in this wicked place.

There is another illustration of what I mean. I say illustration, but in retrospect, it is fitting and sad at the same time. A so-called Christian landed a job in a profane factory in the world.

On the job, he never said a word the whole day. At the end of the day, after arriving home, his wife asked him how it went, and he made the statement that no one knew he was a Christian.

Not only is that our problem today, but it was Lot's problem.

There was no witness for God, no one to cry against the sins of Sodom, no one to warn them of coming judgment.

Lot is a perfect example of "...salt that had lost its savor..." See *Matt. 5:13*. There are many people like Lot in our day. Why do you think that we are witnessing the decline of our great country?

Christians are called to be "salt and light," but by far, we are neither; the salt has lost its savor!

Genesis 19: 9, "And they said, Stand back. And they said again, this one fellow came into sojourn, and he will needs be a judge: now will we deal worse with thee, than with them. And they pressed sore upon the man, even Lot, and came near to break the door."

They had no respect for Lot's witness because of his compromising, accommodating, appeasing lifestyle!

We have been to England where there is a plaque on a church building, which states from the year 1653, a man named Sir Robert Shirley had one desire, and it was to do the best of things in the worst of times.

That should be our desire for the things of God.

In history, that statement made by Sir Robert Shirley was during the worst of times. His king was King Charles; a king tried for treason, and for that crime was beheaded. There was much injustice in the land, Churches harassed, and many had to close. Oh, it was a dark time in history.

Will this be said of America today? So I would ask you, "What are we doing? I see nothing but darkness and only a glimmer of light. Look around you. We are living in perilous times today. War, hatred, anarchy, divorce, child abuse, drug abuse, and pornography seem to be the day's rule. "Everything sacred is being profaned."

The question still must come back to each of us, when the Master returns for the final accounting, what will He realize from His investment in us?

Are we doing the best of things in the worst of times? My friend, we are called to be a witness for Jesus in our beliefs and behavior. We can trumpet our ideas from the rooftops. However, if our behavior is not consistent with what we believe, then we are useless to this God-forsaken, sin-soaked, sin-cursed world, worse than the broken world, for we have the answers to the world needs to hear. However, our witness is rendered ineffectual by our compromising, accommodating ways.

Have you ever been skinned or scalded by a sermon? Have you ever felt like a sermon has stomped on your toes? That's the way I felt when I put this message down on paper.

God has plowed me right and proper, but I needed it, and I'm convinced that I'm not the only one!

The people of God all over this nation need to get on fire for God! The church needs to stop its compromising, accommodating ways and become salt and light once again.

Do you recall our Lord's Word to the lukewarm ones in Laodicea?

He said in **Revelation 3:18-19,** "I counsel thee to buy of me gold tried in the fire, that thou mayest be rich; and white raiment, that thou mayest be clothed, and that the shame of thy nakedness do not appear; and anoint thine eyes with eyesalve, that thou mayest see. As many as I love, I rebuke and chasten: be zealous therefore, and repent."

Thank God there is an answer found in **1 John 1:9,** "If we confess our sins, he is faithful and just to forgive us our sins and cleanse us from all unrighteousness."

Chapter 20

When you begin to look at a person's life, it is not hard to find mistakes one makes and see the Sin embedded in their lives. I'm sure Abraham thought he was doing the right thing. Yet we see God intervening again to protect Abraham and the one he has wronged.

That old saying is so true; old habits die hard. We can see that for Abraham, this is so true.

In the process, you can see the heart of Abraham. Again he is filled with fear. That is his inability to trust God to look after him and Sarah.

It is interesting to note that you will find the seed of his Sin in Ur as you study this chapter. See *verse 13*. If you will go back and explore, you will find this is a sin he had not confessed before God, nor was it forsaken.

Of course, he is not the only one who is not willing to confess Sin. How long has it taken you to see your Sin and admit it? Looking further, you will find it took Israel 40 years in the wilderness to bring out what was in their hearts.

Once a person sins, it is easy to repeat unless you can break that habit and repent. You would think Abraham would learn that lesson the first time. Of course, most of us are pretty hard headed and slow to learn the things of God.

Looking at the text, you will find that at first, Abraham went to Egypt and sinned. It was then there was a famine in the land, and that is why he left the place God wanted him. Now we see a different circumstance. Here in our text, it is another migration.

Interestingly enough, you will find God using two different modes of revelation to speak to the heathens.

Here we find Abimelech, king of Gerar, informed of what Abraham had done through a dream well before the king had surmised the situation.

Also, we find Abraham's reaction is different in each case, which brings about two different conclusions. One the one hand Abraham is excluded from the land. On the other hand, he gets an invitation to remain in the land. Of course, this would not have happened if Abraham had listened to God. But God in His mercy intervenes on behalf of Abraham, and we find God warns Abimelech. See ***verse 3***.

In the context, you can see the hand of God protecting Abimilech providentially from committing adultery. See ***verses 4-6***. Although he was a Gentile, he called God "Lord."

He seems to have been a very exceptional man. God called Abraham a prophet and orders Sarah to be restored by Abimelech. See ***verse 7***.

God sees His failing saints differently than the world sees them. Even though Abimelech did not know Sarah was Abraham's wife, he had sinned by taking her.

Usually, when a person sins against God until they come face to face with it, they will blame that Sin on something.

Generally, you can break it down into groups. We either want to blame people, circumstances or are just willing to lie about the truth. Here Abraham thought the people of Gerar did not fear God, and he must lie to the people to save his own life and that of his wife.

What is the matter with this plan? There is no dependence upon God in this plan. There was some truth in calling her his sister. See ***verse 12***. Some truth mixed with error is very dangerous. We have always said a half-truth is a whole lie. The end does not justify the means.

What he did was according to a prearranged plan. You could call this pre-mediated lying.

Once the truth is known, you would have expected Abimelech to be very harsh on Abraham. After all, it seems he is a just man, and his actions would indicate so. What would you have done is Abimelech's place? What did he do?

He gave Abraham a substantial gift, similar to a dowry, and in the process, he returned Sarah to Abraham. Would this be classed as returning good for evil?

Then we find in our text that he called Abraham, brother. See ***verse 16***. His was payment for the damages of any esteem and respect lost by Sarah. Then he permitted Abraham to dwell in any part of the land. See ***verse 15***. All of this was in answer to Abraham's prayer. See ***verse 17***.

Indeed it is of grace that God would hear the prayer of one who has offended the Almighty God?

In this process, God caused them to be fruitful, as we will see in the next chapter.

It has been said, "Sin works with many instruments. It takes a lie to fit all of them."

The consequences are inevitable. Sin will come like a bee and sting you. You cannot stretch the truth and expect it not come back to you. If the truth is stretched, expect it eventually to fly back and sting you."

Chapter 21

Let me take a moment and share the story leading up to the events related in the passage we are reading now. We have established the promises made to Abraham that his seed would issue forth abundantly and populate a nation set apart for the Lord. See *15:4; 17:4* of *Genesis*.

God promised him and Sarah that the child would be theirs, not the other union's product.

You can see this in *Chapters 17* and *18*, specifically *17:16; 18:10, 14*.

Isaac was born to the great surprise, relief, and wonder of everyone concerned. We will see this in our text in *Genesis 21:1-8*. There are conclusions we each need to understand and follow.

One is to learn to trust God entirely, and then peace will come.

Peace in knowing it was because God was right on time to fulfill His promise to Abraham.

Because of this, Abraham becomes obedient to God and obeys God's command concerning Isaac.

God has revealed His ultimate plan to understand all that He has prepared for us as His people.

As fallen human beings, we are not inclined to pursue the Lord on our own without somehow being called by the Lord, who always takes the first step in reaching out to us.

Remember, when God called Abram, there was a supernatural interaction with God. He spoke to him and showed Himself to him while he was in Ur's land.

In God's divine plan, He includes how He will speak to us, using circumstances in our lives, the testimony of other people, the truth of His Word, the Holy Spirit's urgings in our hearts and minds, and many different ways.

As part of God's divine plan, we can see that He has made way for us to hear His voice calling us to come to know Him and trust Him.

In the case of Abraham and Isaac, God had made an unusual promise that seemed impossible to Abraham and Sarah but was guaranteed because the Promise-maker was God Himself. See *Genesis 18:14.*

So it was in the greater scheme of the Lord that another "seed" would be born, another "Son of Promise" who would be the long-awaited Savior of His people. See *Galatians 3:16.*

Isaac's birth was a miracle for Abraham and Sarah since they were both well past their child-bearing years.

For the birth of the "Seed" from whom Salvation would come, the circumstances were even more miraculous as Mary, a virgin, conceived the child by the Holy Spirit rather than by a human father.

The Lord unfolds the divine plan to ensure that the son of promise in each case was born according to means that could only be attributed to Him, so no mistake about who was at work fulfilling His eternal purposes!

That sounds just like the God I know. How about you?

In the grand plan of the Lord, we find that He will often make a divine intervention when those He loves are in jeopardy.

The description of what is taking place is in Isaac and our Saviour, for intervention was necessary, providing a substitute for our sins.

God is undoubtedly watching over His children. Have you seen that, have you recognized that in your life?

For Isaac, it was a ram in the thicket. What has God done for you?

Later as we will see in God's intervention, instead of death for Isaac, the ram took his place on the altar and died in his place.

Can we see that for us, it was a Lamb on a cross that was our substitute, one who died for us?

Instead of death for us, the lamb took our place on the cross and died for each of us!

Here is a fantastic plan, and what an amazing God to carry it out.

God has demonstrated His sustained passion for calling out people who would know Him, trust Him, and love Him.

As we look back now and see how faithfully the Lord was putting His plan in place, we can recognize the passion which burned in His heart and explains His consistency on behalf of each of us who knows Him.

As you read and study this passage, it is like Abraham's love for Isaac, and yet it is unlike any love the world has ever known. Think of it, as the Father God loves His own Son, the Lord Jesus Christ, but more than that He loves even me. Do you not see the passion He has for His people! A force that broke forth in expressions of love declaring that He loves us with an everlasting love, and demonstrates that love by sending the son to take our place in death.

What kind of passion could this be but the desire of the Almighty God Himself for the people He loves unconditionally and abundantly!

Would you not agree with me in this instance with Abraham and Sarah that beyond a shadow of a doubt, God has given him sufficient proof that shows that He can be trusted absolutely?

For Abraham, I think he needed to see the hand of God.

Remember, there was a man who doubted God, and he needed proof God was who He said he was.

For you and me, the ultimate expression of those proofs can be found in Jesus Christ and confirmed through His resurrection from the dead.

Here at the resurrection, we know that He is who He says by what He has done without question. The proof is in the pudding.

Just as His power gives protection from death for Isaac and victory over death for Jesus, we too can say we believe God. He has kept His promises to the letter through the ages. He has proven trustworthy, so you can always count on what is said to be the truth. God never lies. He keeps His promises.

In these next verses of this chapter, we have the story of Hagar and Ishmael. If we have anything to add, it would be how Hagar reacted to where God was leading her. You can be discouraged, but you can't give in. You may be defeated, but don't give up. You may despair, but don't give up.

I think that pretty well describes the woman Hagar. There is no doubt about Sarah's attitude changing toward Hagar. The problem would not be solved until she left. So she leaves with her son, Ishmael. She went as far as she could humanly go. She was under a bush, ready to die, but God had other plans. She found out that God was with her no matter where she was.

She found out God would meet her and Ishmael's needs.

In our closing verses of **Chapter 21**, we will see the covenant between Abraham and Abimelech. I am sure it did not take much time to be around Abraham that Abimelech recognized God's hand on him.

This covenant is truth; actually, it is the reality of the Living God. Abraham calls the place Beersheba, which means "the well of the oath."

Now I want to give you something to think out. The birth of Isaac foreshadows the birth of Christ. Isaac was the promised seed. We saw this in **Gen. 17:16**. But I would say to you, so was Christ the promised seed. See **Isa. 7:14**. God's fulfillment came to Abraham in the birth of his son, Isaac.

There was a long interval between the first promise and fulfillment. You will see this in **Gen. 12:7** and **Gen. 21**. Think about how long it was from the promise of Christ coming and the completion of that promise. Note it is literally from **Gen. 3:15** to the **N. T.**

Thinking of Isaac, before his birth, they named him. See **Gen. 17:9**. So was Christ. See **Matt. 1:21**. Isaac was born at God's appointed time. We see this in **Gen. 21:2**. But so was Christ. See, **Gal. 4:4**. Isaac's birth was miraculous. See **Rom. 4:19**. So was Christ's birth a miracle. See **Luke 1: 26-36.** Isaac also typifies regeneration. What does the Bible say about the natural man? He is dead in trespasses and sins. In our text, we see Isaac was brought forth from death. See **Rom. 4:19; Eph. 2:1; Rom. 5:6**.

The same miracle performed for Isaac is what God does for us. So it is also with regeneration. The birth of Isaac brought about some conflict in the house of Abraham. When we are born again, it arouses the world's opposition, the flesh, and the devil. The birth of Isaac revealed the real character of Ishmael. The new birth reveals the real nature of the natural man. Isaac grew to be a young man. What did Peter say we should do?

From the day we are born again, our desire needs to understand we should want God's Word to grow by. See **1 Pet. 2:2**.

Chapter 22

Before moving on, I would like to give you some contextual thoughts here. We have the story of Isaac and Abraham up on Mt. Moriah in these first few verses. Remember, God never tempts to do evil but for our good.

God tests man so that man might know what his idols are in his life to learn to deal with them. As far as the mechanics of love, Abraham did love God. But as we have seen, we all doubt at some time in our lives.

There is no doubt that we must learn to die to self as God's children before God can use us.

Just in passing, we know Mount Moriah was the location where the temple was. See *II Chron. 3:1*.

It could have been the same place where Christ hung on the cross. Isaac is the only type in the O.T., which intimated that God required a human sacrifice. While the idol worshiper offered human sacrifice, God's people were never involved in this practice.

Impressively, we have found a man of faith in the man Abraham. As we have studied Abraham's life, we have seen that he exercised faith in God four times.

If you remember, he had to leave his family, for it was the will of God. See *Gen. 12:1*. Later we find him having to surrender his friendship with his nephew, Lot. See *Gen. 13:1-18*.

He was at a seaport city of idolatry and pitched his tent on a mountain between Bethel and Hai.

Later on, we find Abraham in the Plain of Jordan. He then left this and lived in the plain of Mamre. Here was the surrender of his future. See *Gen. 17:17, 18*.

Then here in our text, we see his surrender of his only son. See *Gen. 22:1-19*. Four times his faith was tested in different ways. His obedience was tested. See *Gen. 12:1*. His motives were tested. See *Gen. 13*. His faith was tested. See *Gen. 17:17, 18*. His love was tested. See *Gen. 22:1-19*.

In this passage, we see the simplicity of Faith that Abraham took GOD at His Word.

Strength of Faith in *verse 5*, Abraham said he would come again.

I believe the Scriptures bear it out that Abraham believed God would raise his son from the dead, though he slew him. These are the words by Job in *Job 13:15*, "Though he slay me, yet will I trust in him: but I will maintain mine own ways before him."

His faith source is his conviction of God's real power to do what He said He would do.

Heb. 11:17-19 says, "By faith Abraham when he offered up Isaac: and he that had received the promises offered up his only begotten son. Of whom it was said, That in Isaac shall thy seed be called: Accounting that God was able to raise him up, even from the dead; from whence also he received him in a figure."

Then we see the secret of his faith. He said, "Here Am I" twice. See *verses 1, 11*.

We must have a close fellowship with God to be able to trust Him as Abraham did. Real faith never stops to look at circumstances or ponder the results; it only looks at GOD!! Can you imagine how Abraham must have felt as he traveled with his little group to Mount Moriah for three days, knowing he would do what he had to do? Abraham had told no one what he was planning and what GOD had told him he must do.

A friend of mine's son has cancer in the last stages is close to me. The day before I talked with him, he had heard his son's doctor say, "Son, you have less than two months to live."

He made this statement to me as we talked, "I feel like there is a big knot in the pit of my stomach, and it will not go away."

I don't know, but I believe that must be close to how Abraham must have felt during this time of traveling to Mount Moriah. No matter what, he was going to do what God had asked him to do!!

In this next section, you could write a book, and I am sure many have, but I want to try and be brief and to the point. Have you ever heard a more daunting question than Isaac asked his father? How would you have answered him? I love how Abraham answers his son," And Abraham said, my son, God will provide himself a lamb for a burnt offering: so they went both of them together." In building the altar, arranging the wood, he takes his son and ties him to the altar just built.

He then takes his knife to slay his only son, and then the angel of the Lord speaks to him.

As you think about this, the sacrifice was Abraham's responsibility, but Isaac's raising was God's responsibility alone. Only God has power over death.

Here is a beautiful picture of the sacrifice of Jesus for you and me. Isaac was old enough to carry the wood and thus old enough to resist, but he did not. The angel of the Lord here is the Lord Himself. See ***Gen. 16:7-11; Gen. 18:1-3*** and ***Gen. 21:17, 18***.

In Abraham's obedience, we see a substitute providentially provided.

Without getting too much into typology here, we can say God providentially provided a Lamb for us.

Here is the first time in the Bible we read of a compound name used by God.

It is His name Jehovah-Jireh. The meaning of this name Jehovah-Jireh is God will provide, God will see, God will see to it. Look at the mightiness of this name. God provides the right thing that Abraham needed. It was "a ram." God knew the exact thing Abraham needed. It was in the thicket. Later, according to the Law, this was the sacrifice for the atonement of sins. What more could GOD give than the right sacrifice?

In the Salvation of man, God knew the right thing to give for humanity, The Lamb Of God.

He provides the right place *verse 14*, "in the mount of the Lord."

Abraham didn't need a ram when he came down the mountain, tomorrow, next week, next year; he needed it on the mountain.

When you came under conviction, you needed a Saviour at the altar, beside the bed, or wherever you got saved when you went to the cross. After you got saved, God knew the place where you needed help.

He knew where your mountain was. God knows the place; He knows your address, your street, your street number.

He also provides at the right time. Go back to *verse 10*. Abraham lifts the knife. At that moment, at that instant, God was there. Instantly Abraham obeys, and instead of a knife through his son's heart, God intervenes and provides for him a ram.

Can I say to you God provides for the sinner "in the fulness of time"? Amazing how many testimonies of how God rescued a sinner when all hope was gone. Not only does He provide for the sinner man, but God provides for the saved. We have confidence that God is always right on time. He may not be running on my schedule, but you can be sure His plan is not too slow or too fast!!!

Look at *verse 14* again. It says, "In the Mount of the LORD, it shall be seen." In all of the previous places where Abraham was, there was always someplace to go or someone to replace.

The city Ur of the Chaldees was a seaport. What did he do? He moved to the mountain between Bethel and Hai.

When Lot chose the Plain of Jordan, Abraham moved to the Plain of Mamre. The rejection of Ishmael occurred, but he had Isaac to take his place. You know this is a special place. Now there was no place to go and no person to replace. Everything he loved, he gave up to follow the will of God.

It was here where there was nothing left to give up and nothing to replace it that God revealed himself as the LORD who see to it, as the Hebrew would say.

God has given sufficient proof in tangible ways that show that He can be trusted absolutely.

The ultimate expression of those proofs can be found in Jesus Christ and confirmed through his resurrection.

He presented himself to his disciples even after the resurrection "with many convincing proofs, appearing to them for forty days." See *Acts 1:3*.

Have you noticed God always provides what we need and when we need it? God gives what we need for the perfect accomplishment of His will.

In our text, we see from that point on, Abraham called that place "Jehovah-Jireh," which means, "The Lord will provide." Our text says God "himself" would provide the lamb.

The word "himself" is notable. Think about this, God "himself" sent the Lamb of God to die for the world's sins. The sacrifice came from Him. Can't you see, it was no accident that the ram was in the thicket? God provided the sacrifice. Just as Abraham offered his only son, God himself provided His one and only son's sacrifice on our behalf. The ram was a substitute offering. There was an ultimate price to be paid for our sins.

Through His willingness, Christ became our substitute.

The ram points to the "Lamb of God.

After these verses, we hear no more of Isaac for the next ninety-two verses. He is a picture of the resurrected Christ who is gone and will be coming back one day. After Isaac came down off the mountain, we do not hear about him again until *Gen. 24:63-67*. Isaac is a type of the Son of God waiting for his bride. Note that Rebekah is also a type of the bride of Christ for whom Christ died.

The camel is a type of grace of God that takes us to our heavenly Isaac.

One of these days, we're going home with the father to be a bride for his son. The day will come when the Church's rapture takes place, and we will; Rise by the power of grace.

Ride into Heaven on the camel of grace. Rest in Heaven upon Christ's arm of grace. Reside in Heaven eternally upon God's marvelous grace.

There is one thing more, which must be said before we leave this text. We have too many preachers and colleges who are trying to put the fire out today. They try and water down the Gospel. They try and cut out the Word of God. They will try and compromise the truth of the Word of God. Truth demands we stand on this Word. God can't lie. Justice demands it for the Scriptures say, the soul that sinneth it shall die. Law is needed. The resurrection assures the believer that we become dead to the Law by the bodily resurrection of Christ. Salvation compels it. Preaching demands it. Paul said in preaching, God forbid that I should glory.

Sin necessitates it. If there be no sin, there would have been no need for the cross.

The moment Sin happened, the cross became necessary.

Holiness requires it. Never has God's holiness been more clearly demonstrated than when our perfect substitute bore our sins in his body on the cross.

When we are preaching about the cross, I have noticed that His power can break Sin's shackles. It loosens the clutches of Satan's hold on a hell-bound soul.

It lifts the man from a burning hellfire as it snaps and sizzles and chars the wall of the charcoaled damned. Today, many of the so-called preachers cannot distinguish between the clean and the unclean. They could not tell the unholy from the holy.

They could not tell that which was false or true. They could not tell that which was fake or real.

Abraham could have lit a fire of his own, but God would not have been in that. What we need is a real fire. You know that fire is a picture of the presence of God. See ***Deut. 4:12-15***.

Understand that fire often symbolizes God's presence and is the instrument of His power.

God compared to fire not only because of his glorious brightness but also on his anger toward Sin.

Today we ask where the fire is. I have preached all across the eastern USA and in several foreign countries, and I see nothing but coldness cause there isn't any fire. God help us preach the right kind of fire and have the correct fire to warm us up to God's things. What will it take for you?

Chapter 23

This chapter is the story of the death of Abraham's wife, Sarah. She had lived to a right old age, the Bible says. This whole chapter is devoted to her death and burial in the land of Hebron.

At that time, the owner was a man named Ephron, a Hittite. If you remember, in *Genesis 22*, we saw Isaac's offering, a type of the death and resurrection of Jesus Christ. What a beautiful chapter that was. Here in this chapter, we see that Sarah's death is a type of Israel's death nationally. The reason we say so is that Sarah buried among the children of Heth. They were Gentiles.

So this is a type of Israel buried among the Gentiles, awaiting their restoration by resurrection to come.

Later in the next chapter, *Genesis 24*, we will see Isaac's servant as a type of the Holy Spirit, who goes into the Gentiles' land to seek a bride to comfort Isaac after his mother's death.

The Holy Spirit is now doing for the son what the Holy Spirit did for Isaac's servant.

Today, the Holy Spirit seeks a bride for the Lord Jesus Christ, who will be raptured at the time of His coming.

Sarah died at 127 years of age. Here is the only time in the Old Testament we know a woman's age.

Marriage has been great for us for over fifty years. I am sure to lose her by way of death will be tough to endure, so I know how Abraham must have felt. Here, he lives in Hebron's land and has not thought of where they might bury someone at death. There is nothing new. Abraham had to follow the same process we do today. He had to find a burial plot for the family.

In our text, we find that Abraham wants the land with a cave called Machpelah owned by Ephron. In those days, if one wants a piece of land, they go to that person and offer to buy it.

The owner then refuses to sell but wants to give it. Such was the custom of that day. In buying, the one buying will ask how much it is worth. The owner replies by revealing the worth of the land. The buyer, in turn, gives the owner the amount specified. Note, this was proper trading and dealing in those days. He did not expect Abraham to take it as a gift. Abraham insists upon dealing correctly in financial matters.

He is an excellent example of this for us to follow. He was fair when separating from Lot.

He was correct in refusing the gift of the king of Sodom. He was honest in giving the tithe to Melchizedek. He is careful here in not getting in debt to the Canaanites. The value of the land, according to Ephron, was probably an inflated price. Omri bought the whole hill of Samaria for 6,000 shekels of silver. Secular records show that sometimes the entire village was purchased in those days for 100 to 1,000 shekels.

Abraham pays the price with no bargaining or complaint. So the transaction takes place in front of many witnesses. Later on, in the Scriptures, you will find that Abraham in *Genesis 25:9*, Isaac in *Genesis 35:27, 29*, Rebekah and Leah in *Genesis 49:31*, and Jacob found in *Genesis 50:13* were all buried here.

Looking at Abraham's life, there are many lessons to be learned from his experience.

He believed in immortality. We see this is evident in his care for the dead. If death ended it all, what difference would it make? He believed that God would grant his posterity to inherit this land. There is a mosque built over this burying site today.

Of course, we do not know for sure that it is the same place in Hebron. He believed in a blessed future state for the righteous. His hope was not merely here on this earth, but he looked for a city whose builder and maker is God. See *Heb. 11:13-16*.

Chapter 24

Here is one of the most extended chapters in the Bible, and it reveals one of the most beautiful stories of romance and love. We have been looking at the life of the man Isaac.

The last time we heard of him before this chapter is when he was up on Mount Moriah with his daddy.

Some of the things about his life that are very interesting to learn if you do not already know them and know what I'm about to say today can only stir your heart to understand God's Word!

We have spent time looking at Abraham's obedience, being a father, and Isaac's compliance. Out of *Genesis 22*, we began to understand what real worship is all about.

Worship is based on a revelation from GOD's Word in *Genesis 22:2* where it says, "And GOD said."

Worship is by faith in divine revelation. Here we are talking about the Word of God itself.

Worship frequently involves a costly presentation to GOD.

In the case of Abraham, God wanted his son. Listen to *Genesis 22:2*, "thy son."

Worship necessitates a separation unto GOD.

In Abraham and Isaac's case, we find that he leaves his servants and ass to go up on the mountain. Worship demands an absolute renunciation of self in every form.

This is what it took for Abraham and Isaac, and that is the right direction for us to decide if we want what God wants. See *Genesis 22:5*.

When you study the book of Genesis, you find man's ruin; we're all in trouble.

When you study Exodus's book, when a man is redeemed, He is out of trouble.

Reading the Book of Leviticus, you will find man worshipping, and he is glad to be out of trouble.

Now, as we studied through the sacrifice of Isaac, there was a phrase that caught my attention.

That phrase that Abraham said when he told his servants that he and his son would come again. It was there that Abraham knew reckoned that God would and could raise his son from the dead.

Typology helps understand the previous chapters. Abraham typifies the heavenly father. See *Matt. 22:2* and *John 6:44*. Here is just give you some food for thought about this long chapter, and then we will get into a verse by verse study.

Think of Isaac. He was offered as a sacrifice, and then he went home. Isaac arrives at home, and then the servant was sent to seek and secure a bride for him. Eliezer went to one that was far off. Isaac was the sole possessor, heir to all that belongs to his father.

He was Abraham's only son by Sarah. Isaac stayed at home while the servant sought him a bride.

As you read, you find that he remained in Canaan, a type of Heaven. Rebekah was the father's love gift to the son, Isaac. Isaac met her away from home in the field. He went out to meet her. Read *1 Thess. 4:16-18*.

Isaac was the long-promised son to Abraham and is a type of Christ. Note that his being placed on the altar, as we saw in *Genesis 22*, typified Christ's death. Also, if you remember, he was released and taken off the altar, which typified the resurrection of Christ.

Then as we saw, the death of Sarah in *Genesis 23* typified the national death and blindness of the nation of Israel.

We compare this to the things of Christ and see many parallels. The setting aside of Israel was after the resurrection of Christ and His return to the father. In *Chapter 24*, we will see Isaac, the son and heir, abiding with Canaan's father, a type of the Heavenlies. The bride, who is Rebekah, was taken by Isaac to the father's house.

The servant asked the bride to do three things. It says in *1 Pet. 1:8*, "Whom having not seen; ye love; in whom, though now ye see him not, yet believing, ye rejoice with joy unspeakable and full of glory:" To believe a man she had never met before. To go to a place she had never been to before. Then, to marry a man she had never seen before. When the servant arrived at the well, a miracle took place. See *Verses 11-20*.

There are some fascinating parallels drawn for us here. The well represents Christ. The water is a symbol of Salvation. *John 4:14* says, "But whosoever drinketh of the water that I shall give him shall never thirst, but the water that I shall give him shall be in him a well of water springing up into everlasting life."

We met the Holy Spirit at the well of the water of Salvation. Please read *Isa. 12:1-6* for a beautiful description of what I mean. His job is simple, to select a bride for the son. He searches for the bride. He is a type of what God Holy Spirit is doing today for the Church. See *verses 10-51*. The servant typifies the Holy Spirit in seeking a bride and enriching that bride by the father's wealth. See *John 16:13, 14; Gal. 5:22* and *1 Cor. 12:7-11*.

Think of the message that was delivered by the servant. See *Verses 32-49*. It was a message about the son and no one else. Isaac has now been out of sight for ninety-two verses. The last time we saw him was in *Genesis 22:19*.

From there to this chapter, his name is silent in the Scriptures. It is here that we left him resurrected from the dead and ascended. *Acts 1:9* says, "And when he had spoken these things, while they beheld, he was taken up; and a cloud received him out of their sight."

Notice a couple more things about the bride: He could not get a bride from the Canaanites. We see this in *verses 3* and *37*. Also, see *2 Cor. 6:14-17* for what God means. The bride had to be a chaste virgin. *2 Cor. 11:2* says, "For I am jealous over you with godly jealousy: for I have espoused you to one husband that I may present you as a chaste virgin to Christ." *Eph. 5:27* says, " That he might present it to himself a glorious church, not having spot, or wrinkle, or any such thing; but that it should be holy and without blemish."

Rebekah typifies the bride of Christ. See *Eph. 5:25-32* and *11 Cor. 11:2*.

Isaac stands for the bridegroom (Christ) coming to receive His Bride. See *I Thess. 4:14-16*.

Isaac is now on resurrection ground and that to receive a proper bride, he must have a resurrected bride.

She was Bethuel's daughter, the eighth and youngest son of Milcah and Nahor, Abraham's brother. *Gen. 22:20-23* says, " and it came to pass after these things, that it was told Abraham, saying, Behold, Milcah, she hath also born children unto thy brother Nahor; I Iuz his firstborn, and Buz his brother, and Kemuel the father of Aram, And Chesed, and Hazo, and Pildash, and Jidlaph, and Bethuel. And Bethuel begat Rebekah: these eight Milcah did bear to Nahor, Abraham's brother."

The number eight in the Scriptures is designated as the number of resurrection. Isaac's name is mentioned eight times in *Chapter 24*. He is a type of Christ, the Heavenly bridegroom.

He is called the resurrection and the life.

At this time, Abraham was 140 years old. See *verse 1; Genesis 23:1*, and *Genesis 25:20*.

There is a good possibility that the eldest servant may have been Eliezer. See *verse two* and *Genesis 15:12*.

In the Bible, there is much said of the importance of marrying the right person. See *verses 3, 4*, and then read *11 Cor. 6:14*. We still believe the Scriptures teach marriage a sacred institution that should not happen without God's guidance.

In these next few verses, we see an interaction between Abraham and Isaac and the servant.

The servant asks, "What if the woman will not come? " And in the process, Isaac is told not to go. We find this is well thought about by Abraham, and he knows what to do in providing all the necessary means to do what he has asked of the servant.

We, too, have received the wealth of the heavenly father, and we are to use it in seeking a bride for His Son. See *Matt. 28:18-20*.

He then goes on his journey and arrives at the well. So many beautiful things in the Bible took place by a well. See *John 4*. A servant is a God-fearing man when he asks the Lord in prayer for help, and we find that God answered in the way the servant had prayed. What a wonderful God.

In this case, God answers quickly. See *verse 15*. God sometimes is already working to answer our prayers before we pray. Rebekah was a pure and beautiful young lady, according to the next verses. All in all, we must understand that when we pray, God expects us to be willing to do our part. If you will notice, that is what the servant did. He did his part and left the rest up to God. Follow our thoughts, and you must come to the same conclusion regarding the answering of our prayers.

On one occasion, the Lord furnished the oil, but the woman had to equip the vessels to put it in.

In this case, when the servant met Rebekah, he believed God had directed him and, after talking with her, gave her God a symbol of deity from his master Abraham. She "ran and told."

We should hasten to tell the Gospel. Some run from God, but some run for God.

There are three things that the servant requested of Rebekah. Her identity is asked.

Lodging for him is requested, and hospitality was given to him. In return for answered prayer, the servant worships and prays.

In thinking of this passage, we see a brother of Rebekah's by the name of Laban. The next few chapters will tell us much about him. I think we see his attitude here that will surface again soon. His attitude toward the gifts may be a preview of his greedy nature that stands out later on. See *verse 30*. However, he does recognize that the servant received blessings of the Lord Jehovah.

It is refreshing to see that the custom back them was to accept a stranger is based on his Word.

They seemed to be very hospital people. In this instance, we see provision for the camels and cleansing and refreshment of the body. God wonderfully provides to all that seek Him.

I think this is because the seávant was willing to give glory to those who belonged the glory.

He praises the God of God's.

We find again that the servant is conscientious who gets the praise here. As a type of the Holy Spirit, he does not praise himself, but the one who sent him. See *John 16:13, 14.*

This next section is mostly a re-telling of that which we studied in our last lesson.

There are a few details that are not covered in the earlier section.

In the story, we find that the father prominently mentioned as we might expect.

The fact that the brother and mother are prominent in this passage might indicate that the father was aged or ill.

However, it could be that he gave them a higher place than usual. Believing he had found the right bride, the servant willingly gave his master the dowry and had been instructed to give to the family.

It is always interesting how things take place, and this is no exception. You can easily see the hand of God in all of this. After staying the allotted time, we find Rebekah is willing to go, and the family is willing to let her go.

One of the questions I have always thought about was, what did they talk about on the journey?

It seems natural that they would have talked about Isaac.

On our journey today, we should be talking about Christ, our Saviour. What we know from our text is that Isaac came from the way of the well. It is interesting that "Lahai-Roi" means "The living and seeing one." Have you mediated on something you knew would soon come to pass?

I am sure Isaac was too. No doubt, as he meditated and prayed, his mind would think upon his coming bride. Here comes the bride with his servant.

How can we describe this moving experience? We love Christ but have never seen Him. But one day we will, praise be unto God!! In these last verses here, we see Rebekah getting off the camel and putting on the veil, revealing her modesty, humility, and submission. She then becomes the wife of Isaac. Something interesting here is that we have the first mention of love in the Bible.

Chapter 25

This chapter has many intriguing thoughts. Here was Abraham at the age of one hundred forty years old getting married. I would consider that a miracle all by itself. But in time, he marries a lady by the name of Keturah of the tribe of the Midian's. We find they have several children.

God indeed told Abraham that he would be the father of many nations. He had to get married again for this to be possible.

Throughout the life of Abraham, we have been able to distinguish many types and typologies.

This is no exception to the rule. We can see that Abraham's offspring by Keturah typifies the millennial nations. After Isaac's marriage, which is typical of the union of the lamb, which is after the Church age ends, and this dispensation closes.

One day Israel will be restored to its original order. We also see that the Church will rule with Christ, and then the blessings will come to "all the earth's families."

Isaac, the son, received the blessings when you think of it, and his other brothers received gifts.

We find that Abraham died at the age of one hundred seventy-five years old.

In our text, we find the Scriptures tell us he "was gathered to his people." Here we find six people, including Abraham, Ishmael, Isaac, Jacob, Aaron, and Moses, whom the Bible tells us was buried. After Abraham's death and an interesting fact of the burial, Ishmael, Isaacs's half-brother, helped with the funeral.

Then in the next few verses, we have the generations Of Ishmael. In the genealogy, we have all of his sons listed for us, and then the Bible tells us that he died at the age of one hundred thirty-seven years old. They dwelt in the land of Assyria.

In the next verses, we have the story of Isaac and his sons. It begins with the story of Jacob and Esau. From the Scriptures study, you will find when Isaac married, he was forty years old.

Here is one of those intriguing things. For twenty years, Rebekah had been barren and had no children. Want to know the power of prayer? Isaac prayed, casting himself on the Lord, and God wonderfully blesses. Sometimes though, we find with answered prayer comes trials and testing. Such was the case here.

From the very beginning of these two boys being born, we can see conflict. It probably was not so evident at the beginning of their lives, but soon it would be a conflict between the natural and the spiritual.

Later we will see that these two boys represent two nations as well. Those two nations, and two manners of people, were in her womb, namely, the Israelites and the Edomite's, or Idumeans.

That is, these would be just two men, but they would represent two nations.

They were men of very opposite natures, and their descendants were just as different. Even from the time when they came out of their mother's womb, they were fighting. Is it no wonder they are still fighting today? From the very beginning, these two personally struggled for the pre-eminence. Is it no wonder that their posterity has been and is doing the same today?

In the days of David, the descendants of Esau, the elder brother, were generally subject to those of Jacob the younger; and much more entirely in the latter times of the Jewish state.

Think of Esau and Jacob. There always has and will be a conflict between the two.

It is the same way with women today's struggles with what is known as "rights."

In our case here, we know the younger will rule the elder. Note that the Israelites were of the family of Jacob. On the other hand, the Edomite's were of the offspring of Esau.

Later we will see Jacob had twelve sons, and their descendants were all united and incorporated into one nation. It is not hard to distinguish the fact the Edomite's and the Israelites are very different. Admittedly many differences in manners, customs, and religion, will cause them to be at a constant variance. The struggle of Esau and Jacob in the womb of their mother started the strife between the two nations. If there were two, who were like night and day, we see it in these two. Esau desired to be a hunter. You could say he was an outdoorsman.

On the other hand, Jacob was a plain man, dwelling in tents-minding his sheep and cattle.

The Jews' religion is well known, but whatever the Edomite's were at first, they became idolaters in time.

When Amaziah, king of Judah, overthrew the Edomite's, he brought their gods and set them up to be his gods. The king of Edom has refused passage to the Israelites through his territories on their return from Egypt. The history of the Edomite's afterward is little more than the history of their wars with the Jews. Searching more in-depth, we find that this passage is the beginning of the arguments you will notice about God's Providence. These verses serve to help us explain the challenging passage in *Romans 9*.

I want to deviate a little from my usual explanations of passage and interject a thought here about predestination and election.

From our text here, it is evident that God does not arbitrarily predestinate a particular person to eternal happiness or misery without regard to their merit or demerit. I see God in all that He cannot hate one person and love another. And in that process, give to one what He would not give to another. God has never shown favoritism to anyone.

Indeed, the facts confirm that God knows us and what we will do and bases what He says.

If fact, we are all sinners deserving the same pits of Hell itself. Nor would He give more light to one who is seeking than another one.

I agree with Paul that He gives to every man as He wills, but that is not about grace.

In the context, it is talking about talents. It has nothing to do with Salvation.

I do not believe our text's example in context supports this doctrine called unconditional predestination to eternal life with God's dealings with Esau and Jacob. Nor, for that matter, with the nations of the Edomite's and the Israelites. After long reprobation, the Edomite's cohabitated among the Jews. They have ever since been undistinguishable members of the Jewish Church. Because of their sins, the Jewish people were placed on hold for the church age duration. It will continue until the completion of the period of grace.

When the time comes when the Jews shall all believe in Christ Jesus, then the Edomite's, which they are a part of shall share in this election from God.

Today we know the prodigy of Isaac find a home in the Jewish Church who one day will turn to the promises of Salvation through Jesus Christ. Of course, we know he is the type of the Messiah to come.

Thank God for this age of grace, where we all can come to know Him.

In our text, we find that Esau had come to the place that spiritual things were of no concern to him, and therefore he could care less about the birthright. He never thought of the importance of what it meant. On the other hand, it seems Jacob thought a lot about the birthright and desired it much. On the one hand, we would say he was coveting. On the other hand, we would say he was coveting the best gifts. Yet we cannot justify what he did to acquire the birthright.

From our text, we can see they must have talked about the birthright before because it did not bother Esau in Jacob's bargaining.

The point is Jacob took advantage of Esau. However, Esau should have been wise enough to know better. Jacob was a smart businessman here. He made Esau take an oath. Listen to what Paul had to say about this. *Hebrews 12:16* "Lest there be any fornicator, or profane person, Esau, who for one morsel of meat sold his birthright."

Imagine how foolish Esau was in making and agreeing to the bargaining of his brother? We can add to this and say God often chooses the world's foolish things to confound the wise. There is no doubt that Jacob makes a fool of cunning Esau.

Thus Esau despised his birthright.

He made no appeal to his father about it or proposed to his brother to let him have it back, so to speak later. This shows us his profaneness is confirmed ex post facto, that is, after the deed.

There is a study done by those who despised certain things.

Since I am not necessarily preaching here, it would be an excellent study to take on.

You should stop and think of what Esau did when he gave away his birthright and what it should have meant to him.

The birthright in and of itself was of great importance. It would affect his future. He was the firstborn and had all the rights and would eventually act as a priest. Not only that, but it also had terrible consequences. By birthright, he was the one who held the promise from Eden along with Abel, Seth, Shem, Abraham, and Isaac as the Satan head bruiser.

It also had tragic permanence. By that, I mean, he had a nation that would follow after him one day. What happened was they became haters of the Jews and were conquered many times by them. When he lost his birthright, he lost the opportunity to be in the line of Christ's linage. What a disgrace for he sold it all for a bowl of soup.

In these times at hand, people will say it does not matter whether you sin or not. It will be alright because God is such a loving God. But I am here to tell you that it does costs to sin.

Here we could mention the many things people lost because they sinned against God and the consequences involved.

That would be a sobering study if you would commit yourself to it. Just to give you a hint, think of Saul and how he lost his crown because he sinned against God. The Word of God makes it very understandable that there is a cost to Sin. See verses like *James 1:14, 15*, and ***Rev. 20:11-15*** for more clarification.

How often we have said to those around us never to allow Satan to deceive is thinking there is no consequence to our actions. God will judge your Sin. From the first Sin ever committed, God has judged that Sin continues today just as much. There is a cure for Sin. It is called Repentance. Thank God for the remedy for Sin through Jesus.

Chapter 26

What I want to deal with is how do you learn what the Word of God says? I don't just mean memorizing the Scriptures but getting to the place where you know what it says and what it means.

I'm sure you understand this is only possible by taking GOD's Word's truths and applying it to your own life. Conviction ought to be based on what we know, not on what someone else has told us.

There are four necessary steps that we need to learn to make the application of the Scriptures in our lives. They are first making the facts come alive. That is, you look in detail as to what the Scriptures are saying.

You try and pull a principle out of that text. Listen to **Deut. 6:20** "And when thy son asketh thee in time to come, saying, What mean the testimonies, and the statutes, and the judgments, which the LORD our God hath commanded you?"

Some people may know what the Scriptures say, but do not know its meaning.

What is in it for you? How do we do this? We do this by planning the principle. Once we know a principle, then we can make that principle part of our lives. Put yourselves into it.

Weave that principle into your life. Listen to **2 Cor. 8:11** "Now, therefore, perform the doing of it; that as there was a readiness to will, so there may be a performance out of that which ye have."

Let that principle become part of you.

Now let us reread our text. What do we do? Well, we find every person in that text and find out all we can talk about them.

One principle we can point out for you in our text is that blessing comes after obedience. One way to relate this in our lives would be like what we know about tithing. You do not expect GOD to bless you before you tithe, do you? No, you tithe, and then GOD will bless. So now, let's put these for steps in order: Make the facts come alive. Get all the facts. Remember that the text may not give the whole picture. Therefore, do some research? Shape them so you can understand. Link all the facts together. In other words, when you begin to read now, what does it bring to mind? What have you now learned?

Take, for instance, Isaac. What do you think of when he comes to mind? When I think of Isaac, I think of him as being the sacrifice up on the mountain until GOD intervened uniquely.

The importance of this is that we learn that he was a real man. It was knowing what happened in his life?

Then, of course, there is Abraham. Who was he? What did he do that makes him real to you?

In our text, you can learn several things about this man Isaac. He was a shepherd. He was a leader. He was very wealthy. He was successful. Look at **verse 13**.

What does it mean that he "waxed great"? The next step is to find out all you can, especially if you do not already know.

Who was the herdsman of Gera? What did they do? Where is this place called Gera? Was it a real place? Look on a map and find out.

What does it mean to "pitch" a tent?

How about a well? What is a well? Why was it so important?

First, in this chapter, you will need to find out what was going on. There was a famine taking place. What is a famine? The people were hungry. It takes water to survive. Think about it. Isaac spent a lot of time digging that well. Why would the men of Gera want to fight them anyway? What did they tell Isaac and his men? They said, "It's mine." The ethical principle here is what we say when someone tells us, "it's mine." Amid strife, what did Isaac do? He went and dug another well.

Did that make him a chicken? Was he a coward? What would you have done? If you go back and study God's Word, you will find that his father Abraham had made a covenant with them years before.

No doubt, Isaac may have carried this covenant with him. Why didn't he pull it out and say, "I have my rights."? What did he do? He chose to pursue peace. He went and dug another well. What happened? The same thing happened for the first time. What did he do? He went and dug the third well.

I'm trying to tell you that you need to find a principle that can be used in your daily life.

Next, pull out a principle from all the facts we have learned. Learn to replace Biblical terms with something relevant in your life, like replacing "wells" with "food" today. Then we can all understand what is going on. Facts are like food. You can see the food on the table. What makes the food taste so good? It is all of the seasonings, etc. put into the food that makes it taste the way it does.

Ask yourself a question, how do I know if I have found a Biblical principle in our text instead of misapplying it?

Several things can help us here. You cannot make a mystical meaning out of most of the Scriptures trying to spiritualize principles that are practical applications to something we have learned. Must be Biblical based.

We are not to do everything we read about in the Bible. You will find it does not mean that we are to follow if it is a sin.

If you read the first part of the chapter, you will find that Isaac lied about Rebecca's wife. See **verses 6-10**. Of course, you know that it is wrong to lie.

Now let us go back to our passage of Scripture and learn some more. Of course, Isaac understood the principle that we have before us here. Again, that principle is: Do I keep on giving up, or do I fight?? If I do keep on giving up, am I a chicken??? What is Bible principle here???

See **Rom. 12:18** "If it be possible, as much as lieth in you, live peaceably with all men.

Do you not understand what Isaac said was that as much as is in me, I will try to live peacefully with all me." Now you say that is all right for the first well incident. What about the second well? Isaac had a lot of options here.

He could have pulled out that piece of paper that said that his daddy had dug the wells first and that the king in his day had given him the land where the wells were.

He could have said that one well was enough for him and his men to dig. He could have said that is enough; we will now fight for the possession of the well. However, what Isaac did was what he did the first time; he let them have the well. Do you not see that what he was doing was trying to apply in his life? See **Rom. 12:18**. Also, read **Heb. 12:14** "Follow peace with all men, and holiness, without which no man shall see the Lord:"

There is no doubt that in his heart, this is what he was trying to do.

For you and me today, we need to learn some of the same principles in our lives, but we need good examples to follow to do this. I believe a good example elsewhere in the Bible that teaches this same principle is in **Psa. 136:1-26**. Here we have a Psalm of David: he teaches us of the mercy of GOD. In reading the Word of God, remember you have to get all the facts.

See the first things first. Teach all the facts. In our text here in **Psalms 136**, see **verse 13**.

Like for example, you can see woven into the crossing of the Red Sea, the mercy of GOD. See **verse 15**. The fact is GOD overthrew the army of Pharaoh in the Red Sea. Believe that woven into the destroying of the army of Pharaoh is the mercy of GOD. See **verse 18**.

The fact is that GOD provided manna for the people of Israel after that, they crossed over into the wilderness...Do you get the idea? Your objective is to tie together the third and fourth principles. Plan the way you are going to pull that principle out of the Word. Weave that principle into your life.

Question? Are there ways you can dig another well?? Have you ever said, "That's mine!!?"

That's my basketball. That's my bat. That's my book. That's my idea. That's my seat. That's my parking place. That's my clothes. What should you have said?

What should you have done? Easier to find another basketball. Easier to find another bat. Easier to find another parking place. Easier to find another book. Easier to find another idea.

Easier to find another change of clothes.

Why should we? Well, one of the underlying principles here is that GOD is the one who will make the room if we let Him.

That is the principle of at least one of them that Isaac saw here. Think of our text in *Genesis 26:22* "And he removed from thence, and digged another well; and for that, they strove not: and he called the name of it Rehoboth; and he said, For now, the LORD hath made room for us, and we shall be fruitful in the land."

Instead of demanding your rights, why don't you give space to GOD and let GOD have His way?

Chapter 27

Esau wept because of a lost advantage but found no way to change his mind, though he sought it with many tears. See **Heb. 12:17**. He had remorse. He had regret. But he did not have Repentance.

In this chapter, you could call this chapter trying to help God out. Rebekah may have wanted to comply with God's Word, but she uses unholy means to aid God. See **Genesis 25:23**.

Using this sort of method is never right, for God can do His will without calling on us to lie or cheat to bring it to pass.

She reveals Isaac's plan to Jacob, and she tells her deceptive plan to Jacob. Jacob was afraid of being found out, but Rebekah was willing to bear the curse. Through her scheming, she became separated from her son. Rebekah spent the rest of her days with Isaac. Jacob lies about his identity, and he lies using God's name.

Isaac depends on feeling and is deceived by his son. Today, many people in the religious world rely on feelings for their religion. Not many will accept the facts of Scripture and thus are deceived.

In the blessing of Isaac to his son, we find three things. It contained material blessing. It had governmental and family authority. It contained divine protection.

Esau is also a deceiver, for he claimed a blessing that he had no right to request before God.

Jacob had already received the blessing. Esau wept but did not repent.

What he felt may have been regret or remorse, but not true Repentance.

After all, he had sold the birthright, revealing his lack of appreciation for spiritual things.

Isaac and Esau were far from innocent in all of this.

They were conspiring to deflect to Esau a blessing they both knew that he had forfeited by selling his birthright. See **Genesis 25:23**.

Of course, this does not clear Rebekah and Jacob from the sins they had committed.

It is remarkable that during such unworthy human conduct that the will of God is accomplished.

There are always consequences to Sin. In the end, we see that Esau hates and desires to murder Jacob.

The religious world abounds with deceivers, who speak with Jacob's voice, but whose hands are Esau's hands. These false leaders and movements deceive many to believe that which's not valid according to the Bible.

Unfortunately, there are many like Isaac, whose spiritual vision and discernment is weak.

While depending upon feeling and human reasoning, they lend their influence, money, and blessing to those who are the enemies of Christ and His Church.

In this manner, cults, charismatic, and social Gospel are making inroads in the Church.

Finally, Jacob found acceptance with his father and received his blessing because he sheltered behind the name of the father's firstborn, clothed with his garments.

Likewise, we as sinners find acceptance because we are sheltered behind the name of God's firstborn son, and robed in His righteousness.

Chapter 28

W e need to learn to rejoice more in the Lord. Life is not easy. It is full of hard knocks.

Learning to step out on a limb can be frightening, but sometimes that is what we have to do to submit to the Lord's will.

That is where the fruit of the blessings are. Isaac blesses Jacob and tells him to leave and go back to his uncle Laban and find a wife there.

In our text, we find that Jacob is charged not to marry the Gentiles but to take a bride from his kin. On the other hand, when this charge is extended to Isaac's brothers, we find that Esau goes directly to Ishmael and takes a wife from his family, forbidden by Isaac.

So we see that Esau is in rebellion to the things of God.

Throughout the O.T., the godly are not to marry the ungodly. The wickedness of Noah's day was the result of such unions. See *Gen. 6:4*.

The same is true for us today. We are to have like marriages. See *II Cor. 6:14*.

Jacob leaves, and we know that he will be gone a long time away from his parents.

By this time, Esau was already married to two Canaanite women. See *Gen. 26:34*.

From his brother, Jacob could see that this kind of marriage would not work but be a grief to Isaac and Rebekah. See *Gen. 26:34; 27:46*. The descendants of Ishmael were as rejected in the line of the promised seed as were the Canaanites. See **Gen. 17:18-21.**

Jacob travels to Bethel the first day. Bethel is close to 12 miles north of Jerusalem, and Beer-Sheba is about 25-30 miles south of Jerusalem. Imagine the loneliness that Jacob feels since it was the first time he was away from home.

What a night it must have been. Can you imagine dreaming of a ladder reaching into Heaven?

This ladder is a type of the Lord Jesus Christ. You and I know that Christ alone can span the gap between God and man.

Interestingly this would be the first contact Jacob has with the Lord, personally. I am sure he had heard his father talk about God, but he had not yet had that experience. The same promised blessing was given to Jacob, as was given to Abram and Isaac. You can find this in **Gen. 13:14-18; 17:6-8, and Gen. 26:24.**

Jacob had the promise of God that He would go with him and bring him back. Remember, God made a promise to each of us to never leave us or forsake us. God will perform what He has promised.

Abraham accepted God at face value; that is, he took God at His Word. Herein is the answer to his faith being accounted unto him for righteousness? See **Rom. 4:21.**

What a wonderful feeling to be in the presence of God. Sometimes I have been awed by His presence, and sometimes I have dropped to my knees in fear.

Compare such men as Moses, Aaron, Paul, John. "Dreadful" is from the Hebrew word "yare" (yaw-ray), and it means to fear, morally to revere; cause to frighten.

We see that Jacob understands that he is standing on Holy ground and calls this place Bethel. The firm pillows that he slept on became pillars. There was one to rest upon; the other to make a vow. Bethel is not the first name of this place, but it is the lasting name.

Bethel means the House of God. Later, Jacob calls this place "El-bethel," which is "the God of Bethel." See **Gen. 35:7**. After this night with the Lord, Jacob seems ready to make peace with his adversary, Esau.

Many things occur to Jacob before he does return in peace. This stone represents the Rock of our Salvation. We could call these stones the pillow of rest and the pillar of praise. We may rest upon His promises and stand assured that He alone is able. We must add that the house of God has always been "the pillar of truth." See **1 Tim. 3:15**.

Chapter 29

Jacob begins his years of reaping. Although God chose Jacob, he had not walked according to God's will. Jacob, the supplanter, meets Laban, the schemer, and what a match they made.

Jacob has to learn that the way of the transgressor is hard. Yet, despite it all, Jacob was kept by the Lord. This 500-mile journey seems to have been uneventful after his experience at Bethel. God was indeed with him.

One appealing thought here is that nothing is said of Jacob praying, as did Abraham's servant. See **Gen. 24:15**.

Now we have the meeting of Jacob with Rachel. He finds her at the well watering her fathers' sheep. We cannot believe that Jacob just happened to go to the right well, or that Rachel just happened to come to that well.

God, in His divine plan, was working a great work. Jacob boldly rolls away from the stone.

It seems inevitable that the legal water rights have something to do with all of the shepherds coming, and then the stone is removed.

Jacob is so homesick the first person he sees as kin he kisses. I can only imagine how seeing Rachel brought back thoughts of his mother. During their conversation, Jacob identifies himself and finds out that Laban is her father. We find that it takes a month of visiting and relaxing before Jacob is ready to do business.

There is a principle that is found many times in the Bible. We call that reaping what you sow.

We have a principle which states you will reap what you have sown.

I read about a white-haired man, wrinkled skinned, that walked with the aid of a cane. Someone asked him, 'What is the secret to your long life?" He said, "Drinking, smoking, partying all night, and wild living." "Oh, really," asked the inquirer. "And how old are you?" "I'm 29."

There are inevitable physical consequences to individual lifestyles. There is no escaping the God-given principle of sowing and reaping.

Working at a funeral home for a little while, I have noticed it is the right place to evaluate what a person does with their life. You can tell what a person has done in life by whom and how many attend a person's funeral.

There is the principle of communal life that one reaps what they sow. History has proven that a nation that goes down a specific path is destined to inevitable consequences again and again.

His name was Edward Gibbon, who completed his book in 1787. It took twenty years to finish his book. The book's title is the Decline and Fall of the Roman Empire. By his title, you know he wrote on the fall of the Roman Empire. In his book, he notes what took place in their fall.

It sounds like a read of today's newspaper. There were outlandish divorce rates, the undermining of the home, and the lack of morals. Taxes so high people received free bread just to survive. There was a craze for the pleasure of sports, every year, more extravagant and brutal. Also, there was the building and tearing down statues of people they admired and hated. "The decay of religion, faith is fading into mere form, losing touch with life and becoming impotent to warn and guide the people."

As an American, I shiver when I see the moral decline of our cherished nation. I tremble when our nation's leaders claim to be Christians, endorse alternate lifestyles, and embrace every kind as acceptable forms of behavior.

When the T.V. program "Ellen" proclaimed that Ellen DeGeneres was a lesbian, Vice President Al Gore praised the show suggesting that gay and lesbian practices should be tolerated but accepted and respected as alternative lifestyles.

Our government has pushed God entirely out of our public life, and it will not be without consequences. It has not been without consequences.

There is the principle in spiritual life that one reaps what they sow. Listen to **Gal. 6:7-8**, "Be not deceived; God is not mocked: for whatsoever a man soweth, that shall he also reap. For he that soweth to his flesh shall of the flesh reap corruption, but he that soweth to the Spirit shall of the Spirit reap life everlasting."

How could one sow the seeds of the flesh and not expect God to do something about it?

You cannot expect to reap blessings from the one whom you hate. If you sow a bad seed, you will reap a terrible harvest. If you sow a spiritual seed, you will reap a thrilling harvest.

Job 4:8 says, "Even as I have seen, they that plough iniquity, and sow wickedness, reap the same."

We note this end to end in the Word of God. Remember it was Pharaoh who gave the orders that every Hebrew male child was to be drowned, but he was the one drowned in the end.

Korah caused a rift in Israel's congregation, but God made an aperture in the earth to swallow him in the end.

Ahab slew Naboth, and it was the dogs that licked up his blood. At the end of his life, Ahab had the same results. We read the dogs came and licked up his blood.

We reap what we sow. We reap the same kind of thing as we sow. There is a time for reaping and a different season than when we sow. We reap more than we sow.

We cannot do anything about last years' harvest, but we can about these years. Declared in God's Word is the principle of sowing and reaping.

Jacob is an excellent example of that one reaps what they sow. Here in **Genesis 29**, we see Jacob reaping what he had sown. Think of the ways of Jacob that are remembered by God.

In these chapters, we see Jacob cheated, deceived, and mistreated.

But think back as to what he did with his brother Esau. Remember how he mistreated those around him. See **Genesis 25:29-43**. When you look at his life, he was a crook, a con-artist, and as often as possible, he took advantage of whatever situation at the moment.

That is what he did with his brother in cheating him out of his birthright.

It did not stop there. See *Genesis 27: 18-24*.

On his father's death bed, Jacob deceived him. He had help with the aid of his mother.

What we sow, we will reap likewise. However, remember, we are all held accountable for what we do. His entire life has been one of cheating, conning, and conniving. He did not care how he treated those around him as long as he got his way. Jacob, all his life, has been the boss.
We have mentioned before how these sorts of people think. They will do it their way or bust.

Do you think he would ask God for anything? Where is God in all of this? If he felt it would benefit him, which is what he did.

The rule for the day was to take matters into his hands. No consulting God here. Maybe he understood that somehow he was to receive the birthright. The problem was he was not willing to let God work it out. He chose to do what we would do in taking matters into our own hands. Look at his life, when it came to family matters, where is God? Not in his plans. In *Genesis 29*, how did he receive Rebekah as his wife? He doesn't seek God's will in the matter. He wanted more essential things than God's will.

Look at his finances. At least it appears this is what he thought. Did he consult God? We see him making financial arrangements in *Genesis 30*, without asking God what he should do.

We all know Jacob's life. Don't you see Jacob in your life? He probably reminds us more of ourselves than others. We see the ways of Jacob remembered! The wrongs of Jacob that ware reaped! *Matthew 7:1, 2* says, "Judge not, that ye be not judged For with what judgment ye judge, ye shall be judged: and with what measure ye mete, it shall be measured to you again."

Again *Luke 6:38* says, "Give, and it shall be given unto you; good measure, pressed down, and shaken together, and running over, shall men give into your bosom. For with the same measure that ye mete withal, it shall be measured to you again.

Seeing Jacob's rewards, we can say he got back more than he dished out.

When we come to *Genesis 29*, it is seven years later, and the chickens are starting to go to roost.

Eccles. 8: 11 says, "Because sentence against an evil work is not executed speedily, therefore the heart of the sons of men is fully set in them to do evil."

Do we see this happening overnight? Of course, the answer is no; however, there will be a place to reap what you sow.

Notice this principle at work in Jacob. Then there is the degradation he experienced.

Genesis 29: 15 says, "And Laban said unto Jacob, because thou art my brother, shouldest thou, therefore, serve me for nought? Tell me, what shall thy wages be?" I am pretty sure his mother told him the elder would serve the younger. See Genesis *25: 13*.

If Jacob got the birthright, he would know the elder would serve the younger.

From our passage, we see Jacob must have set his heart on that birthright and get it by any means possible.

Jacob has now been placed in the position of a servant before Laban. The deceiver just was outsmarted. It only took a month as a guest in Laban's house for Laban to devise a plan to keep him there as his servant. Imagine how big this pill was when Jacob began to realize what Laban had done to him. Nothing changes. You reap, you will sow.

Also, note there is the deception he experienced. It seems they were trying to outsmart each other from the beginning. Before Laban could get the words out of his mouth, Jacob already had a plan. The dealer made a bad deal when he chose to serve Laban for seven years to marry one of his daughters, the younger one. We read that Laban tricked him into marrying Leah because of the elder clause. See **Genesis 29:16-26**.

Could there have been more of a shock than what took place after the marriage night?

Consider the story of the man who fell in love with a beautiful woman. He gets married.

The night of the wedding, she takes off her wig, pulls out a glass eye, puts her false teeth in the top drawer. He just sat there looking at her. She looked at him and asked, "Honey, aren't you coming to bed?" He said that sitting on the edge of the bed; I don't know whether to get in the dresser or the bed.

Jacob said to Laban, "Wherefore hast thou beguiled me?" Have you not heard turnabout is fair play? The trickster had been tricked. Isn't that what he did to his brother?

Interestingly, the very thing he has disregarded in Esau, the firstborn's rights, was the same thing God brought face to face to him.

We have discovered that ole saying is true, what goes around comes around.

He ignored his situation with his brother, but now he faces this issue with his wife.

Then there is the delay he experienced. What a story of true love this is.

Just as for the Christian, the most significant motive for service is love. Isn't it interesting what love can do? Jacob's love made seven years seem like a few days. In the same token, service for God will not be dreaded if we love Him.

It has been noted this is one of the greatest love stories of the Bible, but it is marked by tragedy and Sin.

Not only is this love story, but it shows that Sin does have its consequences.

As Jacob had deceived his father, now we see that Laban deceives Jacob.

As Jacob prepares to receive his wife Rachel, we find that Laban has developed an elaborate deception.

Jacob finds out too late that he has been deceived. Under modern marriage customs, such deception would easily be detected. But their traditions made it easy to fool. Jacob finds out the hard way, the rights of the firstborn. Remember how he deceived his father, now he is the victim. He is given Rachel also one week later. Jacob had to serve Laban seven more years for Rachel.

We often find references to polygamy being practiced in the Old Testament, but never with God's approval. In every case, we see that it produced conflict, heartache, and Sin.

Abraham, Jacob, David, and Solomon all furnish examples of the result of this evil.

Now he is going to wait to have what he wanted. Here is the distress he experienced. Through this experience, Jacob acquired two wives instead of one. That created many problems for him. See *Genesis 29:31-32*.

It is evident that there tension, strife, discord, and great division in the home. Remember the conflict he had caused in his own family experienced years before. For seven years, there had been discord and division before he left. There was a great tug of war going on in that family.

What do we see in all this? The point is undeniable.

We reap what we sow.

The ways of Jacob we remembered! The wrongs of Jacob come to pass. We now see the reprehensible words of Jacob! Read *Gen. 29: 25*.

How is it possible he could even question what was happening? Never have you seen one so short-minded. Admittedly, these words by him deserve condemning.

Jacob's words, "Wherefore hast thou beguiled me?" It is a guilty statement.

In his words, we see a lack of personal consideration. I wonder how many times I have heard from my father this statement, "talk about calling the kettle black."

No one wants to face the music. Jacob does not. Most people cannot see the forest for the trees if you know what I mean? He can judge others but not himself. His indeed reminds us of **Matthew 7:3-5**. Mote is the Word meaning a small fragment.

On the other hand, the word beam speaks of a significant timber piece in your eye.

Think of the humor involved here. Here is a man with a tree stuck in his eye. He wants to talk about a person with a toothpick in his eye.

I remember a saying I once heard. It goes something like this, "faults I can see; But praise the Lord, there's none in me."

An illustration I once read says, "A lady showed a friend her neighbor's wash through her back window." "Our neighbor isn't very clean. Look at those streaks on the wash!" Said her friend, "Those streaks aren't on your neighbors' wash. They're on your window."

In his words, we see a lack of personal remorse. Jacob should have realized he was getting what he had sown.

God was using it to bring conviction in his heart. It should have pierced his heart. Instead, we see instead of remorse for his sins; he was angry with Laban. Have you noticed we often react the way Jacob did? We live in a world where it is getting what you can. They don't care about the consequences down the road.

Sensitivity to the things of God has ceased in churches today.

I am sure you thought I would say globally, but the problem is in the churches today. We have studied this passage to expose the way the world has infiltrated the Church of today. But in this, we can see Jacob demonstrates that a person will reap what they sow. You reap what you sow!

Chapter 30

Genesis 30 is not pleasant reading, but it is recorded for our learning.

A thoughtful Christian will read through this chapter and see the awful fruitage and consequences of polygamy, as described herein. We see that a plurality of wives must of necessity produce discord, jealousy, and hatred. We can be thankful that God has left us a better plan, wherein each man should have his wife, and each woman should have her husband.

But that is not the only thing going on in this chapter. You will read of the deception of both Jacob and Laban. One tries to outdo the other, but in the end, it is the will of God that prevails, and so we will see that Jacob and all he has is heading for the Promised Land again.

At the beginning of the chapter, it is not hard to see the envious attitude of Jacob's wives because, at one time or another, one is barren, and another is fruitful. Because of this, we find much hatred in this chapter between the wives of Jacob.

Envy is grieving at the prosperity of another. That sounds godly, doesn't it?

I believe this Sin is a great offense to God, and we see it running rampant in our society.

We used to say God was not within a mile of such an attitude. The problem is what the results will be. God was not in the thinking of everyone involved in this chapter, at least for a while.

We the flesh ruling throughout this chapter, and it should make the true Christian sad.

They could not see that it was God who was making the difference, not their scheming.

Sometimes when things just do not go our way, we need to be careful who we blame and what we do in the process on our own.

What a mess s made here. There is no trusting God at this point. It is just like today, our country is in a crisis, and the last person people turn to is God. He should be the only one we turn too. You will not find much prayer to God in this chapter. It is what man can do, think, or have.

How different we see others in the Word of God when they were in a crisis. Comparing God's Word, we can see the difference between Rachel's asking for mercy versus what Hannah did in *1 Sam. 1:10*. The difference is Rachel envied, and Hannah wept. She pleads with her husband to have children and dies with the second child. Hannah, on the other hand, prayed for one child, and she had four more.

Rachel is presumptuous, but Hannah is submissive and pleads to God alone. Since Rachel was barren, she was willing to give her handmaid to Jacob for a wife to say she had children. In those days, those children would have been hers, not Bilhah's.

If two wives were not enough, we find that Leah, Jacob's first wife, also gave him her handmaid.

What an outrageous thing to do. Where is God in all of this? Rather than seeing God instead, you see the world and the devil in action in the flesh, the world, and the devil. There is nothing but envy, jealousy, and rivalry here.

We stand amazed at the divine appointment's wisdom, which unites one man and one woman only; God hath called us to peace and purity. See *1 Cor. 7:15*.

The Law of Moses reasons it a typical case: if a man had two wives, one would be beloved, and the other hated. See *Deut. 21:15*.

In our text, reaching the end, it is not hard to see Jacob and Laban conniving each other again.

How many times have we said it could be by God's grace only to win the day?

Jacob understood this, as well.

Finally, having accomplished and fulfilled his commitment to Laban, Jacob desires to go back to Canaan's family. Of a truth I can say about the only thing good that comes out of this passage is the fact that Joseph is born. He will be a prominent figure in the rest of the book of Genesis.

Chapter 31

Reading this chapter, you will find a man who wanted to be above others now in a servant's role and that for twenty years of hard labor. You come to the place once in a while when you realize it is time to move on because you have had enough.

At least Jacob had God to tell him when to leave, and that time was now.

There is much to accuse people in today's world. Sometimes we charge justly, other times, not so. We know that riches are a glorious thing in the eyes of carnal people.

However, for the child of God, is it no wonder that things here on this earth do not attract them as it does those of the world?

It is no wonder we see men's over-valuing of worldly wealth, causing the fundamental error that causes the root of covetousness, envy, and evil to spring up inside of them. There is a disadvantage of being wealthy. Think of the envy of those around them. We recall that whom Heaven blesses Hell curses.

Envy is one of those sins you cannot hide. It is not very hard to identify that Sin in a person.

Looking into someone's eyes is often all it takes to know. No doubt, Laban was envious and began to be full of hatred for God was blessing Jacob, and he was tired of what was happening.

Again we see the schemer and the scheme. I am glad that God spoke to Jacob also and told him it was time to leave Haran. He once again confirms to him who He is. He is the God of Bethel. It was there God had met with Jacob and made a covenant with him. There is no way he would forget that night. Remember, Bethel means the "house of God." Bethel stands for fellowship and communion with God.

The backslider should return to Bethel to start over. Laban had certainly mistreated his daughters and took from them. As they packed up and left without Laban's knowledge, it was sure to cause them trouble.

Laban took seven days to catch Jacob and his band, and in the process, God speaks to Laban and tells him not to touch Jacob. Having left the way they did, there was no doubt Laban would be mad and want to pick a fight with Jacob. It is interesting to me that no battle ensued here. There were a lot of tempers flying here, but they left one another in peace. I think one of the reasons why that is Jacob rightfully gave the credit to God. It would be hard to object here. Now they depart in peace.

Chapter 32

Do you know that place called between a rock and a hard place? Jacob had just dealt with his uncle Laban. As he has been heading home, he remembers some unfinished business between himself and his brother Esau. Esau had said he would kill him. So he thinks he will be able to work it out by sending some people ahead and tell Esau he was coming home. Then they are met by an army of four hundred men.

Jacob had instructed his men to call Esau "lord." He was hoping that Esau would accept his offer of grace. When they return to Jacob, they tell him that Esau is coming to meet him; this also brings fear and distress to Jacob.

In the meantime, we find God will intervene for Jacob and sends angels to meet with him to assure him that God will keep His promises. They meet at a place called Mahanaim.

The name means two hosts or camps. Could there have been two hosts of angels, one before Jacob and the other after Jacob? After his men's news, we find Jacob does the one thing left for him: to pray.

It is fascinating the prayer he prays. He pleads the covenant God had made with him. He argues based on God's Word. He confesses his unworthiness and sinfulness. He gives God the glory for all his success. He asks for deliverance for himself and his family. He reminds God of the promises made at Bethel. See *Genesis 28:13-15*.

There is no doubt but that God delights in us clinging to His promises. Now the time is fast approaching when Jacob would meet his brother. It had been many years, and Jacob had not forgotten what he had done to him. Nor had his character changed. He is still the same old Jacob, always planning, always trying to figure out a plan.

I see Jacob in so many of us, always trying to scheme to make things happen the way he wants it to work out. We forget God is really in control and not we. You would think with the angels of God meeting him and him praying such a beautiful prayer that he would have his heart and mind right with God.

But old habits die hard. So Jacob has some lessons to learn, and God will teach him.

Either we lean on God or fail in our plans.

In these next few verses, we see Jacob realizing who he is before the eyes of God. You could say that God wrestled him into submission. I believe that it is wrong to imply that Jacob sought to wrestle with him. It was the man that wrestled with Jacob. Jacob resisted with all his might. He is so much like the rest of us. W Self gets in the way instead of just trusting God to work it out. In our hearts' pride, we are so opinionated that we often fail to or refuse to submit to God's divine will. That shows us our carnal mind and nature yielding only to our self- efforts.

Jacob always strived to supplant his will against the will of God. Of course, it was the Lord that wrestled with Jacob. See **Hosea 12:4**. Though He is called an angel, nevertheless, He is the same one that came to Abraham. See **Gen. 18.2**.

I have often thought that if it was the Lord, then why did it take Him so long to prevail?

I think the answer is God is gracious and long-suffering when dealing with His people. Not to belittle God's power, but rather to show the stubbornness and self-will of Jacob. Early on in this combat, God could have done something to Jacob, but He did not. He touched the hollow of his thigh, showing how quickly the Lord could disable Jacob when He was ready.

Notice this is a good indication of the crippling effect of sin in our lives.

The touch of death must be written on our flesh before the will of God can be accomplished.

The cross and its strength must be entered into before we can walk with God.

Jacob struggled long because his confidence in the flesh was strong. Yet God knows how to touch our strength and write the sentence of death. Until we allow Him to do this, there can be no real power with God. We must become weak before we can be made strong. Once he was resisting, now he is merely holding on. Now, this is the right and proper way to deal with God. Now that his strength broke, may God use this to show him and us the evil of our hearts in acting alone?

May we learn to cling more closely to God? Notice that Jacob says, "I will not let thee go except thou bless me." He had a heartfelt desire to seek God, which was why he was unwilling to let go. God had to touch him before he realized he could not do it alone but by God's power.

Brokenness is the desire of God in each of us. This submissive attitude of our entire dependence is always ready to bring forth the new character of our lives if we let it. Now see him changed.

Before, he had always depended upon his ways and means. We all must learn that lesson of clinging to God alone. Now he becomes Israel and not the supplanter. What is your name, the Lord asks? The Lord knew his name, but the question was asked for Jacob to declare his true nature. He is Jacob, the supplanter, the trickster. His name changed to Israel, which means "Prince with God."

Jacob asks something he should have known, and this he reveals in the next verse.

Interestingly, Jacob calls the place Peniel, "I have seen God face to face." How can anyone see God and live? Instead, God leaves him with a limp for the rest of his life.

What a constant reminder to Jacob so that he would never forget this experience. God was here dealing with Jacob's flesh.

He did not eradicate it, but He only shrank it. All of our life, we will have the battle of our fleshly nature on this earth, but God can undoubtedly cause us to lean upon Him.

His walk reveals to us he was a God conquered man.

Does our walk and conversation in life prove that we are princes with God by or bearing the marks of a life wholly surrendered to God?

If you would read the first part of this chapter, God made a promise, but Jacob did not believe him. After all that has taken place, Jacob is so much like the rest of us. He had not learned to trust God.

Jacob had treated Esau badly, but instead of casting himself on God, he continued to plan and scheme.

We live in a world of manipulation instead of learning to lean on God.

His is the language of a man not focused on God. Jacob's first thought was always to plan, and in him, we have an accurate picture of the human heart. When have you asked God to do something, and you did not like the results, then what did you do?

Esau was not satisfied with what God did about his brother Esau. That is where we are at, fearing, and in Jacob's case, he now fears his brother. That is why he waited behind, alone.

Why do we fear man when we should fear God?

In the case of Jacob, we can see the mercy of God upon him. We must see this as a turning point in the history of his life. That night all alone with almighty God was a fearful thing.

Maybe this was the only way Jacob could face himself. We can never understand our being until we are alone with God.

What do you think about yourself? No matter what others think? That is not the burning question. The most burning question is, what does God think of us?

To answer this question, we must be left alone.

Away from the world, away from all that would influence self, away from thoughts, reasoning, imaginations, and nature. Must be alone with God for however long it takes.

It is here we face reality and truth.

He had forgotten his prayer. We should ask as to whom was Jacob trusting? Was it a few cattle or Jehovah God? We can learn how apt we are to lean on our powers than upon God, but that will not. See *Isa. 40:6*.

Chapter 33

This chapter is the meeting between Jacob and Esau. Once again, we see the old Jacob, full of fear, and with so little faith and trust in God. There is a change in Jacob, the man who prevailed with God, slavishly bows before his brother seven times. Yet, we see the same thing in Elijah, who so heroically stood against Baal's 400 prophets, but a short time later, he flees from the woman Jezebel.

Let this be a lesson for us. One victory does not guarantee a second one. I am sure things would have been different had not God dealt with Esau, as He had done with Laban.

See *Prov. 21:1* for my thinking on this, "The king's heart is in the hand of the LORD, as the rivers of water: he turneth it whithersoever he will."

As they meet, it will surprise you that Jacob is a changed man, and so had his brother, Esau.

In the custom of the day, it is only right for Esau to take things from his brother, and he does as a show of honor and friendship.

So this is the reason for the "why." It is pretty simple. There is forgiveness in the air.

They do not bring up the pass, but it is pretty impressive what they each do here.

Esau wants them to journey together, but I think deep down, Jacob is still afraid of Esau.

He makes some excuses and, in the end, says he will meet with him later back home.

After Esau leaves, we find Jacob being his old self again.

He does not trust anyone, especially his brother. Jacob resides in Succoth. Succoth was the opposite direction from Seir. He had to cross back over the Jabbok to get to Succoth. When he arrives in Succoth, he built a house for himself and booths for his cattle. No short visit here. It speaks of an extended stay. Later we will see his children were mature when he lived in Shechem and indicated they stayed in Succoth for some time. It takes Jacob a while to arrive in Shechem. "Shalem" means "peace" and "safe and sound."

Chapter 34

When you begin to read this chapter, if you are a parent, then you know the heartache that your children can bring to you. As a father and parent, I can tell you many stories of what my children have done.

Would you not agree to be raised in a Christian home is a blessed thing" We tried to teach all of our children the things of God and honor and love Him. We often prayed with them and secretly believed that God would take care of them and protect them. We often remind ourselves that we can only protect them for so long before their seeing what is happening in the world. We pray that as we let them meet and greet the world, we will hold up all of the teachings we have given them in this world's trials.

As parents, we know what they will have to face for the world is a wicked place, and as much as we try to teach them how corrupt the world is, we know that many they will try and experiment with it. My wife and I had four children. For the most part, we homeschooled them and taught them what we felt they should know. But there remains one factor that we cannot teach them: how to live in this wicked world and still hold to Christendom's morals and beliefs on their own. That is something they have to do by themselves. I know I can tell you that it is a hard thing to do.

As a parent, you think back to what you did as you were growing up and what you did wrong and got in to. You know what lies ahead for them, and oh how you pray.

As we read this chapter and the sadness that Jacob and his family were to endure, we too feel the heartache of seeing our children go the way of the world. One thing about it, we each will have to face God with what we have done. One day we each will have to face God with what we have done. There will be no one else with us.

Such a hard lesson to learn, and the more challenging thing about it is we know what is out there, but they do not. We protected our children, sheltered them, loved them, prayed for them, but in the end, they grew up and had to go out on their own. We should try, but we need to understand working hard is not enough. Just knowing we are sinners should be enough. However, sin will find a way to show its ugly head and try and destroy us.

Jacob was no different. He had boys and girls, and boys and girls will do what boys and girls will do.

One of my children can say I was pretty strict with; at least, he kept telling me.

Anyway, just as soon as he was old enough to go, he went to put it simply. He had to find out for himself. And boy did he find out.

Speaking of breaking a mother's heart, Jacob did.

In our text, we find Jacob, who had a daughter, which she wanted to do.

You know what happened if you read the text. In today's terminology, she went to a party and found a guy who hooked up with her.

As a dad, that it will not sit too well with me. Fornication and adultery have always been wrong and always will be wrong. At least the boy had a desire to do the right thing and marry her. The only thing is he was a heathen, and Jacob had forbidden them to associate with them.

Even the father of the son thinks it is a good idea.

That is the way of the world. They think intermingling is not wrong. It was not God's will for them to marry unbelievers. By the way, that is still what God's Word teaches. That has not changed.

When Jacob found out what had happened, he was upset, so he told his sons. Knowing my boys like I do that was not a good thing to do. Just as Jacobs boys devised a plan to get even with the Shechemites, I would think my boys would say something if that situation arose in our family.

Remember, the flesh is wicked, and the heart can devise many things. So the sons of Jacob demands that the men of the Shechemites be circumcised. Oh, how it was a smart but deceitful plan. Hamor's people comply for dishonest reasons as well. But Jacob's sons were quicker to execute their plan. While they were sick and sore from surgery, they were easy victims for slaughter. They killed the men, but they destroyed the city and took captives.

Hearing what was done, Jacob feared the friends and allies of the Shechemites.

If I were Jacob, I would pack my bags and leave, and that is what he did.

When you read this, you will remember that Jacob had told his brother he would go to Bethel.

Of course, he lied to his brother, and that is how he wound up in Shechem.

If you read this, I think you will find that Jacob failed to train and protect his daughter in this heathen land.

Neither Jacob's sins, the sins of the Shechemites, nor his sons' sins kept God from protecting Jacob and his family from oblivion.

It would undoubtedly come if they had intermarried with the heathen.

As we read this, it is understood or should be that the reason Jacob did not go to Bethel at first was that he still had some things to deal with in his own life.

I believe what happened with his children just exemplifies this. He had to get rid of some things in his own life. These things were only substitutes for God. Jacob had to get rid of his old lifestyle. He had to get rid of the old way of doing things and saying things. He had to clean up his act. He could no longer do some things he used to do.

Here at the end of this chapter, Jacob remembered what God had done for him in Bethel.

The altar is mentioned three times in this chapter. See ***Genesis 35:1, 3, 7.***

When you read this chapter, you will find that Jacob was not so worried about the sin but was concerned about its consequences.

There is no doubt he needed to go to Bethel, but you cannot go unless you are willing to shed the world's things.

What does Jacob say? There were strange gods in the house of Jacob. He was God's man, and there was a compromise in his home. Put away the strange gods. There can be no worship at the foot of the cross until this happens. Be clean if you are going up to worship. Change your garments to get clean inside and out. Why'd did they pull off the earrings?

Earrings are always associated with sinful worship in the Bible. See ***Ex. 32:2-4*** and ***Hosea 2:13.***

The cross is always against the old man, the old nature, the old ways. Luz means a departure from God. It means to be in sin.

Now, this is the second time that Jacob found out he was there. Since he had left God, God had not appeared to him. When he was doing the wicked works and doing evil and telling Esau lies, God could not speak to him. God appeared to him only after he stopped his lying and doing evil.

If you will notice, there is a significant gap between ***verses 29*** and ***30.*** Talk about not keeping a promise we see 30 years after he told Esau he was coming. There is a big gap in many of our lives. Bethel is the place where Abraham built his first altar. Then he left and went down into Egypt. He had to go back to Bethel before God blessed him again. See ***Genesis 13:3, 4.***

Chapter 35

Well, Jacob has found himself in a mess once again. He could not return to Haran, he could not go to Esau, and he cannot remain in Shechem.

Like many of us, we have to come to the end of ourselves before the Lord steps in. How many times could we count that the Lord has done that for us too?

God has to tell him what to do. At least he listens and does what God says.

So He tells him to go up to Bethel and dwell there. Make there an altar. Worship is His desire. Now, God will give him the instructions he needs. God gives him instructions as to what to do. The dirty, polluted waters must be cleaned. Now, they were to turn their back on the strange gods. They were to change garments. All this resulted in an outward change.

What did Jacob do? He buried the idols. At least he did not take something wrong and try to make something out of them. Once you obey God, he will take care of you.

They started the journey. The Lord protected them along the way. Once they arrive at Bethel, God continues to instruct Jacob as to what to do. He brought all of his family and people to Bethel. He built an altar and named it El-bethel. The name means the "God of the House of God." In the meantime, we find Deborah has died, and he buries her. We do not know why she was with Jacob.

Perhaps Rebekah was already dead. Rebekah's death is not recorded, and this may be because she is the type of the Church that will not die but be raptured home to be with the Lord. The "oak of weeping buried her."

As God continues to deal with Jacob, we find Jacob receives a new name. For God speaking with him again, he erects another altar. In the meantime, we find that Rachel dies. I think God was preparing him for this by helping him see he was out of fellowship with God and that he needed to repent of his wicked ways.

Once the soul finds restoration, there can be fellowship.

The next step is to find spiritual nourishment. In her death, she gave birth to another son for Jacob. His mother named him Ben-oni (son of sorrow), but Jacob called him Benjamin (son of my right hand). Think about this, as the "son of sorrow," Christ suffered and died, but as the "son of my right hand," He sits at the father's right hand.

Then if that is not enough sorrow added to his life, we find in the rest of the chapter how his sons are once again in trouble for sinning against God. To remember that there are coming consequences to sin, we will see this in the future. Many people sin and think they have gotten away with it.

But alas, we know that sooner or later, the debt will have to be paid.

By this time, Isaac is an older man, and he goes the way of death, just like the rest of us will one day. Imagine, he was 180 years old when he died. The two brothers who had fought so much come together again to bury their father.

Chapter 36

Although this is a long chapter, it can quickly be clarified in just a few words. Once again, we find that Jacob and Esau had separated from each other. This time it is Esau who leaves Bethel. He travels to the land God gave him, which is known as Edom.

Esau goes specifically to Mount Seir. At least this time, it was an honorable separation.

The reason was that God had blessed them both that they had so much the land could not take care of all their flocks.

Now we have in the rest of the chapter the genealogy of Esau.

Two notable points need to be made here. One is that one of the sons of Esau was Amalek.

Later we will hear more of the Amalekites. They became a ruthless and wicked people who hated the Jews. We find this genealogy of the Edomite's inserted in the genealogy of the Horites and the Canaanites or Hittites. They were native to Mount Seir, the land God gave Abraham. You will find them in *Genesis 14:6*, and of their interest in Mount Seir, before the Edomite's took possession of it.

Mentioning them is because of the wickedness among the Edomite's for intermarrying with them, learning their ways, and corrupting themselves. So we find that Esau had sold his birthright, and losing his blessing, must have allied with the Hittites.

Did you notice that his posterity and the sons of Seir are supposed as one nation? We say the apostate Edomite's stand on the same ground with accursed Horites, as we will see later on.

Chapter 37

W e need to go over some background before we get into the life of Joseph. More chapters have been recorded of Joseph than any other O.T. character. We would ask a great question to ask is, why was so much written about him? Because it gives us an explanation of the circumstances of early Israel of which we would not know otherwise.

Without this record, Exodus would be a real puzzle. Joseph is an example of correct Christian conduct. His life gives us valuable insight via instruction and encouragement. Before *Genesis 37*, Joseph is mentioned four times. See *Gen. 30:22-24*.

If you recall, Jacobs's favorite wife was Rachel, who bears him a son. His name is Joseph.

Through Leah, Bilhah, and Zilphah, Jacob had already given birth to 10 sons. See *Genesis 33:2*. Joseph was the 11th son of Jacob.

Rachel had one more son, Benjamin, and she died giving birth to him.

From here to the end of Genesis, the main character is a man named Joseph. I have written much on him, and I have read many books on his life. There are several outstanding characters in the book of Genesis. In interest, more space is given to the life of Joseph than any of the rest. Why? It is because he was a type of Christ in more ways than any other Bible character.

Adam typified Christ in his headship. Abel typified Christ in his death. Noah typified Christ in providing refuge. Melchizedek typified Christ as a priest. Moses typified Christ as a prophet. David typified Christ as a king. But Joseph typified Christ in many, many ways.

I am sure along the way of this study, we will introduce some of them to you.

One of the most compelling things we will see in his life is how to live the Christian life in such a challenging world.

His time was no different from ours. He faces many trials and tribulations, even at an early age. We could call these tests, and they represent many of the trials and tribulations we face in our lives. Just like us, Joseph did not live in the perfect environment. It was a wicked and perverse world he lives in.

How would you like your life exposed in this way? There have been many tests or trials I have had to face in our experience in life, and I am sorry to say I was not as brave and truehearted as Joseph.

However, even in failure, we can learn, and it can make us stronger as we go along in life.

In my life, I am glad that we have had the Word of God to lean on. See *1 Peter 1:7*.

We see Joseph, a man of faith and trust in God, compelled to follow Him wherever he was.

When comparing his life to mine, he was undoubtedly more of faith that what I could muster, for I have God's Word to comfort me; he did not.

If there was ever an individual who trusted the hand of God, indeed, it was Joseph. You must look at *Phil. 4:8* to help understand the meaning.

We can look at our lives seeing many failures, and I am sure Joseph failed too.

However, there are none mentioned in his life for us to read and revel over. No, here is a man who trusted God's hand as He revealed His Word to him. Joseph had only one purpose in his life: to bring glory and honor to the name of Jehovah.

How did he do that? Interestingly, he honored God throughout his whole life from the early years when he became a third ruler in Egypt. What was it the "key" that enabled him to live like that? If we could use but one word to describe the life of Joseph, what would it be? I think it would be purity. Remember this, "sometimes a name carries with it grave consequences." Though he honored God in all he did, it brought persecution and much suffering from his enemies, including his family.

Throughout these next few chapters, there is one question I want you to ask yourself, "What can I do to measure up to the life of Joseph?" Generally, what happens in a Christian's life is that when something doesn't go their way, they begin to question God with that word, "why??"

God, why did you let this happen? What have I done to deserve this? Here seems to be a favorite question of many today who call themselves Christians.

Sure Joseph had questions and thoughts, yet at present, God did not answer or reveal to him the answers he was faced with, not even for a very long time. He knew God had a plan for his life, and he seemed willing to wait until God answered. God did not leave him alone, just like He will not leave us alone. But we have to be willing to wait on him to let him answer in his way and in his time. See *Genesis 39:2, 21*.

It is not for us to know the whole story or the complete set of circumstances, but I know God does. We need to simply believe that God is in control and working everything out for our good. God does have a definite purpose and plan for every one of us. See *James 1:2-6*.

Down the road, in our studies, we will see this in reality in his life. If you would like a sneak peek, read *Genesis 39:2, 21* to understand this. I am reminded again of a favorite verse of mine. See *James 1:2-6*. Joseph believed in God.

God made a promise to his forefathers, and he believed God would keep his promises.

Remember, *Genesis 15:13-15*, "And he said unto Abram, Know of a surety that thy seed shall be a stranger in a land that is not theirs, and shall serve them; and they shall afflict them four hundred years; and also that nation, whom they shall serve, will I judge: and afterward shall they come out with great substance. And thou shalt go to thy fathers in peace; thou shalt be buried in a right old age. "

When you look back to *Genesis 9, 10*, you will see the wickedness of the Canaanites.

On the opposite end of the scale of purity, we see that Israel's little nation had remained pure during that same time.

All Joseph had to do was the will of God for his life. God promised to lead him, be with him every step of the way. All God asks is that each one of us is willing and obedient to him.

Joseph didn't know what God was doing at times in his life, but he was willing to trust him each step.

For Joseph's life, God's plan was simple but very hard to follow.

We often know the course God wants us to take, yet we are not willing to be obedient.

Many times much schooling has to take place before we listen to the voice of God.

In all, God trained Joseph for 30 years. He spent seventeen years at home and thirteen years on the road. In the thirteen years on the road, we will see at least five significant tests that Joseph went through. Now, a turn for the worse is coming.

With the brothers of Joseph, intermarrying was becoming a problem. God's plan was simple: he needed a man to take his people away from Canaan and down into Egypt.

God was looking for the right one he could train to be what he wanted them to be. God plans your life, just like the plan he had for Joseph's life? See *Psalm 139:1-18.*

At the beginning of the story, we find that his father gave him a coat of many colors. The coat tells a story for us as Joseph wore it. But we know that privileges bring responsibility. This coat means position.

Throughout Scripture, the principle tells us the firstborn will give up his right to the heir, and the second born will have it. Throughout the book of Genesis, this principle holds. See Cain and Abel. See Ishmael and Isaac. See Esau and Jacob. See Manasseh and Ephraim. In each case, the second gets the birthright. ***Read Col. 1:15-18***. And *1 Cor. 15:47*, which says, "The first man is of the earth, earthy: the second man is the Lord from heaven."

In each of the cases above, the second gets the blessing over the first.

The reason is that Christ has to receive the birthright and to be the firstborn.

According to the Scripture above, his name on the cross is both the first man, Adam, who failed all of humanity and Christ, the second man who could bring about our redemption.

In Adam, all die. In Christ, all are made alive.

In our text, we see Reuben has already committed incest with one of Jacob's wives.

Listen again to *Genesis 35:22*, And it came to pass, when Israel dwelt in that land, that Reuben went and lay with Bilhah his father's concubine: and Israel heard it. Now the sons of Jacob were twelve:

This is the grounds by which Reuben lost his birthright. Remember, too; Levi and Simeon had led the brutal slaying of the people of Schechem. See *Genesis 34:25-35*.

Later we will see the fate of Judah. He had a child by his daughter-in-law. See *Genesis 38:16*.

In the context, we see then this first test, the test of the soul Joseph must face.

His mind and his will are going to be tested, as we will see later on.

He had to be willing to let God take control of his whole being. He was tested even more after he went through the sufferings by the fact of his exaltation. He was tested on fulfilling God's exact plan and having to wait on God without knowing what God was doing.

Later we will see he even had to wait for two years in jail for God to answer a prayer. After all, was said and done, Joseph saw his brothers and father again, but he waited another two years to reveal himself to his brothers. That was all in the plan of God.

Joseph had to allow time for God to work on the hearts of his brothers. His brothers needed to repent of their sins before God could use them again. Through Joseph's life, we will see how a young man was taken into slavery at age 17. He grows to become the prime minister of Egypt, the most powerful nation on earth at that time.

Joseph had an exciting life. These events happened before the age of 30. No doubt, his home training was influential to him. Hopefully, through this study, we will see his ambitions, temptations, jealousies of his brothers, and suffering at many hands.

We will be able to see the sorrow he faced nearly every day. We will be able to see the suffering at the hands of those whom he tried to serve. We will know his brothers and his sorrow and how he helps his father at the end of his father's life. We will see him live like a nobleman and see the generosity of his life.

Before we go further, I think we need to take another look at his early life. Joseph was possibly around 5 or 6 when his father left his uncle Laban. By this time, many impressions are made on Joseph.

Think about it. He witnessed the life of his father, Jacob. He saw his father's flight from his uncle Laban and then Laban's pursuit of him and the things that took place when they got together. He saw Esau coming to Jacob and how he went out and stayed all night at the place called Peniel. He saw how he came back with a limp and probably wondered what had taken place.

Later you can recall the frightening experience he had at Shechem when his brethren avenged the sins committed against his half-sister Dinah and how they killed so many people. He saw his mother, Rachel, died giving birth to his brother Benjamin, his only full-blooded brother.

I think he had a hard life.

Joseph's life shows us the proper training, and no matter what happens, God can and will be with us to guide and direct us along the way. Keep in mind all those dreams he had were from God. He was not just a dreamer.

Maybe we should ask ourselves what about today; do we have these divine revelations from God? The answer to this question is no. The reason is that God has already given us His written Word. It is our divine revelation from God, and it is final. His word says nothing can be added to them or taken away. We might add that the Word of God is far superior to the dreams Joseph had.

When we think of Joseph's life, we see strict parallels in Christ's life and ministry. See *Matt. 26:63-66*. As Jesus spoke, the Pharisees, scribes, and rulers did not believe him.

In Joseph's life, his brothers and all of his family did not believe him, and even his father will rebuke him for his dreams.

Joseph's first dream was of sheaves bowing down to the head sheaf. His second dream was of the sun, moon, and stars bowing down before him. The image is explicit.

Joseph was superior and would eventually be exalted above his whole family. The coat of many colors was the indicated approval of his earthy father of those dreams. Those dreams had the blessing of God on them as well.

In our text, we find Joseph is in submission to his father's will. Joseph's brethren had taken the flock to Shechem. In the meantime, they moved the flock to Dothan. Jacob worried over his sons and, having concern for them, wanted to know what they were doing. So he sends Joseph to see and to report back to him. See *Genesis 37:12-14*.

It took real sacrifice for Joseph to leave the place of protection and shelter and care to go to where they were.

He knew how they hated him and that it could be dangerous for him to go. Nevertheless, he went as his father instructed. Now starts the second test of Joseph. Expounded is the test of death to self. As we have said, privileges often bring significant responsibilities.

Sometimes there is at a high price to have to pay.

Even before Joseph arrives at his brethren, they see him and start planning to kill him. What are they doing? They mock the Word of God and this proclaimer of the word. They are mocking because they call God's divine truth just dreams. They were more than just dreams.

They were the words of God. They mocked the power of the Word of God. The real character of his brothers now comes out.

Notice the threatenings to Joseph as he comes to them. They ridiculed Joseph. Notice the hatred coming through them. Blindness had set in, and deception is at hand. Their hearts have become hardened against him.

This is where Joseph must learn to die to self. How many of us can say that we have learned to die to self? See **Rom. 6:1-13**. Joseph had to learn God must be foremost in his life.

Have you learned to let go of your dreams for the will of God in your life?

Here he was in the pit. All of his hopes and dreams were being shattered. What comes now is, what will Joseph do? Will he trust God, or will he try to work it out for himself. God gave him those dreams. Cannot God fulfill them as well?

For those dreams to come to pass, Joseph must put them into God's hands alone.

Faithful obedience is becoming a slave to the things of God. A slave has no rights.

He knew it had to be in God's hands if he lived much less those dreams come to pass.

Joseph had to learn faithful obedience and to become a slave to God.

We are purchased and are slaves to God. Do you understand that? Christ shed His blood on the cross for you and me. By that, He paid the ultimate price, giving me freedom from the penalty of sin, thereby making a way to Heaven for us. A slave does not seek his rights because he has no rights.

Herein is a great lesson for us. What does the world say today? Most of the world says, "Give me my rights." But remember that as a child of God, you have none. God owns us as slaves.

So a band of Midianites is seen coming, and Joseph is sold to them as a slave. This is God's plan for his life.

He must become obedient in following it. There is no doubt he did not understand what was happening. Maybe we could ask, "What has happened to Joseph's dreams?"

So far, all of the steps in Joseph's life have been downward. Just because you may have a hard time may not mean you are out of God's will. Remember, Joseph did not know the whole story in his life, just like we do not know the entire story. There is nothing to look up too. No hope. There is no advantage of being the favorite. His brothers have hated him. He has been cast into a pit to die. He has been sold into slavery. He is to be taken to a foreign land without hope. He has been placed into captivity.

All of this took place before he turned 17 years old. How's that for life! Many would cry out and say God could not possibly be in all this. Here was a young man at 17 years of age taken into slavery. We will see him grow to be the prime minister of Egypt by his 30th birthday.

Hopefully, we will see his ambitions, temptations, dreams, jealous brothers, and sufferings at the hands of those he tried to serve through this.

Then we have the misunderstandings and the sorrows he had to go through to get his family into a place where they could once again be blessed of God.

In the end, we will see what real forgiveness is and how God can bless through that heart of mercy.

Here is a key for you. *Genesis 39:2* "and the LORD was with Joseph, and he was a prosperous man: and he was in the house of his master the Egyptian."

Chapter 38

This chapter follows right after the rejection of Joseph. We find that Judah is married to a Canaanite, which means "trafficker." Then we find he marries the daughter of Shuah, which means "riches."

Judah had three sons: Er, which means "enmity," Onan, which means "wickedness," and Shelah, which means "the sprout." Judah is an Israelite.

Who would think God would allow such wickedness to take place in His people. Again we see even in sin the hand of God working and the great grace He offers to His people. Judah certainly shows the depths of depravity where one can fall.

In this chapter, we see his utter rebellion against God. You can see the wickedness of his heart by the way he treats those around him. It seems like when you look at the world today, you hear the name of Christianity used a lot, but I wonder what is in their hearts.

In this chapter, you have Judah's wickedness; you can see that same wickedness in the lives of those around him. There is no doubt that sin is contagious. No wonder God made it very clear to us that we must be careful what we do and say when we call His name.

Granted, we all make bad decisions, but this was an intentional thing Judah did.

Interestingly, one of his sons seemed to have more sense than he did about God's will, yet he did the wrong thing. Wickedness in any form is immortality before God's eyes and he will punish that sin, as you can see in this passage.

However, it is a blessed thing to know that God knows our wickedness and extends grace despite that sin. When you acknowledge your sins before a holy God, I have found He will forgive as long as you repent.

In Tamar's sin, she possibly believed the promise made to Abraham and his seed, understanding the seed of the seed to come from Judah's loins. I think this drove her to do what she did when Judah would not do the right thing, knowing that the seed of the promised one could come.

And in the text, if this was indeed her desire, then God honored that because we know that she is one of the four women mentioned in Christ's genealogy in ***Matthew 1:3***.

From that verse, we can accept the fact that God forgave her hideous sin. Like her father-in-law, we see the deliberate wickedness in all of this but thank God for his great love.

Isn't it such a beautiful thing that God has done?

For a moment, think of this wicked sin Judah committed. First, I believe he knew the will of God and refused to obey it. Because of that, other sins showed up through his sons and his daughter-in-law. Note that you cannot just commit one sin, and then it is done. Is there any doubt the devil knows how it works. You commit one sin, and then you have to commit many more before the deed stops like Judah's case. Second, not only would he not do God's will, but he was also guilty of incest. Also, we can add he was guilty of fornication. He was guilty of the lust of the eye. Note that he saw her.

He was not where he should have been and not doing what he should have been doing.

He was guilty of adultery. Tamar was not his wife, nor in this case, as she was playing the harlot. He was guilty of whoredom; he paid for his sin. He lost that day more than he knew.

Isn't that what sin does?

Satan never tells the result of committing even one unholy sin. However, at the end of the awful story of Tamar's sin, we see God's grace!

Chapter 39

God gave us a break on Joseph's life to inform us of Judah's sins and his family.

Now we take up right where we left off in the life of Joseph. Whatever it seems like Joseph is facing, he still has his eyes on the Lord and believes that God will do good for him. Often in those tests, we take our eyes off God's will and become bitter to the end. What a shame.

I have failed God just like many of you, but you could see God working for the best in your life when you get a chance to look back.

How many times we had said, if we had only listened, things would have been different.

God helps us remember that when we are loyal to Him, that does not mean we will not be tested and tried.

In those trying times, we will see the Almighty Grace of God, enabling us to become overcomers from the assaults of our enemies' enemies.

When we begin to look into this chapter, we will find Joseph stripped of all his possessions and become a slave to those around him, but there is one thing they could not take away from him: his virtue.

I have seen as we are sure you have those that seem to prosper despite their environments.

We took the time to look at Judah's sins in the last chapter to contrast him with his brother Joseph.

There are many today who want to blame society for their wrongdoing. What would you say?

My question to them is who made them do what they did? Yes, Joseph left his father and home, but he did not leave his God. He was faithful to his God, even if he lived in the house with an idolater. "Potiphar" means "devoted to Ra," who was the sun god.

Please note that we can have God's blessings and grace when under severe trials, as we will see in Joseph's life.

Sinners can observe God's blessing if we act like the Christian we are supposed to be.

Admittedly, we find God blesses others for the sake of His people. God is still working out His plans even when they seem to fail. Think of all the problems, circumstances, and even desires we have faced without God. If we had only listened to Him and sought Him to lead us and guide us through the muck and the mire, we might not be in so much trouble.

I guess we all have said at one time or another that life is the pits.

What do you think of Joseph going from one pit to another? It seems he will never get out of trouble with those around him.

How many times trouble has come your way have you stopped and said to God, "why are you doing this to me?' Everything for Joseph looks out of control, and he had no power to do anything about it. As we study his life, you will find that one of the keys to Joseph's growth is his life is that of submission. We read in *Psa. 37:5* "Commit thy way unto the LORD; trust also in him, and he shall bring it to pass."

Who has learned the lesson of waiting on God? I always seem to run ahead of God, yet here is a young man who was willing to submit himself to God's things to work in his life.

Joseph may not have known what was going on, but he was willing to wait on God.

The key to this is he had to believe and trust in God alone. There is no working it out here.

We should stop here and ask ourselves this question, "What would you do in Joseph's place?"

We should view each step we take in life as a school for us in that God is trying to teach us something.

What did Joseph do? Joseph developed a service capacity; he created a character for service. He was willing to serve God wherever He leads. He was ready to serve God, whatever the job God gave him to do. Listen to **Prov. 15:33**, "the fear of the Lord is the instruction of wisdom; and before honour is humility."

We here in America have so much. Sometimes God has to take away things in our lives to get us to serve Him. One of the problems with most of us is that God's will may not be a better standard of living for us as we see it, and many are not willing to give up some things to serve God.

What is needed is a new birth, not a new berth. You have heard it said, "Take him out of the ghetto, and he will change." I don't think so? Just look at the social interjections our society made to those in the ghettos and see if they changed.

Most people would look at the life of Joseph and say God was not in his life. That is contrary to the real truth. The evidence is not valid.

We know by the fact God was with Joseph all the time. We can see this is not true by the fact God was prospering Joseph in all he did.

Later we will see that God turned Joseph's prison into a palace. If you need help in living in this world, all you have to do is ask God.

That is what James said in the New Testament. Listen to his words in **James 1:5** "If any of you lack wisdom, let him ask of God, that giveth to all men liberally, and upbraideth not; and it shall be given him."

In the first part of this chapter, we find Potiphar, who must have bought Joseph off the Midian train and took him to his house to be a servant. It did not take very long before Potiphar realized that God was blessing him because of Joseph. We find that because of this, he treated Joseph better than most and even like a son.

Why did this happen? Because Joseph believed God was in control and would work things out to his good. In the process, we find that Joseph treated all that his master gave him to do as if it was his own.

Notice Joseph did not sit around and moan about his situation. He could have, but he was a man of action. He was honest and proved he could take charge. Looking at Joseph being a slave would make you think he would never have another opportunity to witness God.

As you read, you will see the very opposite of that is true.

Make a note of this; God is interested in our everyday life, no matter the situation.

True Christianity reveals itself best in the typical routines of life.

As Joseph worked, you will find God blessed, and I am sure it was because of Joseph's standard.

Next chapter, you will find that the devil is always relentless. He never gives us.

When you think things have settled down and you have won that test, all I can say is take a deep breath and hold on.

I am sure that it made the devil mad when Joseph held up to Satan's pressures because things were going well. Many times Satan will attack right after you have had a spiritual victory.

Joseph receives his promotion. All was going well. It came from an unexpected source.

Here is the temptation of the eye. Before it was despair, he had to face. Now, this was unexpected. It was the master's wife, not just another slave. It was challenging to defend; she was very persistent.

As children of God, sometimes we will stand alone, even if we have to because God will empower us. Joseph was a slave, and there was a special place for slaves if they had not served their masters well.

They placed Joseph in prison where the king's slaves were when they had done wrong.

The injustice Joseph faced is not uncommon; it happens all of the time, and you can see it from the time of Cain and Abel to today.

Dishonesty is the practice of today, and it was then. Potiphar's wife accused Joseph of rape and shamed her husband by making it appear that he was responsible for the trouble. She did this in front of all of the slaves.

We know because of this, Joseph was innocent. Whenever possible, Satan will use our eye-gate to entice us. Here was Joseph young, handsome, strong, one who took charge. Here lies the making or breaking of many of a man.

Why tempt the body? We find this in *1 Cor. 6:13-15*. The body belongs to the Lord. God wants them pure, healthy, and clean to honor him.

Here was Joseph, all alone. He didn't have anyone to help him at this time. No one had to tell him right from wrong. He didn't have the Bible. The Bible tells us he simply said, "No. "Here, we have the rebuttal of Joseph to sin awaiting him. If you say no to sin, victory is sure to follow.

Even though he did not have the Word of God, he knew the will of God. We know what Paul wrote in *Rom. 6:12* "let not sin therefore reign in your mortal body, that ye should obey it in the lusts thereof."

We should note that this temptation was not just a one-time event. From our text, we learn that it was a continuous thing day by day. That is how Satan operates today against you and me. Why did Joseph not sin? Was he a superman or something? No.

It was because he saw that sin as great wickedness against God, and even though he would have physically enjoyed the moment, it simply was not worth the cost.

Someone once said, "Kill the serpent, and don't stroke his head." What did he do? The Bible tells us he ran. Sometimes that is the only way out.

You would think it was over, but when he ran, he left his garment, and there was no one to witness what he did not do.

You can see what is coming from here. Potiphar has no choice but to believe his wife, and it seems Joseph would not speak up and tell what happened. So because he didn't say a word, he was cast into prison.

What a reward for faithfulness!

God will let things happen to us, just like Joseph, to teach us to trust Him more. The word of God is always accurate. Read *1 Pet. 5:6-7*. We may not understand, but God does. We just have to trust Him. You would think he would get a break about this time. Not so.

The devil will not leave him alone and will see in this next section another test Joseph is going to go through.

The third test that we will look at is the test of the inner soul. What caused Joseph to be victorious in all of this? It was merely his loyalty to God. In his life and ours, there was no room for sin in any form. One of the things we see in his life is he was still shocked by sin.

He saw the great wickedness before the eyes of God.

Today we have become so calloused to sin; it does not bother most of us anymore.

Another thing is he was prepared for sin when it came to facing him. There is a reason for this, and that is he was in constant fellowship with God.

Today, every spare minute is taken away by the world's things and the flesh's lust. If only we could learn to control those things in our lives, we could live a little godlier. Listen to *Gal. 5:16* "this, I say then, walk in the spirit, and ye shall not fulfill the lust of the flesh."

Typically, Joseph was secure because he kept his mind pure. He kept his thoughts, and his actions stayed on God. He was never in doubt that his answer would always be "no."

He was steadfast, not wavering; he never changed his mind about sin.

By this attitude, he honored God.

Through it all, more than all that Joseph lost, there is one thing he did not forget: his character.

If you lose your character, then you have lost everything.

Did Potiphar know? Sure he did. Listen to **Genesis 40:4**, "and the captain of the guard charged Joseph with them, and he served them: and they continued a season inward."

Study what **Prov. 16:1-4** says.

The key to his life was his continual trust in God no matter what he had to endure, for he knew God was with him.

Sin is cunning. It seems natural for most people to allow sin to control them through malice.

Not everyone accused of a particular sin is guilty. However, we should do right regardless of what is going on. If we believe God is in control, he can promote and prosper His people regardless of circumstances.

Just for a moment, think of the types of Christ you see in this passage. Joseph falsely accused. See **verses 16-18**. So was Christ falsely accused? See **Matt. 26:59, 60**. Joseph made no defense for the claims against him. Neither did Christ. See **Isa. 53:7**. Joseph cast into prison. See **verse 20**. Christ was also arrested and as good as thrown into jail for the intent was to kill him. Joseph suffers at the hand of Gentiles. So too, did Christ. See **Acts 4:26, 27**. Joseph won the respect of the jailer. So also did Christ. See **Luke 23:47**. Joseph numbered with transgressors. So was Christ. See **Isa. 53:12**.

Chapter 40

In the last chapter, we saw how Joseph yields his body to God. Now Joseph has to learn another hard lesson. We will call this the test of the mind. How would you react to this kind of test?

You have to consider the atrocities done to him and all the injustice that he had to endure.

In our last chapter, we saw Joseph falsely accused, and he said not a word.

How could he go through so much and still have hope? See *Genesis 39:21*.

I suppose you are wondering what the key to his life is. How could he go through so much and still trust in God? The answer is simple but hard to fulfill. Because he had a right relationship with God, he did not let circumstances dictate his life.

How many times have you heard those around you talk of reputation? Then how many times have you heard the word character?

There is a vast difference between the two. Reputation is what others suppose you to be or think you are, and when you die, that is what they will put on your tombstone. Character is what you are and what God knows you to be. Character is what angels say about you before the throne of God.

Thinking of Joseph, I have always thought about when we get into some kind of trouble, what do we do? Many times we complain to God. Why didn't Joseph complain?

Again, no matter what happened, he believed God was in control of his life.

There is no self-pity here.

So, Joseph receives prison for something he did not do. Potiphar knew this, and I believe he had a hand in helping look after Joseph.

He told the jailer Joseph could be trusted. Therefore, we find that Joseph is placed in authority over the other prisoners right off. In the meantime, Joseph has made up his mind that he will serve God no matter where God may place him.

To serve God well, one must be willing to commit to God in all places. Here he was, placed in a position to help others.

How often have you been sad or discouraged, and then to keep your mind off your situation, God placed you in a position to help others.

He watched the men. He heard of their sadness. He interpreted their dreams. He did so, despite three things: He had his dreams, with little fulfillment.

His previous service had resulted in unjust treatment. His present place of service was in another pit.

Why are you not willing to serve today? Is it because you don't like your circumstances?

Is it because you don't like your place of service? Is it because you don't like the results you are getting?

No doubt, it is not because of a lack of opportunity that keeps us from serving, for there is a world of opportunity before us. Could it be the reason is because of our unfaithfulness toward God in that we don't like the above factors?

There is no doubt Joseph had the patience and was willing to serve God.

Most of us believe that if we serve God in some way or another that God owes us a favor or something and that at the least, he will not let trouble come our way.

That is not the way God operates.

Before God intervened in Joseph's life, he had to wait two full years. By the way, the word "full" in Hebrew indicates that the years were slow in passing. Waiting on God is not an uncommon thing in the life of a Christian.

Moses waited for 80 years. Noah waited for 120 years. John the Baptist waited 30 years. Paul waited for eight years.

Now back in our text, we find that there are a baker and butler. They both had been accused of doing wrong. Now, by the king, they were being punished. They went into prison with Joseph.

In the process of time, they both dreamed dreams. We want to look at these two dreams.

Notice first the pattern of the two dreams. They were natural dreams in the sense that the baker and the butler dreamed dreams in their fields of expertise.

First, we have the dream of the chief butler. See **verses 9-15**. His dream revealed a vine with grapes. In his dream, he pressed the grapes in the king's cup. The three branches represent three days. So Joseph tells him restoration would soon come putting him in his former position. He asks the butler to use his influence to help get him out of prison.

Joseph tells them after listening to the baker that shortly they would return to their jobs before Pharaoh.

What would be more natural than for Pharaoh to consider the cases against his two officers?

Being innocent of his charges, the butler suggested reinstatement to the king's table while the baker, having a guilty conscience, would dream that birds would eat the food off the tray?

The two dreams were much the same. In their dreams, they pointed to three days.

Both would be restored to their former positions before any charges were brought against them. One dreamed Pharaoh accepted him back, and the other dreamed of his rejection and his death. Upon hearing the good news of the butler, the baker decided to share his dream with Joseph. See *verse 16*.

Studying the text, it is apparent the butler did not care about Joseph. You can see right off he had a guilty conscience. Joseph tells him the truth, even though it was hard. As Joseph told the truth, even though it was not suitable for one of the men, we should ask why we should speak the truth, knowing it will hurt. The answer is because of God's just sentence upon this wicked world.

Most people want to hear good news. Most people want to hear about grace. Most people want to hear about Heaven. Most people want to hear about love. Most people want to hear positive things.

So we see that a big feast was prepared for the two men. See *verse 20*. The butler gets his old job back during these activities, and the baker is taken out and hanged just like Joseph had said.

In today's world and probably in the world which Joseph lived, we should remember in the times of testing that: God's way is always the best. God's time is right. God's grace is still sufficient. God has a purpose in every life.

However, we need to remind ourselves that with a purpose, there is always discipline.

I am sure no one wants discipline, but we will find that discipline brings faithfulness, no matter the circumstances.

One of the lessons Joseph was facing and had to ask himself was, where was God in all of this? As with Joseph, we must be willing to serve in the capacity God places us.

If you look closely at our text, Joseph could not see God's plan for his life while here in prison.

He was doing what you or I would be doing, looking for a way out of prison. He thought if liberty were to come then, he could return to his father. If he had gotten out, you can see that he would not have followed God's will. However, he could not get out unless God allowed it.

The purpose of God's will in our lives takes place in God's own time, not ours.

Even though Joseph had given an accurate interpretation of this dream, the butler still forgot Joseph.

But God did not.

As a saint of God, he finds those who are having trouble and offers his sympathetic aid.

As for Joseph as a prophet of God, he interprets the dreams given to him. As a true prophet, he gives the bad news as well as the good. Joseph is a true prophet for his interpretation is fulfilled in every detail. See *Deut. 18:22; 13:1-5*.

Joseph becomes a blessing to one but pronounces judgment upon the other. So did Christ, regarding the two thieves, one saved, one lost. Joseph knew the future about these specific things. Christ knows the end of all things. See *John 12:49 and Mk. 13:31*. Joseph's predictions came true. Christ's predictions will all come true.

Just as a thought think on this, salvation comes to believers; unbelievers are damned. See *John 3:18*. In our text, we find that even though Joseph told the butler to remember him, we see he did not.

Chapter 41

Y ou could very well start this chapter by saying Joseph certainly had been going through the mill. Many today would say, "Poor old Joseph." Injustice had been served to him again, right? Here he was, thrown into the prison at no fault of his own. Then there for a while, and he had a chance to get out with others' help. But there was no help for Joseph. Man forgot him.

However, God did not forget him. Surely we can see we are not to put trust in man, for that the very best man will fail you. We know this truth expounded by the butler and the fact he forgot Joseph. Remember *Jer. 17:5-10* and what God said?

I wonder how many today trust the Word of God instead of the way of the world.

We need to remember to turn from the failures of man to the faithfulness of God. *Read Isa. 49:15, 16.*

What God does may sometimes be slow in our thinking before it comes to pass, but that which God does, he does well. Not only that, but we read in *Isa. 40:31* these words, "but they that wait upon the Lord shall renew their strength; they shall mount up with wings as eagles; they shall run, and not be weary, and they shall walk, and not faint."

Have you thought about how Joseph must feel?

Here he has been waiting for two years. Have you ever noticed that sometimes years go by as days? Not here for the Bible indicates to us that these two years that each day that passed to Joseph was years of days. But later on, Joseph would be called the revealer of secret things.

Here is the continuing test of the mind.

This test is to put us into such a position as to have nothing human to trust. It is becoming very obvious to Joseph without God; he had no hope. The mind's test is hard, but God will test you to see if you are willing to give him your all.

The purpose of the butler and baker's dreams was to get Joseph into a position that God could use. Finally, the butler remembered Joseph and what he had done for him. In the process, we see that the butler repents of not remembering Joseph. How many times have you heard of trusting in the Lord, and you will receive your reward. In the dreams of the baker and butler, we found that these dreams were about something natural. Once told, they could understand them. They were dreams to underline the truth of Joseph's interpretation of those dreams. They were dreams to grant a blessing God was going to give.

Now in our text in this chapter, we see the dreams of Pharaoh. These were not natural dreams.

These dreams came from God himself for a particular purpose. He had two dreams. The second dream gave more light and truth to the first vision of Pharaoh.

God got his attention. Did he know who sent the dreams? No, because he called for the magicians, etc. It is fascinating that he remembered his dream in detail. As he told it to the magicians and wise men, none could give him a reasonable interpretation. I believe they were hindered by God not to provide the king with a satisfactory answer to what he had dreamed.

Here was the opportunity God would use to open the door to bring to memory the butler's dreams again.

It would be at this time Joseph would be brought before the king. What was the reason for them not being able to interpret the dreams? I think one of the reasons is that God intervened.

Another reason would be it is here we see the cloudy vision of man because of sin.

Only the man of God would be capable of giving the interpretation of the dreams.

That is why the magicians and all the others failed.

God allowed it to happen this way so that Pharaoh would want to know what the dreams involved. These were instructional dreams that came directly from God to learn more about what to do in the future.

Sometimes God presents truth to an unbelieving man to help others to understand the will of God. It was an honor for Pharaoh to get this dream. Even the enemies of God can be used to perform the will of God.

Generally, when God does this, he does so in such a way as to relate to them in their present life situation. It should not surprise us then that carnal man can use words that only link to Christianity.

The first dream gave Pharaoh something to make him think. The second was to clarify the first dream. Soon we will see that in these two dreams show God is in control of future events.

We know this is not what the average person believes, even today. As Pharaoh calls his magicians to interpret his dreams, he does not want to acknowledge these dreams' origins. You see, man believes they do not need God. We see this as evidenced by the fact of what Pharaoh does.

Do you think that man would do anything differently today? I think not. Sin in our lives causes man to have impaired judgment.

Pharaoh believed he could get the answer. How can sinful men find a Holy God? They can't. Neither could Pharaoh. Is God in control? Sure He is.

See it in the fact God would not allow the magicians to find the answer to the dreams.

None could interpret. We know God's plan never fails. It is interesting to me as to how it is that all of Egypt's learned men could not give the king an answer?

Where is their knowledge now? God struck them dumb, for they did not answer the king a word. They didn't even present the king as an excuse for not solving the dreams.

Why did it happen this way?

It was to show Pharaoh that God in heaven is supreme and all-knowing. It was to show him the wise men were not so smart after all. We can see the reasoning of God behind this.

It was to stir Pharaoh's desire to know the truth.

By the way, God can silence anyone he chooses, even the most knowledgeable of our time.

Now it is time for the butler to remember Joseph. He says, "I do remember." Notice the thought of the butler. He had wronged the king, and so in prison, he went. Then he had been released by the king, but while in prison, he had a dream.

Joseph was able to tell him what would come to pass. He told him he would take place and that he would gain his former position. Why would he speak up now? He remembered!!

There are other reasons too. One is that Joseph will find freedom from the jail cell by way of elevation.

Why do I say that? The answer will be coming forthwith.

Because another reason is, Joseph might interpret the dreams.

Another reason is that Egypt would have plenty of food for the coming years and the many people who would need food, including his family. Had it not been for Joseph, we can see that God would not have received the honor and praise due His name. It is interesting to note that now Pharaoh is ready and willing to listen to someone other than his wise men about the meaning of his dreams.

We can see this on the testimony of the butler. Before this time, if Joseph stood before Pharaoh, he would not have listened to him. Again it is fascinating to notice the confidence of Pharaoh in Joseph, sight unseen. Why is that?

Now Joseph is called in as a prophet of God. Notice the importance, for only the prophet of God, can discern the Word of God. True men of God will only try and honor God in all things. He had to show Pharaoh that no one had power over God. Joseph could not instruct; only God could. God should receive all of the glory. Herein then, is wisdom.

So we could say this happened to bring comfort to Pharaoh as well.

You will see that Pharaoh does not panic when people come to him for food in about seven years.

He will calmly send them to Joseph. Pharaoh's dreams were significant for him, for his country, and the known world at that time.

Next, we see the first step of wisdom, acknowledging that God is the answer to all man's problems. The interpretation of the dreams tells us what is going to happen to Egypt. Famine is on the way. So we can see the two dreams are just one dream. One dream helps clarify the other.

God divinely gave it, for God is about to act. In his wisdom, Joseph tells Pharaoh to look out a man. Joseph is not just the interpreter of the dream; he adds instruction and council.

All true prophets of God not only interpret but should propose remedies and solutions.

He then advises Pharaoh.

He tells him to lay the grain up and has rulers to look after it. Even though we have a problem laid out, there is also a cure for the issue presented. Again the interpretation is given by the grace of God.

As a preacher of the Gospel, it is our responsibility to give the interpretations and then give the purpose and then remedy the problem.

Joseph then advised Pharaoh to heed the counsel of God and to do what Joseph instructs.

From this, we can see Joseph did not want any personal gain. For Joseph, it was a plan of preservation. The interpretation by Joseph spelled doom but not without being given a declaration of salvation to the lost. See *John 12:27-36.*

All Pharaoh had to do was follow the advice of God.

Remember, God had a plan, a plan of preservation. Joseph's message predicted doom, but it also provided for deliverance. If we denounce sin without declaring salvation, it is going to produce only fear, not faith. It is true, sin needs condemnation, and conviction needs to come.

But we can't stop there; we must get the convicted to Calvary.

We have to show the sinner the solution for sin. There is only one answer, and that answer is Jesus.

Joseph told Pharaoh there would be a famine in the land, but he also told Pharaoh what to do to keep from starving to death. To do this, he added that Pharaoh needed someone in charge, someone to make decisions, one who understood the immediate problem, and how to handle it.

The choice for Pharaoh was an easy one to make.

Who but the one who could interpret the dreams would be better suited to meet the need?

We know that Joseph would be his choice and what a great one it would turn out to be.

We have looked at Joseph's life and the trials that he had to go through, but now we come to an exciting part.

No longer would he be the hated one in the pit. No longer would Joseph be a slave in the pit of trials. No longer would Joseph be sold into slavery. No longer would a pure, innocent man be put into prison. No longer would he be the forgotten one in a pit.

Think about four things that Joseph told the butler while in prison. The first thing was meditation. He told the butler to remember him. See **Gen. 40:14**.

What do you think about it? Remember **Prov. 23:7** says, "for as he thinketh in his heart, so is he: Eat and drink, saith he to thee; but his heart is not with thee."

The butler's failure to remember Joseph is this.

Next, there is an obligation. He asked the butler to show kindness. Studying Joseph, if faced with the same problems, would you do what he did?

The third thing Joseph said to the butler was what I would call proclamation. That is what Joseph asked him to do, and that made mention of him before Pharaoh.

So we ask you, "What do you like to talk about most in your life?"

The fourth thing Joseph said to the butler to do is what I would call exaltation.

Wouldn't you want to get out of prison? He did, and I know so would you.

As we will soon see, God brought Joseph out of the pit and placed him in a palace.

Should we not ask you, "What has Christ done for you?"

Joseph is about to make a radical change as one could make. He went from being that of being a slave to that of being the second ruler in a world kingdom. How is that for a promotion?

From the time Joseph's brothers cast him into the pit until now is approximately 13 years.

Joseph is now 30 years old.

Here is the 4th time Joseph becomes the overseer of a house. He was an overseer over his father's house. Remember the coat of many colors? See *Genesis 37:3*. Then he was placed as overseer of Potiphar's house. See *Genesis 39:4*. He was just the overseer of the prison. See *Genesis 39:22*. Now he is going to be put as overseer of Pharaoh's house. See *verse 40* of our text.

He had proven his faithfulness to serve in whatever capacity God wills. As we think back, we wished Joseph was released from prison earlier, but that was not in God's plan.

Suppose he had been delivered earlier, especially before the two dreams of the butler and the baker. He would have gone back to Canaan land and would not have been available to answer Pharaoh's dreams.

Joseph went through the test to put him in a position that God could use unusually and bring great glory to God's name. What is it that God is after in your life today?

I am sure you see that God's timing is vital in a person's life, and that is only possible if we are in His will.

Now before we move on, there are some things I would like to mention about the promotion Joseph is about to receive. Think of his reign. He once was in jail, but now he finds himself ruler over the house of Pharaoh. See *verse 40*. Not only is he ruling, but he also needed recognition of that rule. Most of the time, a ruler would wear a ring to signify a place of authority. See *verse 42*. Many times this ring would be used to seal a document before the citizens, becoming law. It was as if Pharaoh had himself put the seal in it.

He also got a change of clothes. He got a new coat or, in this instance, a new robe. See *verse 42*. Note the change of garments; once he wore slave's clothes, now kingly garments.

Notice his position changed. He received a position of authority over others, giving him a high rank of power.

Next, Joseph received a chain of importance. When he wore this chain around his neck, all had to bow before him. See *verse 42*. Think about it, once he had to walk as a slave everywhere. Now the king gave him a chariot to ride in. See *verse 43*. A chariot to ride is another symbol of his authority. When Joseph now rode down the streets, there were runners in front of him, crying, "Bow the knee."

Up till this time, Joseph was the one who had to bow. Until this time, Joseph did not have much of a reputation. See *verse 45*.

Now Joseph got a new name.

He left the old name and ways behind. Part of his new name means "to be thrust out."

Pharaoh made sure Joseph had a good reputation. Pharaoh knew Joseph to be a man of character, but he had come from prison, giving Joseph the name change.

Pharaoh knew Joseph was a Jew, and Potiphar's wife had slandered his Jewish name.

The new name solved the problem. The other part of Joseph's new name means "prime minister." From *verse 45*, we know that Pharaoh gave Joseph a wife. Her name is Asenath, daughter of Poti-Pherah. Not Potiphar's wife. Potiphar and Poti-Pherah both have a woman Joseph could have had.

I am glad he made the right choice. Then there is something interesting about the seven things Joseph received in our lives today. Think about these things:

In his reign, as a Christian, we are to let Christ reign over our lives from day to day.

In his ring, remember that is a sign of authority. We are to let Christ have the rule over our lives simply because we are no longer a slave to the bondage of sin.

He has purchased us, but he has sealed us unto the redemption day by the Holy Spirit.

In his robe, we see as a Christian that we have changed garments from sin to righteousness.

We see that we have become joint-heirs with Jesus by his precious shed blood as a Christian in his rank.

In his ride, we can see that we are to ride to the four corners of the earth, proclaiming the good news just as Joseph had men telling the whole world that they had food.

In his reputation, we see as Christians, we are to live a life for Christ because our past has been wiped clean, and we have received a new name.

In his romance, we see a new book, a new Saviour, a new king, and that we should fall in love with all that he is because that is what he has done for us.

We are now his bride.

Why did Pharaoh accept the interpretation of his dream from Joseph knowing that the magicians could not answer? I believe one reason is that God still wanted a peculiar people he could work through. Going down into Egypt would suit that well because, for the most part, the Egyptians hated the Jews. So why was there the switch of accepting Joseph as "one of them"?

I think that a little history lesson here might help. At this particular time in history, the Hyksos kings were the kings of Egypt. They were not native Egyptians but were the Bedouins tribes from the Arabian Desert. These people were a nomadic group, and for some time, they controlled Egypt. Probably Joseph was now speaking with one of them. Perhaps their languages were close as well.

There is another reason Joseph could have validity here. These kings probably found it hard to find people to trust, and Joseph had proven he could be trusted. If ever there was a story to tell about rags to riches, this is it. Thinking of these tests that Joseph has gone through could be viewed from two sides.

We could say that that from a personal point of view, his sufferings and injustice were due to his brother's hatred of him, to Potiphar's neglect, to the butler's ingratitude. We know that Joseph was innocent of every charge made against him.

However, if we try and take a spiritual point of view believing that **Rom. 8:28** is still real, we would have to say that in all, these 13 years were spent as a training ground for some future work that God had in store for Joseph. God does have a plan for our lives.

We can say of a truth that most of the time, it is not an easy road we have to go down as children of God.

However, it will be the best road. From the human standpoint, we can see the course of events in the average person's life-shaping up like this:

First, there is anger; why did you let this happen to me? Then there is discouragement, why do I have to go through so much. Finally, we see rebellion allowing that person to become hard-hearted, cold, and calloused to Godly things.

That would be the average so-called Christian but not Joseph.

In closing this chapter, there are at least five things to learn in Joseph's life. Always remember God has a purpose, whether we see it or not. Still, there is a purpose, and this purpose calls for discipline and tests. What God expects in this life is faithfulness. Remember what God starts. He always finishes. What matters is if we are in God's will, we can bring glory and honor to his name.

In the last part of this chapter, we have an intriguing thought that Moses gives to us. That is the mention of the age of Joseph when he came to power. Joseph was now respected, even though he was young by ruling standards. Thirteen years had gone by since he had last seen his father.

During these next seven years, we will see Joseph is a man of action, going from place to place ordering and storing the food for survival. These first seven years are years of plenty.

In the wisdom God gave to Joseph, he did what God told him to do. In the process, we see his power and wisdom demonstrated to Pharaoh and the people around him.

The food is stored for the years of famine. It would be interesting to precisely see how Joseph held up the grain, not only for the people but also for the animals.

Soon we will see the years of famine coming and then what a change in the world.

God, in His mercy, told Joseph his plan so that the world would not go hungry.

Chapter 42

This chapter starts with the faith of Jacob, for he heard there was grain in Egypt. So during the famine, Jacob did two things. He believed the story of grain in Egypt. Then he acted upon that belief.

Now we see the beginnings of God's plan not only for Joseph but for the little nation of Israel.

In the context of this chapter, you will see that Joseph's brothers had never repented for the wrong they had done to Joseph and their family.

We can see this because Jacob was unwilling to send Benjamin with his brothers into Egypt to buy grain to live. It had been 20 years now, and still, Jacob knew nothing of the events other than the lie all the brothers concocted together all those years ago.

They would be shocked Joseph was living and that he was now a ruler in Egypt. Upon their arrival in the land of Egypt, they must have been afraid and worried deep down. Their brother had learned the ways and language of Egypt. I am sure he must have looked like those around him. His brothers knew he must have wound up in Egypt by the Midianites but had no idea what God had done with Joseph.

I find it very interesting that the brothers' reaction was fear when Jacob told them to go down into Egypt. I am sure it struck a nerve in their hearts and brought the remembrance of the past.

With their reaction, we can quickly learn that they had not changed.

You know that there is a bigger picture here than just a family and their present situation.

Remember that Joseph is a type of Christ, and his brothers are a type of Israel.

This type is correct whether we look to the past, present, or future of Israel.

In the beginning, as we said, it was the famine that brought them to Joseph. But behind all of this is the hand of the unseen God at work.

In one sense of the word, we can say this is judgment.

If you think with me, it will be a judgment that will finally drive Israel to the Lord Jesus Christ in the end times. We see Jacob's sons delivered Joseph into the Gentiles' hands to compare and consider these events. Thinking it was the Jews who gave Christ into the hands of Gentiles as the Roman guard came to get Jesus and take him before Pilate.

Concerning the brothers, it was essential to get to the "ruler" who had the grain in Egypt, or else they would soon die.

It was a simple matter of life and death. Spiritually speaking, we can say of a truth that whether Jew or Gentile, each need Christ, and it is a matter of life or death.

Looking at the parallel, we can see that neither the Jews nor Gentiles had the bread of life.

Joseph, as a type of Christ, had the bread of life to give.

After Joseph's rejection, his brethren left Canaan's land to where they would soon be in Egypt's land.

Looking at history, we can see that after rejecting Christ, the Jews were driven from the land in 70 A.D.

Here in this chapter, we will see that Joseph faced with more tests. We all know that as long as we have breath and want to do God's will, there will be some tests in this life.

These all are to bring us closer to God.

We know that once we graduate from one test, there will be another one coming soon.

Joseph was no different from us.

How is he going to serve God? Had he learned the lessons God wanted him to know?

Was he willing to take another step in serving God?

Now we have exposure at last. When he sees his brothers, how will he react?

I know how most of us would have reacted if we saw those who had been cruel to us and tried to harm you.

Joseph could have done something to his brothers when they came when he recognized them.

Interestingly they did not recognize him.

More than likely, they thought he was dead. It was because they were not looking for him.

It was because he was not dressed like them, remember he was an Egyptian. It was because he spoke a different language from them very fluently. At least 20 years had gone by, and the last time they saw him was when he was 17 and in a pit. He was at least 37 years old now.

No doubt by this time, they had forgotten Joseph. Why didn't Joseph reveal himself to his brothers?

I think one of the reasons is that he wanted to know what had become of Benjamin.

He also wanted to know if his brothers had a change of heart. I believe Joseph had a right to be afraid of them and wise to be cautious.

Therefore, it was important for Joseph to discover some facts about them before revealing himself to them. As long as his family had plenty, they had no desire to come to Egypt.

Now, famine is at hand. Famine leaves a deep desire in one's heart, and whether they knew it or not, a conviction was coming.

This is what Joseph needed to know. Often God works in this way; he has to take something away from us to get our attention. Do you remember what took place in **verse 1?**

From the text, you can see that just the mention of Egypt stirred their hearts. And we see that Jacob was still suspicious of his sons. Now we see God working. He is working in two directions.

He works from the standpoint of Joseph and second from the perspective of his brothers.

Joseph was now going through another test in his life. He was not in training anymore.

Would Joseph, as his brothers, stood before him, retaliate and have his brothers killed?

He certainly had the authority and the power to do so.

Or would he humble himself?

If you think of these trials that Joseph had come through, none of them are related to his salvation.

These are trials of life. All of these trials were to bring him to a closer fellowship with God. See **2 Timothy. 1: 12** and 2 **Tim. 2:9, 10**.

Joseph calls them spies. They said they were true men. Really? It is a shame they did not know who they were talking too.

Even though we find Joseph speaking very rough to his brothers and accused them of being spies, we see no vengeance.

Joseph remembered his dreams. But he had no pleasure in his brothers bowing before him and giving him such honor. Maybe Joseph saw the hand of God in all of his life now.

God works the same way today. No matter what others say, little details are essential.

Think of the interrogation by Joseph.

What were the conditions back home? Would his father be living, or is he dead?

Before Joseph could reveal himself to his brothers, God had to bring about repentance for past and present sins.

So we find that Joseph decides to put his brothers to the test.

In this test, it is to imprison his brothers and then changes his mind sound familiar? See *verses 16, 17*.

Originally Joseph's brothers had wanted to kill him. Then, because of Reuben, instead of killing him, they sold him as a slave. God has a way of reminding us of every little detail of our sins to have to confess them as sin and repent of that wickedness as we know.

Who were the "true ones" now?

Notice they say Benjamin is alive, and one is not. In other words, they were still covering up their past sins. From this statement, it is evident that there is no fear of God in their lives. *See verses 22, 23*. Do you remember what *Prov. 13:15* says? "Good understanding giveth favour: but the way of transgressors is hard."

There were, and we could say for today, four things necessary for reconciliation. We need the conscience awakened. We need a confession of sin. We need to repent genuinely.

Repentance must produce a change in one's life. Our minds are wonderfully made. God has made us so that we can remember things, or we can forget things. Joseph's brothers needed to remember.

In jail it would be an excellent place to remember. So he puts them in jail for three days. See *verse 17*. While they were there, he was hoping that their conscience would awaken.

Now would be a good time to admit their guilt of what they had done to their brother. I am sure you have heard that saying, "what goes around comes around." Listen to the following verses. *Matt. 7:2* "for with what judgment ye judge, ye shall be judged: and with what measure ye mete, it shall be measured to you again." *Prov. 21:13* "whoso stoppeth his ears at the cry of the poor, he also shall cry himself, but shall not be heard."

If one is to repent genuinely, you will see three things take place, as we said.

Think about what Joseph's brothers said to each other while in jail. They admitted they were very guilty of a crime. They thought back and said, "We saw the anguish of his soul." Then they thought of why this has come upon them. This is called reasoning.

Now notice the response of Joseph. They had spent three days in jail to get them to think about their past and what they had done. Now he releases them but takes one more step toward getting them to repent. He tells them to go and get his brother Benjamin and bring him back. In the process, he would keep one of them with him. That was to be Simeon, so he bound him in their presence. I am sure they are afraid by now.

Joseph gave them provision for the journey home and food to take with them.

They did not know that he had returned their money, which made them more afraid once they found the money back in their bags. Outwardly he bound Simeon in their presence. Outwardly they only saw harshness. The others are set free, but only to watch Simeon tied.

Inwardly is a different story. We find Joseph is broken-hearted over these events but does not let it show for he had heard and understood their conversations in the jail. Inwardly Joseph weeps so no one could see him.

We can genuinely say he was a hard man, but he was a man of great compassion inwardly.

Again we find he fills their bags for the trip and does not charge them for the provisions.

Their money was returned, causing great fear and conviction. See **verses 25-28**.

A guilty conscience is now evident from his brothers. As we see the hand of God, we know God's first objective is now complete. That is, their conscience has now been awakened.

Before moving on to the next chapter, I want to remind you of the types Joseph is of Christ once again.

This chapter is primarily about them. Think about the following: Joseph's brethren come before his face. See **verses 6-17**. Joseph was unknown and unrecognized by his brethren. See **verses 6-8**. Christ is unknown and unrecognized by the Jews today. See **John 1:11**. Joseph knew and recognized his brethren. They did not know him. See **verse 8**. Today we know Christ knows and looks after the Jews. See **Jer. 5:3; Jer. 16:17** and **Hosea 5:3**. Joseph punished his brethren and brought justice to them. See **verses 7-17**. For centuries now, the Jews have been punished by our Lord. See the following verses: **Hosea 9:17** and **Matt. 23:35-38**. Joseph's brethren wanted to pay for the grain they received. See **verse 10**.

Throughout history, Jews and Gentiles alike want to pay for salvation and God's blessings.

In the beginning, Joseph's brethren indeed tried to assume a self-righteous attitude. See **Verses 10, 11**.

Today is no different. Those we call sinners today, both Jews and Gentiles, do not want to admit they are sinners in need of a Saviour. If you have noticed in our text, Joseph's brothers did not confess their sin to him. See **verse 13**.

It does not take very long to understand that sinners do not want to be honest about what they have done to Christ. Because of their sin, God wants his brothers to repentance, and we find that Joseph cast his brethren into prison for three days. See **Verse 17**.

The sinner must be put into the proper place and brought to the place that he will humble himself, thereby bringing God glory and honor.

In the context, we see that Simeon is left behind, held until Joseph sees Benjamin.

In type, we see the only way sinners can be saved through our substitute, the Lord Jesus Christ.

In the end, what is needed to be accomplished happened?

We see that the brother's conscience is smitten deep in their hearts.

I remind you that this was not repentance, but it was a step in the right direction.

In type, we also saw Joseph weeps over his brethren. See *verse 24*. I am sure you remember that Christ wept over Jerusalem. The only way the brothers of Joseph could be forgiven is through grace. We see this in *verses 25-28*.

In the last few verses, we see Joseph's brothers returning to their father. See *verses 29-34*.

We know that Joseph's brothers are blind to the true meaning of his dealing with them. We know that today in Israel's spiritual blindness, which they are in, they cannot see God's purpose in their lives through His Son Jesus Christ.

Chapter 43

Think back over the first visit that Joseph's brothers had with him. If you remember, just the name of Egypt brought fear to their minds. Then when they got to Egypt, they had a rough time from Joseph. Right at the beginning, they were spies; it was determined. Then they were cast into prison for three days. What was going on?

It will frequently make you wonder what was that the length of time Joseph was in the pit.

Was it for three days, and that is why they were in jail for three days? It was after three days that they were all are set free except Simeon. God used this to get them to the point they would admit their sin against Joseph. See *Gen 42:21*.

Here is a key to the beginning of their repentance of past sins. God uses this to stir their conscience. It did not take long for them to admit they were guilty before God.

Isn't it interesting that they remember the very anguish of his soul after all of those years?

Therefore they understood that perhaps this is the judgment from God for what they had done. See *Gen. 42:28*.

Herein is another key. The brothers had confessed their sins privately, but not yet publicly.

They still needed open confession of their sins. God was doing a work. The money returned to them brought great fear to them.

In the meantime, we find that Joseph believed God's hand was in what he had done. Up to this point, we see that they think everything they had done God was using to bring judgment upon them. Now all of the grain they had received is gone again.

There is no doubt that if they did not eat, they would starve to death.

So Jacob says the only thing he knows to say is, "go buy some food." They understood that they had to go to the only place where there was any food, Egypt. Yet we also know Joseph had told them not to come back without Benjamin. Judah speaks up for the rest of his brothers and states he will be surety for Benjamin. Think back at what Reuben had said earlier to his father.

You will find that in *Genesis 42:37*, where Reuben said, "And Reuben spake unto his father, saying, Slay my two sons if I bring him not to thee: deliver him into my hand, and I will bring him to thee again."

That is totally unlike that of what Reuben had said. Notice the difference? Why was Judah ready to be a surety for Benjamin? He will do it, for it is a life and death matter. See *verses 8, 9*. He pledges his own life as a surety for Benjamin's. "Surety" means "to exchange, to become surety for anyone." Judah said that if it came down to it, he would be willing to exchange his life for his, to stand in his place; to become surety for one's life, in this case for Benjamin, it means to pledge oneself for the life of another"

Herein is a beautiful type of Christ. Let us remember that one from the tribe of Judah, who became surety for us. See *Heb. 7:22*.

In reading what Reuben said and Judah said, you could see that Judah means every word spoken here.

I have given my life to believe that Christ is our surety today. Also, a surety is a person who takes responsibility for another whose credit is not good.

Don't you know, without Christ; the whole world is guilty before God? When the sinner comes face-to-face with the truth about his sin, he understands that God is righteous in all that he does. God indeed loves, but His is a righteous love.

Sin is rebellion against God, and we must deal with it.

One of the reasons for him being our surety is that he can be our surety in the first place. He is God in the flesh.

Listen to these words in *John 1:14*, which says, "and the Word was made flesh, and dwelt among us, (and we beheld his glory, the glory as of the only begotten of the Father,) full of grace and truth."

Then we have these Old Testament words in *Isa. 53:7* "He was oppressed, and he was afflicted, yet he opened not his mouth: he is brought as a lamb to the slaughter, and as a sheep before her shearers is dumb, so he openeth not his mouth."

Judah being willing to become surety for his brother, proves he has a change of heart.

We call it genuine repentance.

I believe this is because he has made up his mind never to treat anyone like he treated his brother Joseph years before.

Repentance is a change of mind that directs a difference in a course. It is a mental change that affects moral growth. Penance may make one weep over their sins, but only true repentance makes one forsake the sin. Penance is merely an act of sorrow, not a turning away.

Where there is no repentance, there is no forgiveness.

Jacob would see he had no choice in letting Benjamin go. As we said, it was a life or death situation. There could be no blessing or deliverance until they accept responsibility.

You have to let sometimes go and just trust God. It is full surrender to Christ or nothing.

If Christ is not Lord of all, then he is not Lord at all.

Now in our text comes the time that Jacob has to surrender his will to God's will.

Notice the usage of "the man" in *verses 11, 13, 14*.

To them, Joseph was just "the man." Tragically, this is how many Jews and Gentiles look upon Christ, just as "the man." He was a man when he walked the earth, but in fact, he was God-man. Even in his earthly state, He was just as much God as He was a man.

Joseph's brothers feared the Egyptians' visit again, so should we fear our meeting with Christ at the Judgment seat.

However, if one has truly repented of their sins and has a heart change, there is nothing to fear.

We see several steps taken as they arrive back to Egypt and stand before Joseph. Notice the change indicated by Judah's willingness in this scene to take care of Benjamin. Not only that, but it is also where they want to return the money that was in their bags originally.

Then in **verses 19, 20**, you have their confession of sin outwardly. Just like us, we make mistakes along the way, and they are no different. They made mistakes along the way.

They took a present to Joseph. What can you bring before a Holy God?

They also are confessing their sin to a servant instead of to Joseph. Who should we confess our sins too; there is only one person, Jesus Christ.

We see the process beginning. A sinner has to come to the place they will either accept or reject the truth.

Sin strikes a deadly blow. So you would ask, "How can we escape the consequences of sin?"

The only way is through Calvary and accepting the one who died for us.

Only can Christ meet the price required for my or your sins. There is nothing we can pay. See **John 1:14; Isa. 53:7** and **Heb. 10:10, 12**, and **18**.

It is interesting to me that the steward has a good knowledge of who God is.

Joseph must have taught the steward about God. The brothers return with Simeon, and I am sure he tells them of the events that have taken place.

Then they are brought into Joseph's house after they confessed.

It is at this point they fulfill the dream of the sheaves. See ***Gen. 37:7-9.***

Maybe we should ask what it will take to bring you to God's place to speak to your heart.

I can only imagine the mixture of pain and joy as Joseph asks his brothers about his father and then sees Benjamin for the first time.

He is so overcome with joy; he has to go out and weep. You know there is nothing wrong with a man crying.

Here at the end of the chapter, we see the feast is made ready and set to the table. Notice the custom that is taking place here. The Hebrews at one table, the Egyptians at another table, and Joseph is sitting all alone. They must have wondered why Joseph did not sit with the Egyptians. Having been to foreign countries, I know it is wise to follow the land's customs if they do not cause one to sin against God. Then they marveled that Joseph knew the order of their ages. We should remember that the Lord knows everything about us.

They were not all treated alike, but there is no complaint.

Here was a test, to see if the brothers had changed, or whether they would be resentful of Benjamin, as they had of Joseph.

Here in these few verses, we have the evidence of true repentance.

They did not mind that Benjamin had a better portion than the rest of them had.

Chapter 44

Many of the things that happen to us in life happen to bring us to the light to know our condition and turn us to the Lord. See **Deut. 8:2, 3**. In this case, I am sure the brothers were glad this visit turned out better than the first visit with the man in charge of the food. It seemed that all was going well with the brothers.

They had the corn. They had everything they needed. All the brothers were together. The trip would be easy, and the home was not far away.

But God is not through with them yet. They are in for a great surprise. Having spoken again to Joseph and getting the provisions, they needed and the preparations finished; they prepared to return home. Joseph had been gracious enough to fill their sacks to the limit.

Undeservingly the Lord gave graciously to us. Not only did they get provisions, but were they about to have a rude awakening.

Just as they get ready to leave, Joseph instructs his steward of something he wanted him to do.

Discreetly we find that a trap lay on the brothers. There are still yet more tests for them to endure. Joseph instructs his steward to place his cup into the bag of Benjamin. How else could he see the reaction and response of his brothers? This cup was divining, used to foretell the future, but it is highly unlikely that Joseph ever used it.

Joseph instructs his steward to go and overtake his brothers and look in each bag after he told the steward what to say to his brothers.

No doubt, they were rejoicing that their trip had proven so successful.

So when the steward approaches, I think their hearts must have sunk, and they knew something was amiss.

The steward gives them the words of Joseph, and now they are petrified. Indeed they were innocent of the charges against them, especially after what had happened the first time.

They were indeed innocent of the charge, but they were guilty in many other things.

Many today are the same way. How confident could they be? None of them had done wrong.

What a reckless and robust agreement they made together.

Searching through the bags, they discovered the money returned and that the cup was in Benjamin's sack.

Now you can begin to see a change in the brothers. Earlier, they were full of accusations, but not now. They could have accused or abandoned Benjamin, but they did not. So they return to the city in sorrow. Little did they know that sorrow was bringing them to repentance? See **II Cor. 7:9, 10.**

Do you know that one day the "sack" of our life will be examined by God? Every secret will come to light before Him.

Now they take their correct place before Joseph. In this, we see that the steward is a type of the Holy Spirit. He brings them to the feet of Joseph, who is a type of our Lord Jesus Christ.

Why? They needed to confess their sins before him, and this is their opportunity to acknowledge their sins.

Genesis 43:16 is another key verse. Listen to what God says, "And Judah said, what shall we say unto my Lord? What shall we speak? Or how shall we clear ourselves? God hath found out the iniquity of thy servants: behold, we are my Lord's servants, both we, and he also with whom the cup s found."

Notice Judah's three questions to Joseph as he stands before him. Here is the place they need to be. What does he do? He confessed, "God hath found out the iniquity." Think of ***Ezek. 20:42, 43***. The Lord always finds out.

Has Judah changed? True repentance brings outward confession. Do we know the heart of Judah? It is in words, "we...also." Judah puts them all together as if they are one.

Note this is an act that had not been accomplished before. Now begins the challenge before him.

Now Judah becomes the Advocate, a beautiful picture of the Lord Jesus Christ.

Will he keep his promise to his father; will he become surety for his brother? Seldom will we ever find a plea that will equal Judah's? Here we see Judah at his best. It foreshadows the great future of his tribe. See the following verses: ***Deut. 33:7; Gen. 49:10*** and ***Psa. 78:67, 68*** for more information.

I think it is essential that we look more closely at the plea of Judah.

Seven times he says thy servant.

Fourteen times he mentions his father.

Four times he says, father and thy servant.

One time he says the father is an older man.

One time he speaks of his mother.

Three times he speaks and says that Benjamin is the youngest brother.

One time he says he is the son of the old age of his father.

One time he speaks as being the little one.

Three times Benjamin is called the lad.

One time he speaks of one brother being dead.

One time he speaks of the torture of Joseph.

Two times he speaks of his father's sorrow.

Two times he speaks of his father's dead if Benjamin does not come back with them.

One time he speaks of Benjamin bound up as the father.

Judah now speaks and says he will be surety for his brother Benjamin.

Notice what a change made in his life. He shows love toward his brother Benjamin. He shows humility toward his father back home. Notice now Judah's offer that they all would serve with Benjamin.

At the end of this conversation, Judah tells Joseph he thought his brother was dead and guilty of murder.

Gladness fills our hearts for God will forgive us for our sins we committed against His only son, Jesus Christ.

Notice Joseph was willing to become their Saviour. Being willing to become their Saviour meant he was ready to save them from the just penalty of death.

The result of the gifts they brought was not what caused this. It was not because they confessed guilt. It was not because of the sacrifices that brought them salvation. His suffering purchased Joseph's gracious forgiveness for them for the past 20 years that brought them salvation.

All this was necessary that they should evidence repentance and change of heart before Joseph would reveal himself to them. The entire company of brothers seems to be broken and melted.

Chapter 45

A study of Joseph's life is a great way to see our wonderful Lord Jesus Christ typified in the Old Testament.

Some preachers declare that Joseph and Christ are alike in at least two hundred different ways, but we will limit our study to Joseph and his brethren.

The chapter opens with Joseph in the Palace ruling over all the land of Egypt.

However, this is a tremendous change from the position he once held in prison.

Now, he has an elevated position beside the Pharaoh. Joseph, twenty years earlier, we see his brothers had stripped him of his beautiful coat of many colors, then put in a pit, sold as a servant into Potiphar's house in Egypt, lied on by Potiphar's wicked wife.

Then, put in prison and then elevated to a leadership position that we find him in this chapter.

We might say Joseph's path led through the pit, to Potiphar's house, to the prison, and finally to the Palace.

How could Joseph be so successful and live so pure before the Lord through all these ups and downs? We find the answer in *Gen. 39:2, 3,* and *21*. Four times we are reminded that "The LORD was with Joseph."

The land of Egypt had received blessings of seven years of plenty, and had it not been for God's mighty hand working in the life of Joseph, and the whole world would have starved to death in the next seven years.

But God intervened through Joseph, and he gave Pharaoh a plan from God to save the day.

Whereby grain was stockpiled while the crops were doing well, and all of Egypt could eat from the surplus when the crops failed to yield.

Pharaoh liked the plan so well that he brought Joseph out of prison and implemented the program. Sure enough, during the years of plenty, they stockpiled the grain, and just like Joseph had predicted, the crops then failed, and Egypt was the only place to find food.

Back in the homeland, Joseph's father, Jacob, and his eleven brothers needed food.

Jacob heard about corn in Egypt, so he sent the boys down to get food for the family, and who do you think they found ruling the land of Egypt.

Here is one of the most heart touching human experiences found in the Bible or anywhere else.

Indeed it abounds with many lessons that we are at a loss about how we can mention them all in such a short space. From our previous chapter, we find the events of this chapter only take place after their repentance. **See Genesis 44.**

Joseph's object in dealing with his brethren brought success. They are now sorrowful and repentant. Did you know that an unrepentant sinner can't know Jesus Christ as Lord?

As a type of Christ, we find Joseph was made known to them in time to save them. See **Gen. 44:9, 10, 33**, and **34**.

In our text, we see that Joseph commands his servants to leave for what he was about to reveal he needed to say in private. We still see Joseph being the compassionate one, for I am sure he must have considered their feelings before the Egyptians.

He didn't want his servants to know how his brothers had treated him.

If they had known, they might have resented the forgiveness of Joseph to his brothers.

The sinner must first go before the Lord in private confession before made public.

Now we find three little words, "I am Joseph."

Can you imagine the shock of these words when his brothers hear them?

Here is the 2n^d ruler of all of Egypt, crying before them saying he is Joseph. How did they feel? I think the first thing they felt was fear in knowing it was Joseph in the first place. Then I think they were confused, how could it be possible? Look at *verse 3*. How could they answer him? What would Joseph now do?

Sometimes we just have to accept what Revelation brings. Notice here is the triumph of righteousness; it does pay to live right. Notice also the victory of grace, and Joseph replaces fear with love. Grace is the outflow of love from God.

In all of the things that had happened to Joseph, he saw God's hand in it all, even though he did not know how God would do what he was going to do.

Joseph knew from early on that what mattered most was that God's will had to be first. See, *Gal. 2:20*.

Joseph was not ashamed of his brothers for what they had done to him. Only the love of God could give a person the heart to do that. Throughout his whole life, we have seen his eyes fixed on God. It did not matter what the circumstances about him were. See *Phil. 3:10-14*.

As we think of our lives, I would say that one of the most significant trials we will ever face is being ill-treated, especially by the ones that we generally love the most.

The natural man would only retaliate if given a chance.

In the Christian life, we find that Christ teaches good for evil. Do we see in Joseph's real character, what he wants his whole life to represent? Through everything he has gone through, Joseph knew God had a purpose in all of this.

Now, after finally getting his brothers all together instead of seeking revenge, he weeps. See **Genesis 45:7**.

I would love to present some more likenesses of Joseph and Christ. Like Christ and Moses, rejection came the first time. See **Ex. 2:14; Luke 19:14** and **John 1:12**. Like Christ, he wept over others. Like Christ, he sent for his own. See **I Thess. 4:13-18**. Like Christ, he came to preserve life.

Joseph dealt with them in marvelous grace. He invited them to come near. See **verse 4**.

So will the Lord when He deals with Israel in grace in the future. See **Zech. 13** and **Isa. 54:7, 8**.

Remember, God also invites the trembling repentant sinner to come near the blood of Jesus.

Even though they were responsible for their sin, God sent Joseph ahead of them to have the opportunity to confess that sin.

The same comparison can be made of Christ and the Jews. Compare **Acts 2:23** and **36**.

Even in seemingly unfortunate circumstances, we have seen how the Lord will take care of His children in our lifetime.

The rest of this chapter gives rise to this in that even Pharaoh had an open heart and mind to the Jews who would become a nation one day.

God promised Abraham that he would provide and take care of that little Jewish nation and give them a place to stay. But along the way in the tests and trials of life, we find that many times even before they reach the Promised Land, God is wonderfully and marvelously taking care of and providing for His children.

We each have a lot to be thankful for, and often we forget the everyday things God does for us as He did for that little nation.

Joseph's attitude so honored God that he laid it on a Gentile king's heart to give those few people a beautiful place to live while God is at work behind the scenes, getting them ready for the next adventure they will face as a nation.

In the process of this story, we now see Joseph wanting to see all of his family, and then he sends his brothers to get them to move to Egypt, where he can provide and take care of them.

After so many years, we find Jacob was shocked and in disbelief, but the brothers finally convinced him to move.

Now no more deception but honestly and truth rule the day. The brothers gather all of their families and head south.

Again this chapter is loaded with types and symbols of Christ. For instance, we have Joseph sending for his father, Jacob. One day Christ is going to re-gather Israel to their homeland, where he will reign. Joseph's brethren go forth to declare his glory. So should we go forth today and declare His glory. Joseph shared his joy with others, and so should we share our happiness with others. Joseph's brethren go forth, seeking others to bring to Joseph. So should we be seeking to bring others to our Joseph?

Joseph had a prepared place for them, and we should remember Christ prepared a place for us. See *John 14:1-3*. They testified of one who was thought to be dead but now is alive.

That is the message of the New Testament Church.

In our text, the command was "haste ye, and go up to my father, and say unto him, thus saith thy son Joseph, God hath made me lord of all Egypt: come down unto me, tarry not." See **Gen. 45:9**. Listen to **Gen. 45:25, 26**, "and they went up out of Egypt, and came into the land of Canaan unto Jacob, their father, and told him, saying, Joseph is yet alive."

The boys could have told Jacob nothing more important than the truth about Joseph being alive. Likewise, as Christians, you and I have no more important story to say to this world than the death, burial, and resurrection of our heavenly Joseph, the Lord Jesus Christ.

Praise the Lord for the virgin birth, the perfect life, and the substitutionary death on the cross, but it would all have been in vain if he did not rise from the dead.

Note the following verses: *I Cor. 15:17* "if Christ be not raised, your faith is vain; ye are yet in your sins." And *Rom. 1:4* "declared to be the Son of God with power, according to the spirit of holiness, by the resurrection from the dead." Then *read I Cor. 15:1-4.*

Thank God we have a living Saviour.

There is an illustration I once heard. The story goes like this: I once listened to a black preacher preaching on the Resurrection of Christ. He said words like this. "Before I enter into my message on death's impossible predicament, I would like to have a dialogue with Mr. Death.

Mr. Death, I have four very pertinent questions I would like to ask you.

Where were you born would be the first question?

And Mr. Death replied, "In the Garden of Eden, I made my entrance into this world."

Another question would be what your address is? Where do you reside? Mr. Death said, "My speech is universal. I live all over the world. Nowhere on this earth is my presence not known.

Mr. Death, the third question for you is, "what do you work? Mr. Death said, "I intend to destroy the world and the people in it."

Mr. Death, I only have one more question. I would like to know if you have ever failed.

And Mr. Death replied, "Only once." Mr. Death said, "But you know from the very moment I saw the one named Jesus I knew he was off-limits for me. You see, the only strength I have is through sin, but there was no sin in Him to get my hands on. We went into the tomb together, but somehow I knew that my stay in the tomb was temporary. I knew I was there as a visitor and would have to leave before long".

Another commenting on the resurrection said, "after twenty-four hours in the tomb with Christ, Mr. Death said to Rigimortis, "you're slow in your old age, go to work on Jesus, but there was no shift change that day, and Rigimortis found no place to go work on him.

After forty-eight hours, Mr. Death said, "try again."

On that second day, Rigimortis had to set and look as a spectator only at the body of Jesus.

On the third and final day, Mr. Death said, "Rigimortis try one more time," and Rigimortis straddled the body of Jesus just in time to see the color come to his face and feel the body began to move beneath him.

He said, "Mr. Death, I don't know about you, but I am leaving here, I am vacating this tomb."

Mr. Death said, "I am going with you," and they left the tomb while Jesus Christ got up and walked out victorious over death, hell, and the grave.

Herein is the message we must give to the world! Jesus Christ is alive! Amen.

In our text, then we see that yes, the brothers told Jacob that Joseph was the "lord," and you and I should say the same thing about our heavenly Joseph, the Lord Jesus Christ.

Vance Havner once said that men who try to make him "either, or" are in reality trying to make him "neither, nor."

I'm glad the Bible gives no alternatives or options for the lordship of Jesus Christ. It just gives a plan. We can understand, as emphatic a statement is that "he compared the Bible to "Saviour" tells me that God wants this world to know that Jesus Christ is Lord.

In the New Testament, "lord" is used six hundred and fifty-seven times while "Saviour" is only found twenty four times.

I suppose the book of Romans is used for soul-winning more than any other book in the Bible, and the word "Saviour" does not appear one time in the book. But "Lord" is found thirty-nine times. Number two on the list for soul-winning is probably the book of Acts. In Acts, the Holy Ghost only said "Saviour" two times, but he said "lord" one hundred and two times.

Number three in popularity would probably be the Gospel of John. In the Apostle of John, "Saviour" is found one time while "lord" is found forty-four times. Just for the record, the entire Bible has the word "Saviour" thirty-seven times and the word "lord" or "lord" six thousand seven hundred and sixty-one times. He is our Lord!

As you think of the brothers, I have a good idea that when these eleven sons of Jacob stood before the Lord of all the land of Egypt and heard him say, "I am Joseph your brother, whom ye sold into Egypt" brought great fear to them all. See *Gen. 45:4.*

There is no doubt that their minds instantly replay some events that happened twenty years before.

They remembered their animosity and hatred toward Joseph that caused them to sell him as a slave into Egypt then deceive their father Jacob into believing that Joseph was dead.

And now Joseph is in control.

At this point, the boys didn't have much hope for the future.

They probably thought Joseph would get even with them by having them killed, or at least thrown into prison, but Joseph very quickly said, "now, therefore, be not grieved, nor angry with yourselves, that ye sold me hither: for God did send me before you to preserve life." See *Gen. 45:5.*

Joseph revealed his love for his brothers and the Lord Jesus, whom you and I have so drastically sinned against still loves us.

We have all the authority of the Bible behind us when we tell this world that God loves sinners.

Someone once said, "There is nothing in the best of men to cause God to love them and nothing in the worst of men to keep God from loving them."

God is not motivated to love sinners because of what he sees in them.

God's reason for loving sinners is within Himself for "God is love." See *I John 4:8.*

Therefore, he loves them because he is God. See the following verses in ***Eph. 2:4; Eph. 5:2*** and ***1 John 4:9, 10, 16***. He loves us, and now their final statement about Joseph to their father.

Let me give you another illustration. A little boy was lost and frightened, almost to the state of hysteria. The police picked the little fellow up, but he was so scared he couldn't even tell them his name.

They couldn't get any information from him that would help them locate his parents or home.

They took him to the police station, which only frightened him that much more. So they put him back in the police car and began driving around town hoping to find his home. After several minutes of riding around town, the little boy leaned up from the car's back seat, tapped the officer on the shoulder, and said, "Officer, let me out, I can go home from here."

The officer stopped the car and said. "Son, before we let you out of the car, you will have to convince us that you know where you are and go home from here."

The little boy said, "Oh yes sir, officer, I can go home from here. He said to the officer, "Look across the tracks officer. You see that church with the cross on it, that's my church.

There's a cemetery just the other side of the church, and I live only on the other side of the cemetery.

Let me out officer, and I'll go by the cross then through the cemetery, and I'll be home".

The officer said. "Son, are you not afraid that you won't be accepted when you get home?"

"Oh no, officer. That was taken care of when I was born. They're just waiting for me to get home, and they'll be glad to see me".

My friend that it is with us who know the Lord Jesus Christ as our personal Saviour.

We have already been by the cross, and if the Lord Jesus doesn't soon come, we will go through the cemetery and find the home just on the other side, and we too have already been accepted. Listen to Paul's words "to the praise of the glory of his grace, wherein he hath made us accepted in the beloved." *Eph. 1:6.*

After telling this story in service, a little boy came to me and asked, "What happened to that little boy?" I said, you know I have an idea. He started home and made it by the cross but met his father coming to meet him before he got out of the cemetery. Amen!

I believe that's what will happen to me. I'm on my way to the cemetery, but I think I will meet the Lord coming for me on this side of the grave. "And when he saw the wagons which Joseph had sent to carry him, the spirit of Jacob their father revived: and Israel said it is enough; Joseph, my son, is yet alive: I will go and see him before I die. See *Gen. 45:27, 28.*

Jacob didn't have to go one inch toward Joseph in the energy of his flesh.

The blessing of Joseph was simple. He got on board the wagon that Joseph had provided and enjoyed the ride. Likewise, the Lord Jesus Christ has provided all that's needed to get you and me from earth to glory.

There are grace and mercy sufficient for the journey. If you are saved, I trust you are enjoying the journey to where Jesus is.

If you are not saved, please believe that Christ died for you before that dead takes over you.

He's alive; he's the Lord, loves you, and wants you to live with him.

Chapter 46

The task at hand was taking a trip for Jacob. They had to bring every-thing they had, for they were not coming back. For Jacob to leave his home, this was a big thing, but he knew that he could trust God's will. Think of all the memories there.

As the journey begins, we find that Jacob wants to stop at Beersheba and sacrifice unto the Lord. That is the right thing to do, for it is there that God meets with him again and tells him not to be afraid of going down into Egypt.

Now, he will be able to see his long, lost son again if he goes.

One thing to note about this trip was that he did not leave Canaan's borders without sacrificing and knowing God's will. We could each stop here and think about what we do.

Do we stop and ask God to make decisions, whether financial, emo-tional, spiritual, or in a move? It would probably be wise on our part and ask God what He wants us to do.

Interestingly God calls Jacob by that name and not Israel. I think this is just a little subtle way of reminding him that he is just an ordinary man, but he can be significant with God.

With his meeting with God here at Beersheba, we find that God assures him of protection for his journey and, in the process, explains to him why he is supposed to make the trip.

Once again, God makes a promise to Jacob that God will bless him.

Again, all this is in the plan of God to fulfill the remarkable prophecy given to Abraham.

We have now entered into another step in God's plan for the little nation of Israel.

Interestingly we find that as they begin their journey to Egypt, God calls Jacob by his new name Israel.

He is the beginning of a new era. Now God lists each of the sons of Israel and their families that come with them. So what would be the reason for the list of names? There is a historical significance to the names because they are the beginning of the nation of Israel. And it marked the tribe of the coming Messiah.

I think there is a practical application in the listing of the names, and that is God is concerned about every person on this planet. The number of names is significant. Seventy is the number of 7 times 10. Seven is the number of holiness's, and 10 is the number of completeness.

Seventy is the promised span of life, and Israel had 70 elders.

Sometimes you will find discrepancies within numbers mentioned in the Bible. There is a list of sixty-six souls that came with Jacob. Altogether there will be seventy if you include Jacob, Joseph, and Joseph's two sons. Stephen's seventy-five have all of the above numbers plus the five grandsons of Joseph born later. See *Acts 7:14* and *I Chron. 7:14-22*.

There are no contradictions in the Bible. What a sight this must have been. Already God was preparing the way for them to live in the land of Goshen.

God's purpose was to separate them from the Egyptians, so there would be no intermarrying.

To live in Goshen would allow them to multiply greatly in a prosperous, protected, and segregated part of Egypt. In Joseph's meeting with his family, it is interesting that they do not meet him in judgment but love.

Chapter 47

Beginning our search of this chapter Joseph and his family are getting together and Joseph placing them in Goshen's land before they met the King. Imagine meeting the President. What an honor. Maybe he felt the same way. That should remind us that we will meet the King of Kings and Lord of Lords one day.

Because Joseph had so much power and possessions, he could make it possible to provide for the whole family. Think of what a blessing it is to move literally from rags to riches lacking nothing. In a literal sense, Joseph was able to save his family's lives, for had they not come to Egypt, all would die.

It is here in Goshen God was preparing them for what lay ahead in the future. In getting his family established, we find that Joseph brings his father to meet with the King. What a meeting it must have been!!

Think of it, the mighty monarch and the aged but wise and dignified Jacob meet. If you remember, Jacob had sent gifts to Pharaoh, but now instead of bringing gifts, we find Jacob pronounces a blessing upon Pharaoh. He involves Jacob's religion and his God before a heathen king. Very interesting, we would say.

It is also true that one day Christ will, at His second advent, present His brethren, the Jews, in the court of Heaven, restoring them to the place of blessing in the earth.

As Jacob here blesses King Pharaoh, so Israel's portion will be in the Millennium that of blessing the kings of the earth.

When you read through this chapter and try and read between the lines, it is undeniable at the onset that Joseph was very wise in the counsel he gave to Pharaoh but also in his dealings with his family and what might be the reaction of the Egyptians toward them.

In the counsel of his family, it is admirable what he did for them all.

He gave them the best of the land, he gave them protection, and he gave them provisions for all of them.

We also see that he was very wise in his dealings with the Egyptians about looking after them during famine years. Once all of the monies ran out of buying grain, we find that he traded grain to eat for their livestock for their land, and he allowed them to move from the country to the cities so they would not be so far away from provisions.

Interestingly enough, we find that when Joseph knew that the famine was about over, he began to sell seed to the Egyptians so they might once again grow crops.

Of course, he charged them for it, which was only appropriate.

Ending the chapter, we know that Jacob lived a good life with his family, and now he knows that the end is near.

He makes a special request to Joseph that he should not be buried in Egypt but wanted the final resting place to be in the Promised Land.

In the process, Joseph tells him that his bones would not rest forever in Egypt. Note **Heb. 11:21**.

Chapter 48

What an excellent chapter this is in the midst of sorry.

I have seen God work many times in people's lives in the sense that during some sorrowful event, out of it becomes a great blessing from God.

Joseph works as prime minister, and his family is dwelling in Goshen's land not very far away.

Jacob is sick, and they send for Joseph. We would do what Joseph did. He takes his sons with him to see his father. He may not have known how sick his father was, but in God's excellent plan, we see He will work out. We understand that this was providential, regardless of whether Joseph had any prior knowledge of what was about to occur.

So Joseph sends word that he is coming to see his father, and Jacob is like most of us he needs to show them that he is willing to see them no matter how he feels.

It is interesting the word changes for Jacob, whose name is now Israel.

Jacob gets the news of Joseph's coming.

However, in a close reading of the text, you will see that Israel strengthened himself.

I understand the significance here because Jacob, the father, is the fleshly man who receives the message. Still, Israel is the theocratic and divinely appointed head of the nation, the spiritual man who "strengthened himself."

When Joseph arrives and goes in to see his father tells him what God had done for him in Luz, how God had made a promise to him and blessed him. See *Genesis 28:10-19* and *Genesis 35:6-13*.

The significance here is that it was El Shaddai "God Almighty" that appeared unto him.

There is no doubt we need to see God as God Almighty, the all-powerful, all-sufficient one.

In today's world, we are almost overwhelmed by the immorality and hatred for God's things. The reason behind this is pretty simple.

We have allowed the world to believe God is not who He says He is and thereby have degraded His Name.

Today, modern theology has put it in the minds of the world's people that He is just a man, just like you, and I show this in our actions, instead of Him being Almighty God!

God help us open our eyes and see God for who He is once again and stand up for that belief.

In our text, we find a beautiful thing that takes place in that Jacob considers the sons of Joseph to be just like his sons, giving them birthright to Jacob's heritage. See *I Chron. 5:1, 2*.

You know there are some things you will never forget, and it was a good thing that Jacob tells of Joseph's mother.

Now Jacob wants to bless Joseph's children and have Joseph bring them near to him to bless them.

Now the Bible indicates the blessing is by Israel and not by Jacob, Note again what was said earlier in this chapter, As the boys presented to Jacob, his eyesight is so that he has to ask which son he is. As Jacob (the supplanter), he had no power to bless, but as Israel (Prince with God), he did have the right to bless. As for Israel, Prince with God pronounced the blessing; the boys' noted the divine order. As has been the principle of the second getting the more incredible blessing, we see this here too. Isaac was preferred above Ishmael, and Jacob before Esau. It was so of Cain that Abel, the second born, was the accepted one.

It was also true of the first Adam and the Last Adam. It is also true of redeemed men that the flesh is born first, but the second born (the spiritual man) has first place.

Especially note in **verses 15, 16**, how the Trinity of God is involved in this blessing.

We have God the Father, God the Son, and God Holy Spirit taking part here.

Notice it was God before whom my fathers walked. God, which led me by the Holy Spirit, brought Sanctification. Then the Angel which redeemed me we see Christ in His Redemption.

Here is introduced, the Hebrew word "gaal," translated, redeemer. It carries the idea of a kinsman-redeemer. What a beautiful picture of Christ presented to Joseph and his sons here. Note here a couple of verses. See **Isa. 43:1**; **Isa. 49:26** and **Job 19:25**.

It is again interesting to note that Israel's blessing to Joseph's son has his right hand on the younger and his left hand on the older, Joseph notices this and tries to change it, but you and I know that it is impossible to change God's will.

So Ephraim is placed before Manasseh. We see this fulfilled in the history of the tribes. Ephraim was not only more numerous but was more powerful and influential.

Israel leaves parting words to his son and tells us something we should never forget.

I am sure Joseph would never forget Israel's last words to him.

He said to Joseph, "Behold, I die, but God shall be with you, and bring you again unto the land of your fathers. Moreover, I have given o thee one portion above thy brethren, which I took out of the hand of the Amorite with my sword and with my bow."

In other words, to put it in my terms, he says, "I die, but God will remain. I die and can no longer be with you, but God will never leave you. I die, and cannot bring you into the land, but God can, because He lives.

At the end of this excellent chapter, we find that Joseph received a double blessing in that he would be the father of two tribes.

Chapter 49

As much as the last chapter was a blessing, we find that this next chapter contains the opposite. In prophecy, Jacob reveals the sins of his sons in the blessings he gives them.

Jacob starts with the oldest and works his way down the ranks.

We do not ordinarily think of Jacob as a prophet, yet this chapter contains some remarkable prophecies.

Like many other prophecies, there is a double fulfillment. We note the completion of these in part, yet there is much to be accomplished in the last days. Much of the Old Testament history unfolded just as prophesied in this chapter. It is very noticeable in the book of Joshua, as well as elsewhere.

So Jacob starts with his son Reuben, the firstborn. As the firstborn, he would have the first rank among his brethren, the tribes' leadership, and a double share of the inheritance.

But through his sinful acts, he forfeited these blessings that should have been his.

Here, in the end, the sins are listed for all to know and the results. Lust in *Genesis 35:22* and *Deut. 27:20* along with what we would say instability as listed in *James 1:6-8* and *II Pet. 2:14*. From *1 Chron. 5:1, 2*, we know Reuben did not get the birthright.

In actuality, Reuben prevailed in nothing. No king, no prophet or judge came from Reuben.

They also settled on the wilderness side of Jordan. See *Num. 32:5* and *Judges 5:15, 16*.

They received the smallest portion.

They were numerically weak, and according to *Num. 1:21*, they only numbered 46,500.

Yet in *Numbers 26:7*, they had shrunk to 43,000, although other tribes had grown.

The next two brothers were Simeon and Levi. Jacob considered them instruments of cruelty, and we have their sins described for us in *Gen. 34:25*. We see God's judgment upon them.

Simeon received his inheritance within the tribe of Judah. See *Josh. 19:1-8*.

Also, their number shrank from 59,300 in *Num. 1*, to 22,200. See *Num. 26* and *I Chron. 4:24, 27*.

Levi only received cities scattered throughout the land. See *Josh. 14:4*.

Levi joined Simeon in his cruelty, but he later joined to the Lord in grace. See the following passages: *Ex. 32:26-28* and *Num. 25:6-13*.

Jacob now calls his son Judah Lion's Whelp. That just means to be praised by brethren.

In the end, the coming Messiah would come through this tribe. You can also read in the book of the Revelation of his power. See *Rev. 5:5*.

Two words describe him, the first, the ruling hand, and second Shiloh. The scepter means that as a tribe, they would rule. See *2 Sam. 5:1-3*. And the word Shiloh means, as I said, Messiah. See *Isa. 63:1-3*.

Next, we have Zebulun, which means by the sea. Here we note that Jacob passes from the 4th son to the 10th.

Christ was to come out of Judah but to live in the land of Zebulun.

Later you will find that Deborah praised Zebulun. See *Jud. 5:18*.

They were faithful to David and were not of a double heart. See *I Chron. 12:33, 40*.

Zebulun means a haven of ships and seafaring people. See also, *Matt. 4:15* and *Isa. 9:1-7*.

Next, you have Issachar. His name means strong. He was to bear burdens. This tribe grew to be numerous and influential. See *Num. 26:25*. They numbered 64,300, but they increased to 87,000. See *I Chron. 7:5*.

Dan is the next tribe or son mentioned, and you will find that his tribe was the first to go into idolatry. See *Judges 18:30*. Remember the story of Samson? He was of the tribe of Dan.

Could the anti-Christ come from this tribe?

Next, you have Gad. Gad means overcomer. See *Deut. 33:20-21*. Gad's inheritance was in Gilead's land, and they were subject to constant attacks by the Ammonites and Midianites.

According to God's Word, they were the first tribe to go into captivity. See *I Chron. 5:18-26*.

Asher was able to provide olive oil and petroleum in his inheritance. See *Luke. 2:36-38*.

Naphtali means wrestling, lack of self-control, and goodly words not used wisely.

Capernaum, Bethsaida, and Chorazin are in the territory of Naphtali.

Then you have Joseph, who is envied and persecuted by the rest. But he was blessed of God and given a double inheritance through his sons. See *Ezek. 47:13*.

Just for the record, you have Joshua from Ephraim, one of Joseph's tribes. See *Num. 13:8*.

Then there is Benjamin, whose name means warlike, and you will find his tribe generally allied with Judah in times of trouble. See the following verses: *Judges 20:16, 21, 22; II Sam. 2:15, 16; I Chron. 8:42; 12:2* and *II Chron. 17:17*.

Ehud was from the tribe of Benjamin. See *Jud. 3:15-22*. King Saul was also from that tribe. See *I Samuel 9:1, 2*. So was Saul of Tarsus, now called Paul. See *Phil. 3:5*.

Now in the last part of this chapter, you have Jacob's request concerning his death.

He went to Egypt when he was 130, and he lived another 17 years after seeing Joseph. In the first 17 years of Joseph's life, Jacob looked after his son Joseph. In the last 17 years of Jacob's life, Joseph looked after Jacob. At the end of the first 17 years, Jacob mourned for Joseph many days. At the end of the second 17 years, Joseph wept for his father many days.

Each of the two periods began with great joy. In the 1st period, Jacob gave Joseph much honor. In the 2nd period, Joseph gave Jacob much recognition. In the end, the Egyptians honor Jacob because of Joseph.

Chapter 50

This first half of the last chapter of Genesis takes up the ceremony and mourning of Israel.

According to Egyptian custom, there is mourning for forty days, and then a considerable entourage takes Israel's body back to Canaan to be buried.

What a sight that must have been to those who came in contact with them.

Even some of the Egyptians went with Joseph and his family to do the honoring of his father.

Losing a loved one is never easy.

I am sure you know how they all felt.

We are not sad that they are in Heaven; we are sorry because we will miss them here on earth.

All in all, I would say Jacob had a beautiful life.

His life was like many of ours with its ups and downs, but the fact remains that God was faithful to him and blessed him tremendously.

As children of God, we have to look back at how we have seen God intervene on our behalf and say the same thing Jacob told about God and his faithfulness.

I have thought about the mistakes we make in life.

Yes, they can bring on some hard times and a lot of trouble, especially when we are out of God's will.

But in the end, if we listen to the small still voice of the Holy Spirit stirring our hearts, nudging us to come back to Him, we will find out as Jacob and Joseph did that "all things do work for our good."

Often, when going through things we cannot see, we are looking at ground level instead of looking up where we are looking for guidance and direction.

Today troublesome times are here, and we should learn to trust God more and more in this world we live in instead of the flesh, the devil, and the world itself.

I know I have said that before but I need to remind myself to be different from those around us.

Often, we hear others say, "oh me," when we should be saying, "oh God."

Study the Word of God. See verses like the following: ***Rom. 1:17; 2 Cor. 5:7; Isa. 57:13,*** and many more. What we have learned is; there are two kinds of trouble in our lives. One brought on by sin and the other one brought on by God wanting to build us up and make us more reliable.

We look at the church today, and sure we can say it is weak. Maybe what the church is going through now, rather than tearing us down, will build us up and help us realize we have taken for granted too many things?

We should now be able to see that our freedoms could be taken from us quickly.

I have always heard that what Christians need is a little persecution to move them in the right direction.

Maybe what is going on with us today is God's unseen hand trying to lead us in the right direction. I sure pray so.

Back in our text, there is no doubt as wicked and cruel as some of Jacob's sons were they still loved their father and did all they could to honor his last wishes.

We all have that sin nature, and many times we let it win over us and lead us down the wrong path in life, but I am convinced that if we have been taught right and know the Lord, then, in the end, we will come back to the place God wants us to be.

Now that the father is gone, the brothers begin to worry about their past again.

Sometimes when others have forgiven us, it is tough to forgive ourselves, and because of the guilt we carry over our sins, we find it problematic that others would genuinely forgive us for the wrongs we have done.

It was the case with the brothers. Now that their father is dead, they begin to think that Joseph will turn on them and do what they did to him. I would suggest you read the following verses: *Rom. 12:19; Eph. 4:32*, and *Heb. 7:25*.

With a sincere heart, we can say that God's forgiveness has nothing to do with your sins' size, only with the Savior's mercy. The brother's mistake was to judge Joseph's forgiveness by guilt and not by Joseph's grace. No wonder Joseph wept before his brothers.

Thank God for the blood.

Judgment is gone; however, we know that we have to face the consequences in every sin. Joseph replies to his brothers and admonishes all of them not to fear him.

We need a heart like Joseph's.

How many times in our lives have we not been willing to forgive others when they wronged us?

As a dedicated child of God, it has been interesting to see how Joseph had responded in the entire test he has gone through.

One thing that stands out about him, and I should say there are many things, but the one thing was beyond a shadow of a doubt God had a plan, and he was willing to wait on Him to show him what to do.

I can say many times; God has made me wait for Him to reveal His will to me.

Waiting is so hard, but willingness brings blessings in the end.

For the brothers, they based their fears on what someone else said and not God's Word.

Why is it that God is the last one we trust?

In the context, we see the brothers once again confess to Joseph.

I, too, had come before God many times and asked Him to forgive me for a sin I had committed against Him. One day long ago, I talked to a wise ole preacher about that, and he made a statement to me that has rung true the rest of my life. That statement was this, "when did God forgive you of your sin?" I answered that he forgave me the first time I asked Him.

His reply was, "why do you keep asking Him over and over again to do the same thing."

Well, the answer to that is I did not believe God would forgive me, and only till I got that straight with God did I know what peace was. We know that God had forgiven the brothers, and we know that Joseph had forgiven his brothers. How it nearly broke his heart, and he weeps openly before them.

One important thing here is that Joseph does not deny their evil intent, but God's goodwill and sense overshadowed their sins. In the end, we see again that Joseph promises to take care of them.

There is no doubt he handled the whole problem with the utmost kindness. Now here, in the end, we see the death of Joseph. He lived for 110 years.

Just for observation purposes, notice how the span of human life was shortening.

Isaac lived to be 180, Jacob 147, and Joseph 110.

We know he lived to see Ephraim's grand-children and held Manasseh's grand-children on his knees from our text. As a grandfather, I can relate to this and what a joy it is.

It was the dying request of Joseph to be buried with his family in Canaan land. See *Heb. 11:22.*

Here was a man who believed the promises of God and was faithful to the end.

Time, labor, or joy could shake Joseph's faith in God's eventual deliverance of His people.

Though dying, he knew the promises of God were sure.

At the end of this chapter, we find how the children of Israel honored Joseph's request.

Genesis begins with the creation in all its beauty and perfection, but ends with "a coffin in Egypt."

Only one word is needed to describe the reason for the profound change, and it is "SIN."

I think you would have to agree with Joseph's insight into God's will, and the future was incredible.

Sometimes I plead for discernment such as Joseph had. If we all did what a change in this world, there would be. He was able to look beyond his death, and in it, he saw slavery come to his people.

He saw Moses, maybe not by name, but believed there was a coming kinsman-redeemer.

In this, he saw there would be a need to take his body with them, and that was his final request.

We know from *Exodus 13:19* that Moses took the bones of Joseph at the departure.

One of the impressive things about Joseph's death is he left them a memorial to his body.

Yes, they embalmed him and laid him in a coffin in Egypt.

But notice they did not have as an unusual burial service for him as they did with his father.

He was not staying there forever.

He, too, wanted his body transferred from Egypt to the Promised Land. It is important to remember the coffin of Joseph. The reason is that over 400 years later, Moses knew right where it was and was able to get it with no trouble to take it with them in the Exodus. See *Ex. 1:8*.

Later in the Bible, you will find that there will be a time when the pharaohs of Egypt did not know Joseph. With this King came slavery, bondage, hardships, tears, heartaches.

There is no doubt there must have been many times that little nation of Israel would look at that coffin and remember the promise that their forefather Joseph had made to them that they would one day leave Egypt.

One day they would long for that day. One day that day came. It was the Passover night, and Moses carries Joseph's bones out of Egypt, across the Red Sea, through the wilderness to Jordan. The day came, now they were at Jordan, and Joshua carries Joseph's bones across Jordan into the Promised Land.

Ending there is a consummated redemption for that little nation.

Remember, Redemption has two parts. We can say there is an outward and then inward part.

Why because there are two parts, the body, and soul. Joseph had confidence in God that he would take him out of Egypt someday. That day arrived, and it happened just a God had promised.

Think of the book of Genesis. It begins with creation and ends with a coffin. It starts with glory and ends with a grave. It starts with the nastiness of eternity for those who have not trusted God and ends with shortness. It starts with a living God and ends with a dead man, and so we ask, "Is there a hope of glory?"

Interestingly, if you look at the word "coffin" in the Hebrew means chest, and in this instance, we could have a hope chest for Israel's nation. We, too, can say there is hope in this hopeless world.

May God help us through these studies to learn to know and trust the hope that God has given to each of us and make a difference in our lives.

About the Author

anny K. Hill is a seasoned pastor, now semi-retired. He is a former missionary to the Republic of Ireland staying nine years, and a professor for three years at Clarksville Theological Seminary, with over forty-five years' experience in the ministry. He has Bachelor's Degree in Bible, a Masters in Religious Education and a Doctorate in Theology. He has preached the Gospel in many foreign countries and several States in the USA. Danny and his wife Brenda reside in Eastern North Carolina with their three living children and four grandchildren.

References and Endnotes

Chapter One

"Celebrating the Life of Robert Ned Thomas, Sr." Jackson Advocate, vol. 80, no. 9, Jackson Advocate, 30 Nov. 2017, p. 13A.

Goldberg, Elisa. "Bringing Light to the World." Jewish Exponent, vol. 237, no. 22, Jewish Exponent, 26 Feb. 2015, p. 29.

The Experience of Christ - by Witness Lee. https://www.ministrybooks.org/books.cfm?xid=KA5Q8NG8LFISY

Chapter Three

Breen, Margaret. "Race, Dissent, and Literary Imagination in John Bunyan and James Baldwin." Bunyan Studies, no. 21, Northumbria University, Department of Humanities, Faculty of Arts, Design and Social Sciences, Jan. 2017, p. 9.

Daily Thorn at PO Box 51644, 87181. https://addr.ws/daily-thorn-religious-organization--albuquerque-us.html

Stolen waters are sweet, and bread eaten in secret is ... https://biblehub.com/commentaries/proverbs/9-17.htm

Anderson, Judith. "Doers of the Word: Shakespeare, Macbeth, and the Epistle of James." Christian Scholar's Review, vol. 46, no. 4, Christian Scholar's Review, July 2017, p. 341.

Genesis 4:5 But unto Cain and to his offering he had not ... https://www.bible.com/bible/1/GEN.4.5.kjv

Blog | God and Country Radio. https://www.godandcountryradio.org/blog/

Man in His Fall, part I - SLJ Institute. https://sljinstitute.net/systematic-theology/anthropology/man-in-his-fall-part-i/

GENESIS 3:13 KJV "And the LORD God said unto the woman ... https://www.kingjamesbibleonline.org/Genesis-3-13/

Christlike Communications - Church Of Jesus Christ. https://www. churchofjesuschrist.org/study/general-conference/1988/10/ christlike-communications?lang=eng

Whose Fault Is Our Temptation?. https://www.gty.org/library/sermons-library/59-7

Genesis 3:15 AKJV - and I will put enmity between thee and ... https://www. biblegateway.com/passage/?search=Genesis+3%3A15&version=AKJV

When Isaiah says we are healed by his stripes is he ... https://ebible.com/ questions/19755-when-isaiah-says-we-are-healed-by-his-stripes-is-he-talking-about-a-physical-healing-or-a-spiritual-healing

Dubins, Jerry, and Mark Novak. "SHOSTAKOVICH: Violin Concertos Nos. 1 1 and 2 2." Fanfare, vol. 40, no. 4, Fanfare, Inc., Mar. 2017, p. 421.

The Distinction between the Lord's Table and the Lord's ... https://www. stempublishing.com/authors/RF_Kingscote/RFK_Table_Supper.html

Sessions 9 and 10. https://ibs.cru.org/index.php/download_file/view/1048/

Understanding God's Divine Protection – biblicalview59. https:// biblicalview59.wordpress.com/article/understanding-god-s-divine-protection-1pf06wvr9ri3n-19/

Duties of a Christian in the Government - Home | Facebook. https:// www.facebook.com/Duties-of-a-Christian-in-the-Government -255738934955332/

Reversing Obama, Trump EPA reaches deal with Pebble mine ... https:// www.adn.com/politics/2017/05/12/pebble-is-on-epa-reaches-deal-with-bristol-bay-gold-mine-company/

Christians: Can you enjoy Heaven knowing that someone you ... https:// answers.yahoo.com/question/index?qid=20091207160331AArGkec

Free will, Depends on your point of view - Sermon Index. http:// www.sermonindex.net/modules/newbb/viewtopic.php?topic_i d=8669&forum=36&start=0

HEBREWS 2:15 KJV "And deliver them who through fear of ... https://www. kingjamesbibleonline.org/Hebrews-2-15/

ROMANS 5:20 KJV "Moreover the law entered, that the ... https://www. kingjamesbibleonline.org/Romans-5-20/

Chapter Four

Ladakh: 'Modi could lose public opinion' - Rediff.com ... https://www.rediff.com/news/interview/ladakh-modi-could-lose-public-opinion/20200618.htm

THEO UFND3100 Study Guide (2011-12 D) - Instructor D at ... https://www.studyblue.com/notes/note/n/theo-ufnd3100-study-guide-2011-12-d/deck/9734389

Psalm 27 – Discover Books of The Bible. https://bible-studys.org/psalm-27/

Prince of Creative Anachronism | Unofficial Royalty. http://www.unofficialroyalty.com/columnists/the-laird-othistle/prince-of-creative-anachronism/

Le 'Coco' Chanel Opened Her First Shop In 1910, No One ... https://jocelynflosvv.wordpress.com/2013/06/25/le-coco-chanel-opened-her-first-shop-in-1910 no one-could/

World Church: Adventists Condemn London Acts of Terror ... https://news.adventist.org/en/all-news/news/go/2005-07-06/world-church-adventists-condemn-london-acts-of-terror-pray-for-victims/

ROMANS 5:20 KJV "Moreover the law entered, that the ... https://www.kingjamesbibleonline.org/Romans-5-20/

Mendelsohn, Steve. "Dear Cornel West ..." Jewish Exponent, vol. 238, no. 68, Jewish Exponent, 21 July 2016, p. 15.

1 John 3:12 Parallel: Not as Cain, who was of that wicked ... https://biblehub.com/parallel/1_john/3-12.htm

Clarke, Colin. "GEORGIEV: Symphonic Triptych No. 1. Percussion Concerto No. 3, 'Genesis' 1." Fanfare, vol. 42, no. 5, Fanfare, Inc., May 2019, p. 277.

Luhr, Eileen. "Redeemer: The Life of Jimmy Carter." The Christian Century, vol. 131, no. 15, Christian Century Foundation, July 2014, p. 37.

Gap Theories of Creation - Geocentricity. https://www.geocentricity.com/ba1/no117/gap.html

Chapter Five

if you have not done this then you have missed something ... https://www.tripadvisor.com/ShowUserReviews-g274707-d1576262-r301401634-Prague_On_Segway_on_E_Scooter_on_Quad-Prague_Bohemia.html

JUDE 1:15 KJV "To execute judgment upon all, and to ... https://www.kingjamesbibleonline.org/Jude-1-15/

Hebrews 11:6 KJV - But without faith it is impossible to ... https://www.biblegateway.com/passage/?search=Hebrews%2011:6&version=KJV

Chapter Six

Genesis 6:5 Then the LORD saw that the wickedness of man ... https://www.biblehub.com/genesis/6-5.htm

Scottish Bike Show Meet. http://www.ducati-upnorth.com/forum/showthread.php?618-Scottish-Bike-Show-Meet/page4

Job 42:6 KJV: Wherefore I abhor myself, and repent in dust ... https://biblehub.com/kjv/job/42-6.htm

Debates - Issue 117 - May 8, 2017. https://sencanada.ca/en/content/sen/chamber/421/debates/117db_2017-05-08-e

First Week of Advent: Hope. https://bogbit.com/first-week-of-advent-hope/

Ephesians 2:8-10 For by grace are ye saved through faith ... https://www.bible.com/bible/1/EPH.2.8-10.kjv

Sometimes all it takes is for you to make up your mind ... https://www.pinterest.com/pin/14847873755851074/

Chapter Seven

And The Spirit Of God Moved Upon The Face Of The Waters. http://www.jasher.com/Insights%20page/Godmoved.htm

Oscarson, Christopher. "Dominion In The Anthropocene." Dialogue: A Journal of Mormon Thought, vol. 52, no. 4, Dialogue Foundation, Dec. 2019, p. 1.

Less Than Zero (1987) - Less Than Zero (1987) - User ... https://www.imdb.com/title/tt0093407/reviews

Genesis 7:20 KJV: Fifteen cubits upward did the waters ... https://biblehub.com/kjv/genesis/7-20.htm

Does Gen. 7:11, Noah's Flood point to Sudden Destruction ... http://www.fivedoves.com/letters/oct2011/ronr1029.htm

Chapter Eight

How do I get this question through the Yahoo filter (some ... https://answers.yahoo.com/question/index?qid=20080908102703AAhsrlT

Chapter Nine

3 Elements to Reducing Lockdown Fatigue | What is Lockdown ... https://www.cardinus.com/us/insights/covid-19-hs-response/lockdown-fatigue-what-is-it/

Why Hunt The Backcountry – High Country Ministries. http://highcountryministries.org/thoughts/why-hunt-the-backcountry/

Chapter Eleven

GENESIS 10:10 KJV "And the beginning of his kingdom was ... https://www.kingjamesbibleonline.org/Genesis-10-10/

Genesis 10:10 His kingdom began in Babylon, Erech, Accad ... https://www.biblehub.com/genesis/10-10.htm

GENESIS 11:9 KJV "Therefore is the name of it called Babel ... https://www.kingjamesbibleonline.org/Genesis-11-9/

Revelation 13:15 - Bible Gateway. https://www.biblegateway.com/verse/en/Revelation%2013%3A15

Genesis 10:9 He was a mighty hunter before the LORD; so it ... https://www.biblehub.com/genesis/10-9.htm

7 Awesome Promises about God's Unchanging Character. https://www.crosswalk.com/faith/spiritual-life/awesome-promises-about-gods-unchanging-character.html

Jeremiah 29:11 For I know the thoughts and plans that I ... https://www.bible.com/bible/8/JER.29.11.ampc

Chapter Twelve

Laugh Thru It - angiesthatsthat.blogspot.com. https://angiesthatsthat.blogspot.com/2013/08/laugh-thru-it.html

Ezekiel 37 Commentary | Precept Austin. https://www.preceptaustin.org/ezekiel_37_commentary

Chapter Thirteen

Anderson, Judith. "Doers of the Word: Shakespeare, Macbeth, and the Epistle of James." Christian Scholar's Review, vol. 46, no. 4, Christian Scholar's Review, July 2017, p. 341.

Chapter Nineteen

Hosea 7:9 KJV: Strangers have devoured his strength, and ... https://biblehub.com/kjv/hosea/7-9.htm

Chapter Twenty-two

Hebrews 11:18-20 KJV - Of whom it was said, That in Isaac ... https://www.biblegateway.com/passage/?search=Hebrews%2011:18-20&version=KJV

The Angel of the Lord – adaughtersgiftoflove. https://adaughtersgiftoflove.wordpress.com/2019/07/05/the-angel-of-the-lord-2/

Chapter Twenty-five

Carla: May 2013. https://carlacrosby.blogspot.com/2013/05/

SDF arrests ISIS suspect near Syrian-Iraqi border. https://npasyria.com/en/blog.php?id_blog=2732&sub_blog=15&name_blog=SDF%20arrests%20ISIS%20suspect%20near%20Syrian-Iraqi%20border

HEBREWS 12:16 KJV "Lest there [be] any fornicator, or ... https://www.kingjamesbibleonline.org/Hebrews-12-16/

Chapter Twenty-six

Chapter 16: Interviewing basics - The News. http://www.thenewsmanual.net/Manuals%20Volume%201/volume1_16.htm

HEBREWS 12:14 KJV "Follow peace with all [men], and ... https://www.kingjamesbibleonline.org/Hebrews-12-14/

Chapter Twenty-nine

Reaping What You Sow Genesis 29 - PDF Free Download. https://docplayer.net/20770254-Reaping-what-you-sow-genesis-29.html

The Measure You Mete... - A New Thing Ministries. https://anewthingministries.com/the-measure-you-mete/

Yes this is a "conspiracy" sub. However, all plots can be ... https://www.reddit.com/r/conspiracy/comments/6454a8/yes_this_is_a_conspiracy_sub_however_all_plots/

Chapter Thirty

How Spider-Man: Far From Home Can Wrap Up Marvel's Phase ... https://www.cinemablend.com/news/2471618/how-spider-man-far-from-home-can-wrap-up-marvels-phase-three

Chapter Thirty-seven

4 Bible Characters Who Chose Joy - Bible Study. https://www.crosswalk.com/faith/bible-study/4-bible-characters-who-chose-joy.html

Genesis 15:15 KJV - And thou shalt go to thy fathers in ... https://classic. biblegateway.com/passage/?search=Genesis+15:15&version=KJV

ADENIKE SALAKO BLOG'S WORLD: Are You Investing in Heaven ... https://adenikematt.blogspot.com/2014/04/are-you-investing-in-heaven-or-where.html

4 Steps To Change Your Behavior For Good. https://www.forbes.com/ sites/work-in-progress/2018/07/19/4-steps-to-change-your-behavior-for-good/

Read Tangled in His Embrace by Sherri Hayes (1) Page 1 ... https://thenovelfree. com/book/tangled-in-his-embrace-by-sherri-hayes/1

Chapter Thirty-nine

ROMANS 6:12 KJV "Let not sin therefore reign in your ... https://www. kingjamesbible.me/Romans-6-12/

Chapter Forty-one

The Plan. https://www.harpercollinschristian.com/9780849929168/ the-plan/

Chapter Forty-two

Matthew 7:2 - KJV - For with what judgment ye judge, ye... https://www. studylight.org/bible/kjv/matthew/7-2.html

Chapter Forty-four

Numbers 32:23 KJV: But if ye will not do so, behold, ye ... https://biblehub. com/kjv/numbers/32-23.htm

Chapter Forty-five

Genesis 45:27 However, when they relayed all that Joseph ... https://biblehub. com/genesis/45-27.htm

Chapter Fifty

TBC Food Sales. https://www.tbcfoodsales.com/

A coffin in Egypt (Joseph – Genesis 50:22-26) | Flaming ... https:// ezrachimts.wordpress.com/2019/06/09/a-coffin-in-egypt-joseph-genesis-5022-26/

CPSIA information can be obtained
at www.ICGtesting.com
Printed in the USA
BVHW030941250321
603410BV00006B/30